ANCIENT INDIAN TRADITION & MYTHOLOGY

Translated by
A BOARD OF SCHOLARS

Edited by
Prof. J. L. SHASTRI

VOLUME 28

ANCIENT INDIAN TRADITION AND MYTHOLOGY SERIES

[PURĀṆAS IN TRANSLATION]

VOLUMES

ŚIVA 1-4
LIṄGA 5-6
BHĀGAVATA 7-11
GARUḌA 12-14
NĀRADA 15-19
KŪRMA 20-21
BRAHMĀṆḌA 22-26
AGNI 27-30
VARĀHA 31-32
BRAHMA 33-36
VĀYU 37-38
PADMA 39-48
SKANDA, PARTS I-XIV 49-61

VOLUMES UNDER PREPARATION

SKANDA, PARTS XV-XXIV
BHAVIṢYA
BRAHMAVAIVARTA
DEVĪBHĀGAVATA
KĀLIKĀ
MĀRKAṆḌEYA
MATSYA
VĀMANA
VIṢṆU
VIṢṆUDHARMOTTARA

THE

AGNI PURĀṆA

Translated and Annotated by
N. GANGADHARAN

PART II

MOTILAL BANARSIDASS PUBLISHERS
PRIVATE LIMITED • DELHI

Reprint: Delhi, 1998, 2013
First Edition: Delhi, 1985

ISBN: 978-81-208-0360-2

MOTILAL BANARSIDASS
41 U.A. Bungalow Road, Jawahar Nagar, Delhi 110 007
8 Mahalaxmi Chamber, 22 Bhulabhai Desai Road, Mumbai 400 026
203 Royapettah High Road, Mylapore, Chennai 600 004
236, 9th Main III Block, Jayanagar, Bengaluru 560 011
Sanas Plaza, 1302 Baji Rao Road, Pune 411 002
8 Camac Street, Kolkata 700 017
Ashok Rajpath, Patna 800 004
Chowk, Varanasi 221 001

UNESCO COLLECTION OF REPRESENTATIVE WORK—*Indian Series*
This book has been accepted in the Indian Translation Series
of the UNESCO Collection of Representative Works,
jointly sponsored by the United Nations Educational,
Scientific and Cultural Organization
(UNESCO) and the Government of India

Printed in India

By RP Jain at NAB Printing Unit,
A-44, Naraina, Phase-I, New Delhi 110 028
and Published by JP Jain for
Motilal Banarsidass Publishers (P) Ltd, 40-41 U.A.
Bungalow Road, Jawahar Nagar, Delhi 110 007

PUBLISHER'S NOTE

The Purest gems lie hidden in the bottom of the ocean or in the depth of rocks. One has to dive into the ocean or delve into the rocks to find them out. Similarly, truth lies concealed in the language which with the passage of time has become obsolete. Man has to learn that language before he discovers that truth.

But he has neither the means nor the leisure to embark on that course. We have, therefore, planned to help him acquire knowledge by an easier course. We have started the series of Ancient Indian Tradition and Mythology in English Translation. Our goal is to universalize knowledge through the most popular international medium of expression. The publication of the Purāṇas in English Translation is a step towards that goal.

PREFACE

The present volume contains the *Agni Purāṇa* Part II (Chapters 101 to 251) in *English Translation*. This is the twenty-eighth Volume in the series on *Ancient Indian Tradition and Mythology*.

The project of the Series was envisaged and planned in 1970 by Lala Sundar Lal Jain of Messrs Motilal Banarsidass. Hitherto twentyseven volumes of the Series (comprising English translation of *Śiva, Liṅga, Bhāgavata, Garuḍa, Nārada, Kūrma, Brahmāṇḍa* and *Agni* Part 1) have been published and released for sale.

This Purāṇa, like most of the other Purāṇas, is of encyclopaedic character. Like the first part, this part of the Agni Purāṇa contains topics of diverse nature. Nevertheless, there is unity under diversity. For example, Chapters 101-106 which open this part deal with the subject of architecture in relation to temple-edifice, house-building and town-planning. Chs. 107-108 describe Svāyambhuva creation and the Cosmographical account of the Universe. Chs. 109-116 deal with the sacred places of pilgrimage on the Ganges and Narmadā as well as on the Śrīśaila mountain. Among the holy places, Vārāṇasī, Puṣkara, Kurukṣetra, Rājagṛha, Prayāga and Gayā figure prominently. Ch.117 describes the mode of performing ancestral rites at these places. Chs. 118 to 120 are devoted to the description of Continents with special reference to Bhārata, the sub-continent of Jambūdvīpa. Chs. 121 to 149 relate to astrology and astronomy in relation to war. They also outline a number of stratagems and tantric rites for running administration and gaining victory in war. From the study of these and other chapters on polity it appears that the statesman of the Agnipurāṇa is in favour of Imperial power to be vested in the Sovereign who is ambitious for world conquest. The ambitious monarch is asked to seek success from all quarters, specially from super powers such as Kubjikā, Cāmuṇḍā, Aghorā and Varadā, these being the various forms of goddess Śivā, the consort of Lord Śiva.

From these topics the Agnipurāṇa proceeds to the description of Manvantaras (giving names of Manus, sages, Indra for each cycle of Manu), Āśramas (stages of life), Saṁskāras (purificatory rites) from birth to death (150-167). Chs. 168 to 174 relate to atonements for various offences and expiations for sins. Chs. 175 to 207 describe religious vows—obligatory and occasional, some of which are not found in the Smṛtigranthas. Chs. 208-213 dwell upon gifts and corporeal austerities (Vratas) of pious nature. Ch. 214 describes the system of veins in the body and their functions. Chs 15-16 recount the mode of reciting Gāyatrī and its greatness. Ch. 217 contains Vasiṣṭha's prayer to lord Śiva. Chs. 218 to 237 constitute discourse of Puṣkara to Vasiṣṭha on the king's coronation, appointment of assistants and the code of their conduct, fortification, kings' duties, policy, code of law, military expedition, omens presaging victory or defeat in war, six expedients, rites preceding the march of the army and a hymn to Lakṣmī for success. Chs. 238 to 242 include Rāma's discourse to Lakṣmaṇa on the eve of battle in Laṅkā, on the duties of the monarch, six expedients and four ways of policy and a harangue on king's statesmanship.

From these topics the Agnipurāṇa proceeds to some miscellaneous topics such as the description of physiognomy of men and women (Chs. 243-244), royal fan, bow and sword (245), testing of gems (246), site for building (247), worship of Viṣṇu (248), science of archery and the method of using a noose (249-251).

This wide range of subjects is most interesting and informative. The treatment of each topic comprising one or more chapters is lucid and unitary in expression and thought.

ACKNOWLEDGEMENT OF OBLIGATIONS

It is our pleasant duty to put on record our sincere thanks to Dr. R. N. Dandekar and the UNESCO authorities for their kind encouragement and valuable help which render this work more useful than it would otherwise have been. We are extremely grateful to Dr. Gangadharan of Sanskrit Department, University of Madras, for his lucid translation of the text and exegetical notes. We are grateful to Dr. K. V. Sharma for translating Chapter 122 on *Pañcāṅga: the Almanac* and writing notes thereon. We also thank those persons who have offered suggestions for improving the work. —EDITOR

CONTENTS

PART II

ABBREVIATIONS

Common and self-evident abbreviations such as Ch(s)-Chapter(s), p—page, pp—pages, V—Verse, VV—Verses, Ftn—footnote, Hist. Ind. Philo—History of Indian Philosophy are not included in this list.

ABORI	*Annals of the Bhandarkar Oriental Research Institute*, Poona
AGP	S. M. Ali's *The Geography of Purāṇas*, PPH, New Delhi, 1973
AIHT	*Ancient Indian Historical Tradition*, F. E. Pargiter, Motilal Banarsidass (MLBD), Delhi.
AITM	*Ancient Indian Tradition and Mythology* Series MLBD, Delhi.
AP	*Agni Purāṇa*, Guru Mandal Edition (GM), Calcutta, 1957
Arch.S.Rep.	Archaeological Survey Report
AV	*Atharva Veda*, Svadhyaya Mandal, Aundh
Bd. P.	*Brahmāṇḍa Purāṇa*, (MLBD), Delhi 1973
BG	*Bhagavadgītā*
Bh. P.	*Bhāgavata Purāṇa*, Bhagavat Vidyapeeth, Ahmedabad
Br.	*Brāhmaṇa* (preceded by name such as Śatapatha
BS. P.	*Bhaviṣya Purāṇa*, Vishnu Shastri Bapat, Wai.
BV. P.	*Brahma Vaivarta Purāṇa*, GM, 1955-57
CC.	*Caturvarga Cintāmaṇi* by Hemādri
CVS	*Caraṇa Vyūha* Sūtra by Śaunaka; Com. by Mahidāsa
DB	*Devī Bhāgavata*, GM, 1960-61
De or GDAMI.	*The Geographical Dictionary of Ancient and Mediaeval India*, N. L. De, Orienta Reprint, Delhi, 1971
Dh. S.	*Dharma Sūtra* (preceded by the author's name such as Gautama)
ERE	*Encyclopaedia of Religion and Ethics*—Hastings.
GP	*Garuḍa Purāṇa* Ed. R. S. Bhattacharya Chowkhamba, Varanasi, 1964

GS	*Gṛhya Sūtra* (preceded by the name of the author such as Āpastamba)
HD	*History of Dharma Śāstra*, P. V. Kane, G. O. S.
IA	*The Indian Antiquary*.
IHQ	*The Indian Historical Quarterly*
JP	*Purāṇa* (Journal of the Kashiraj Trust) Varanasi
KA	*Kauṭilya Arthaśāstra*
KP	*Kūrma Purāṇa*, Veṅkaṭeśvara Press Edt. Bombay, also Kashiraj Trust Edt., Varanasi 1971
LP	*Liṅga Purāṇa*, GM, 1960; also MLBD, Delhi, 1981
Manu.	*Manusmṛti*
Mbh.	*Mahābhārata*, Gītā Press, Gorakhpur, VS 2014
MkP	*Mārkaṇḍeya Purāṇa*
MN	*Mahābhārata Nāmānukramaṇī*, Gītā Press Gorakhpur, VS 2016
MtP.	*Matsya Purāṇa*, GM, 1954
MW	*Monier Williams Sk. English Dictionary* MLBD, Delhi, 1976
NP.	*Nāradīya or Nārada Purāṇa*, Veṅkaṭeśvar Press, Bombay
PCK	*Bhāratavarṣiya Prācīna Caritrakośa*, Siddheshwar Shastri, Poona, 1968
Pd. P.	*Padma Purāṇa*, GM, 1957-59
PE	*Puranic Encyclopaedia*, V. Mani, English, MLBD, Delhi, 1975
PR or PRHRC	*Puranic Records on Hindu Rites and Customs* R. C. Hazra, Calcutta, 1948
ṚV	*Ṛg-Veda*, Svādhyāya Mandal, Aundh
Śat. Br.	*Śatapatha Brāhmaṇa*
SC or SMC	*Smṛti Candrikā*—Devanna Bhaṭṭa
SEP	*Studies in Epics and Purāṇas*, A.D. Pusalkar Bharatiya Vidya Bhavan (BVB), Bombay

CHAPTER ONE HUNDRED AND ONE

Mode of consecration of a temple

The Lord said :

1-5. I shall describe the mode of consecrating a temple. By that itself it would become permeated by the divine force. After the angular projection is completed, the preceptor should locate a pitcher made of gold or other metals at the middle of the eastern altar. It should be filled with the *pañcagavya* (five things got from a cow), honey and milk. Five kinds of gems should be placed under (the pitcher). (The pitcher) should be adorned with garland and cloth. It should be besmeared with fragrance. It should be decorated with fragrant flowers. The temple should be decorated with tender leaves of trees like mango etc. After having finished the accomplishing rite in his body, the preceptor should gather (his soul energy) with the breath drawn in. The preceptor should then convey to (lord) Śambhu (Śiva) by his command with the exhalation of breath after the soul had been conceived as different from all the (other) souls with (the recitation of) its own *mantra.*

6. After having gathered the same from the twelve-petalled, that one shining like a spark of fire, the beatific states should be located in the pitcher as laid down in the *tantras.*

7. The image, its qualities, the beatific states, the letters upto *kṣa* and their lords and the collection of fundamental principles should be located.

8. The ten *nāḍis* (tubular organs of the body), ten vital winds and the thirteen sense-organs as well as their presiding deities (should be located) after having united the syllable *om* with their names.

9. (The two fundamental principles of) illusion and universal space which stand in relationship of cause and effect towards each other, the gods of learning who direct the pervad-

ing (lord) Śambhu (Śiva) (should also be located therein) with the (recitation of) *mantras*.

10-12. After having located the accessories, the preceptor should prevent (the deity) from going away by showing the *rodhamudrā* (posture made with the fingers denoting restraint). Otherwise an image of the god (should be made) of gold or other metals and it should be purified as before with the five things got from a cow etc. After having placed the pitcher on the bed and contemplating (lord) Rudra, the consort of Umā, (the lord) should be located in that (image) as the pervasive (lord). Oblation, sprinkling, touching and repetition (of *mantras*) (should be done) for accomplishing (lord's) stay therein permanently.

13. After having completed thus the announcement of invocation in its three divisions, the preceptor should place the image in the pitcher.

CHAPTER ONE HUNDRED AND TWO

Mode of consecrating the flagstaff

The Lord said :

1. O Skanda ! I shall describe (the mode of) consecration of the pinnacle, the banner and the flag-staff relating to a temple as laid down.

2. Either it should be half the depth of the tank or of the whole edifice. The banner-staff should be made of wood in the case of (a temple) built of brick and of stone in the case of that built of stone.

3. In the case of a temple of Viṣṇu, the pitcher should have the mark of a disc and be proportionate to the image of the deity. If it is with a trident it is known as *agracūla* (the tip of the top portion).

4. If the (mark of a) *liṅga* is found on the top it is called *īśaśūla* (the banner-staff of Śiva). This kind (of flagstaff) is

also found to be described in saivite texts as having the *bījapūraka* (of the shape of common citron)

5. The coloured banner should be made to reach down to the half of the plinth (of the temple), or to commensurate with its entire length, or of the same length with its rod, according to the option (of the consecrator).

6-7. That banner is known as the *mahādhvaja* (great banner) which flaps around the platform of the edifice. The rod measuring fourteen, nine or six cubits in length should be known as the excellent etc. by learned men. A flagstaff made of a bamboo or of wood etc. yields all desires.

8. A flagstaff breaking down in the middle at the time of planting the same augurs evil to the sovereign of the country or to the consecrator.

9. It should be remedied by (the repetition of) the *bahu-rūpamantra.* Then the guardian deities of the door should be worshipped and appeasement with the *mantras* (should be done).

10-12. After having placed the flagstaff, it should be bathed with (the repetition of) the *mantra* of the weapon. After having sprinkled the flagstaff (with water) with (the repetition of) the same *mantra*, the preceptor should then bathe (it) with herbal waters and make the divine edifice. After having smeared (the rod) with juice and laid on the bed as before, the location (of the *mantras*) (is done) in the flagstaff as in the case of the *liṅga.* But one should not locate the energies of knowledge and action. There is no need to use the fourth case (of inflection) indicating speciality. There is also no need for constructing an altar.

13-14. Then the principle of *artha* (sense), the second principle of knowledge and the faces (of Śiva) such as Sadyojāta etc. and the principle of Śiva (should be located) in the flagstaff. Lord Śiva, the indivisible, whose attendants have been located should be worshipped. Then oblations should be made with the vedic *mantras* for the sake of the presence of the flagstaff and ending with (the word) *phaṭ* for every part of the flagstaff. The flagstaff is also consecrated in a different way.

15-17. All about this has been described in the mode of

the *astrayāga*. After the temple has been made, the bedstead and the quadrangle having been decorated at the (decided) place, and the three fundamental principles have been located therein, the oblations etc. should be offered and then (lord) Śiva should be worshipped as before.

18-22. After having meditated on (lord) Śiva as the repository of all the principles, the all-pervasive god should be located (therein). The (gods) Ananta (serpent chief) and Kālarudra (a form of lord Śiva) should be considered as lying at the lotus feet, the (lords) Kūṣmāṇḍa and Hāṭaka at the platform at the top of the plinth and the guardian deities along with the nether worlds, hells, other worlds and the hundred Rudras representing the cosmic egg having been contemplated should be considered at the plinth. Then (the preceptor) should contemplate the picture of a man on the cloth with a lion on the left along with the forty such as principles of water, lustre, and wind, that which is known as enclosing all things, the eight resultant of the intellect, the eight kinds of *yoga*, and the three qualities ending with destruction. The four (principles of) learning etc. (should be considered) as located in the cornice of the temple.

23. The (principle of) illusion along with (lord) Rudra (are located) in the neck, the learning in the threshold, the mystic circle, the master along with the lord of learning in the (ornamental) pot above.

24. It should be conceived as the matted hair and the crescent (on the top) as the trident (of the lord). The three energies (should be located) in the flagstaff and should be looked upon (as permeated) with the sound.

25-26. (The preceptor) should also conceive that the energy (known as) *kuṇḍalī* is present in the banner. Thus (the different gods) should be conceived as present in that abode. After having lifted the *liṅga* along with its pedestal or with the earth (lying at its bottom) with (the recitation of) the *mantras*, it should be placed in its seat namely the lotus of energy after having placed the gems etc.

27. After the banner staff has thus been fixed, the person for whom the rite is performed gets the desired fruits after cir-

cumambulating the edifice along with his relatives and friends.

28. After having contemplated (the *mantra*) *pāśupata*, along with the presiding deities of the *mantras*, the preceptor should invoke the presiding deities possessing the weapons for the sake of protection.

29. After having made oblation for the removal of defects of deficiency etc. and making offerings to the quarters, fees should be paid to the preceptor. The *yajamāna* (the person for whom the rite is done) would go to the heavens.

30. Such a person would enjoy comforts for so many thousand *yugas* as the number of atoms in the structures of the image, *liṅga* and the altar.

CHAPTER ONE HUNDRED AND THREE

Mode of repair of old or broken liṅgas

The Lord said :

1-2. I shall describe the repairing of the *liṅgas* which have become old etc. as laid down. That one which is devoid of the characteristics, or broken or whose outlines have become blunt or that which is struck by lightning or cracked or broken or mutilated or damaged in any other way should be installed on its pedestal as also its bull.

3-5. The *liṅgas* which have been shaken (from their position) or which have become unsteady or which have been slantingly fixed or which lean towards a particular direction or those which have been fixed exactly at the centre (of the temple) should be re-installed (in their places) if they are devoid of any cracks or if they have been washed by floods of river water etc. A *liṅga* of Śiva duly reinstalled at a different place as laid down should not be removed whether it has been perfectly fixed or improperly fixed.

6. A *liṅga* should be established by (offering) a hundred (oblations) and be removed by (offering) a thousand (oblations). If the *liṅga* is worshipped, it would set right even the old ones.

7. After having erected a sacrificial shed either in the southern part or in the north-eastern part of the ground and an arch on the door on the western side and completed the worship of the guardian deities, worship with the *mantras* (is done) on the (sacrificial) ground.

8-10. After having appeased with the *mantras* and worshipped the presiding deities of the ground as before and made offerings for the quarters outside, the preceptor should sip waters (thrice). After having fed the brahmins, (lord) Śambhu (Śiva) should then be informed, "O (lord) Śambhu ! This *liṅga* is defective and is to be removed. O (lord) Śiva graciously take thy seat in myself for a while if it pleases you". After having submitted to the lord thus one should offer oblation of appeasement.

11-12. (The preceptor) (should offer) one hundred and eight oblations with honey, clarified butter, milk, and *dūrvā* (a kind of grass). After having established the *liṅga*, it should be worshipped on the ground then. (The Śiva *mantras* for the worship are (as follows): "*Om*, to the all-pervading etc." "*Om*, obeisance to the lord of the heart, the pervading." The *aṅga mantras* (those for assigning on the different parts of the body) are "*Om* obeisance to the pervading lord, to the head." etc. Then the principle abiding therein should be addressed with the *mantras* of the weapon.

13-17. (Then the preceptor should say as follows): "Whichever good spirit that is lodged in this *liṅga* may go to its place of liking after leaving this *liṅga* by the command of (lord) Śiva. (Lord) Bhava (Śiva) being attended to by the learning and the presiding deities of learning would remain here." Then having made thousand oblations for each one of the (three) parts with the *pāśupata mantra*, sprinkled waters of appeasement and touched with the *kuśa*, (the preceptor) should repeat (the mantras). After having offered the *arghya* (waters for washing) in the reverse order to the (fundamental) principles and to the presiding deities of the principles, the preceptor should bid farewell to the presiding deities of the eight manifestations (of lord Śiva) located in the *liṅga* and the pedestal by binding them with a golden noose placed on the shoulders of the bull and leading them with the repetition of the *mantras* of (lord) Śiva and should put it in the waters. Then the preceptor should offer hundred oblations in order to confer prosperity.

18-22. One hundred oblations each (should be offered) to satisfy the presiding deities of the quarters and for the purification of the sacrificial ground. After having laid protection for that building with the (repetition of the *mantra* of) *pāśupata* weapon, the preceptor should establish another *liṅga* therein as laid down. (*Liṅgas*) established by demons, sages, brahmins belonging to the clan of renowned sages and those well-versed in the *Tantras* (class of literature dealing with magic and mystic formulations for the worship of different deities) should not be removed even as laid down, even though they may be old or broken. This is the procedure to be followed for replacing an old edifice. After having located the collection of *mantras* on the sword another edifice should be made. If (the edifice is) made less spacious it is said to confer death (on the consecrator) and if made too spacious it would cause loss of wealth. Whether the same materials (are used) or better materials it should be done well to be of the same measure as before.

CHAPTER ONE HUNDRED AND FOUR

General characteristic of a divine edifice :

The Lord said :

1. One who has peacock on the banner ! I shall describe you the general characteristics of a divine edifice. In a ground divided into four parts, the breadth of the walls should comprise a part.

2. The adytum should be one-seventh of this. The pedestal (should be) a quarter of its extent. The pedestal should occupy the central part of the ground divided into five parts.

3. The aperture and the wall should be one part each. Two adytums in two parts is medium. One adytum in two parts is excellent.

4-6. According to some the vault of the adytum should occupy three such parts and the walls the rest. In the case of a plot divided into six parts the walls (should comprise) one such part. The breadth of the adytum (should be) one part and that of the pedestal two parts. The height of the temple (should be) double or greater than twice (the breadth) by a quarter or in certain cases triple (that of the breadth). Sometimes it would be half the breadth or one-third of (the entire area of) the ground.

7. The (inner) circumference (of the vault would be) a quarter less than the area of the temple. The outer circumference (would be) a third of it. Small chariots should be got ready at the centre.

8-9. Lords Cāmuṇḍa, Bhairava and Nāṭyeśa (different forms of Lord Śiva) should be placed in them. Images of eight or four deities should be made outside to surround (the main temple) and they should occupy half the space of the temple. They may or may not be within the temples. The (images of) Ādityas (the 12 suns, progeny of Aditi and Kaśyapa) should be placed at the east. The (images of) Skanda and Agni (should be placed) in the north-west.

10. In this way, images of Yama (lord of death) and other deities should be placed in the respective directions over which they preside. After having divided the pinnacle into four parts, the region of the vault (should be made to comprise) two such parts.

11-13. The top platform of (god of) fire should be in the third part. The flat cushion (should be placed above that) with a cornice. The five (classes of temples) are *vairāja*, *puṣpaka*, *kailāsa*, *maṇika* and *triviṣṭapa* (characterised by structures of different shapes) built over the top platform. The first (among the above) is a square, the second one a rectangle, (the third one) circular, the next one oval and the fifth one is octagonal. Each one of these is divided into nine (thereby) giving rise to forty-five divisions.

14-15. The temples belonging to the *vairāja* class are—the first one *meru*, *mandara* the second one, *vimāna*, *bhadra*, *sarvatobhadra*, *caruka*, *nandika*, *nandivardhana* and *śrīvatsa*.

16-17. The nine temples belonging to the *puṣpaka* (class) are *valabhī*, *gṛharāja*, *śālāgṛha*, *mandira*, *viśāla*, *brahmamandira*, *bhavana*, *prabhava* and *śibikāveśma*. The circular shaped temples—

valaya, dundubhi, padma, mahāpadma, varddhanī, uṣṇīṣa, śaṅkha, kalaśa and *khavṛkṣa* belong to the *kailāsa* class.

18-21. The nine—*gaja, vṛṣabha, haṁsa, garutmān, ṛkṣanāyaka, bhūṣaṇa, bhūdhara, śrījaya* and *pṛthivīdhara* are oval-shaped and belong to (the class called) *maṇika. Vajra, cakra, svastika, vajra-svastika, citra, avastika-khaḍga, gadā, śrīkaṇṭha* and *vijaya* are the names of those which belong to *triviṣṭapa* (class).

22. These are the names given to the towns of Lāṭas etc. The top portion should be half the height of the neck and proportionately broad.

23. After having made the top platform into ten parts, the breadth of the shoulder portion (should be made to comprise) five parts. The neck portion should be made (to comprise) three parts, and the *pracaṇḍaka* (?) should be four such parts.

24. The doors should be made so as to face the cardinal points and never on the intermediate points. The pedestal should extend to two corners (of the temple) and to the middle part of the adytum.

25. Sometimes (the pedestals) extend upto the fifth part of the adytum from the posterior edge thereof, their height being double of their length. A different type (of construction) is described now.

26-30. Four doors should be made so as to measure ten fingers less than one hundred and sixty fingers known as the *uttama* (excellent ones). Three (doors) would be of the *madhyama* (middle) order and three (doors) of the *kanīyasa* (inferior ones). The breadth (would be) equal to half the height or height greater than (the breadth) by a third part. The height may be four or eight or ten fingers more. The breadth may be a fourth (part) of the height. There should be ornamental indents on the threshold. It has been stated that the breadth of all of them (should be) half the breadth (of the doors). The door with two, five, seven or nine ornamental indents confers the desired (fruit). Two warders should be carved in the doorframe to occupy a quarter part of the latter below the lower (ornamental) branch. The ends of the (ornamental) branches should be decorated with (the images) of the fairy twins.

31. (In a temple) if the post has been encroached (the consecrator) would be a slave and if the tree has been impeded

in its growth it would confer poverty, if it has encroached on a well at the gate it portends fear and if it protrudes over the ground (it augurs) loss of wealth.

32. If it has encroached a thoroughfare it would get captivity (for the consecrator). One would get poverty if the temple had been built to make the hall (in front) as narrow. If it obstructs the *varṇa* (?) it will make one deformed.

33-34. If a mortar causes an obstruction it would give poverty. If a stone-block causes obstruction it would cause enmity. If it is shadowed (by some other building) it gives poverty. There will not be defects of obstruction (in the following cases) —by felling a tree, uprooting (of stone) or by leaving intervening space equal to twice that of the original compound.

CHAPTER ONE HUNDRED AND FIVE

Mode of worship of the presiding deity of a place

The Lord said :

1. The presiding deity of the ground should be worshipped in (a mystic diagram) of eightyone squares for the prosperity of a city, village, fort, house or temple and their definite accomplishment.

2-4. I shall narrate the names of the ten occult nerves which face the east. (They are) *śāntā*, *yaśovatī*, *kāntā*, *viśālā*, *prāṇavāhinī*, *satī*, *vasumatī*, *nandā*, *subhadrā* and *manoramā*. (The following occult nerves) are remembered in the north in twelve of the eighty-one squares—*hariṇī*, *suprabhā*, *lakṣmī*, *vibhūti*, *vimalā*, *priyā*, *jayā*, *jvālā* and *viśokā*.

5. (Gods) Īśa and others should be worshipped in the eight directions. (Gods) Īśa, Dhanañjaya, Śakra (Indra), Arka (Sun), Satya (truth), Bhṛśa (strong) and Vyoma (sky) (should be worshipped) in the east.

6. (Gods) Havyavāha (fire), Pūṣan, Vitatha, (untruth), Bhauma (Mars), Kṛtānta (god of death), Gandharva (a semi-divine being), Bhṛṅga and Mṛga (should be worshipped) in the south.

7. The Pitṛs, the door-keepers, Sugrīva, Puṣpadanta, Varuṇa, Daitya (demon), Śeṣa (the serpent-god), and yakṣman (consumption) (should be worshipped) always in the west.

8. The diseases, the serpent-chief, Bhallāṭa, fortune, Aditi, and Diti should occupy six half squares. (God) Brahmā should be worshipped in the nine squares (at the centre).

9-10. (God) known as ĀYĀ (should be worshipped) in the two north-eastern squares of Brahmā. (God) known as Apavatsa (should be located) in the six squares below that between the central points. (God) Savitā should occupy two squares in between those of Marīci and Fire-god. (God) Sāvitrī should occupy two places below that and (God) Vivasvān six places below that.

11. (One should worship) (the gods), Viṣṇu, Indra, Jaya and the moon in the squares belonging to Pitṛs and (lord) Brahmā. (The god) Mitra should be worshipped in the six squares in between those of (gods) Brahmā and Varuṇa.

12. The attendant of (god) Rudra (should be worshipped) always in the ten (squares) in between those of the diseases and (god) Brahmā. (The disease) *yakṣman* (consumption) (should be worshipped) in the two squares below that and *dharādhara* in the six squares on the north.

13. (The demonesses and demons) Carakī, Skandavikaṭa Vidārī, Pūtanā, Jambha, Pāpa and Pili-piccha should be worshipped outside in the directions of north-east etc.

14. There should be eightyone divisions of squares (in the case of a site relating to) a house. The same should be one hundred divisions (if it relates to) a (temple) pavilion. As before, the gods should be worshipped. (Lord) Brahmā (should be worshipped) in the sixteen squares (at the centre).

15-16. (The gods) Marīci, Vivasvat, Mitra and Pṛthvīdhara should be (worshipped) in ten squares in the (four) directions. Diti, Īśānī, Mṛga, Mukhya, Pitṛs, Pāpa (spirit of sin), yakṣman (consumption) and fire-god should be (worshipped) in one and a half square each in the (eight) directions north-east etc.

17. O Guha (Kumāra, son of Lord Śiva and Pārvatī)! I shall briefly describe the measures (of different forms of temples) in order. It should measure twentyeight cubits in length and twentyeight cubits in breadth.

18. The entire circumference would measure twenty-two cubits. The width of the wall would measure nine. The above measures would hold good in the case of pavilions known as *śivāśraya*, *śivākhya*, *rudra-hīna* and *sadobhaya*.

19. (The pavilions of) the Sāvitra class would measure eighteen cubits in length and fifteen in breadth, and the width of the walls would be made equal to a thirtieth part of the above.

20. The height of the walls above the plinth would measure thrice the width thereof. The ground elevation of manifold kinds depending on the passages should be in a same line with the foot of the wall.

21. In the Bhadra (type of temples) there should be passages (on all sides) except at the front. There should be a passage at the entrance. The Śrījaya (class) would be devoid of the hinder (passage). If there are no passages on the sides it is Bhadra class.

22. The passage (should be) as wide as the adytum or half of it. The supplementary passage (should be) half (that) of the (main) passage and should link one, two or three chambers.

23. I shall describe the common features of the temples which would confer all the desires (on the consecrator). (It should have) one, two, three, four or eight rooms in order.

24. In a temple having one room the southern part should face the north. If there are two, one of them should have its western part facing the east. If there are four rooms there should be one room each as stated above facing the north and east respectively.

25. If it faces the west it is known as Śiva, the east (it is known as) Yamasūryaka, the east and north (it is known as) Daṇḍa, and the east and south (it is) known as Vāta.

26. If it faces the west and north it is called Bali. That which is (known as) the Triśūla will get destruction of wealth. A house devoid of its eastern wing will be Sukṣetra which confers prosperity.

27. One devoid of southern rooms is (known as) Śūlī. That are having three rooms confers excessive prosperity. The building without any room on the west destroys the progeny of the consecrator) and also creates many enemies.

28-29. I shall describe the eight chambers commencing with the east (known as) *dhvaja* etc. The washing and fragrance chambers as well as the kitchen (should be) on the south-east. The parlour and bed chambers (should be) in the south. (The chamber) for bows and weapons (should be) at the south-west. (The chamber) for costly articles (should be) at the west. (Room) for articles of perfume (should be) at the north-west.

30. (The chamber) for wealth and cattle should be made in the north. The excellent place for initiation (should be) on the north-east. The building (should be made) according to (a standard) measured with the consecrator's hand and co-extensive with the pedestal.

31. The cubit measures should be tripled and then divided by eight. Then the remainder should (be the measure) of the *dhvaja* etc. upto the end of *vāyasa*.

32. A building (raised on) the second, third, fourth, sixth, seventh and the eighth (parts of the ground) as well as in the middle and end will be ruinous.

33. Hence, the divine edifice built on the ninth part is deemed to be auspicious. The pavilion built at the centre thereof having a breadth equal to or twice the breadth (of the edifice) is commendable.

34-38. Eight rooms each should be built on the east, west, north and south. The effects of these from east onwards are respectively (described). Fear, association with woman, victory, prosperity, fame, righteousness, strife and poverty are the eight effects of the door on the east. The eight effects of the door on the south are conflagration, unhappiness, annihilation of friends, loss of property, death, (gain of) wealth, becoming a sculptor and (birth of) children. Long life, banishment, grains, wealth, peace, destruction of wealth, emaciation, enjoyment, progeny are the effects of the door on the west. Illness, intoxication affliction, prominence, wealth, longevity, intelligence and honour are the effects of the door on the north.

CHAPTER ONE HUNDRED AND SIX

Vāstu relating to Cities

The Lord said :

1. I shall describe the *vāstu* (worship of the presiding deity) relating to a city for the prosperity of the kingdom. Land measuring eight miles or half of it or a quarter of it should be set apart.

2. After having worshipped the presiding deity of the city, enclosure should be made ready in the thirty squares of lord Īśa (Śiva) and others. The eastern gate (should be) on that of (lord) Sun.

3. The southern (gate) should be (raised) on (the squares) of the *gandharvas* (semi divine beings) while the western one (should be raised) on that of (lord) Varuṇa. The northern gate (should be) made on that of (lord) Soma. The low-roofed chambers should be made extensive.

4. The doors should be six (cubits wide) so that the elephants and other (animals) could easily pass through. A city should never be founded (on grounds) far away from one another, or of shape of the crescent moon or hypotenuse (of the plot) broken.

5. (A city of the shape) of the face of a *vajrasūci* (diamond needle) or having two or three easy ways is not favourable. The frontage of a city resembling (the shape of) a bow or *vajranāga* is beneficiary.

6. After having worshipped (the gods) Viṣṇu, Śiva, Sun and others and bowing down, the founder (of a city) should make the offerings. The goldsmiths and blacksmiths should be provided for at the south-eastern quarter of the city.

7. The houses of professional dancers and courtesans (should be located) in the southern quarter. (The houses) of actors, potters and fishermen (should be located) in the south-western quarter.

8. (Space) should be (set apart for) war-chariots, weapons and swords in the western quarter (of a city). Distillers of liquor and those engaged in the service (of the state) (should be located) in the north-western quarter.

9. Brahmins, ascetics and holymen (should be provided for) in the northern quarter. Those who sell fruits and other articles and merchant community in general should be located in the north-eastern quarter.

10. The commanders of army (should be given quarters) in the eastern quarter. Different regiments of the army (should be provided) in the south-eastern quarter. The officers who attend upon the ladies (should have their residence) in the southern quarter. Royal camps should be located in the south-western part.

11. The chief ministers, treasurers and architects (should be located) in the western direction. Men of judiciary belonging to the clan of brahmins and eminent men (should be located) in the northern part.

12. The military men (should be located) in the southern part, the tradesmen and *śūdras* (fourth class of men) in the western part. The physicians (should be provided with quarters) in all directions and horses and army should be placed in all quarters.

13. The movable class of *liṅgas* (should be placed) in the east and the cremation ground in the south. Cattle-sheds (should be located) in the western part and farmers in the northern part.

14. Foreigners should be located in the angular points. This should be observed even in small villages. Those who see (the goddess) Lakṣmī and Kubera at (each side of) the eastern gate-way (of the city) obtain prosperity.

15. The temples of gods (should be established) in the western part facing the east. (The divine edifices should) face towards the west and north respectively in the east and the south.

16-17. The temples of gods Brahmā, Īśa (Śiva) and Viṣṇu (should be built in the city) for the protection of the city. A city, a village, a fortress or a house not having a (guardian) deity will be swallowed by the goblins etc. and becomes infected by diseases. The cities protected by deities confer victory, enjoyment and emancipation.

18. The treasure-house should be in the east, the kitchen in the south-east, the bed-chamber in the south and the arsenal on the west.

19. The dining (chamber) (should be) in the western part,

the granary in the north-west, store-house in the north and the chamber for the deities in the north-east.

20-23. The palaces may have four chambers or three or two or one. In the case of palaces having four chambers there are two hundred and fiftyfive subdivisions based on the terraces in front of the buildings, whereas those having three chambers (will have) four (sub-divisions) and those having two chambers (will have) five (sub-divisions) and those having one chamber (will have) four. The terraces should number twentyeight both in a house and city or they should be four, seven, fiftyfive, six, twenty-eight or eight only.

CHAPTER ONE HUNDRED AND SEVEN

The creation of Svāyambhuva Manu

Fire-god said :

1-3. I shall describe the different worlds, the earth and the continents. King Priyavrata had ten sons Agnīdhra, Agnibāhu, Vapuṣmān, Dyutimān, Medhā, Medhātithi, Bhavya, Savana, Jyotiṣmān, and Satya. The father gave them seven continents as follows: He gave Jambūdvīpa to Agnīdhra and Plakṣa to Medhātithi.

4. He gave (the continent of) Śālmala to Vapuṣmān, (continent) Kuśa to Jyotiṣmān, continent of Krauñca to Dyutimān and (continent of) Śāka to Bhavya.

5. He gave Puṣkara to Savana. What Jambūdvīpa was given to Agnīdhra by his father (was divided by him and given to his sons). He gave (the country) called Hima to Nābhi.

6. (He gave) Hemakūṭa to Kimpuruṣa, Naiṣadha to Harivarṣa, central Meru to Ilāvṛta, Nīlācala (Nīla mountains) to Ramya.

7. (He gave) Śvetavarṣa to Hiraṇvat, Kuru to Kuru, Bhadrāśva to Bhadrāśva, western (countries) to Ketumāla.

8. The king having established the sons of Priyavrata (in the regions) of Meru, went to the forest. After having performed penance, he reached god Hari.

9. O Foremost among beings ! the eight countries Kimpuruṣa and others by nature abound in happiness and felicity and have natural perfection.

10. There is no fear of old age or death, (adherence or non-observance of) moral obligations relating to *yuga* periods, or lower or middle class of beings in (the country) of Hima.

11. Ṛṣabha was born to Nābhi through Meru. Bharata was born to Ṛṣabha. After having entrusted the kingdom to his son, Ṛṣabha resorted to Śālagrāma and attained Hari.

12. The country was called Bhārata after the name Bharata. Sumati was born to Bharata. Bharata resorted to Śālagrāma (to worship) Hari after entrusting his kingdom (to his son).

13. He became a yogin (on practising *yoga*). I shall describe his life later at the time of narration of *yoga*. From Sumati, Tejas (was born). Indradyumna was born from him.

14-15. Parameṣṭhī was born from him and Pratīhāra was born then. Pratihartā (was born) from Pratīhāra and then Bhuva, Udgītha and Prastāra from Pratihartā. Vibhu was the son of Prastāra. Then (was born) Pṛthu and Nakta. Gaya was the son of Nakta.

16. Nara was the son of Gaya. Then Virāṭ was his son. Mahāvīrya was the son (of Virāṭ). Dhīmān was born to him.

17. Mahānta was his son. Manasya was his (Mahānta's) son. (Then) Tvaṣṭā (was born to him). Virajā (was born) to Tvaṣṭā. Raja was his son.

18. Satyajit (was born) to Raja. O Sage ! one hundred sons were born to him. They were the lights of the universe. The (country of) Bhārata was well-developed by them. The creation of the Svāyambhuva (Manu) was remembered (so far) relating to Kṛta and Tretā (yugas).

CHAPTER ONE HUNDRED AND EIGHT

Cosmographical account

Fire-god said :

1. The seven continents are Jambū, Plakṣa, Śālmali, Kuśa, Krauñca, Śāka and Puṣkara.

2. These continents are surrounded by seven oceans namely, Lavaṇa (salt), Ikṣu (sugarcane juice), Surā (nectar), Sarpiṣ (clarified butter), Dadhi (curd), Dugdha (milk) and Jala (water) of even proportions.

3. The Jambūdvīpa (continent of Jambū) is situated at the centre of continents. The Meru mountain which is the kind of sixteen mountains towers majestically extending to eighty-four (*yojanas*).

4. The mountain rises to thirtytwo thousand (*yojanas*) above (the earth) and spreads to sixteen thousand (*yojanas*) under the earth. Its peaks are in the shape of a pericarp of a lotus.

5. Himavān, Hemakūṭa and Niṣadha are in the southern part. Nīla, Śveta and Śṛṅgī are the *varṣaparvatas* (boundary mountains) in the northern part.

6. Two of the above (mountains) extend to two lakhs (*yojanas*) at their middle, while the others are ten thousand (*yojanas*) less. Their altitude is two thousand *yojanas* and they have an equal breadth at the base.

7. O Twice-born one ! Bhārata is the first mountain. Kimpuruṣa is known as the next one. Harivarṣa is the next one to the south of Meru.

8. Ramyaka, Hiraṇyaka and Uttara Kuru are in the north just as the Bhārata (in the south).

9. O Excellent sage ! Each one of them is nine thousand (*yojanas*) in their extent. Ilāvṛta is at the middle. Meru rises up from the centre with its golden peak.

10. O Fortunate one ! Ilāvṛta spreads to nine thousand (*yojanas*) all around Meru. There are four mountains here.

11. They are beams of support for the Meru, each one extending to one lakh (*yojanas*). (Among these) the Mandara (mountain) is in the east and the Gandhamādana is in the south.

12-13. The Vipula (mountain) is in the west and the Supārśva (mountain) is in the north. The Kadamba, Jambū, Pippala and Vaṭa are the trees in these extending to eleven hundred (*yojanas*) (serving as) their banners. Jambūdvīpa gets its appellation on account of the Jambū fruit of the size of an elephant.

14. The waters of the river Jambū deposit the golden ores.

The Supārśva (mountain lies) on the east of Meru and the Ketumāla (mountain) on the west.

15. The forest of Caitraratha (lies) on the east, Gandhamādana on the south, Vaibhrāja on the west and Nandana on the north. (I shall describe) the lakes herein.

16. (They are) Aruṇoda, Mahābhadra, Śītoda, Mānasa, Sitāmbha, Cakra and Muñja. The mountains known as Keśarācala[1] are in the east.

17-18. The mountains (called) Trikūṭa[2] (group) lie on the south. The Śikhivāsa[3] (group) (lie) on the west. The Śaṅkhakūṭa[4] (group) lie on the north. The abode of lord Brahmā is on the Meru (mountain) extending to fourteen thousand *yojanas* above. (The abodes) of Indra and other guardian deities are around the abode of Brahmā.

19. The river Sītā, after falling from the feet of (lord) Viṣṇu, washes the lunar region and falls from heavens on the east (on the Bhadrāśva mountain). It falls from Bhadrāśva on the hills below successively and reaches the ocean.

20-21. Similarly, (the river) Alakanandā flows in Bhārata through the south and reaches the ocean after dividing itself into seven branches.

(The river) Cakṣu reaches the ocean on the west. So also (the river) Bhadrā (passes through) the Uttara Kuru (country) and reaches the northern ocean. (The mountains) Mālyavat and Gandhamādana extend upto the Nīla and Niṣadha (mountains in the north and south respectively).

22-27. The Meru (mountain) lies in between them in the shape of a lotus. (The countries) Bhārata, Ketumāla, Bhadrāśva, and Kurus situated outside these boundary mountains are the petals of this lotus of the world. The two boundary mountains Jaṭhara and Devakūṭa extend upto the Nīla and Niṣadha mountains on the north and south. The Gandhamādana and Kailāsa

---

1. They are Śitāmbha, Kumuda, Kurarī, Mālyavān and Vaikaṅka. See *Vi.P.* II.ii.26.

2. They are Trikūṭa, Śiśira, Pataṅga, Rucaka and Niṣāda. See *Vi. P.* II.ii.27.

3. They are Śikhivāsa, Vaiḍūrya, Kapila, Gandhamādana and Jārudhi. See *Vi.P.* II.ii.28.

4. They are Śaṅkhakūṭa, Ṛṣabha, Haṁsa, Nāga and Kālañjara. See *ib.* 29.

(mountains) spreading in the east and west to eighty *yojanas* lie in the ocean. The two boundary mountains Niṣadha and Pāriyātra are situated on the west as in the east. (Similarly), the boundary mountains Jaṭhara and others (are situated) around Meru in four directions.

28. O Excellent sage ! Abodes of (goddess) Lakṣmī, (lords) Viṣṇu, Agni and Sūrya and other gods are situated in the caves in the mountains Keśara and others.

29-30. They are the abodes of gods on the earth. Sinners do not go there. Lord Viṣṇu resides in Bhadrāśva as Hayagrīva, in Ketumāla as Varāha, in Bhārata in the form of Kūrma (tortoise) and in Kurus in the form of Matsya (fish). Lord Hari is worshipped everywhere in his universal form.

31. In the eight countries Kimpuruṣa and others, there is no (misery such as) hunger, fear, grief and others. The twenty-four thousand inhabitants live without diseases.

32. There is no imaginary division of time such as the *Kṛta* (*yuga*) etc., the division of worlds, waters and clouds. There are seven principal mountains in each one of these countries.

33. Hundreds of rivers rise from them giving rise to sacred waters. I shall describe the sacred spots situated in Bhārata.

CHAPTER ONE HUNDRED AND NINE

The greatness of sacred spots

Fire-god said :

1-4. I shall describe the greatness of all sacred spots which confer enjoyment and emancipation. One, whose hands, feet and mind are well-disciplined and one who possesses learning, austerity and penance, reaps the fruits of pilgrimage. One who has restrained from accepting alms, one who eats less, one who has conquered his senses, one who is devoid of sins, such a person on pilgrimage would get the fruits of all sacrificial rites. One would be born as poor, if he has not fasted three nights, had not gone on pilgrimage and had not given gold and cows as gift. Whatever fruit is got by doing sacrificial rites will be gained by going on pilgrimage.

5. O Brahmin ! Puṣkara is the excellent sacred spot. One should dwell there atleast for three nights. There are thousand crores of sacred places in Puṣkara.

6. Lord Brahmā resides here along with celestials. The sages who desire for everything and the celestials have had perfection here after bathing and worshipping the ancestors and celestials.

7. They attain the fruits of performing Aśvamedha rite and reach Brahmaloka. One who gifts food in (the month of) Kārttika, gets free from sins and reaches Brahmaloka.

8. It is difficult to go to Puṣkara and the austerity at Puṣkara is still more difficult. It is difficult to give gift at Puṣkara and it is still more difficult to stay at Puṣkara.

9. One elevates hundreds of manes by staying therein, by repetition (of divine names) and by doing ancestoral rites. The path to Jambū also lies therein, as also the sacred spot of Taṇḍulikāśrama.

10-11. The Kaṇvāśrama, Koṭitīrtha, (river) Narmadā, Arbuda, Carmaṇvatī, Sindhu, Somanātha, Prabhāsa, confluence of (river) Sarasvatī at the ocean, the ocean, Piṇḍāraka, Dvārakā and Gomatī yield all fruits.

12-13. The Bhūmitīrtha, Brahmatuṅga and the (land of) five rivers, the king of mountains, Devikā, the destroyer of sins, the meritorious Vinaśana, Nagodbheda, the destroyer of sins the Kumārakoṭi are spoken as bestowers of all benefits.

14. Whoever always says, "I will go to Kurukṣetra and live, therein", becomes free of sin and goes to heaven.

15. The gods Viṣṇu and others dwell there. (One who) lives therein reaches lord Viṣṇu. One who bathes in the river Sarasvatī and Sannihata reaches the region of Brahmā.

16. Even the dust particles at Kurukṣetra confer excellent position. The Dharmatīrtha, Suvarṇa and Haridvāra are excellent places.

17. The sacred places Kanakhala and Bhadrakarṇahrada are meritorious. The confluence of the rivers Ganges and Sarasvatī and the Brahmāvarta destroy sins.

18. The Bhṛgutuṅga, Kubjāmra and the place of origin of Ganges destroy sins. Vārāṇasī is an excellent sacred spot. Avimukta is unsurpassed.

19. The sacred Kapālamocana and Prayāga, the excellent sacred spot, the confluence of Gomatī and Gaṅgā and (the river) Gaṅgā throughout do not confer hell.

20. The sacred Rājagṛha is meritorious. Śālagrāma removes sins. Vaṭeśa, the sacred Vāmana and the confluence of Kālikā are excellent places.

21. Lauhitya, (river) Karatoyā, Śoṇa, Ṛṣabha (hills) are excellent places. Śrīparvata, Kolbagiri, Sahyādri and Malayagiri (are sacred).

22. The rivers Godāvarī, Tuṅgabhadrā, Kāverī, Tāpī, Payoṣṇī and Revā are the bestowers (of fruits). The Daṇḍaka forest is excellent.

23. Kālañjara, Muñjavaṭa, Sūrpāraka, (river) Mandākinī, Citrakūṭa and Śṛṅgaverapura are excellent spots.

24. Avantī is an excellent place. Ayodhyā destroys one's sins. Naimiṣa is an excellent place which yields enjoyment and liberation.

CHAPTER ONE HUNDRED AND TEN

The greatness of Gaṅgā

Fire-god said :

1. I shall describe the greatness of (river) Gaṅgā. She should be worshipped. She yields enjoyment and liberation. The countries through which she flows are holy and excellent.

2. The (river) Ganges is the succour for the beings who resort to it always. The (river) Ganges duly worshipped, succours the two lines of ancestors.

3. The drinking of the waters of Ganges (confers the merits of performance of) thousands of Cāndrāyaṇa. One who worships the Ganges for a month gets the fruits of all sacrificial rites.

4. The goddess (Ganges) destroys all sins and confers (access to) heavens. One continues to stay in heavens as long as (his) bones remain in the (waters of the) Ganges.

5. Blind people and others attain equal status with the

celestials by worshipping her. The carrying of the earth dug up from the beds of Ganges destroys one's sins just as the Sun.

6. (The river) purifies hundreds and thousands of holy men who look at it, touch it, drink (its waters) and repeat (the word) Ganges.

CHAPTER ONE HUNDRED AND ELEVEN

The Greatness of Prayāga

Fire-god said :

1. I shall describe the greatness of Prayāga, the excellent place, which confers enjoyment and emancipation. O Excellent sages ! the gods Brahmā , Viṣṇu and others stay at Prayāga.

2. So also the rivers, oceans, *siddhas* (accomplished persons), gandharvas (semi-divine beings) (stay there). There are three fire-pits and the Ganges (flows) in the middle.

3. (The river Yamunā), the daughter of Sun, renowned in the three worlds flows there with force having all sacred spots before her.

4. (The land) in between (the rivers) Ganges and Yamunā is known to be the thigh of (goddess) earth. The sages knew that Prayāga is the generative organ situated in the thigh.

5. Prayāga and Pratiṣṭhāna are the woollen blanket and the mule. The holy place of Bhogavatī is the platform for the god of creation (Brahmā).

6-7. The scriptures and sacrificial rites are endowed with forms at Prayāga. By singing in praise of this sacred place, or by the repetition of (lord's) names or by touching the earth here (one) gets free from all sins. Charity, ancestral rites and recitation (of names of the god) done at Prayāga, the place of confluence (of the two rivers), has undecaying merits.

8. O Twice-born ! One who has resolved to die at Prayāga at the end (of his term of life) should not change his mind on the authority of scriptures or on the words of the people.

9-12. Ten thousand and six crores of sacred places are present only here. Hence Prayāga is the foremost (place). The

Bhogavatī, sacred spot of Vāsuki (serpent chief) and the flight of swans are present here. One reaps the fruits of making a charity of a crores of cows by bathing at Prayāga three days in the month of *māgha* (February-March). The learned have declared thus. It is easy to have access to Ganges all along its course, but very difficult at the (following) three places—Gaṅgādvāra (Haridvāra), Prayāga and the confluence of Ganges with the ocean. One goes to heaven by giving alms here and one will become a monarch here itself.

13-14. One who dies at the root of the banyan tree and the confluence goes to the abode oflord Viṣṇu. The sacred sands on which Urvaśī (a nymph) had sported, the Sandhyāvaṭa, the Koṭitīrtha, the Aśvamedha, the pure Mānasa, and Vāsaraka are all excellent places.

CHAPTER ONE HUNDRED AND TWELVE

The greatness of Vārāṇasi

Fire-god said :

1. (Lord) Maheśvara (Śiva) said to Gaurī (consort of Śiva) that Vārāṇasī is the sacred place. It confers enjoyment and emancipation on those who reside there and recite (the name of god) Hari (Viṣṇu).

Rudra (*Śiva*) *said* :

2. "The sacred place, O Gaurī, has never been forsaken (by me) and hence it is called Avimukta[1]. The repetition (of god's names), the performance of penance and giving alms at Avimukta indeed (yields) undiminishing benefits.

3-5. After rubbing away dust from the feet with a stone, one should stay at Kāśī (Vārāṇasī). He should never forsake it. The eight holy spots —Hariścandra, Āmrātakeśvara, Japyeśvara, Śrīparvata, Mahālaya, Bhṛgu, Caṇḍeśvara and Kedāra, remain concealed at Avimuktaka (Vārāṇasī). Avimuktaka is the most sacred place among all sacred places.

6. It extends to two *yojanas* in the east and half a *yojana* in

1. Avimukta is one of the names of Vārāṇasī.

the opposite direction. The (two) rivers Varaṇā and Asī (flow) and Vārāṇasī lies between the two.

7. Bathing, muttering (of divine names), oblations (to gods), (one's) death, worship of gods, ancestral rites, alms-giving and stay and whatsoever done here is capable of conferring enjoyment and emancipation.

CHAPTER ONE HUNDRED AND THIRTEEN

The greatness of Narmadā

Fire-god said :

1. I shall describe the greatness of Narmadā which yields great pleasure. The water of the Ganges purifies the bather at once. The water of the river Narmadā (purifies) at the mere sight of it.

2-3. It extends (in length) to one hundred *yojana* and two *yojanas* in breadth. There are sixty thousand holy places and sixty crores on the hills on either side at Amarakaṇṭaka. (The place of) confluence with Kāverī is meritorious. Listen to me. I shall describe about Śrīparvata.

4-5. (Goddess) Gaurī in the guise of (goddess) Śrī (Lakṣmī) did penance here. Lord Hari told her, who was doing penance, that she would attain salvation, and that hill will be known after her name as Śrīparvata. Hundred *yojanas* all along (the hill) would become greatly meritorious. Charity, penance, chants and ceremony done here all yield undiminishing merits.

6. Death at this place (conveys one) to the world of Śiva. This excellent sacred place yields everything. Lord Śiva sports here with his consort. (The demon) Hiraṇyakaśipu performed penance here and became mighty. The sages attained perfection here.

CHAPTER ONE HUNDRED AND FOURTEEN

The greatness of Gayā

The Fire-god said :

1-2. I shall describe the greatness of Gayā. It is the most excellent among the sacred places. The demon Gaya practised penance. Being tormented by the heat of his penance, the celestials (approached lord) Viṣṇu who was lying in the milky ocean and told him "Kindly protect us from the demon Gaya." (Lord) Hari (Viṣṇu) said yes. He met the demon and asked him to request for a boon.

3-4. The demon requested that he would be the holiest of all places. Lord Viṣṇu granted his request. Having seen that the demon (was on the earth) and the earth had become deserted without Lord Viṣṇu, the celestials, Brahmā and others in the heaven met lord Hari (Viṣṇu) and said, "O (lord) Hari ! The earth has become deserted."

5. On seeing the demon's presence, lord Hari (Viṣṇu) asked (lord) Brahmā, "You go to the demon along with the celestials and request for his body for the purpose of a sacrifice."

6. After having heard that, Brahmā went to the demon Gaya along with the celestials and said to him as follows: "I am your guest. I request you (to give me your) pure body for (the sake of being offered in) a sacrifice."

7. The demon Gaya granted the request. He fell down. (Lord Brahmā) did the sacrifice on the skull. As it was moving, (lord Viṣṇu) asked lord Brahmā to offer the final oblation.

8-9. Even as the final oblation was being offered, the demon moved. Hence lord Brahmā asked Lord Viṣṇu. Lord Viṣṇu then called Dharma (the god of virtue) and said, "O celestials ! you all support this divine stone. The club-wielding form of mine along with the gods will be present on this slab."

10-11. Having heard that, lord Dharma supported that excellent divine slab. Marīci, the son of Brahmā married Dharmavratā, the daughter of Dharma and Dharmavatī. She was devoted to doing penance. (They two spent happily) just as (lord) Hari sported with (goddess) Śrī (Lakṣmī) and (lord) Śambhu (Śiva) with (goddess) Gaurī (Pārvatī).

12. (Once) he returned from the forest with *kuśa* (grass)

and flowers and was very tired. After taking food he said to Dharmavratā, "Massage my feet."

13. The dear wife accordingly was massaging the feet of the sage who was taking rest. In the meanwhile, as the sage fell into a nap, lord Brahmā came there.

14. Dharmavratā began to think, "Shall I worship lord Brahmā ? Or shall I continue to massage the feet (of my lord) ? Brahmā who is the lord of my lord should be worshipped."

15-17. After thinking (for some time) she began to worship lord Brahmā with all the honours. Marīci (woke up and) saw her (doing service to Brahmā). As she was not doing as directed he cursed her angrily, "You will become a stone". Dharmavratā also said to him, "After having stopped massaging your feet, I had worshipped (Brahmā) your lord. As you have cursed me, a faultless person, you will be cursed by (lord) Śaṅkara (Śiva)". Dharmavratā bore the curse singly and resorted to fire-god.

18. She performed penance for a long period. Then Viṣṇu and other celestials appeared in front of her and asked her to request for a boon.

19-22. Dharmavratā said to the celestials, "O Gods let my curse come to an end. The celestials said, "The curse given by Marīci will not be otherwise. You will become a sacred stone bearing the marks of the foot-prints of lord (Viṣṇu). You will be endowed with the essence of the gods, O Devavratā (Dharmavratā) ! You will be representing the forms of all celestials, You will be meritorious for making the demon motionless". Devavratā said, "If you are pleased with me, may Brahmā, Viṣṇu, Rudra, Gaurī, Lakṣmī and other gods stay in me ever." The fire-god said, "Having heard the words of Devavratā, the celestials said in affirmative and repaired to the heavens."

23. That divine stone slab of the demon was supported by (lord) Dharma. The demon began to move with the stone slab on which (the gods) Rudra and others remained.

24. The demon was still moving along with celestials. Then lord Hari (Viṣṇu), who was reclining in the milky ocean, was requested by celestials and he gave his form of wielding a mace.

25. (He said) "You all may go. I shall myself go there with the form known to all celestials." There lord Gadādhara

manifested (in the form of) manifest, unmanifest and both mani fest and unmanifest.

26-30. (Lord) Ādigadādhara was himself present in order to make (the stone slab) steady. There was a demon named Gadā. He was killed by lord Viṣṇu. Viśvakarmā (the celestial architect) made a mace from the bones (of that demon). (Lord) Gadādhara killed Heti and other demons with that first mace duly. Hence, he is known as Ādigadādhara. When lord Ādigadādhara was manifest in the divine stone slab and the demon remained steady, then lord Brahmā offered the final oblation. The demon Gaya asked celestials "Why I was deceived ? By the more command of lord Viṣṇu I would have remained steady. Because you have tormented me you should give me a boon".

The celestials said:

31-32. "Since you have been made steady by us, this will become a holy place of the lords Viṣṇu, Śambhu (Śiva) and Brahmā. (It would become) more renowned than all other sacred places. It would confer the region of Brahmā on the (departed) ancestors". Having spoken thus, the gods and goddesses remained there. All the sacred places also were present there.

33-35. After having performed the sacrifice, Brahmā gave fees to the priests. The sacred place of Gayā (extends to) five *krośas* (ten miles). Fiftyfive villages were endowed with (the following): Golden hills flowing with rivers, milk and honey, reservoirs of curd, clarified butter, plenty of hills of food, *kāmadhenu* (the celestial cow), *kalpataru* (the celestial tree) and abodes made of gold and silver. Let the brahmins here do not seek alms. The lord gave all these things after having spoken very little.

36-37. (The brahmins) at Gayā were cursed by lord Brahmā when they on account of their greed received gifts of money and other things of the righteous sacrifice "You will be deprived of learning. You will be greedy. The rivers will be bereft of milk and other things. The mountains will become mere rocks."

38-40. The brahmins said to (lord) Brahmā, "Everything has been lost on account of the curse. Kindly be gracions to us for the sake of our livelihood". He replied to the Brahmins, "You will be dependent on (the pilgrims to) the sacred place as long as the moon and sun (exist). The people who come to Gayā and worship you by offering gifts of food, wealth etc. and ancestral rights shall elevate hundreds of their families to heaven from hell and excellent position after heaven."

41. Gaya also performed a sacrifice offering plenty of food and profuse fees. The place has been named as Gayā after him. The Pāṇḍavas worshipped lord Viṣṇu.

CHAPTER ONE HUNDRED FIFTEEN

Mode of making a pilgrimage to Gayā

Fire-god said :

1-7. When he has decided to go to Gayā after having duly performed the ancestral rite, he should wear ochre robes and do circumambulation of the village. He should control his mind and should not seek alms as he proceeds on the journey everyday. As soon as he has started from his house to go to Gayā, he secures for his ancestors the steps to ascend to heaven at each one of his steps. What is that to be done by acquiring knowledge about the *brahman* (the absolute) ? What is the benefit of dying at a cowshed ? What is the use of stay at Kurukṣetra ? If the son goes to Gayā, the ancestors celebrate it on seeing that the son has reached Gayā. (They would think), will they (the sons) offer us waters atleast by touching with their feet ? The knowledge about *brahman*, the ancestral rite at Gayā, the death at the cowshed and stay at Kurukṣetra are the four ways of attaining liberation. The ancestors who are afraid of hell desire that their sons who go to Gayā would be their saviours. Tonsure and fasting is a general rule (to be adhered) at all the sacred places.

8. There is no restriction about time at Gayā. The oblations may be offered always. One who stays there for three fortnights purifies seven generations.

9. In the *aṣṭaka* ceremony and in the *vṛddhi* rite at Gayā on the day of death, separate rite is performed for the mother at Gayā. But it is performed along with the husband at other places.

10. So also with the rites for the nine relatives such as the father etc. and for the twelve relatives. One should bathe in the sacred water of Uttaramānasa on the first day.

11. One should bathe in the sacred Uttaramānasa for the sake of increase of longevity and good health, for the destruction of all sins and for liberation.

12. By satisfying gods and ancestors with offerings, the doer of ancestral rite is deemed to have offered them the balls (of rice) "I am satisfying gods remaining in heaven, sky and earth."

13-16. One should satisfy beings in heaven, sky and earth, and father and mother (with the words), "I make these offerings of balls (of rice) for (my) father, grandfather, greatgrandfather, mother, (paternal) grandmother, (paternal) great-grandfather, (maternal) grandfather, (maternal) great-grandfather and (maternal) great great grandfather and others for their uplift. "Our salutations to the Sun-god who is of the forms of (the planets) Moon, Mars, Mercury, Jupiter, Venus, Saturn, Rāhu and Ketu. Whoever bathes in the Uttaramānasa elevates his entire family.

17-18. After having saluted Sun (god) one should go to the Dakṣiṇamānasa without speaking (any word). (One should contemplate as follows): "I bathe in the Dakṣinamānasa for the satisfaction of (my) ancestors. I have come to Gayā. May all my ancestors ascend heaven." After having performed ancestral rite and offered balls (of rice), one should utter as follows after worshipping Sun (god) :

19. "Om, salutation to Sun (god), lord (of the universe. O Supreme god ! get me the cherished end. Graciously grant enjoyment and emancipation to all my ancestors.

20-21. May the most propitious Fire-god, the conveyor of oblations, Soma, Yama, Aryamā, and groups of manes—Agniṣvāttāḥ, Barhiṣadaḥ, Ājyapāḥ come here. My ancestors such as mother, (maternal) grandfather and others were protected here by all of you.

22-24. I am the person to offer them balls (of rice). I have come to this Gayā (Kṣetra). The sacred place named Kanakhala, renowned in three worlds and being worshipped by celestials, sages and *gaṇas*, lies to the north of Muṇḍapṛṣṭha (the place where tonsure is done). It is being guarded always by the licking great serpents that give pleasure to accomplished persons and frighten sinners. The mortals on earth go to heavens and sport there by bathing there (in the waters of Kanakhala).

25. Then one should go to Phalgutīrtha situated on the Mahānadī after having visited Uttaramānasa, Nāga, Janārdana, sacred well and banyan tree.

26. This is spoken as the Gayāśira. It is also called Phalgutīrtha. The Muṇḍapṛṣṭha, Naga hill and other places are the most excellent among outstanding.

27. The water on the earth is veritable Kāmadhenu which yields prosperity and heaven. The Phalgutīrtha causes delight to the eyes. No other place is like the Phalgu (tīrtha).

28. The man who bathes in the Phalgutīrtha and worships lord Gadādhara (Viṣṇu) is deemed to have achieved all things got by the doers of good deeds.

29. The sacred places on earth, commencing with oceans and ending with tanks go to Phalgutīrtha once everyday.

30. Whoever bathes reverentially at the Phalgutīrtha, the foremost among tīrthas, causes forefathers to reach the region of Brahmā and the own self to get enjoyment and emancipation.

31-33. One who performs the ancestral rite here should bathe, offer balls (of rice) and worship (lord) Brahmā. In this Kaliyuga, all regions (of the universe) are presided over by (lord) Maheśvara (Śiva). But (lord) Gadādhara (Viṣṇu) is the presiding deity here. (Lord) Brahmā (remains here) in the form of a *liṅga*. (One should say), "I make obeisance to (lords) (Maheśvara) Śiva, Gadādhara (Viṣṇu), Bala, Kāma (god of love), Aniruddha (a form of Viṣṇu) and Nārāyaṇa. I also make obeisance to Brahmā, Viṣṇu, Nṛsiṁha and Varāha (forms of Viṣṇu) and others." Then one elevates hundreds of his family after worshipping (lord) Gadādhara.

34. Then one should go to Dharmāraṇya on the second day, bathe in Mataṅgavāpī at the excellent Mataṅgāśrama, do the ancestral rite and offer balls (of rice).

35-36. One should utter the following (words), after worshipping gods Mataṅgeśa and Siddheśa: "Let the gods and guardian deities be the witness (to the fact) that I had come here and performed rites at this Mataṅga for the liberation of my fore-fathers. Bathing, offerring waters of liberation, performance of ancestral rite and other acts (should be performed) at Brahmatīrtha and the sacred well.

37. The performance of ancestral rite between the well and the sacrificial post lifts hundreds of fore-fathers. The righteous person who salutes the Mahābodhi tree gets the region of heaven.

38-39. On the third day, having control over the senses, one should bathe in the Brahmasaras, with the words, "I bathe in the sacred Brahmasaras for the favour of lord Brahmā and convey forefathers to the region of Brahmā served by the brahmarṣis and gaṇas. The doer of ancestral rite should offer waters of libation, offer balls (of rice) and sprinkle (water over his body). One who wants to have Vājapeya (rite) should circumambulate the *brahmay ūpa* (post).

40. One sage offers water at the root of the mango tree holding a pitcher and *kuśa* in his hand. The mango trees are watered and the forefathers are satisfied. One act is well known as yielding two fruits.

41-42. By making obeisance to lord Brahmā one elevates hundreds of generations. On the fourth day, after having bathed in the Phalgutīrtha and offering *tarpaṇa* to gods, one should do the ancestral rite together with (the offering of) balls (of rice) at the Gayāśiras. The extent of sacred Gayā is five *krośas* (ten miles) and the extent of Gayāśira is one *krośa* (two miles).

43. By offering balls (of rice) there, one elevates hundreds of generations. The great lord Mahādeva (Śiva) has placed his foot at the Muṇḍapṛṣṭha.

44. The Gayāśira is said to be the sanctuary at Muṇḍapṛṣṭha. The Gayāśira itself has been made the hermitage at Phalgutīrtha.

45-48. The nectar flows therein. Whatever is offered there to the forefathers never decreases. After having bathed at Daśāśvamedha and worshipped lord Brahmā, whoever touches the Rudrapāda (the foot mark of lord Rudra) will not be born again. Having offered the ball of rice of the measure of a *śamī* leaf at Gayāśira, those who are in the hell go to heaven and those who are in heaven attain liberation. The offer of ball (of rice) (is made) along with *pāyasa*, (sweet porridge) flour made into a paste, gruel, rice and wheat and mixed with sesamum. By offering the ball (of rice) at Rudrapada, one elevates hundreds of generations.

49. Similarly, one who offers the ball (of rice) at the ancestral rite at Viṣṇupada gets released from debts (due to ancestors). One will elevate hundreds of fore-fathers as also his own self.

50-53. So also, one who does the ancestral rite at the Brahmapada (the place where the footmarks of Brahmā are situated) conveys the forefathers to the region of Brahmā. Similarly, (the performance of) ancestral rite at the *dakṣiṇāgnipada*, *gārhapatyapada* and the *āhavanīyapada*[1] confers the fruits of (performance of a) sacrificial rite. One who does the ancestral rite to *āvasthya*[2] (fire), (gods) moon, sun, *gaṇa*, (sage) Agastya and Kārttikeya elevate the family. After having saluted the chariot of Sun, one should make obeisance to Karṇāditya. After having worshipped the foot of (lord) Kanakeśa, one should make obeisance to Gayākedāra. (By such acts) one gets freed from all sins and conveys his fore-fathers to the region of Brahmā.

54-55. Prince Viśāla at Viśālā became father of children by offering balls (of rice) at Gayāśiras. He asked the brahmins, "How can I have children ?" The brahmins told Viśāla, "All things will be got by offering balls (of rice) at Gayā."

56-59. Then Viśāla also offered balls (of rice) to the forefathers at Gayāśiras. Having seen white and red (coloured) souls in the sky, he asked them, "Who are you ?". One among them, the white person, said to Viśāla, "I, the white person, am your father now going to the region of Indra on account of (your) good deeds. O son ! the red coloured (person) is my father and the black coloured is my grand-father. We had reached hell and we are liberated by you. Because you have offered balls (of rice) we are going to the region of Brahmā". After saying thus they went away. Viśāla got progeny, ruled the kingdom and (finally) reached lord Hari (Viṣṇu).

60-62. The foremost among the pretas said to the merchant for his liberation, "Good fruits are enjoyed by all *pretas*, who

1. The places associated with the fires of the household.
2. A household fire.

are tormented by sufferings. Once, a pitcher together with food and water was given on a Śrāvaṇadvādaśī day at noon. That has been sustaining (us ever since). You go to Gayā with money and offer us balls (of rice)". The merchant went to Gayā with money and offered balls (of rice).

63-64. The foremost among the *pretas* was led to the region of (lord) Hari (Viṣṇu) along with the other *pretas*. (One liberates) his own self, his forefathers and those who have died on the paternal and maternal side, as also those related to the preceptor, the father-in-law and other relatives, by the offer of balls (of rice) at Gayāśiras.

65-67. (One should utter the following words): "Those who have been deprived of the offer of balls for their sake, those who do not have a wife or children, those for whom the rites could not be done, those who were blind, lame or of deformed limbs, those who were born prematurely and other known and unknown (relatives) in my family, for their sake, I have offered the ball (of rice). Let it remain undecaying. Those fore-fathers of mine who remain in the form of a *preta*, let all of them be pleased for ever by the offer of the ball (of rice)".

68. All those who desire to elevate the family should offer balls (of rice) to all. So also one desirous of (elevating his own self) and getting imperishable place should offer (ball of rice).

69-70. The wise man should bathe at Gadālola with the (repetition of) *mantras*. O lord Janārdana ! I bathe in this sacred Gadāprakṣālana at the extremely sacred Gadālola in order to appease sufferings due to mundane existence. Obeisance to the *Akṣayavaṭa* (banyan) tree, which yields undecaying heaven.

71. One should do the ancestral rite at the spot of the banyan tree and feed brahmins for (securing) undecaying position of forefathers and for the destruction of all sins.

72. If one brahmin has been fed, crores (of brahmins) would become fed. What more to say ? If many are fed, the offerings done to the fore-fathers become undecaying.

73. The fathers of those who offer food at Gayā become virtually the *putriṇa* (i.e. having sons). After having saluted the

1. The word *putra* means—one who saves parents from the hell called *put*.

banyan tree and the lord of the banyan tree, one should worship the great grand-father.

74. One would attain imperishable position and elevate hundreds of his family members. The pilgrimage made to Gayā always (bears) fruit whether it is done in the proper way or not.

CHAPTER ONE HUNDRED AND SIXTEEN

Mode of making a pilgrimage to Gayā

The Fire-god said :

1. One should do *sandhyā* (twilight worship) after bathing in (the river) Mahānadī with (the recitation of) *gāyatrī* (*mantra*). The ancestral rite and offer of balls (of rice) in the morning preceded by (the recitation of) *gāyatrī* (*mantra*) yields undiminishing (fruits).

2. Having bathed in the noon (as the sun remains up) and having worshipped with songs and (playing of) musical instruments, the (evening) twilight worship is done there itself in front of the sun and the offer of balls (of rice) is made.

3. (Similarly) one should (offer) at the place of Agastya. One, who has come out after having entered the *yonidvāra* (the fissure in the hill), does not enter the *yoni* (the womb) again and will be liberated from the cycles of birth and death.

4. (He) should then pay obeisance to Bali (a demon king) at Kākaśilā and (lord) Kumāra (Subrahmaṇya).Then one should offer balls (of rice) at Svargadvāra, Somakuṇḍa and Vāyutīrtha.

5. Then (he) should offer balls (of rice) at Ākāśagaṅgā and Kapilā. After having paid obeisance to Śiva, the lord of Kapilā, one should offer balls (of rice) at Rukmikuṇḍa.

6. After having worshipped (lord) Koṭīśa at Koṭitīrtha, one (should offer balls of rice) at Amoghapada. Then the balls (of rice) should be offered at Gadālola, Vānaraka and Gopracāra.

7. After the worship of the cow, one who does the ancestral rite and offers balls (of rice) at (the river) Vaitariṇī, elevates twentyone generations. Then one should offer balls (of rice) at Krauñcapāda.

8-11. (The pilgrim) should then offer balls (of rice) at Viśālā and Niścirā on the third day. One who bathes in the Ṛṇamokṣa and Pāpamokṣa and with the sacred ash at the Bhasmakuṇḍa gets free from sin. One should then worship lord Janārdana (uttering as follows): "I have placed this ball (of rice) on your hand. O Janārdana ! When I die let this remain without decay." (Lord) Janārdana himself (remains) at Gayā in the form of forefathers. Having worshipped that lotus-eyed lord one gets liberated from three debts. After having worshipped (lord) Mārkaṇḍeyeśvara, one should worship (lord) Gṛdhreśvara.

12. Then the balls (of rice) should be offered to (lord) Maheśa at the Mūlakṣetra at Dhārā. Balls (of rice) should be offered at Gṛdhrakūṭa, Gṛdhravaṭa and Dhautapāda.

13. (The pilgrim) should then offer balls (of rice) at the Puṣkariṇī, Kardamāla and Rāmatīrtha. One should make obeisance to (lord) Prabhāseśa and offer *piṇḍa* (balls of rice) at Pretaśilā.

14. (The following words should be recited on these occasions) : "May all (my) fore-fathers and relatives who are still in the form of *pretas* (the dead people still in the state of a spirit) in the heavens, sky or earth get released from that state by my offer of *piṇḍas*."

15. One who offers *piṇḍa* at the following three places-Pretaśilā, the sacred Gayāśiras and Pretakuṇḍa at Prabhāsa, liberates his family.

16. (The pilgrim) should pay obeisance to (lord) Vasiṣṭheśa and offer *piṇḍa* in front of that (deity). He should then offer *piṇḍa* at Gayānābhi, Suṣumṇā and Mahākoṭi.

17. (*Piṇḍa* should be offered) in front of (lord Gadādhara), at Muṇḍapṛṣṭha and in the presence of the goddess. The Muṇḍapṛṣṭha together with the guardian deities should be worshipped first.

18. By doing such worship, one will not have fear and the effects of disease and poison will be destroyed. One who worships (lord) Brahmā conveys his family to the region of Brahmā.

19. One who worships Subhadrā (sister of lord Kṛṣṇa), Balabhadra (brother of lord Kṛṣṇa) and Puruṣottama (here refers to lord Kṛṣṇa), gets all his desires fulfilled, elevates his family and attains heaven.

20. One should pay obeisance to (lord) Hṛṣīkeśa and offer *piṇḍa* in front of that (deity). Having worshipped (lord) Mādhava, one becomes honoured by the celestials.

21. One who worships (the goddesses) Mahālakṣmī, Gaurī, Maṅgalā and Sarasvatī elevates his fore-fathers and enjoys all pleasures in heaven and becomes a learned man (in his next birth).

22-24. One who worships the twelve Ādityas (suns), Fire-god, Revanta and Indra, gets free from diseases etc. and attains heaven. One who worships Kapardi, Vināyaka and (lord) Kārttikeya (Subrahmaṇya nourished the six Kṛttikās) gets his desire accomplished without any impediment. One would get everything by worshipping the eight mysterious *liṅgas*—Somanātha, Kāleśa, Kedāra, Prapitāmaha, Siddheśvara, Rudreśa, Rāmeśa and Brahmakeśvara.

25. By worshipping (lords) Nārāyaṇa, Varāha and Nārasiṁha one would get prosperity. By worshipping (lords) Brahmā, Viṣṇu, Maheśa and Tripuraghna (destroyer of Tripura) one would get all things.

26. He who worships Sītā, Rāma, Garuḍa and Vāmana gets all the desired things and conveys his forefathers to the region of Brahmā.

27. By worshipping lord Ādigadādhara in the company of celestials, one gets free from three debts[1] and redeems the entire family.

28. The stone slab is of the form of celestials and it is hence meritorious. There is no place in Gayā where there is no sacred spot.

29-32. That person in whose name a *piṇḍa* is offered, is conveyed to (the region of) Brahmā eternally. After having paid obeisance to Phalgvīśa, Phalgucaṇḍī and Aṅgārakeśvara, one should perform the ancestral rite at the place of Mataṅga and

1. They are due to the sages, gods and manes.

Bharatāśrama. So also one should offer food at Haṁsatīrtha, Koṭitīrtha and Pāṇḍuśilā. There, at the Agnidhārā, and at Madhusravas, *piṇḍa* should be offered. One should offer *piṇḍa* at the forest of Dhenukā and worship the cow at Dhenupada. One who offers *piṇḍa* in the Sarasvatī (river) redeems all the fore-fathers.

33. After having worshipped the evening twilight, one should pay obeisance to (goddess) Sarasvatī. The brahmins proficient in the Vedas and Vedāṅgas should do the three twilight worships.

34. After having done circumambulation of Gayā and having worshipped the brahmins at Gayā, offer of food or any-thing else becomes undecaying.

35-42. The lord Ādigadādhara should be glorified and prayed to as follows: "I pray to the conferer of *yoga*, (lord) Gadādhara, the resident of Gayā, who redeems the fore-fathers for the sake of *dharma* (righteousness), *artha* (prosperity) *kāma* (pleasure) and *mokṣa* (redemption). I salute that true *brahman*, who is devoid of a body, organs, mind, intellect, life-force and ego who is always pure, and who is endowed with intellect. I always salute the lord who is bliss, without a second form, who is wor-shipped by the celestials and demons, and who is surrounded by gods and goddesses. I pay obeisance to the destroyer of the sinful propensities of the *Kali* period, the person wearing the garland of wild flowers, the protector of all the worlds, the one bent on the redemption of the family, the one divided himself into the manifest and unmanifest. I worship that destroyer of frightful sins and one who remains as the permanent essence. O lord ! Gadādhara ! I have come to Gayā in order to do the ancestral rite. You be the witness for me here today. Let me be free from three kinds of debts. May the gods Brahmā, Īśāna and others be the witness for me. I have come to Gayā and have redeemed my forefathers. Whoever reads (about) the greatness of Gayā at the time of (doing) the ancestral rite, attains the region of Brahmā. The ancestral rite done to the forefathers becomes undecaying and it confers the region of Brahmā.

CHAPTER ONE HUNDRED AND SEVENTEEN

Mode of performing the ancestral rites

Fire-god said :

1-5. I shall describe (the mode of performing) *śrāddha* (ancestral rite) as described by sage Kātyāyana to the sages. One should do *śrāddha* at Gayā especially on the *saṅkrānti*[1] etc. or on the day of the new moon or on days after the fourth day. After having reached there, one should invite (any one of the following for the *śrāddha*): the mendicants, pious householders one who has completed his studies, learned brahmins, those who are faultless, those who strictly observe the propriety of conduct. Persons afflicted by white leprosy or leprosy should not be invited. So also people who are present uninvited should not be entertained. They should have bathed, be pure and have self-control. They should face the east while doing divine acts. The three fore-fathers (father, grand-father and great grand-father) should separately be invoked. So also the fore-fathers on the maternal side (to whom one is entitled to offer) should be invoked.

6. The performer of the *śrāddha* should observe continence that day. (He should be) gentle, calm, not hasty, true and not intoxicated. (He should) not stir out. (He should) not read the scriptures and practice silence.

7. Kind enquiries should be made of the chief among those seated. Even number of *darbha* should be spread for the fore-fathers. The (appropriate) deity should be invoked.

8. One should ask, "Shall I invoke Viśvedevas ?" (He should be replied), "you invoke". After having invoked Viśvedevas, and having spread barley, one should repeat the following :

9. O Viśvedevas ! You hear this. I invoke the fore-fathers. Having asked thus and being permitted to invoke, one should invoke them (saying) "You be pleased."

10-12. After having spread the sesamum, one should invoke the fore-fathers with the repetition of (the *mantra*), "Fore-fathers" One should sprinkle on the *kuśa* with the mantra *śaṁ no devī*.

1. The day on which the sun enters a new sign of the zodiac.

After having scattered the grains of barley with the (repetition of the *mantra*) "You are the barley grains", the sesamum (is scattered) (with the repetition of the *mantra*) "You are the sesamum. You are permeated with the essence of Soma. Graciously gratify the souls of forefathers. Salutations." Flowers should be offered with (the *mantra* "śrīśca te" in a golden or silver vessel or a wooden (vessel) or sword or vessel made of a leaf. The circumambulation is done clockwise in the case of celestials and anticlockwise in the case of fore-fathers, wearing the *pavitra* (made of *darbha*) on the hand, one for each one (of the fore-fathers).

13. (Then he should recite the following *mantra*): "May the celestial waters together with the waters of the earth and sky and the golden sacrificial waters confer blessing on you." (Then the waters of respectful offering should be offered to the Viśvedevas with the *mantra*): "O Viśvedevas ! Here are the offerings for each one of you". (Similarly, offerings should be made to the forefathers saying) "Here is the offering for you, O Forefathers !

14. Similarly, offerings should be made (to the grand-fathers) with (the *mantra*) "Obeisance to the grand-fathers." The sacrificial vessel is lowered with (the repetition of the *mantra*) "You are the seats of my forefathers."

15. Then perfumes, flowers, incense sticks, lamps, shawls and food with clarified butter should be raised up (by the performer of ancestral rite). (The brahmins should then be asked) "Shall I offer them in the sacrifice ?"

16. Being permitted (by the brahmins) to do so, those things should be offered to the fire in the case of those who maintain fire and on the hands of forefathers in the case of those who do not maintain fire with the repetition of the following *mantra* and (wearing) the *pavitra* (made of *darbha* worn on the finger).

17. The first oblation is (made with the *mantra*): "Obeisance to the Fire-god, the conveyor of offerings." The subsequent (*mantras*) are to Soma, to forefathers, to the god of death and Aṅgiras.

18. The remnants of oblations should be collected in the food vessel. "O Nectar ! this earth is your receptacle, the sky is the covering. The brahmin is your mouth. I am casting in that mouth permeated with the nectar." After having repeated (the

mantra) "This Viṣṇu", the thumb of the brahmin is placed in the food.

19. The sesamum should be scattered with (the *mantra*) "Removed", and the food should be given. After saying, "Be pleased", the *gāyatrī* and other *mantras* should be repeated.

20. "Obeisance to the gods, the forefathers, great yogins, Svadhā and Svāhā always."

21. After having known that they are satisfied, the food must be scattered and water should be given to each one of them. After repeating the *gāyatrī* (*mantra*) as before, (the *mantra*) "honey, honey" should be repeated.

22-23. They should be asked, "Are you all satisfied?". They should say, "We are satisfied.' Being permitted by them the residual food should be gathered together and water should be sprinkled by the side of the place where food was eaten. Three *piṇḍas* should be placed on *kuśa*, after they have done the *ācamana* (rinsing of the mouth).

24. After the rinsing of the mouth, water, flowers and unbroken rice should be offered. The water given may be undiminishing. Then (the forefathers) should be requested (as follows):

25-31. "May the forefathers be gracious: May our progeny prosper always. May the donors enjoy prosperity. So also (may) the *Vedas* and progeny (prosper). May our earnestness never fail.. May we have plenty to give. May our food get profuse. May we get (enough) guests. May there be (plenty) seeking alms. May we not seek alms from anybody. The stems of *kuśa* over which the (term) svadhā (obeisance) has been repeated are then gathered along with the *pavitras* and (permission) should be asked to say obeisance (to forefathers). After having been permitted, (the following *mantra*) should be recited: "Obeisance to the fathers (includes the brothers and cousin of the father) grandfathers and great-grand fathers. Obeisance." As one is repeating this, water should be sprinkled from the raised pot and fees should be paid according to one's means. In the ceremonies related to the gods and forefathers one should say : "May the Viśve devas be pleased". They should be bid adieu (with the *mantra*) "Vāje vāje". Then one should accompany the brahmins (with the repetition) of (the *mantra*) "āmāvājasya," do circumambulation of them and enter the house. One should do this on the new moon day every month.

32. I shall describe (the mode of doing) *ekoddiṣṭa* (rite done for an individual only). The *śrāddha* rite is done as before. One *pavitra*, *argha* and one *piṇḍa* are offered.

33-34. In this rite, there is no invocation and the offering is not made in the fire. The Viśvedevas are not (invited) here. At the (time of) query about satisfaction (one should ask) "May it be relished". The brahmin should say, "well relished". They should be asked to be seated and be pleased with the offering. They (should say), "We are pleased". The remaining (part of the ceremony) should be done as before.

35-37. I shall describe (the mode of performing) the *sapiṇḍikaraṇa* (a rite in honour of the dead person done on the 12th day after death or at the end of one year). (It is done) at the end of a year or in the middle. Three vessels should be kept for the forefathers and one vessel for the dead person. The four (vessels) should be provided with the sesamum and flowers along with the *pavitra*. Having filled them with scented water, sprinkle the vessel of the dead person with the *mantra* "ye samānā". The offering of the *piṇḍa* should be (done) as before. By this rite (the soul of) the dead person attains the position of fathers.

38-49. I shall describe (the mode of doing) the *śrāddha* rite which confers prosperity. Everything is done as before. One should repeat (the *mantras*) except the *mantra* of the father and (do) circumambulation in the forenoon. The materials (required are) good *kuśa*, and barley grains instead of sesamum in this rite. The query about satisfaction is "Is it well done". The brahmin should say, "well done". The *piṇḍas* should be composed of curd, broken rice and the jujube. One should ask, "Shall I invoke the ancestors who are fit to receive *nāndī* (rite)". They should be requested to be satisfied with the offerings. The manes (who are) the *nāndīmukhas*, I shall describe. One should ask the clan of manes, the *nāndīmukhas* to be pleased. The *nāndīmukhas* are—father, grand-father, great-grandfather, maternal grandfather, maternal great grand-father and maternal great great grand-father. (In this ceremony) the term *svadhā* should not be added. Even number of brahmins should be fed. I shall describe the country herbs which would satisfy the manes. They would get satisfied with the roots and fruits of the forest for a month, with the fish for two months,/with the ominous bird for three months, with the deer for four (months), with the goat for five or six, with the tortoise for seven or eight, with the boar for nine (months), with the meat of the ram, (meat) of the buffalo and the spotted antelope for ten months, with the milk of a cow and *pāyasa* (sweat gruel) for one year. They would be satisfied for twelve years with the meat of a sacrificial goat. The meat of a rhinoceros, the *kālaśāka* (a kind of vegetable), (meat) of a red goat, honey and sea crabs offered in the rainy season and *śrāddha* (done) in the (asterism) of *maghā* (tenth in the cycle) (yields) undiminishing benefits. The brahmins who study the *Vedas*, who do *agnihotra*, who study their own branch of *Vedas*, those who are learned in the six ancillary texts (of the *Vedas*), one who worships the Nāciketa fire thrice a day, the three *madhu* (ṛks of the *Ṛgveda*), those who read the *dharmadroṇa*, one who knows the *trisuparṇa* (*sūkta*) and the *jyeṣṭhasāman* are those spoken as the *paṅktipāvanas* (the purifiers of an assembly).

50-53. I shall describe the mode of performing fruit-bearing (rites). (The *śrāddha* done) on the first lunar day confers plenty of wealth, on the second day (gets) beautiful wives, on the fourth day the fulfilment of heartfelt desires, on the fifth day (confers) progeny, on the sixth day (makes the doer) thrive well, on the seventh day (increases) agricultural prospects, on the eighth day (confers) material prosperity, on the ninth day mules, on the tenth day plenty of cows, on the eleventh day off-springs, on the twelfth day wealth and grains, on the thirteenth day (ensures) excellent position among one's kinsmen. The *śrāddha* of those dead by means of weapons (should be done) on the fourteenth. It is said that one gets all (desires fulfilled by doing *śrāddha*) on the new moon day.

54-58. "The seven hunters (who resided) in Daśārṇa, the deer (which dwelt) upon the mountain Kālañjara, the *cakravāka* (a species of water birds) in the Śaradvīpa, the *haṁsas* (ganders) in the Mānasa lake were born at Kurukṣetra as brahmins well-versed in the Vedas. They had gone a long way. May you excel them." When this verse is read at the (time of) *śrāddha* etc., the *śrāddha* gets completed and it yields the region of Brahmā. A son may perform *śrāddha* of his grandfather even as his father is alive, or of the grandfather when the great grandfather is living, or of the great grandfather when the great great grandfather is living. So also (*śrāddha* is done) for the mother, maternal grandfather etc. Whoever reads the *śrāddhakalpa* (that relating to performance of *śrāddha*) gets the fruits of performing a *śrāddha*.

59-63. A *śrāddha* performed at a sacred place, or on the days of the commencement of the *yuga* or Manu period gets undiminishing fruits. Similarly, (śrāddha done) on the ninth day of bright fortnight in (the month of) Āśvayuk (October-November), on the twelfth day in Kārttika (November-December), on third day in Māgha and Bhādrapada (February-March and September-October), on the new moon day in Phālguna (March-April), on the eleventh day in Pauṣa (January-February), on the tenth day in Āṣāḍha (July-August), on the seventh day in the month of Māgha (February-March), on the eighth day of dark fortnight in Śrāvaṇa (August-September), on the full moon day in Āṣāḍha (July-August) and on the full moon days in Kārttika, Phālguna and Jyeṣṭha (June-July) (confer manifold benefits). The days of commencement of the Svāyambhuva Manu periods are also of undiminishing benefits. Gayā, Prayāga, (river) Gaṅgā, Kurukṣetra, (river) Narmadā, Śrīparvata, Prabhāsa, Śālagrāma, Vārāṇasī and river Godāvarī (are sacred places). *Śrāddha* (done) at those places and also at the Puruṣottama (*kṣetra*) (Puri) (yields manifold fruits).

CHAPTER ONE HUNDRED AND EIGHTEEN

The country of Bhārata

Fire-god said :

1. That country which (lies) to the north of ocean and south of Himādri (Himālaya) is known as the Bhāratavarṣa extending to nine thousand (*yojanas*).

2-4. This is a land of religious rites. It gives accomplishment of action in getting redemption. Mahendra, Malaya, Sahya, Śuktimat, Hemaparvata, Vindhya and Pāriyātra are the seven principal mountains here. Indradvīpa, Kaseru, Tāmravarṇa, Gabhastimān, Nāgadvīpa, Saumya, Gāndharva, Varuṇa and Bhārata are the nine territories here surrounded by the ocean.

5-8. The continent extends to one thousand *yojanas* from north to south. There are nine divisions of the Bhārata lying around the central part. The *kirātas* (hunting tribes) (are) in the east. The *yavanas* (the foreigners) (are in the west). The brahmins and others devoted to the *Vedas* and *smṛtis* (code books) (are) in the central part. The rivers rise from the Pāriyātra (mountains). Narmadā and other (rivers) flow from the Vindhya. (The rivers) Tāpī, Payoṣṇikā, Godāvarī, Bhīmarathī and Kṛṣṇaveṇī and others flow from the Sahya (mountains). (The rivers) Kṛtamālā and others flow from the Malaya (mountains). (The rivers) Trisāmā and others originate from the Mahendra (mountain). (The rivers) Kumāra and others rise from Śuktimat (mountain). (The river) Candrabhāgā rises from the Himālaya (mountains). The countries Kuru and Pāñcāla and the Madhyadeśa are situated in the western part.

CHAPTER ONE HUNDRED AND NINETEEN

Description of different continents

Fire-god said :

1. The Jambūdvīpa extends to a lakh of *yojanas*. It is surrounded by the Kṣīroda (ocean) measuring one lakh *yojanas*.

2. The Plakṣadvīpa is surrounded by the Kṣāra ocean. The seven sons of Medhātithi are the rulers of Plakṣadvīpa.

3. They are Śāntabhaya, Śiśira, Sukhodaya, Ānanda, Śiva, Kṣema and Dhruva after whom the countries are named.

4. Gomedha, Candra, Nārada, Dundubhī, Somaka, Sumanā and Vaibhrāja are the boundary mountains. The inhabitants are good.

5. There are seven principal rivers here. The inhabitants from Plakṣa to Śāka live for five thousand years and they adhere to righteous way of life adhering to the institutions of caste and stages of life.

6-7. Āryakas, Kurus, Viviṁśas and Bhāvins are respectively the brahmins and others (*kṣatriyas, vaiśyas* and *śūdras*) here. They worship (lord) Soma (moon). Its extent is two lakhs *yojanas* and it is surrounded by the ocean of *ikṣurasa* of equal measure. The Śālmala (dvīpa) is twice that. The seven sons of Vapuṣmat were the rulers of Śālmala.

8-12. Śveta, Harita, Jīmūta, Lohita, Vaidyuta, Mānasa and Suprabha are their names and the countries were known by their names. This twice bigger continent is surrounded by the Suroda (ocean) of equal measure. The seven (boundary mountains) are Kumuda, Anala, Balāhaka, Droṇa, Kaṅka, Mahiṣa and Kakudmat. The brahmins and other (three castes) are Kapila, Aruṇa, Pīta and Kṛṣṇa (respectively). They worship (the lord) in the form of Vāyu (wind god). This is surrounded by Suroda. Udbhida, Dhenumat, Dvairatha, Lambana, Dhairya, Kapila and Prabhākara, (the sons) of Jyotiṣmat were the rulers of Kuśa (dvīpa). Dadhimukhya[1] and others are the brahmins and others. They worship (the lord) in the form of Brahmā.

13. Vidruma, Hemaśaila, Dyutimat, Puṣpavat, Kuśeśaya, Hariśaila and Mandara are the boundary mountains.

14-16. This is surrounded by the Ghṛtoda ocean as well as the Krauñcadvīpa. The sons of Dyutimat were the rulers of Krauñca and the countries (ruled by them) were named after them. They are seven—Kuśala, Manonuga, Uṣṇa, Pradhāna, Andhakāraka, Muni and Dundubhi. (The names of) the seven mountains here are Krauñca, Vāmana, Andhakāraka, Devāvṛt, Puṇḍarīka and Dundubhi. Each one of them is twice as big as the other.

17-19. The mountains in the respective continents are also twice as the corresponding one in the others. The brahmins and others (three castes) are Puṣkara, Puṣkala, Dhanya and Tiṣya and (they) worship Hari. The Krauñcadvīpa is surrounded by Dadhimaṇḍodaka (ocean) and the Śākadvīpa. The sons of Havya and the rulers of Śākadvīpa were Jalada, Kumāra, Sukumāra, Maṇīvaka, Kuśottara, Modākī and Druma. The countries were known by their names.

20-21. Udaya, Jaladhara, Raivata, Śyāma, Kodraka, Āmbikeya and the beautiful Keśarī are the seven (boundary) mountains. The brahmins and others are Maga, Magadha, Mānasa and Mandaga. They worship (the lord) in the form of the Sun. The Śāka *dvīpa* is surrounded by the Kṣīrābdhi.

1. These are Daminaḥ, Śuṣmiṇaḥ, Snehāḥ and Mandehāḥ.

22-24. It is also surrounded by Puṣkara (*dvīpa*). (The ruler of Puṣkara), Savana had two sons—Mahāvīta and Dhātaki. They ruled over two countries known by their name. There is one boundary mountain called Mānasa at the centre in the shape of a bracelet. It extends to one thousand *yojanas* and is of equal height. (The people here) live for ten thousand years. (Lord) Brahmā is worshipped here by celestials. This continent is surrounded by the Svādūdaka ocean of equal measure.

25-26. The waters of the ocean neither decrease nor increase. O Sage ! At the moon-rise or moon-set and at the white and dark fortnights, an increase or decrease of waters by five hundred and ten *aṅgulas* (equal to one finger-breadth) is seen in the oceans.

27-28. The Svādūdaka is of many good qualities. The land is golden and is devoid of living beings. The peak (called) Lokāloka extends to a lakh of *yojanas*. It is engulfed in darkness in the form of the pan of the egg-shaped (universe). This land found with this pan of the egg-shaped (universe) extends to fifty crores.

CHAPTER ONE HUNDRED AND TWENTY

The extent of the universe

The Fire-god said :

1. The extent of the earth is believed to be seventy-thousand (*yojanas*). Its height is ten thousand. The nether worlds (extend) to one thousand each.

2-3. The seven nether worlds are Atala, Vitala, Nitala, Gabhastimat, Mahātala, Sutala and Pātāla. The demons dwell in those pleasant lands which are respectively coloured black, yellow, red, white, stony and golden.

4. Lord Viṣṇu in the *tāmasa* (darkness) form as Śeṣa (the serpent) lies under the nether worlds. He, the Ananta (infinite) on account of his infinite (good) qualities, (lies there) supporting the earth with his head.

5. There are many hells under the earth. A *vaiṣṇava* (devo-

tee of lord Viṣṇu) should not fall therein. The extent upto which the earth is illuminated by the sun is known as the sky.

6. O Vasiṣṭha ! The region of the sun is at (a distance of) one lakh (*yojanas*) from the earth, the region of the Moon at one lakh (*yojanas*) from the Sun, and the region of the stars at one lakh (*yojanas*) from the moon.

7-8. (Planet) Mercury is at two lakhs (*yojanas*) from the region of the stars. (Planet) Venus (is) at two lakhs from Mercury. (Planet) Mars (is) at two lakhs from Venus. (Planet) Jupiter (is) at two lakhs from Mars. (Planet) Saturn (is) at two lakhs from Jupiter. (The region of) the seven sages (ursa Major) (is) at one lakh from Saturn, the polestar (is) at one lakh from the sages (Ursa Major) and is at the apex of the three worlds.

9. The Maharloka (lies)at a crore (*yojanas*) from the pole-star, where those who have seen a full cycle of time reside. The Jana (loka), wherein dwell (the sages) Sanaka and others, (lies) at two crores (of *yojanas*) from that.

10-11. The Tapo (loka) (is) at eight crores from Jana (loka) where Vairājas (a class of celestial beings) are the presiding deities. The Satyaloka is at ninetysix crores from the Tapo (loka). It is known as the Brahmaloka where dwell celestials who do not die. The region fit for one to move on foot is the Bhūloka (the earth). The region of Bhuvarloka is said to be between (the earth and) the Sun.

12. The Svargaloka lies between the Sun and the pole-star in the fourteen lakhs (*yojanas* of space). These regions cover as an exterior shell of the universe.

13. They are again covered by ten-fold layers of elements water, fire, wind and ether.

14. O Great sage ! Each one of the ten latter regions lie enfolded in one another and thus form an exterior cover of the primary thing.

15. O sage ! One does not have any knowledge about the limit of that infinite. That nature has been the source of everything else.

16. This kind of innumerable eggs had come into being there. The *pumān* (*brahman*) exists in a potent state in the universal nature just as the fire in the wood and oil in the sesamum.

17-19. This *pumān* lies embedded in the nature as a conscious onlooker and knower. O Wiseman ! The nature and the brahman are held together by the force of Viṣṇu, the form of the essential virtues of all beings. That is the cause for their separate existence as well as union. O Great sage ! That is the cause for the agitation at the time of creation (of beings). It is similar to the wind sustaining hundreds of water particles after its contact with water.

20. The celestial beings and others are born through the concerted action of the nature and the effect of the force of Viṣṇu acted upon by the force of the former.

21-29. Viṣṇu is identical with brahman itself from whom this entire universe (has come into being). The chariots of the Sun are nine (occupying) thousand *yojanas*. O Excellent sages ! The axis is double that (measure). The axle of its wheel is one and half crores and seven lakhs (*yojanas*). The wheel is fixed there. It has three naves[1], five spokes[2], six circumferences[3], two movements[4] consisting in the cycle of period. O Great intellectual ! The second axis of the Sun's chariot is twentytwo thousand seven hundred and fifty (*yojanas*). The measurement of the two axles is equal to its yoke. The shorter axis and its yoke rest on the polestar. O Best disciplined ! The seven metres *gāyatrī*[5] and others are its horses. Sun's rise and setting are his being perceived and not being perceived. O Vasiṣṭha ! The regions from the earth to those where the polestar remains get lost at the time of deluge. The region where the polestar is stationed to the north of Ursa major is the excellent shining third place of (lord) Viṣṇu in heaven. This is the excellent place of ascetics who have become free from impurities.

30. The river Gaṅgā which purifies one by mere remembrance flows from there. It is to be known that the porpoise shape of the planets in the sky is that of lord Viṣṇu.

31-32. The polestar is situated at its tail. It revolves (on its non axis) and causes the planets to go round. That chariot

1. Forenoon, midday and afternoon.
2. *Parivatsara* etc.
3. The seasons.
4. Northern and southern.
5. *gāyatrī, bṛhatī, uṣṇik, jagatī, triṣṭup, anuṣṭup* and *paṅkti*.

of the Sun is ridden by different celestials, *Ādityas* (sons of Aditi), sages, *gandharvas* (semi-divine beings), *apsaras* (semi-divine beings), *grāmaṇī* (semi-divine beings), serpents and demons. Lord sun is the cause of snow, heat and rain.

33-36. He is the manifestation of lord Viṣṇu of the form of *Ṛgveda* and other (*vedas*) and is the cause of good and evil. The chariot of moon has three wheels drawn by ten horses yoked to its left and right and of the colour of jasmine. Thirtysix thousand three hundred and thirty-three celestials drink (the phases of) the moon. The manes (drink) one phase. One (phase) (is lost) being associated with the rays of the new moon. The chariot of the son of the Moon Mercury is composed of the fiery and windy material. Mercury moves on drawn by its eight horses.

37-41. The chariot of Venus (has got) eight horses, as also the chariots of Mars, Jupiter and Saturn (drawn) by horses. The chariot of Rāhu (ascending node of the Moon) (has) eight horses. The chariot of Ketu (descending node of the Moon) (has) eight horses. O Brahmin ! From this body of (lord) Viṣṇu this lotus-shaped earth with the mountains etc. has originated. (Lord) Hari (Viṣṇu) is the galaxy, worlds, rivers, mountains, oceans and forest. Whatever exists or ceases to exist is (lord) Viṣṇu, known through true knowledge about (lord), Viṣṇu. There is nothing beyond the purview of knowledge. Knowledge is the supreme place, the (lord) Viṣṇu. One has to do that act by which that true and infinite knowledge, namely, (lord) Viṣṇu, may be attained. Whoever reads (the section on) cosmogony would attain happiness.

CHAPTER ONE HUNDRED AND TWENTYONE

The science of Jyotiṣa (Astronomy and Astrology)

Fire-god said:

1. I shall describe the science of astrology which gives discrimination of good and bad events. It is the quintessence of four lakhs (of treatises). By knowing this (science) one becomes omniscient.

2. The marriage of girls should not be done when there is *ṣaḍaṣṭaka*[1] or *dvidvādaśa*[2] as well as in *trikoṇa*[3]. In other cases as well as in *samasaptaka*, there will be happiness.

3. If there is friendship between the lords of the second and twelfth (houses) or the trines or there is single lordship, then there will be prosperity in the married life even if there be hostility.

4. Even in such a condition the union may be made, but not in sixth-eighth (*ṣaḍaṣṭaka*) condition. (If the marriage is done) when Jupiter or Venus has set, the bridegroom and bride would die.

5. A marriage is not commendable when the Sun is in the house of Jupiter or Jupiter is in the house of the Sun.

6. The marriage should be postponed by three fortnights or by four months respectively when there is transit (of a planet from one house to another) or retrograde motion (of a planet). A vow or marriage should not be done when there is retrograde motion or transit of Jupiter.

7. (Marriages done) in (the months of) Caitra (April-May), Pauṣa (January-February) on the *riktā* days (fourth, ninth and the fourteenth day of a fortnight) or when (lord) Hari (Viṣṇu) is asleep, or on Tuesdays and Sundays or on the new moon day would bring forth unfavourable result. But the twilight (time) is auspicious.

8. A marriage is said to be commendable in the asterisms *rohiṇī*, *uttarā*, *mūla*, *svātī*, *hasta* and *revatī* (when the Sun is) in Libra or Gemini.

9. One should avoid a *viddharkṣa*[4] in celebrating a marriage, piercing the ears, vow, rite to determine the sex of a child before its birth, the first feeding of the child, and the tonsure.

10. The rite to determine the sex of the child before its birth should be done in (the asterism) *śravaṇa*, *mūla* and *puṣya*, on Sundays, Tuesdays and Jupiter and in (the signs of) Aquarius, Leo and Pisces.

---

1. The sixth and eighth; counting from the ascendant in the horoscope of the proposed life partners the ascendant in the other person's horoscope gives sixth or eighth.

2. The second and twelfth; counting as before which gets the second or twelfth.

3. The trine, Leo, Taurus, Virgo, Sagittarius, Libra and Aquarious are the trines for the planets sun etc.

4. Certain asterisms said to be opposed to certain other asterisms.

11. The discharge of a debt (should be done) in (the asterisms) *hasta*, *mūla*, *mṛga* (*śirṣa*) and *revatī* and on Wednesday and Friday. The (rite of) chewing of betal leaf should be done on Sunday, Monday, Thursday and Friday and in (the asterism) *mūla*.

12. The first feeding (of a child) (should be done) on a Friday or Thursday or in (the asterism) *mṛga* (*śirṣa*) in (the sign of) Pisces, in the five asterisms (beginning with *hasta* (citrā and svātī) and in the three asterisms beginning with *kṛttikā* (*rohiṇī* and *mṛgaśirṣa*).

13. New fruits and food should be eaten in (the asterisms of) *aśvinī* or *revatī*, *puṣya*, *hasta*, *jyeṣṭha*, *rohiṇī*, *śravaṇa* and *aśvinī*.

14. Medicine should be administered in (the asterisms of) *svāti*, *saumya* (name of the five stars in orion's head), the three *pūrvas* (*Pūrvaphālgunī*, *pūrvabhādrapada* and *pūrvāṣāḍha*, *maghā*, *yāmya* (*bharaṇi*) and the three (beginning with) *śravaṇa* which are auspicious.

15-20. One should bathe first after becoming free from illness on Tuesday or Sunday or Saturn. One should write eight times the syllable 'hrīm' and the name (of the enemy) in the middle and the (names of the eight) *vasus* as well as the (syllable) *hrīm* in the (eight) angular points on a Tuesday and wear it in his cloth on the neck with the *gorocanā* (pigment got from the cow) and saffron. It is certain that one's enemies get subjugated by this *mantra*. *Śrīm hrīm* is the protective (*mantra*) when the (*mantras*) *śrīm* and *hrīm* are written on the *bhūrja* leaf as stated above in the eight (points) together with *gorocanā* and saffron and covered by turmeric. (Similar writing) on a stone slab kept buried under the soil with its face downwards nullifies them. *Om hūm saḥ* is the *mantra*. This *mantra* written on a *bhūrja* leaf along with *gorocanā* and saffron wards off death. The first, fifth and ninth houses confer satisfaction and second, sixth and twelfth confer general welfare.

21-23. The third, seventh and eleventh cause acquisition; fourth, eighth and twelfth cause enmity. (The twelve houses Meṣa etc. denote) respectively the body, wealth, brothers, friendship, progeny, enmity, wife, death, righteousness, activity, income and expenditure. One should speak about the nine *tārābala*[1] (as follows): the *janma* (birth), *sampat* (prosperity), *vipat* (misfortune), *kṣema* (welfare), *pratyari* (enmity), *sādhaka* (seeker or accomplisher), *nidhana* (death), *mitra* (friend) and *paramamitra* (close friend).

24. The first shave (of a child) is commended on Sunday, Monday, Wednesday, Thursday and Friday in the six months commencing with *Māgha* (February-March).

25-26. The *karṇavedha* (piercing of the ear) (should be done) on Wednesday and Thursday in the (asterisms of) *puṣya*, *śravaṇa* and *citrā*. The commencement of study in the fifth year (should be done) after worshipping (lord) Hari (Viṣṇu) and (goddesses) Vāṇī (goddess of speech) and Śrī (Lakṣmī, goddess of wealth), avoiding the sixth, first and the fifteenth, the *riktā* days (fourth, ninth and fourteenth days) and Tuesday. The tying up of the girdle is auspicious (if done) in the six months commencing with *Māgha*.

27-31. The tonsure and other (rites) are not commended in (the asterisms) *śravaṇa* etc. The investiture of a brahmin (boy) performed when the Jupiter or Venus has set and the Moon is waning brings forth death or stupidity. The rite marking conclusion of the study should be done on an auspicious day, in the asterism suitable for shaving, at an auspicious place on the rising constellations in a good house. The imparting of the science of archery in the asterisms *aśvinī*, *maghā*, *citrā*, *svātī*, *yāmya* (*bharaṇī*), *uttarā*, *punarvasu* and *puṣya* is commendable. One who desires to live should not wear new clothes in the asterisms *bharaṇī*, *ārdrā*, *maghā*, *āśleṣā*, *kṛttikā* and *uttaraphālgunī*. (Wearing of new) clothes on Wednesday, Thursday and Friday is not objectionable at (the time of) marriage (and other festive occasions).

32. Wearing of gems like conch-shell and coral is commendable in (the asterisms of) *revatī*, *aśvinī*, *dhaniṣṭhā*, and the five commencing with *hasta*.

33. Anything bought in (the asterisms of) *bharaṇī*, *sarpa* (a particular constellation), *dhaniṣṭhā*, the three *pūrva* (*pūrva*-

1. Counting from the birth asterism to the asterism of that day that number should be divided by nine, the remainder indicates the *tārābala* as shown above.

phālguni, *pūrvabhādrapada* and *pūrvāṣāḍha*) and *vāruṇa* (*śatabhiṣak*) causes adversity. Also its sale causes adversity.

34. Anything bought in (the asterisms of) *aśvinī*, *svātī*, *citrā*, *revatī* and *śatabhiṣak* and on Sunday causes profit. If anything is sold (on the days ruled by these asterisms) causes adversity.

35. An employer should not be attended upon in (the asterisms of *bharaṇī*, the three *pūrvas* (see verse 33 above), *ārdrā*, *āśleṣā*, *maghā*, *svātī*, *kṛttikā*, *jyeṣṭhā* and *viśākhā*.

36. Money is deposited or articles are given or taken back in (the asterisms of) *uttara*, *śravaṇa* and *śākra* (*jyeṣṭha*). The coronation of a king should be done (in these asterisms).

37. Entering a house (for the first time) is auspicious in the months other than *Caitra* (April-May), *Jyeṣṭha* (June-July), *Bhādra*(*pada*) (September-October), *Āśvina* (October-November), *Pauṣa* (January-February) and *Māgha* (February-March).

38. The commencement (of the construction) of a house in (the asterisms of) *aśvinī*, *rohiṇī*, *mūla*, the three *uttaras* (*uttaraphalguni*, *uttarabhādrapada*, and *uttarāṣāḍha*), *mṛgaśirṣa*, *svātī*, *hasta* and *anurādhā* is commendable.

39-40. Sundays and Tuesdays should be avoided for (the excavation of) a tank or (the construction of) a palace. So also the building of a house should be avoided when Jupiter is in Leo or in (the conjunction of) Jupiter and Sun or in an intercalary month or when Venus is in the transit ascension or descension or has set. (It would cause) burning by fire, fear, disease, affliction from the sovereign or loss of wealth.

41. Hay should be gathered in the five (asterisms of *śravaṇa* etc.). One should enter the (new) house in the asterisms of *dhaniṣṭhā*, *uttarā* and *vāruṇa* (*śatabhiṣak*).

42. The second, third, fifth, seventh and thirteenth days (of a fortnight are commendable) for the construction of a boat. A sovereign should be seen in (the asterisms of) *hasta*, *revatī* and *aśvinī*.

43. Pilgrimage undertaken in (the asterisms of) the three *uttara* (*uttarāṣāḍha*, *uttaraphālguni*, and *uttarabhādrapada*), *dhaniṣṭhā*, *ārdrā*, *kṛttikā*, *saumya* (*mṛgaśirṣa*), *viśākhā*, *āśleṣā* and *aśvinī* accomplishes prosperity.

44-47. One should not graze the cows in the three (asterisms of) *uttarā*, *rohiṇī* or on *sinīvālī caturdaśī* (day prior to new moon) or in (the asterisms of) *śravaṇa*, *hasta*, *citrā* and *vaiṣṇavī* (*śravaṇa*). One should not enter (the cow-pen) in (the asterisms of) *anila* (*svāti*), *uttarā*, *rohiṇī*, *mṛga* (*śirṣa*), *punarvasa*, *śravaṇa* and *hasta*. One should do agriculture in (the asterisms of) *punarvasu*, *uttarā*, *svātī*, *Bhaga* (*pūrvaphālgunī*), *mūla*, *Indra* (*pūrvāṣāḍha*) and *vāruṇa* (*śatabhiṣak*) or on Thursday or Friday or Monday or Sunday or in (the zodiacal signs of) Taurus, Virgo and Gemini.

48-51. One who desires fortune should sow seeds except that of the mandāra (coral) on the second, third, fifth, seventh, tenth and thirteenth (days of the fortnight) and in (the asterisms of) *revatī*, *rohiṇī*, *Indra* (*pūrvāṣāḍha*), *Agni* (*kṛttikā*), *hasta*, *maitra* (*anurādhā*) and *uttarā*. Harvest of grains should be done in (the asterisms of) *revatī*, *hasta*, *mūla*, *śravaṇa*. Bhaga (*pūrva-phālgunī*), *maitra* (anurādhā), *pitṛdaiva* (*maghā*) and *saumya* (*mṛgaśirṣa*). One should take them into the house at the time of the rise of (the asterism) *mṛgaśirṣa* or in (the asterisms of) *hasta*, *citrā*, *Aditi* (*punarvasu*), *svātī*, *revatī* or in the three stars (commencing with) *śravaṇa* or in a fixed sign or on Thursdays, Fridays and Wednesdays or in (the asterisms of) *yāmya* (*bharaṇī*) *Aditi* (*punarvasu*), *maghā*, *jyeṣṭhā* and *uttara*.

52. (The following *mantras*) written on a leaf and placed amidst the heap of grains in (the asterisms of) the three *pūrvas* (*pūrvāṣāḍha*, *pūrvaphālgunī* and *pūrvabhādrapada*), *viśākhā*, *dhaniṣṭhā* and *vāruṇa* (*śatabhiṣak*) increases the grains "*Om*, (salutation) to the bestower of wealth and the lord of all wealth. Give me wealth. Oblations. O goddess Ilā (Lakṣmī) ! One who makes the world thrive ! The desire incarnate ! Grant me wealth in the new year ! Oblations.

53. Wisemen know that grains should be taken out in the (above) six asterisms. Tanks, gardens and (images of) gods should be consecrated when the Sun is in the Cancer. (Lord) Cakrapāṇi (the wielder of the disc) (Viṣṇu) should always be laid down when the Sun is in the (sign of) Gemini and it is the twelfth day after the new moon.

54. When the Sun is in the (sign of) Leo and in Libra and the two twelfth days after the new-moon, the first is the day of getting up of (lord) Indra and (the second one) is the waking up of (lord) Hari.

55-57. Similarly, (the goddess) Durgā is made to get up when the Sun enters (the sign of) Virgo. When a *bhadrātithi* (the second, seventh and twelfth days of a lunar fortnight) occurs on a Tuesday, Sunday or Saturday and is marked by three fourth of a constellation that (combination) is known as *tripuṣkara*. All ceremonies should be done when the moon and star are pure.

58. One has to forecast prosperity for those in whose (chart), the Moon is situated in the sixth, seventh, tenth or eleventh house from the ascendant.

59-60. The second, fifth and ninth in the bright fortnight brings good. The asterisms are (known to be) friendly, extremely friendly, accomplisher of riches and welfare etc. (The one known as friendly) causes death by its ascendancy. That which is calamitous (causes) destruction of wealth. One should know that which is *pratyari* (enemy) (causes) death. One gets death in that which is (known as) destruction.

61. The period from the eighth day of the dark (fortnight) till the eighth day of the bright (fortnight), the moon is known to be waning and is known to be full thereafter.

62. It is known to be *mahājyaiṣṭhī* if the Sun is in (the signs of) Taurus or Gemini and Jupiter is in (the asterisms of) *mṛga-śirṣa* or *jyeṣṭhā* and the full moon (occurs) on a Thursday.

63. It is also called *mahājyaiṣṭhī* when Jupiter and Moon are in (the asterism of) *jyeṣṭhā* and the Sun is in (the asterism of) *rohiṇī* on the full moon day in the month of *jyeṣṭhā* (June-July).

64. The banner of (lord) Indra fastened to the support should be hoisted in (the asterism of) *svāti*. It should be lowered down after a week in (the asterism of) *aśvinī* and in the sign of Leo.

65. When the Sun is eclipsed by Rāhu (the ascending node) any gift is deemed to be gold, all the brahmins are equal to (lord) Brahmā and all the waters are equal to Gaṅgā.

66. O Brahmins ! The entry of the Sun in the different signs is known by the names of *dhvāṅkṣī*, *mahodarī*, *ghorā*, *mandā*, *mandā-kinī* and *rājasī*.

67. If the Sun passes (from one sign to the other) in the *karaṇas* (divisions of a day) *bālava*, *kaulava* and *taitila*, then the people would be happy.

68. People would suffer from poverty and harassment by

the sovereign if (the Sun) enters (the astral combinations known as) *gara, vava, vaṇik, viṣṭi, kintughna* and *śakuna.*

69. If the Sun makes a transit in lying position in *catuṣpada, viṣṭi* or *vāṇijya* (*karaṇas*[1] or divisions of the day), it would cause famine or war between sovereigns or quarrel among husbands and wives.

70. If (the Sun) stays in one's birth-star it would cause disease or mental anguish, while (its presence) in the asterisms of *kṛttikā* and *rohiṇī* would cause misery for nine nights and three nights respectively.

71-76. It is said that the transit in (the asterism of) *mṛgaśira* (causes misery) for five nights, in *ārdrā* (causes) death, and in *punarvasu* or *puṣya* (causes) (misery) for seven nights. Its entry in (the asterism of) *āśleṣā* (causes misery) for nine nights, in *maghā* (causes misery) until one's death, in *pūrvaphālgunī* (causes misery) for two months and in *uttarā* (causes misery) for fifteen (days). While the sun is in (the asterism of) *hasta*, the (asterisms) *citrā, svāti* and *viśākhā* would bring misery for a fortnight, two months and twenty days respectively. Its transit in (the asterisms of) *anurādhā, jyeṣṭhā, mūla* and *pūrvāṣāḍha* (would cause misery) for ten days, a fortnight, no relief (from misery) or fifteen days respectively. (The Sun's transit) in (the asterisms of) *uttarā, śravaṇa, dhaniṣṭā* and *śatabhiṣak* (would cause misery) for twenty days, two months, fifteen days or ten days respectively. There will not be relief (from misery) if it enters (the asterism) *bhādrapada.* (The Sun's transit) in (the asterisms of) *uttarā, revatī* and *aśvinī* would (cause misery) for fifteen days or ten days or a single day respectively.

77. Its transit in (the asterism) *bharaṇī* causes danger to life and it becomes auspicious by doing oblations with the *gāyatrī* (*mantra*). Making a gift of a cow with five kinds of grains, sesamum, clarified butter to a brahmin compensates (the evil influences).

78-79. The periods of influence of the Sun, Moon, Mars, Mercury, Saturn, Jupiter, Rāhu and Venus are six, fifteen, eight, seventeen, ten, nineteen, twelve and twentyone years respectively.

---

1. These are different *karaṇas* or eleven divisions of the day.

CHAPTER ONE HUNDRED AND TWENTYTWO

*Pañcāṅga : The Almanac**

God Agni said:

1a. Time is (reckoned by) the accumulated number of years, (months etc., from the epoch up to the point of time under consideration). I shall set forth the calculation involved in reckoning time.

1b. The accumulated (i.e. elapsed) number of years (up to the required point of time) is to be multiplied by 12 (*arka*) and the (number of months elapsed in the current year from) Citrā is to be added to the product)[1]

2a. The sum obtained is doubled and placed at two places. To one is added 4 (*veda*) and to the other 865 (*pañcāṅgāṣṭa*). (The latter figure is to be divided by 60 and the quotient added to the first, while the remainder is kept as the second figure). The resultant is to be called '*guṇa*'.[2]

**General* : *Pañcāṅga* or the five aspects of reckoning time for each day, computed and recorded in Hindu almanacs are: (i) *Vāra* (day of the week), (ii) *Tithi* (lunar day), (iii) *Nakṣatra* (the Constellation through which the moon moves), (iv) *Yoga* (Sum of the longitudes of the Sun and the Moon), and (v) *Karaṇa* (half-*tithi*). All these reckonings have religious and ritualistic significances.

The verses in this chapter are all of a highly cryptic nature and, like philosophical aphorisms, imply much more than what is actually expressed, and can be correctly understood only with suitable explanations. While the implied information is given brackets in the translation, an example is worked out in the Notes illustrating the working, step by step.

1. Any epoch or starting point in time might be adopted, like, for instance the *Kalpa* or the beginning of creation, the Caturyuga, Kaliyuga etc. or any of the eras like the Śaka.

Let the point of time taken for consideration, for which the *Pañcāṅga* is required be Śaka 10 (elapsed), in the month of Vaiśākha, 1st *tithi* of the bright fortnight.

Multiplying by 12, the elapsed years,	10×12	=120
Adding the 1 month, Meṣa, elapsed,		= 1
Total months elapsed from epoch		=121

2. Multiplying the months from epoch by 2 (i.e. 121 × 2=242) and plactng them in two places:

and plactng them in two places:	242		242
Adding 4 and 865	4		865
	246		1107
Dividing the second figure by 60 and adding to the first	264	27	(*Guṇa*)

2b. (The *guṇa*) is placed at three places (one below the other, in the serpentine fashion, each being written one step to the right of the preceding one). The 'middle' is multiplied by 8 (*vasu*) and the product again multiplied by 4 (veda). (The columns are to be added up.) and again written as 'upper', 'middle' and 'lower'.[1]

3. Subtract 398 (*aṣṭa-randhra-agni*) from the *lower* and 87 (*saika-rasāṣṭaka*) from the 'middle'. Divide (the 'middle' and the 'lower') by 60 and add the quotients to the preceding, (keeping the remainders in their places).[2]

4a. *Vāra-tithi correction.* The first (i.e. 'upper)' when divided by 7 will give the week-day constant for *tithi.* (The quotient is to be rejected as of no more use.) The resultant is to be used as the Vāra-correction for *tithi-nāḍikās*'.[3]

4b-5. *Nakṣatra-Yoga* constants. The '*guṇa*' derived above is to be multiplied by 2, and 3 subtracted from the second figure. *Guṇa* is set down before the result (in the serpentine fashion). 30 (*kha-rāma*) is set down below the last figure, and 6, 12 and 8 (*rasa-arka-aṣṭa*), respectively, below the three figures, (and the columns added up and elevated by dividing by 60). Divide the first figure by 28 and place it below the 'correction for *tithi*' (obtained in verse 4a). (add and take the result as a second 'upper').[4]

---

1. Placing the *guṇa*) in three places in the serpentine fashion:

	264	27		(upper)
		264	27	(middle)
		264	27	(lower)

Multiplying the 'middle' by 8 (i.e. 2112-216) and again by 4 (i.e. 8448-864), and setting it down in the above scheme:

	264	27		
		8448	864	
			264	27
Adding the columns, the new 'upper', 'middle' and 'lower' are:	264	8475	1128	27 (27 is rejected)
2. Subtracting 398 and 87		87	398	
	264	8388	730	
Elevating by 60	404	0	10	

3. Dividing the 'upper' by 7 for week-days and rejecting the quotient, we get the *vāra*-correction for *tithi* as 5-0-10.

4. Multiplying the '*guṇa*' (264-27) by 2 (i.e. 528-54 and subtracting 3

	528	51	
Setting down the '*guṇa*' below		264	27
Adding 30 to the last figure			30
Adding 6-12-8 to the expression	6	12	8

6-8a. The 'guṇa' is halved, 3 subtracted (from its second figure) and the whole expression multiplied by 2. The first figure here is multiplied by 11 (*rudra*); the second figure is increased by 1 and divided by 39, the quotient being subtracted from the first figure and the remainder kept in its place. The resultant is termed *madhya*. Subtract 22 from the first figure and divide it by 60; the remainder is deductive; the quotient is added to the (second) 'upper' (of verses 4b-5). The first figure is divided by 27 and the remainder set down in its place. The resultant expression is the constant for the correction of *nakṣatra* and *yoga*.[1]

8b-9a. Nakṣatra. For the calculation of *tithi*, there is a monthly constant, being 2 *piṇḍas* (i.e. whole units) and 32 *nāḍikās* (which has to be added to the *tithi* correction contained in verses 4a). Similarly, for the *nakṣatra*, there is a monthly constant, being 2 *nakṣatras* and 11 *nāḍikās*, (which, when added to the *nakṣatra* correction of verse 8a, will give the elapsed *nakṣatra* and the *nāḍikās* gone in the current *nakṣatra*.)[2]

Adding the whole	534	327	65
Elevating by 60	539	28	5
Dividing the first figure by 28 and rejecting the quotient	35	28	5
Adding the correction for *tithi*, i.e. the second 'upper'	5	0	10
Adding	40	28	15

1. The *guṇa* (264-27) is halved (132-14), 3 subtracted from the second figure (132-11) and multiplied by 2 (i.e. 264-22). The first figure is multiplied by 11 (i.e. 2904); to the second figure 1 is added (i.e. 23) and divided by 39 and the remainder (i.e. 23) is retained. This is termed the new 'middle'. Subtracting 22 from the first figure (i.e. 2882-23) and elevating by 60, we get 48-2-23.

Applying this	48	2	23
to the new second 'upper'	40	28	15
we have	88	30	38
Dividing by 27 and ignoring the quotient, the correction for *nakṣatra* and *yoga*:	7	30	38

2. Adding the *tithi*-constant (2-32-00) to the *vāra-tithi* correction (5-0-10), we have 7-32-10, being the *vārādi* (week, day etc.) correction for the point of time taken for consideration. For the *nakṣatra* of that point of time, add the *nakṣatra* constant (2-11-00) to the *nakṣatra* correction (got in verses 6-8a), i.e. 7-30-38, and we have the *nakṣatra* as 9-41-38. In other words, at the point of time taken, nine *nakṣatras* have passed by, and in the current 10th *nakṣatra*, maghā, it is 41 *nāḍikās* and 38 *vināḍikās*.

9b-10. *Weekday and commencing point of Tithi.* Add the *tithi*-correction above (to the *vārādi-tithi* correction got in verse 4a), placing the *tithi* number below the *vāra* number. Divide by 7 (if *vāra* plus *tīthi* exceeds 7); the remainder will give the elapsed week-day counted from Sunday, and the *nāḍikās* gone in the next day at the point of the commencement of the relevant *tīthi*) In the case of *tithis* after adding the complete units (*piṇḍakas*), the sum should be divided by 14 (if the sum exceeds 14, and the remainder taken as the *tithi*.)[1]

11-14a. *True-Tithi correction.* The correction, in *nāḍikās*, for the fourteen *tithis* would be, in order, minus, plus, plus, minus, (minus and so on). Whi e the correction for the 14th *tithi* is zero), the correction for the thirteenth and the first is 5 (*vinā-ḍikās*) (each, minus and plus, respectively), that for the 12th and the 2nd, 10 (*vināḍikās*), that for the 11th and 3rd, 15 (*vinā-ḍikās*), that for the 10th and 4th, 19 (*vināḍikās*), that for the 9th and 5th, 22 (*vināḍikās*), that for the 8th and the 6th, 24 (*vinā-ḍikās*), and that for the 7th, 25 (*vināḍikās*). These *khaṇḍakas* (correction-bits) are to be applied appropriately to the *piṇḍakas* (full units).[2]

14b-17a. *Vikālā correction.* In the case of (the three), Karka-ṭaka, (Siṃha and Kanyā), divide the *rāśis*, respectively, by 6 (*ṛtu*), 4 (*veda*) and 3 (*traya*); in the case of Tulā, (Vṛścika and Dhanus), divide, respectively, in the reverse, i.e. by 3, 4 and 6; in the case of Makara, (Kumbha and Mīna), respectively, by 3, 4 and 6; and in the case of Meṣa, (Ṛṣabha and Mithuna), divide, respectively, in the reverse, i.e. by 6, 4 and 3. The correction, in *vikalās*, which is positive in the case of the three, Meṣa etc., are 50 (*kha-iṣu*), 40 (*kha-yuga*) and 12 (*mitra*); in the case

1. Adding the *tithi* constant (2-32-00) to the *vāra-tithi* correction (5-0-10). we get 7-32-10 for the week,day, which means that 7 days have elapsed as / counted from Sunday, and at the point of time in consideration, i.e. Śukla-pratipad in Vaiśākha, it is Sunday at 32 *nāḍikās* and 10 *vināḍikās* (Mean).

2. The *nāḍikā* corrections enunciated are:

Tithi	*Nāḍikā corr.*	*Tithi*	*Nāḍikā corr'*
14	0		
13	− 5	1	+ 5
12	− 10	2	+ 10
11	− 15	3	+ 15
10	− 19	4	+ 19
9	− 22	5	+ 22
8	− 24	6	+ 24
		7	+ 25

of the three, Karkaṭaka etc., it is in the reverse order, (i.e. 12, 40 and 50, but positive); in the case of the three, Tulā etc., (it is 50, 40 and 12), negative; (and, in the case of the three, Makara etc., it is 12, 40 and 50, negative).[1]

17b-19a. *Application of the vikalā correction.* The *vikalā* correction is to be applied to the *tithi* multiplied by 4. Multiply their eleven *vikalās* by the difference in *liptās* (i.e. *kalās*) between the elapsed and to-elapse portions of the *tithi* and divide by 60. If the elapsed portion is less than/the portion to-elapse, treat the correction as positive even if it be negative and or positive, retain it as positive; while, in the case of the portion to-elapse being greater, the reverse is the case (i.e. the correction is to be taken as negative both if it is negative or positive).

19b-21a. *Further correction to the Tithi.* Double (?Treble) (the *nāḍikās* of) the *tithi* and subtract from it one-sixth of (the product). Apply to it the *tīthi-nāḍikās* obtained for the sun in the reverse order, and subtract the result from 60; the true *nāḍis* of the *tithi* would be obtained. If not subtractible, add 60 and subtract; if more than 60, reduce it by 60 and subtract.[2]

21b-22. *Yoga.* The *tithi* is associated with the constellation The *tithi* multiplied by 4 and a third (of the *tithi*) added to it. Apply to it the negative correction. (By dividing it by 27, the *yoga* elapsed and the *nāḍikās* in the current *yoga* are obtained.) True *tithi* has be to be used as the means for calculating the *yoga*.[3]

23a. The *yoga* is, indeed, got also by adding (the longitudes

---

1. The *vikālā* corrections enunciated are:

Month	*Divisor*	*Corr.*	*Month*	*Divisor*	*Corr.*
Karkaṭaka	6	+ 12"	Makara	6	− 12"
Siṁha	4	+ 40"	Kumbha	4	− 40"
Kanyā	3	+ 50"	Mīna	3	− 50"
Tulā	3	+ 50"	Meṣa	3	− 50"
Vṛścika	4	+ 40"	Ṛṣabha	4	− 40"
Dhanus	6	+ 12"	Mithuna	6	− 12"

2. For the third *tithi* correction, multiply the *tithi-nāḍikās*, 32-10 (of verses 9b-10) by 3 (i.e. 96-30), and deduct a sixth thereof (i.e. 16-5), resulting in 80-25. Adding to this the tithi -*nāḍikās* (32-10), we get 112-35. The correction for one *tithi* (viz. 5 *nāḍikās*, of verse 11-14a) being applied negatively, we get 107-35. Dividing it by 60, the true *nāḍikās* in the current *tithi* is got at 47-35.

3. *Yogas* form variable divisions of time during which the joint motion of the Sun and the Moon in longitude is 13° 20' or 800 *kalās*. In a cycle there are 27 *yogas*, some of them being considered as auspicious and others inauspicious. Their significances are taken due note of in deciding upon the times for rituals and domestic ceremonies. The 27 *yogas* are:

of) the sun and the moon (in *kalās* and dividing by 800).[1]

23b-24a. *Karaṇa*. (The number of) the *tithi* reduced by 1 and multiplied by 2, and the product divided by 7, gives the *karaṇa* of day-time. The *tithi*-number multiplied by 2 and the product reduced by 1 and divided by 6 (*kṛta*) gives the *karaṇa* of the night.[2]

24b-c. The *karaṇa* of the end (i.e. seeond half) of the 14th *tithi* of the dark fortnight is called Śakuni; (that of the first half of the full moon day is called Catuṣpada; that of the end (i.e. second half of the full moon day) is called Ahi (Nāga); and that of the beginning (i.e. first half) of the prathamā (of the bright fortnight) is called Kiṁstughna.

1.	Viṣkambha	10.	Gaṇḍa	19.	Parigha
2.	Prīti	11.	Vṛddhi	20.	Śiva
3.	Āyuṣmān	12.	Dhruva	21.	Siddha
4.	Saubhāgya	13.	Vyāghāta	22.	sādhya
5.	Śobhana	14.	Harṣaṇa	23.	Śubha
6.	Atigaṇḍa	15.	Vajra	24.	Śukra
7.	Sukarmā	16.	Siddhi	25.	Brahma
8.	Dhṛti	17.	Vyatīpāta	26.	Indra
9.	Śūla	18.	Varīyān	27.	Vaidhṛti

Multiplying the true *tithi* (viz. 47-35 of verses 19-20) by 4 (i.e. 190-20) and adding a third of the *tithi* (viz. 15-52), we get 206-12. Dividing by 27 (which is the total number of *yogas* in a cycle) and rejecting the quotient, we have 7-12. i.e. 7 *yogas* up to Sukarmā have gone by and, in the current 8th *yoga*, Dhṛti, 12 *nāḍikās* too are over.

1. In the alternative method of calculating the *yoga*, the longitudes of the Sun and the Moon are added and the sum divided by 800 (which is the said sum in terms of six *kalās*). The quotient will give the number of the *yogas* elapsed and the remainder the *nāḍikās* etc. elapsed in the current *yoga*.

2. The *Karaṇa* is a measure of time extending over half a *tithi*, having astrological significance. They carry eleven names, being: (1) Bava, (2) Bālava, (3) Kaulava, (4) Taitila, (5) Gara., (6) Vaṇija, (7) Viṣṭi, (8) Śakuni, (9) Catuṣpada, (10) Nāga and (11) Kiṁstughna. A cycle consists of 60 *karaṇas* (during the 30 *tithis* or 60 half-*tithis*). The last four *karaṇas* occur only once and occupy the four half-*tithis* from the second half of the 14th of the dark fortnight to the first half of the/1st *tithi* of the bright fortnight, and, so, are called *sthira* or 'fixed' *karaṇas*, while the other seven *karaṇas* occupy the remaining 56 half-*tithis*, by repeating themselves eight times, and, so, are called *cala* or 'moving' *karaṇas*.

CORRECTIONS TO THE PRINTED TEXT (SV Edn).

Verse	*For*	*Read*
3b	षष्टिहतो	षष्टिहृतो
7b	-मूर्ध्वं	-मूर्ध्वे
10a	शेषवाराश्च	शेषा वाराश्च
14b	पिण्डकाद्	पिण्डका
19a	तिथिर्द्वि	तिथिर्द्वि (? स्त्व)
22a	तिथिस्त्वि	तिथित्वि
22b	शोधनम्	साधनम्
23b	कृतिर्द्विधा	कृतिर्दिवा
24c	–तो हि	–तोऽहिः

CHAPTER ONE HUNDRED AND TWENTYTHREE

Description of the Svarodayacakra, Śanicakra, Kūrmacakra and Rāhucakra

The Fire-God said :

1. I shall describe the (*svarodayacakra*) in order to know the victory and welfare in a military expedition. The vowels a, i, u, e and o (should be written) in order (in the different squares) and then the days (*tithis*) *nandā* and others (should be written below) in order.

2. (The names of) the planets Mars, Sun, Mercury, Moon, Jupiter and Venus (are marked) on the right-hand side and Mars, Sun and Saturn on the other side in the letters 'ka' to 'ha'.

3-7. The time between the rising of the Sun to its rising on the next day should be multiplied by thirty-nine and then divided by twelve, and the quotient should be divided by nine and three respectively, the quotient being the time of predominance of the vowels or the principles they represent from day to day. The *tithi* on which the predominance takes place, brings death (to the organiser of any expedition).

Three *sphuraṇas* (throbs) make up one *ucchvāsa* (breath). Three *ucchvāsas* make up one *pala* (a measure of time). Sixty *palas* constitute one *liptā*. Sixty *liptās* (make up) a day.

The five (vowels are known to be) child, boy, youth, old and death in their half-rising state. It is said to be rising and setting when it is in the eleventh place and together with the fifth (place) brings death and reverses.

(Thus-far the *Svarodayacakra*)

8. In the *Śanicakra* (the diagram of Saturn) the rise of the planets is taken into account in a fortnight. There will be fifteen squares herein. Therein the place of Saturn indicates death.

(Thus ends the *Śanicakra*)

9. (The *Kūrmacakra*) is in the shape of a tortoise. (The result is known) from the position of Saturn in the asterisms beginning with *maghā* and ending with *kṛttikā*.

(Thus ends the *Kūrmacakra*)

10-11. In the *Rāhucakra*, one should write seven (squares) above and seven below. On the full-moon day, Rāhu travels from the south-east by the north-west to the south-west occupying the north-west on the new-moon day. The letter 'ra' should be written in the southern part and the letter 'ha' in the north-west. The letters 'ka' etc. (are marked) on the first lunar day and other (days) and the letter 'sa' in the north-west.

12-20. When it happens to be in the face of Rāhu it brings reverses. On the full-moon day and in the south-east it is *viṣṭi*. It is *karālī* in the east and on the third day. It is (known as) *ghorā* in the south and on the seventh day. It is (known as) *saumya* in the north-east and on the tenth day. One should avoid travel towards the north-west on the fourteenth day, towards the west on the fourth day, towards the south on the eighth day of the bright fortnight, and on the eleventh day. The (names of the) fifteen *muhūrtas* (a period of fortyeight minutes) are *Raudra*, *Śveta*, *Maitra*, *Sārabhaṭa*, *Sāvitra*, *Virocana*, *Jayadeva*, *Abhijit*, *Rāvaṇa*, *Vijaya*, *Nandin*, *Varuṇa*, *Yama*, *Saumya* and *Bhava*. One should do violent deeds in the *Raudra*, ceremonial bathing in the *Śveta*, the marriage of one's daughter etc., in the *Maitra*, auspicious deeds in the *Sārabhaṭa*, establishing in the *Sāvitra*, deeds relating to the monarch in the *Virocana*, victorious deeds in the *Jayadeva*, battles in the *Rāvaṇa*, agriculture and commerce in the *Vijaya*, wearing the turban in *Nandin*, the digging of tanks in the *Varuṇa*, acts of destruction in the *Yama* and good acts in the *Saumya*.

21-22. The *yogas* (a division of time) are known to be indicating good or bad from their names. *Rāhu* (ascending node) (travels) from the east to north-west and thence to the south. From the south (it goes) to the north-east, and from the north-west to the west, then to the south-east, then to the north for three (*ghaṭikas*). Then after four *ghaṭikas* it affects the (point of) concurrence.

(Thus ends the *Rāhucakra*)

23-24. The (following) excellent herbs (should be) worn for victory *caṇḍī*, *indrāṇī*, *vārāhi*, *musalī*, *girikarṇikā*, *balā*, *atibalā*, *kṣīrī*, *mallikā*, *yūthikā*, *śvetārka*, *śatāvarī* and *guḍūcī*.

25. One should tie up the tuft of hair with (the repetition of) the *mantra*, "*Om*, salutations to (lord) Bhairava (a form of Śiva), the wielder of a sword and axe in his hands; '*Om, hrūm*', (salutation) to the destroyer of obstacles, ("*Om, hrūm, phaṭ*", for success. With the same *mantra*, mark on the forehead, collyrium to the eyes and scented fumes should be applied.

26-32. Listen to me. (I shall describe) the different kinds of unguents for bathing and drinking and powdered drugs. A mark on the forehead composed of *subhagā*, *manaḥśilā* (arsenic) *tāla*, shellac and the milk of *taruṇī* (gives) conquest (over one's enemy). *Viṣṇukrānta*, *sarpākṣi*, *sahadeva* and *rocanā* made into a paste with the milk of goat and worn on the forehead gains success (over one's enemy). *Priyaṅgu*, saffron, *kuṣṭha*, *mohani* and *tagara* worn along with clarified butter subjugates (the enemy). *Rocanā*, red sandal, *niśā*, *manaḥśilā*, *tāla*, *priyaṅgu* and mustard (made into a paste and worn) also yields the same result. *Mohinī*, *haritā*, *kāntā*, *sahadevī* and *śikhā* made into a paste in the juice of pomegranate and worn on the forehead as a mark subjugates (all). Even the celestials including Indra are subjugated. Then what about the poor mortals? *Mañjiṣṭhā*, red sandal, *kaṭukandā* and *vilāsinī* together with *punarnavā* as a paste subjugates even the Sun (god). Sandal, *nāgapuṣpa*, *mañjiṣṭhā*, *tagara*, *vacā*, *lodhra*, *priyaṅgu* and *rajanī* mixed with oil of *masī* controls others.

CHAPTER ONE HUNDRED AND TWENTYFOUR

The essence of astrology as described in the science of victory in battles

Fire-God said :

1. I shall describe the essence of astrology as propounded in the (science) of victory in battles, without the employment of *mantra* and herbs and as narrated by Īśvara (Lord Śiva) to Umā.

The Goddess said :

2. Explain to me the strategy by which the demons were conquered by celestials. So also (explain to me) the knowledge relating to success in battles which give discrimination about good and bad.

The Lord said :

3. Energy comprising fifteen letters was born by the desire of the chief god. The movable and immovable were born then. One finds one's desire fulfilled by the worship (of the energy).

4. I shall explain the base of the *mantra* which is produced from five *mantras*. Those *mantras* remain in all the *mantras* in their beginning and end.

5-6. They are the *mantras* of *Ṛk*, *Yajus*, *Sāman*, and *Atharva vedas* in order. The *mantras* of lords Brahmā, Viṣṇu, Rudra, Īśa (Śiva), Indra and others who are (known as) Saptaśikha devas are these five *mantras*. 'a, i, u, e, o' (are) the parts. The fundamental (*mantra*) is stated to be Brahma.

7. Just as the fire in the wood which has not developed fully is not seen, the energy of lord Śiva remaining in the body is not seen.

8. The energy adorned with the syllable of '*Om*' is first born. O Great lady ! the *bindu* (dot) (was) then (born) together with the letter 'e'.

9. The letter 'u' which is the soul of the sound was born then. It produces the sound remaining in the heart. Then the letter 'i' of the shape of a crescent, which gives knowledge about the path of release, (was born).

10. The letter 'a' which is the supreme one giving enjoyment and emancipation, was born manifest. The letter 'a' is under the power of control of the lord. It is remembered as the part of cessation of activity.

11-12. The fragrance, the mystical letter 'na', *prāṇa* (life breath), *iḍā* (a tubular vessel in the body) and the energy known as fixed rest in this. The letter 'i' is known as the stable part. The essence, the *apāna* (one of the five life-winds) in the body), *piṅgalā* (a tubular vessel in the body), the energy (known as) *krūrā* and the mystical letter '*i*' remain united inside. The letter 'u' is the knowledge part. The form which is the characteristic of fire, the mystic letter 'ra', the *samāna* (one of the five life-winds in the body), the *gāndhārī* (one of the tubular verse in the body), and the energy *damanī* (rest therein).

13. The letter 'e' is the tranquil part. The sense of touch which is the characteristic of the wind, the *udāna* (one of the five life-winds in the body), the *calā* (one of the tubular organs of the body) and the energy (called) *kriyā* (rest therein). The syllable '*om*' is that beyond the tranquil part. The sound which is the characteristic of the sky and the *vyāna* (one of the five life-winds in the body) (rest therein).

14. The (above-mentioned) are the five kinds of letters. The (planets) Mars, Mercury, Jupiter, Venus and Saturn respectively (preside over) the letters 'a' etc. The letters 'ka' and others are placed below these.

15. Everything relating to the movable and immovable (objects of the world) is known through these. I shall describe the knowledge-base. The *praṇava* (syllable '*om*') is stated to be (lord) Śiva.

16. (When we say) Umā, it denotes (lord) Śiva along with (his consort) Umā. Umā is the energy (of Śiva) This energy remains (in three forms) as Vāmā, Jyeṣṭhā and Raudrī. (It remains in the three forms of) Brahmā, Viṣṇu and Rudra duly. Creation etc. are the three qualities (associated with them).

17-18. Three *nāḍīs* (tubular vessels in the body) which are gem-like (are also present). (The *praṇava*) is moreover gross and subtle (which are respectively) highest and lowest. One should contemplate (on) that (*praṇava*)day and night as white-coloured, as showering the excellent ambrosia and flooding the soul. O Goddess ! One would become unaging and attains the qualities of lord Śiva.

19. The limbs (of the body) (are assigned) in (the fingers) beginning with the thumb and the eye at the centre. Then one should worship (lord) Mṛtyuñjaya (Śiva, conqueror of earth) and become victorious in the battles.

20. The sound is void and without any support. The *sparśa* (consonants ka to ma) should be touched bending horizontally. The form is stated to be having upward motion and rests under the water.

21. The fragrance remains detached from all places. The principal part is at the centre. The bulbous root, which is of the form of (lord) Śiva remains at the base of the navel.

22. The formation with energy houses the moon, sun and (lord) Hari (Viṣṇu). It is endowed with the ten winds and the five primary elements.

23. (That bulbous root) which is the soul of lord Śiva is of the shape of the destructive fire that is shining. That is the life of the entire world of living beings of the immovables and movables. When that one having the fire as its soul is lost, I consider that it is dead.

CHAPTER ONE HUNDRED AND TWENTYFIVE

Different circles which get success in battle

The Lord said :

1. "*Oṁ hrīṁ* (Goddess) Karṇamoṭani ! Manifest in different forms ! Possessor of many teeth ! *hrūm phaṭ om haḥ. Om* devour devour. Cut cut. Suck suck. *Hrūm phaṭ* salutation". When this *mantra* is repeated by persons angrily and with red eyes, it would bring about the death or the downfall (of his enemy) or stupefy (his mental calibre).

2. The great incantation of (Goddess) Karṇamoṭinī is the protector of all castes. I shall describe the rise of five principles which rests on the *svarodaya* (science of sound).

3. The wind moves in the space between the navel and the heat. One should repeat this at the time of battle etc. It would pierce the ears and eyes (of the enemy).

4. The accomplisher should be bent on repetition (of *mantras*) and oblation (to fire). When the wind (moves) from the heart (downwards) to the anus and (upwards) to the throat, the acts of bringing fever on the enemies or causing their death (should be undertaken).

5. When the wind blows through the larynx with the essence, (the votary) should do rites conferring peace and prosperity. When (the wind flowing) from the eyebrows to the nostrils (known as) *gandha* (smell) (is present) one should practise the divine paralysing or drawal.

6. There is no doubt that one would be able to paralyse by making the mind absorbed in the smell. The votary should perform the (acts of) paralysing and wedging.

7. (To accomplish this he) should worship (the divinities) Caṇḍā, Ghaṇḍā, Karālī, Sumukhī, Durmukhī, Revatī, Prathamā and Ghorā in the wind-circle.

8-10. The goddesses who accomplish the charm remain well-established in lustre. They (are) Saumyā, Bhīṣaṇī, Jayā, Vijayā, Ajitā, Aparājitā, Mahākoṭī and Raudrī. (These goddesses who possess) dry bodies take away life. (The goddesses) dwelling in the essence are Virūpākṣī, Parā, Divyā, Ākāśamātṛs, Saṁhārī, Daṁṣṭrālā and Śuṣkarevatī.

11-12. Pipīlikā, Puṣṭiharā, Mahāpuṣṭipravardhanā, Bhadrakālī, Subhadrā, Bhadrabhīmā, Subhadrikā, Sthirā, (Niṣṭhurā, Divyā, Niṣkampā and Gadinī) (are the goddesses staying in the circle of smell. These thirty-two mothers reside in the circles at the rate of eight in each.

13. There is only one Sun and only one Moon (in the world). Each one of these goddesses preside over each one of the sacred places on the earth.

14. The one (universal) life force remains divided through (different) circles among created beings. It remains in tenfold forms on account of division into left and right.

15. Out of the skull (cup) of the universe (they) drink the supreme nectar, the mystical drops, encircled by the apparel of principles.

16-18. Listen to those five groups of letters which give victory in battle. (The letters), a, ā, ka, ca, ṭa, ta, pa, ya and śa are said to be the first group; i, ī, kha, cha, ṭha, tha, pha, ra, and ṣa (form) the second group; u, ū, ga, ja, ḍa, da, ba, la and sa (form) the third group, e, ai, gha, jha, ḍha, dha, bha, va and ha form the fourth group and o, au, am, aḥ, ṅa, ña, ṇa, na and ma form the fifth group.

19-20. These fortyfive letters (indicate) the prosperity of men. (These letters in each group) are respectively) known as the child, boy, youth, old, death, affliction to one's self, emaciation, indifference and destroyer. The (asterism) *kṛttikā*, the first day of a fortnight and (the planet) Mars are known as beneficial to one's self.

21-22. The sixth day (of a fortnight) and (the asterism) *maghā* (occurring) on a Tuesday and the eleventh day (of a fortnight) and (the asterism) *ārdrā* (occurring) on a Tuesday (cause) affliction. (The asterism) *maghā* and the second day (of a fortnight) occurring on Tuesday (yields) gain. (The asterism) *ārdrā* and the seventh day on a Wednesday bring loss. The asterisms *bharaṇī* and *śravaṇa* on a Tuesday (are) also of the same type. A Thursday marked by (the asterism) *pūrvaphālguna* and third day is profitable.

23. A Thursday (marked) by (the asterism) *dhaniṣṭhā* and *ārdrā* on the eighth day, and the same day (ruled) by (the asterism) *āśleṣā* on the thirteenth day causes death. A Friday

(marked) by (the asterism) *pūrvabhādrapada* on the fourth day (also yields the same).

24. A Friday ruled by (the asterism) *pūrvāṣāḍhā* and the ninth day as also by (the asterism) *bharaṇī* and the fourteenth day causes affliction.

25. The fifth day and the (asterism) *kṛttikā* occurring on a Saturday is said to be prosperous. The tenth day together with the (asterism) *āśleṣā* in conjunction with Saturday would be causing affliction.

26-27. The conjunction of (asterism) *maghā*, Saturday and full moon is held as fatal. First to the ninth have (the directions) east, north, south-east, south-west, south, north-west, moon and Brahmā as the aspects. If they have aspects together with the signs (artificial division of the ecliptic) as well as the planets that would confer perfection.

28. The four constellations *meṣa* to *kumbha* cause victory if full and death if otherwise. It is to be duly calculated, the absence of Sun etc. as well as whether they are full.

29. The Sun has no influence in the case of war. The Moon influences to appease defeat. One should know that Mars causes riot. Mercury (influences) to realise desire. Jupiter influences to get success.

30-31. Venus influences to get mental happiness. Saturn would influence to get defeat in battle. In the *piṅgalācakra*, the asterisms in which the Sun moves should be arranged (in the shape of a human figure), at the face, eyes, forehead, head, hands, thighs and feet. If the three stars at the foot (are identical with the natal star of the person concerned) (it indicates) death. (It indicates) loss of prosperity if on the sides.

32. (If the three asterisms) on the face (are identical with the natal star) (it indicates) affliction. If that on the head (is identical) (it indicates) failure of the task undertaken, and that on the head (indicates) fruitfulness. (I shall) describe the *Rāhu-cakra* now.

33-35. It goes from the east to the south-west, from the south-west to the north, from the north to the south-east, from the south-east to the west, from the west to the north-east, from the north-east to the south, from the south to the north-west and then again to the north, during (the period of) four (*ghaṭikas* every day). O dear ! I shall now tell you about the lunar phases which act as the above said Rāhu and about different directions south-east to north-east and from the full-moon etc. to which a journey should be held inauspicious during their respective continuance. (An expedition commenced) at the back of Rāhu brings success in battle, (while that undertaken) at its front brings death.

36. Till the eighth day of the dark fortnight, the east aspected by Rāhu would cause fright. (Similarly) Rāhu acts in the north-east, south-east, north-west and south-west (on the same day).

37-38. If the constellations Aries etc. are in the directions east etc., and when the Sun is (present) there it causes death, The third day in the dark fortnight, the seventh day, the tenth day, the fourteenth day in the bright (fortnight); fourth day, the eleventh day and the fifteenth day *viṣṭi* (a kind of adverse period) in the south-east and north-west.

39-42. (The letters) a, ka, ca, ṭa, ta, pa, ya and śa are the (five) groups (of letters) (standing for) the planets Sun etc. The vulture, owl, hawk, a small owl, owl (*kauśika*), crane, peacock and the water-fowl are known to be birds (in the diagram). At first the mystic syllable should be accomplished by means of oblation. Then it is known as expansion when it is *uccāṭa* (a kind of charm which drives away one's enemy). Then the application (of the mystic syllable) accomplishes (the desired results) in bringing another under one's control, in fever and in attraction. The syllable 'salutations' should be used in acts of bliss and peace-making, the syllable *vauṣaṭ* in (rites for) nourishment and in controlling etc. (The syllable) *hum* (is used) for (causing) death, breaking amity (between two persons), while (the syllable) *phaṭ* (is used) for driving away one's enemies. (The syllable) *vaṣaṭ* (is used) in (connection with) progeny and bringing splendour etc. Thus there are six kinds of mystic syllables.

43-45. I shall now describe the medicinal plants which provide good protection. *Mahākālī*, *caṇḍī*, *vārāhī*, *īśvarī*, *sudarśanā* and *indrāṇī* when worn on the body protect. *Balā*, *atibalā*, *bhīru*, *musalī*, *sahadevī*, *jātī*, *mallikā*, *yūthi*, *gāruḍī*, *bhṛṅgarāja* and *cakra-*

rūpā are great herbs which confer victory when worn (on the body).

46-48. O Greatest Goddess ! if these are gathered during an eclipse they confer good. Making an elephant endowed with all characteristics out of earth, one's enemy should be benumbed by doing the rite at its foot. After having gathered earth from an ant-hill (the rite should be done) at the summit of a mountain or at (a place having) a single tree or at a place struck by lightning. Then (the previously invoked) two divine mothers should be attached. *Om* ! obeisance to *Mahābhairava* ! to the Fierce form with deformed tooth ! to the Yellow-eyed ! to the Bearer of trident and sword ! *Vauṣaṭ*. O Goddess ! One should worship the mud and benumb multitudinous weapons (of the enemy).

49-50. I shall describe rites relating to fire which ensures victory in battle etc. The votary should remain nude, have the tuft untied, face the south and offer human flesh, blood and poison mixed with chaff of grain, pieces of bone as oblations to fire kindled with logs of wood at the cremation ground in the night uttering the name of the enemy one hundred and eight times. "*Om* obeisance to Goddess Kaumāri ! (You) dally, (You) coax ! O Ghaṇṭādevī ! (You) kill this person at once. Obeisance to you O Goddess of knowledge ! Oblations." By oblations made with this formula the enemy gets fettered.

Om ! One having a hardy frame ! One having a fierce mouth ! One possessing a tawny complexion ! One having a dreadful face ! One possessing erect hairs ! One having great strength ! One possessing a red face ! One having the lightning as the tongue ! Most fierce ! Possessing large teeth ! Having dreadful form ! One who strikes very firmly (at the battle) ! One who built the bridge to the city of Laṅkā ! The carrier of the mountain ! One who moves about in the ethereal space ! You come O lord ! Possessor of great strength ! Valiant ! The Bhairava makes known (his presence). O Great Raudra (fierce) you come ! You encircle this person with the long tail, pierce and trample him. *Hrūm phaṭ*. O Goddess ! (oblation should be made) one hundred and thirty-eight times (with the above). Hanumat (monkey-faced god) accomplishes all acts. The enemies get routed on seeing Hanumat in the picture.

CHAPTER ONE HUNDRED AND TWENTYSIX

Combinations of good and bad asterisms

The Lord said :

1-2. I shall describe combinations of asterisms determining good and bad. One should count the asterism in which the Sun is present and assign three (asterisms) from that at the head (of human figure drawn), one at the face, two in the place of the eyes, four at the hands and feet, five at the heart, the genital organ and the knee. Then one should determine one's longevity etc. (based on that).

3. The presence of the natal star on the head or at the face indicates acquisition of kingdom. (Its location) on the eyes (indicates) fortune and lustre. (Its location) at the heart (indicates) acquisition of wealth.

4. (Its presence) on the arms (indicates) that one would be a thief. (Its presence) on one of the feet (indicates) death or (the natal would be) a wanderer.

5. (Commencing with the asterism in which the Sun is stationed, the respective names of the days associated should be written on eight pitchers leaving the pitcher for the Sun as empty). The pitcher of the Sun exerts malignant influence and the pitchers in the east and other directions benevolent influence. I shall describe the (method known as) *Phaṇi Rāhu*, which indicates success or failure (in battle).

6-10. Twenty-eight circles should be drawn, intersected by four lines. The asterisms should be arranged therein in rows of three. The asterism occupied by Rāhu (the ascending node) should be deemed as the head of the serpent. Commencing with that, the twenty-seven asterisms are arranged in successive order. The presence of seven asterisms at the face (of the serpent) (indicates) that one will die in the battle. The presence of seven asterisms at the shoulders as well as the middle part (of the body) (portends) complete rout. Their presence at the belly foretells honour and success for the native. Their presence about the waist indicates success over rivals in the battle. One would get fame if (the asterisms) are situated on the tail. The asterisms aspected by Rāhu indicate death. I shall describe you a different (combination) known as the strength of the Sun and Rāhu.

11-12. Sun, Venus, Mercury, Moon, Saturn, Jupiter, Mars and Rāhu respectively preside over one-sixteenth part of a day. One who (sets out) after the expiry of (the periods of) Saturn, Sun and Rāhu, conquers battalions of army, and a marching force and wins in gambling.

13-15. (The asterisms) Rohiṇī and the three Uttarās (Uttaraphālgunī, Uttarāṣāḍha and Uttaraproṣṭapada) and the Mṛgaśīrṣa are the five fixed (asterisms). (The asterisms) Aśvinī, Revatī, Svātī, Dhaniṣṭhā and the Śatabhiṣak are the five movable (asterisms). One should undertake journeys in these (asterisms). Anurādhā, Hasta, Mūla, Mṛgaśīrṣa), Puṣya and Punarvasu are (commended) for all acts. Jyeṣṭhā, Citrā, Viśākhā, the three Pūrvas (Pūrvaphālgunī, Pūrvāṣāḍha and Pūrvaproṣṭapada), Kṛttikā, Bharaṇī, Maghā, Ārdrā and Āśleṣā are evil.

16. (All acts) at fixed places (should be done under the influence) of fixed asterisms. Movable asterisms are excellent for journeys. One should do (acts) in mild (asterisms) for conferring prosperity and frightful (deeds) in malignant (asterisms).

17-21. An evil (act) should be done (under the influence) of an evil asterism. I shall now describe (the asterisms known to) have their faces downwards etc. (The asterisms) Kṛttikā, Bharaṇī, Āśleṣā, Viśākhā, Maghā, Mūla, the three Pūrvas (Pūrvāṣāḍha, Pūrvaphālgunī and Pūrvaproṣṭapada) (are known to be) downward-faced. One should do such acts (which require) keeping one's face downwards. (Digging) of wells and tanks, acts relating to imparting knowledge and preparation of medicine, the launching of a boat, installation of a prince and pitching (of a royal camp) etc. (should be performed) in these (asterisms). (The nine (asterisms) Revatī, Aśvinī, Citrā, Hasta, Svātī, Punarvasu, Anurādhā, Mṛga(śīrṣa), Jyeṣṭhā are known as having their faces lateral. One should perform coronation of kings, construction of stables for elephants and horses, laying of garden houses, building of palaces, walls, doorways, fixing of flagstaff and banner etc. under these (asterisms).

22-26. The twelfth day falling on a Sunday, the eleventh day on a Monday, the tenth day on a Tuesday, the third day on a Wednesday, the sixth day on a Thursday, the second day on a Friday, and the seventh day on a Saturday are inauspicious.

I shall now describe the (combination known as) *tripuṣkara.* The second, twelfth, seventh and the third day with the Sunday, Tuesday and Saturday, these six (are known to be *tripuṣkara.* (The asterisms) Viśākhā, Kṛttikā, the two Uttarās, Punarvasu and the Pūrvabhādrapada, these six (are known to be) *tripuṣkara.* Any profit, loss, victory, disease, birth of a son, loss, something which has slipped and that which has strayed, all these get multiplied thrice (during the *tripuṣkara* period).

27-28. The seven (asterisms) Aśvinī, Bharaṇī, Āśleṣā, Puṣya, Svātī, Viśākhā and Śravaṇa are known (to be having) firm look. They have their look in ten directions. The journey undertaken to a far off place at an auspicious moment (is followed by a safe) return journey.

29-31. The five asterisms—the two Āṣāḍhas (Pūrvāṣāḍha and Uttarāṣāḍha), Revatī, Citrā and Punarvasu (are) squint-eyed. The person undertaking a journey under these asterisms (has a safe) return. Kṛttikā, Rohiṇī, Saumya (the five stars on the orion's head), Phālguni, Maghā, Mūla, Jyeṣṭhā, Anurādhā, Dhaniṣṭhā, Śatabhiṣak and Pūrvabhādrapada are known as blunted. One who undertakes journey under these asterisms would again return home.

32. Anything lost (on days ruled by the asterisms) Hasta, Uttarabhādra (pada), Ārdrā and Āṣāḍha cannot be recovered and a battle commenced in these asterisms) would not continue.

33-36. I shall again describe the *gaṇḍānta* (the first fourth of an asterism preceded by a node of asterisms) in the midst of asterisms as such. The four *nāḍīs* (one *nāḍī* equals 24 minutes) of the (asterism) Revatī and the four (*nāḍīs*) of Aśvinī (are known as *gaṇḍas*). One has to avoid with great care those *yāmas* (three hours) (in undertaking a journey etc). The four *ghaṭikās* (one *ghaṭikā* equals 24 minutes) forming last part of Āśleṣā and the first part of Maghā are called the second *gaṇḍa.* Listen to me ! O Bhairavī ! The third (*gaṇḍa*) is between the asterisms of Jyeṣṭhā and Mūla, and that is of the form extremely malignant for three hours. One should not do auspicious acts in these, if he wants to live. At the time of birth of a child in these periods the parents would die.

CHAPTER ONE HUNDRED AND TWENTYSEVEN

The auspicious and inauspicious periods of the day based on certain combinations

The Lord said :

1. The three *ghaṭikās* (one *ghaṭikā* is equal to 24 minutes) (from the commencement) of *viṣkambha* (an inauspicious period), the five *ghaṭikās* of *śūla* (an adverse period), the six (*ghaṭikās*) respectively in the *gaṇḍa* and *atigaṇḍa* (types of impediments) and the nine (*ghaṭikās*) in the *vyāghāta* and *vajra* (a kind of adverse period) should be avoided.

2. One should avoid all undertakings when the whole day is ruled by both *parigha* and *vyatīpāta* (obstacles) and the undertaking of any journey or commencing a battle on the day ruled by *vaidhṛta* (obstacle).

3. O Goddess ! I shall describe the good or bad (effects of the positions of planets) in the constellations of *Meṣa* and others. The Moon and Venus occupying the first house confer good when they leave (the same).

4. One has to forecast loss of property, absence of gain and reverses in the battle if the Mars, Sun, Saturn and Rāhu (occupy) the second house.

5-6. The second (house) occupied by the Moon, Mercury Venus and Jupiter confers good. Just as the Sun, Saturn, Mars and Venus in the third (house) confer good so also all the planets. Mercury, Moon and Rāhu yield benefits. Mercury and Venus in the fourth (house) are beneficial. All other planets are ominous.

7. Just like Jupiter in the fifth, the presence of Venus, Mercury and Moon yield the desired gains. The Sun is auspicious in the sixth (place).

8. O Goddess ! The planets Moon, Saturn, Mars and Mercury confer good (if they remain) in the sixth (place) from the native sign. One should avoid Jupiter and Venus in the sixth (house).

9. The Sun, Saturn, Mars and Rāhu in the seventh (house) (indicate) misery and Jupiter, Venus and Mercury (in the seventh house) indicate happiness. The Mars and Venus are

auspicious in the eighth (house).

10. All other planets (in the eighth house) (indicate) evil propensities. The Mars and Venus in the ninth (house) are auspicious. The other (planets) (in the ninth) (exercise) evil influences. The Venus and Sun in the tenth (house) confer gains.

11. The Saturn, Mars, Rāhu, Moon and Mercury bring good. All planets are good in the eleventh (house). One should avoid Jupiter in the tenth (house).

12. The Mercury and Venus in the twelfth (are beneficial). One should avoid all other planets in the twelfth. The twelve zodiacal signs exercise influence over the whole day (in order). I will describe them (now).

13-14. (It takes) four *nāḍis* for the Sun to traverse the (zodiacal signs). Pisces, Aries, Taurus and Gemini, six *nāḍis* (to traverse) Cancer, Leo, Virgo and Libra and five *nāḍis* (to traverse) Scorpio, Sagittarius, Capricorn and Aquarius. The (Zodiacal signs) Aries and others are respectively movable, fixed and of dual nature.

15. The Cancer, Capricorn, Libra and Aries are movable. One should do all acts involving movement and permanent victory, both good and bad.

16. The Taurus, Leo, Acquarius and Scorpio are the fixed signs and all acts of fixed nature (should be done in them). (A person going away under their influence) will not return quickly. (One who) falls sick (under their influence) will not get cured.

17. The Gemini, Virgo, Pisces and Sagittarius are of dual nature. These dual-natured (signs) are always auspicious for all acts.

18. One would get increase, victory and gains in sojourn, trade, battle, marriage and royal audience. One would get victory in battle.

19. (The asterisms) Aśvinī (consisting of) three stars is of the form of a horse. If it rains in this (asterism), it would rain for a night. If it rains in the asterism presided over by Yama (god of death) (Bharaṇī) it would rain for a fortnight.

CHAPTER ONE HUNDRED AND TWENTYEIGHT

The koṭacakra—a drawing to forecast results

The Lord said :

1. I shall describe *koṭacakra*. One should draw a square. One should draw another square inside that (square) and again another square inside the second.

2. The zodiacal signs Aries etc. (should be assigned) to the directions east etc. (in the three squares) which are the symbols of the three *nāḍis* (tubular organs in the body). The (asterism) Kṛttikā (is located) in the east and the (asterism) Āśleṣā in the south-east.

3. (Asterism) Bharaṇī should be placed in the south. Viśākhā should be assigned in the south-west. (Asterism) Anurādhā (should be located) in the west and Śravaṇa in the north-west.

4. (Asterism) Dhaniṣṭhā should be located in the north and Revatī in the north-east. These eight asterisms are located in the outer *nāḍī* carefully.

5. The asterisms Rohiṇī, Puṣya, (Pūrva) Phālgunī, Svātī, Jyeṣṭhā, Abhijit, Śatatārā and Aśvinī (are located) in the middle square in order.

6. I shall describe the *nāḍī* at the middle of the drawing. In that inner square, the (asterism) Mṛga(śīrṣa) (is located) at the east, and Punarvasu at the south-east.

7-8. The Uttaraphālgunī (is placed) in the south. (The asterism) Citrā (is located) in the south-west. Having placed Mūla in the west, the Uttarāṣāḍha in the north-west, the Pūrvabhādrapada in the north and Revatī in the north-east, the central square should be thus made to contain the eight asterisms.

9. (The asterisms) Ārdrā, Hasta, the four Āṣāḍha[1] and the three Uttara[2] should be placed inside the central square as four pillars.

10. Fortifications should be made thus. A belligerent coming from outside from the direction of lord (planet) (that presides over the day) and the asterisms (representing that

---

1. The Pūrvāṣāḍha and Uttarāṣāḍha.
2. The Uttaraphālgunī, Uttarāṣāḍha and Uttaraproṣṭapada.

quarter) is sure to get the benefits.

11. If the planets and asterisms at the innermost square are good, it is known that those remaining in the inner square would be victorious and defeat for that person coming (from outside).

12-13. One should enter the fort when the conducive asterism (rules) and one should come out under the influence of conducive asterism. One should know if the battle commenced when the planets Venus, Mercury and Mars leave their respective asterism one would face defeat. If the battle commenced when the asterism held auspicious for entering the castle was ruling, then that fort would be captured. One need not get surprised.

CHAPTER ONE HUNDRED AND TWENTYNINE

Guidelines for storing and selling grains

The Lord said :

1-2. I shall describe the quantity of food-grains to be gathered when there may be fall of meteors, earthquake, hurricane, eclipse, entry of foreign matter and conflagration in different directions in different months (of the year). If these occur in the (month of) Caitra (April-May), the ornaments etc. gathered (would become) four-fold (worth) in (the course of) six months.

3. All things collected in the (month of) Vaiśākha (May-June) would become six-fold (worth) in eight months. In the same way, the grains such as barley and wheat (stocked) in the (months of) Jyeṣṭha (June-July) and Āṣāḍha (July-August) (would fetch more).

4. (Similarly) one would get (increased returns) in the month of Mārgaśīrṣa (December-January) from ghee, oil etc. purchased in (the month of) Śrāvaṇa (August-September), apparels and grains in Āśvina (October-November) and grains (purchased) in Kārttika (November-December).

5. (One would get) profit by the purchase of saffron and perfumes in Puṣya (January-February), food grains in Māgha (February-March) and perfumes in Phālguna (March-April). Thus the *arghakāṇḍa* (section on storing and selling of grains and goods) has been described.

CHAPTER ONE HUNDRED AND THIRTY

Different spheres marked by asterisms indicating victory in battle etc.

The Lord said :

1-2. O Good-natured Goddess ! I shall describe the four kinds of spheres (to find) one's victory. (The asterisms) Kṛttikā, Maghā, Puṣya, Pūrva (phālguni), Viśākhā, Bharaṇī and Pūrva-bhādrapadā belong to the sphere of fire. I shall describe its characteristic.

3-9. If the wind blows, holes (are noticed) in the disc of the Sun and Moon, earthquakes (occur), hurricanes (strike), (there be) the eclipses of Sun and Moon, smoky flames, conflagration in (different) quarters, and comets are sighted and (there be) blood-like red showers, heat waves and fall of meteorites (under these asterisms), (there would follow) epidemics of eye diseases and hiarrhoea. The fire would rage. The cows would yield reduced (quantity of) milk. The trees (would bear) lesser (quantity) of flowers and fruits. The food grains would get destroyed. One should foresee little rain. The four castes of people would be harassed. The entire humanity would suffer hunger. The inhabitants of (the regions of) Sindhu, Yamunā, Gurjara, Bhoja, Vāhlīka, Jālandhara, Kaśmīra and the Uttarā-patha as well as these countries would be destroyed when these portents are noticed. (The asterisms) Hasta, Citrā, Maghā, Svāti, Mṛga (śīrṣa) or Punarvasu, Uttaraphālgunī and Aśvinī are spoken as comprising the sphere of wind.

10-12. The people would become bereft of virtues. All would lament in despair. (The countries) Dāhala, Kāmarūpa, Kaliṅga, Kośala, Ayodhyā, Avanti, Koṅkaṇa and Āndhra would get destroyed. (The asterisms) Āśleṣā, Mūla, Pūrvāṣāḍha, Revatī, Bhādrapada and Uttarā (form the regions where) water reigns supreme. If something unusual takes place under their influence, it should be spoken as resultant of their respective influences.

13-14. Cows would have plenty of milk and trees would abound with flowers and fruits. There would be good health. The earth would abound with grains. The grains would be highly valuable. The kingdom would be prosperous. There would be grave battles among kings.

15-19. (The asterisms) Jyeṣṭhā, Rohiṇī, Anurādhā, Dhaniṣṭhā, Uttarāṣāḍhā and Abhijit witnessing any unusual commotion are said to be related to celestial (region). The subjects would be jubiliant being free from all diseases. Kings would conclude treaties and the kingdom would be prosperous. The eclipses are known to be of two kinds—by the head or by the tail of Rāhu. If the Sun or Moon and ascending node of Moon are in the same sign, it is known to be eclipse by the head. If it is the *jāmitra* (the seventh sign of Zodiac) it is said to be by the tail. When the Moon stays at the fifteenth asterism from the one occupied by the Sun and if the lunar day begins and ends in between two sunrises, one should indicate the lunar eclipse.

CHAPTER ONE HUNDRED AND THIRTYONE

Diagrams known as Ghātakacakra, Naracakra and Jayacakra indicating failure or success in battle etc.

The lord said :

1-3. The vowels commencing with 'a' should be written in a circular form commencing from the east. One should write such circles for the months Caitra (April-May) and the other months. The vowels should be considered as representing the lunar days first to thirteenth. If the (names of) lunar days of first, full moon, thirteenth, fourteenth, eighth, eleventh and seventh in the circle of Caitra happened to be touched, one should know about one's victory or gains. One should know that it augurs well if odd numbers (of vowels are present). It is said that it augurs bad if even numbers (of vowels are present).

4-5. When the name of a person is pronounced at the time of commencement of the battle, if one's name begins with a long vowel, he will always have victory even in dreadful battles. If the name of the warrior (commences with) short vowel, he would die without any prevention.

6. If the first letter is long and the middle letter is also long (both indicate) death. If two letters at the middle are first (among the letters), it would end in the death (of the person) without any doubt.

7. If there are vowels at the beginning and the end, one should know (impending) death (if the vowels are) short and victory (if the vowels are) long.

8. I shall describe *Naracakra* (the figure of a man) consisting of asterisms. A human figure is drawn first and the asterisms are arranged (in order).

9-11. Three asterisms are placed at the head (of the figure) one at its face, two at the eyes, four on the arms and two at the ears. Five asterisms (are placed) at the heart and six asterisms at the feet. The asterism for one's name should be found out and be placed at the centre of the drawing, at the eyes, head, right-ear, right-hand, feet, heart, neck, left hand, secret organ and feet (of the human figure).

12. One should know that fatality is certain at that asterism occupied by the Sun, Saturn, Mars or Rāhu (the ascending node).

13. I shall (now) describe the *Jayacakra* (the circle of victory). One should draw letters *a* to *ha*. One should draw thirteen lines (on a plane) and six lines obliquely.

14-15. The quarters, planets, sages, Sun, priest and the lunar days are placed (in the chambers above) in order. Stupefaction, remembrance, scriptures, asterisms etc. and the letters *a, ka, ḍa, ma* etc. (are written) below them. The Sun and other planets when placed in seven places, the planets are powerful at the end of the name. (The planets) Sun, Saturn and Mars (are) for victory and the planet Mercury for truce.

16-18. Twelve lines are drawn, six on the right and six on the left. Fourteen, twentyseven, two, one, fifteen, six, four, three and seventeen are known as weak points for wealth. The letters *a, ka, ṭa* and *pa* should be located below. After having assigned letters one by one the rest should be located as follows: the figure made up of letters comprising the name should be divided by eight.

19-20. The quotient if identical with the number represented by a crow (fourteen) would signify the diagram a strong one, while the same equal to the numbers represented by an ass, bull, elephant, lion, horse and camel would signify greater success respectively than the preceding one.

CHAPTER ONE HUNDRED AND THIRTYTWO

Description of Sevācakra and the indication of accrual of benefits

The Lord said :

1. I shall describe the *Sevācakra* that indicates the gain or loss from the father, mother, brother, husband or wife.

2. One should know from that from whom one would get benefits. One should draw six vertical lines and eight different lines obliquely.

3-4. Then there would be thirty-five chambers. The letters should be written in these (chambers). The five vowels are drawn and afterwards one should discard the three (consonants known as) hīnāṅga (diminutive) and write letters *ka* to *ha* in groups of *siddha, sādhya, susiddha, ari* and *mṛtyu.*

5. Names (which begin with letters) falling under (the chambers) *ari* and *mṛtyu* should be avoided in all acts by one's efforts.

6-7. (The letter) falling in the first place (should be deemed) as yielding good. The second place would be a supporter and the third one would confer materials. The fourth one causes one's own destruction, while the fifth one gives death. The chambers occupied by friendly, servile and related letters would indicate acquisition of wealth.

8. All the letters respectively occupying the *siddha*, *sādhya* and *susiddha* always yield fruits and the two *ari* and *mṛtyu*, should be rejected in all undertakings.

9. The vowels *a*, *i*, *u*, *e* and *o* are known as included in the term *akārānta* as told now. Now I shall describe the different species of beings for which the different groups of letters stand for.

10-11. The celestials occupy letters falling under the group of letter '*a*', the demons occupy letters of '*ka*' group, the serpents letters of '*ca*' group and the *gandharvas* (a kind of semi-divine beings) letters of '*ṭa*' group. The sages are stated to be in letters of '*ta*' group, the demons are known to be in letters of '*pa*' group, the goblins in letters of '*ya*' group and the men in letters of '*sa*' group.

12-13. Demons are stronger than celestials, serpents than demons, *gandharvas* than serpents and sages than *gandharvas*. Demons are stronger than sages, goblins than demons and men than goblins. One (under the influence) of a stronger species should avoid (contact with one of) the weaker.

14-18. Listen again duly (to the narration) about *Tārācakra* which indicates friendship. As before it is calculated from the star and the first letter of the name of a person. The nine stars which should duly be ascertained from the natal star of a person are—*janma*, *sampat*, *vipat*, *kṣema*, *pratyari*, *dhanadā*, *ṣaṣṭhī*, *nidhana*, *mitra* and *paramitra*. The star known as the *janma* is inauspicious. The star (known as) *sampat* yields extremely great result. The star (known as) *vipat* makes (one's attempts) futile. The star (known as) *kṣema* is favourable for all undertakings and *pratyari* destroys one's wealth. The star (known as) *dhanadā* gets the benefit of kingdom etc., and the *nidhana* makes all attempts futile. The effect of the star (known as)*mitra* is friendship and that of *paramitra* is conferring benefits.

19. O dear, the number of syllables which are the numerical equivalents of vowels in the names of two persons (to be related in any way), should be counted and added and (the total) be divided by twenty. The remainder indicates the result.

20. One should find the debt and credit between the two names from the debt being indicated by lesser number of

syllables and the credit by greater number of syllables.

21. Friendship (would grow between two persons) whose names stand in relationship of credit and indifference in the case of relationship of debt. This is said to be the *Bevācakra* which indicates benefits or the contrary.

22. (There would be) friendliness (between those born under the constellations) of Aries and Gemini as also between those of Gemini and Leo. There would be great amity (between the born under the constellations) of Libra and Leo as also between Sagittarius and Acquarius.

23-25. One should not accept the service of a person if his natal sign and that of the other person are in (relationship of) friendship. There is friendship between the following Taurus and Cancer, Cancer and Acquarius, Virgo and Scorpion, Capricorn and Scorpion, Pisces and Capricorn when they are respectively the third and eleventh signs. The constellations Libra and Aries would be in great friendship, Taurus and Scorpion would be in great enmity. There would be friendship between Gemini and Sagittarius, Cancer and Capricorn, Capricorn and Acquarius as also Virgo and Pisces.

CHAPTER ONE HUNDRED AND THIRTYTHREE

Different traits in infants and combinations indicating success in battle

The Lord said :

1-5. I shall describe the character (of an infant) from the nature of planets presiding over nativity. One would be born not extremely tall, neither lean nor stout, possess even loins, of a reddish yellow complexion, having reddish eyes and would be possessing good qualities and brave in the house of the Sun. One who was born in the house of the Moon would have good fortune and be of mild disposition. One who was born in the house of Mars would be flatulent and greedy. A person born in the house of Mercury would be intelligent, fortunate and respectable. A person born in the house of Jupiter would be extremely irascible and fortunate. One born when the Venus was rising would be charitable, enjoy comforts and fortune. A person born in the house of Saturn would be intelligent, fortunate and respectable. One born in a good-natured *lagna* (the rising point at the east at the time of one's birth) would be good-natured and one (born) in cruel-natured *lagna* would be cruel-natured.

6-11. O Gaurī ! I shall describe the effect of the presence (of the planets) in the sign of one's nativity according to one's name. The presence of Sun in such a position would get the native elephants, horses, wealth, grains, wide sovereignty and recovery of lost wealth. The period of Moon would get (the native) a damsel of celestial beauty. In (the period of) Mars one acquires land and happiness. One (gets) land, grains and wealth in (that of) Mercury. One (gets) elephant, horse etc. and wealth in (that of) Jupiter. In (that of) Venus one (is blessed with) plenty of food and drink and wealth. One is afflicted with diseases etc. in (that of) Saturn. (One is blessed with) good services with unguents etc. and good trade if Rāhu (ascending node of the Moon) is seen (in the nativity) even if the name of person contained odd number of letters or if it be in the flow of left *nāḍī*. Similarly, the presence of Saturn, Mars and Rāhu (in the left *nāḍī*) would make the native victorious in the battle. The presence of the Sun in the flow of the right *nāḍī* would augur loss in trade. A person would certainly be victorious in battle if his name contains even (number of letters). One should know victory in battle if the movement is downwards and death if the movement is upwards. *Om hūm om hrām om sphem* break down the weapons. *Om* break to pieces. *Om* rout all enemies. *Om hrūm om hraḥ phaṭ*.

12-14. One should place (the above) *mantra* (on his body) repeating seven times and should meditate on his self as lord Bhairava, auspicious, possessing four or ten or twenty hands, wielding in the hands a spike, a club, a sword, raised *kaṭṭāri*, devouring the army of others and having his back on his own forces. One should repeat this one hundred and eight times in front of the army of enemies. By the repetition of this and the sound of small drum the enemy force would run away abandoning their weapons.

15-24. Listen ! I shall again describe another application that breaks the army of others. After having collected the charcoal from the cremation ground and the excrements of owl and crow one should draw the image of Bhairava on a cloth. The name of the enemy together with the letters are to be written at nine places such as the head, face, forehead, heart, genital organ, feet, back and between arms. (The image) should be broken down at the time of battle with the repetition of the above sacred syllable.

I shall describe *Tārkṣyacakra* for the sake of victory and which is (known as) *trimukhākṣara* (three-faced syllable). Throw away. *Om* oblations. Tārkṣya is destroyer of enemies, disease and poison. It also sets right one possessed by an evil spirit or afflicted by diseases or grief-stricken. One would accomplish results proportional to his actions through the bird (Tārkṣya). All poisons such as those due to a plant, movable beings and spiders and artificial poison get destroyed by the look of an accomplisher. One should again contemplate on the great Tārkṣya having two wings and of the form of a man, having two arms and a curved beak, supporting an elephant and tortoise and coming in the middle of the sky having innumerable serpents at its feet. One would see the enemies being swallowed, eaten, hit and struck by the beak in the battle, some crushed by the feet, some crushed by being struck by the wings and some running away in ten directions. One who contemplates on Tārkṣya would be invincible in the three worlds.

25-26. I shall describe the work to be done to accomplish the sanctity of the bunch of peacock's feathers. *Om hrūm* bird ! Cast away ! *Om hūm saḥ* ! The most valiant and of great strength ! Devour all forces (of the enemy). *Om* trample down. *Om* break to pieces. *Om* melt away. *Om hūm khaḥ om* ! Bhairava may accept oblations. One should repeat this at the (time of) lunar eclipse and the bunch of peacock's feathers should be sanctified and waved in front of the army. Just as the one riding the lion would do the herds of deer, one would rout (the army of enemies) by the sound and contemplation on the elephant and lion.

27-33. I shall describe the invocation with the sacred syllable (which would rout the enemy force) from a distance by its sound. Porridge should be offered to the divine mothers, especially to Kālarātrī. One should invoke (the goddess) from a distance with the flowers *mālatī* and *cāmarī* together with the ashes from the cremation ground and the roots of cotton (plant). *Om ahe he* Mahendrī ! Break ! *hi om* discard ! Devour the enemy ! *lili kili om hum phaṭ* ! By this breaking sacred syllable (*bhaṅga-vidyā*) repeated from a distance the enemy would be destroyed. A mark on the forehead made up of *aparājitā* and *dhattūra* (should be made use of) together (with the *mantra*). *Om kili kili vikili icchākili* ! (Goddess) Umā ! Destroyer of goblins ! Śaṅkhini (woman fairy) ! Wielder of a club ! Ferocious ! Māheśvarī (Great goddess) ! Projecting meteors from the mouth ! Emitting fires from the mouth ! Possessing ears like the conch ! Possessing emaciated thighs ! One who vomits (Alambuṣa) ! Take away ! *Om* dug up all wicked persons. *Om* ! O Goddess ! whoever looks at me (you) stupefy them. *Oṁ* ! the terrible (goddess) remaining in the heart of Rudra (Śiva) ! By your gracious disposition protect me then. Oblations. After having drawn the divine mothers surrounded by all their forms outside, the (above) sacred syllable, which accomplishes all desires, should be written on a betel leaf. It was worn by (gods) Brahmā, Rudra, Indra and Viṣṇu on the hand before. The celestials were adorned with this protective potent of (goddesses) Nārasiṁhī, Bhairavī, all goddesses of the form of Śakti, (goddess) Trailokyamohinī and Gaurī at the time of great battle between celestials and demons.

O auspicious one ! It is known as the protective amulet in which the letters consisting of the name (of the wearer) sanctified by the principle sacred syllable on the petals of a lotus (shaped diagram) and duly worshipped with the accessories.

34-41. I shall describe *mṛtyuñjaya* (conquering death). The name surrounded by *kalās* (syllables) should be in the midst of sacred syllable and preceded by the letter *sa*. The letter *ja* coupled with the dot and the syllable *om*, containing the letter *dha* at the middle and with the letter *va* together with the sanctified Moon at the middle that routs all the wicked (should be placed). Otherwise one should write the name and the object on the petals. The syllable *om* should be written on the petal on the east, one's right and north. The syllable *hum* (should be written) on the south-east etc. and the (other) syllables on the sixteen petals. (The consonants) *ka* etc. (should be written) in the thirtyfour petals. One should write this sacred syllable of conquering death outside on a *bhūrja* leaf together with *rocanā* (yellow pigment), saffron, camphor and sandal. It should be enclosed with a white thread, covered by bee-wax and worshipped on a pitcher. By wearing this amulet one gets cured of his diseases and his enemies would perish. I shall explain the sacred syllable known as Bhelakhī that wards off separation and death. *Ām* Vātala (windy) ! Vitala (located in the lower region ! Cat-faced ! Daughter of Indra ! Born through the agency of wind god ! Obstruct. Come. *Hājā* in me, *Vāha ityādi duḥkha nityakaṇṭhoccairmuhūrtānvayā aha māṁ yasmahcṁ upādi* om Bhelakhi ! Om ! oblations. (Similarly) the sacred syllable of Navadurgā repeated seven times if worn on one's mouth paralyses the mouth (of the enemy). *Om hūm phaṭ* oblations. One undefeated in a battle with a word if held after repetition for seven times.

CHAPTER ONE HUNDRED AND THIRTY-FOUR

Sacred formula for the conquest of three worlds

The Lord said :

1-3. I shall describe (the formula) that conquers three worlds and crushes all (other) amulets. *Om hūm kṣūm hrūm om* obeisance. O Goddess ! Possessing (frightful) teeth ! Possessing fierce face ! One having a very fierce form ! *Hili, hili* ! Possessing red eyes ! *Kili, kili* ! Possessing great sound ! *kulu om* ! Possessing a tongue resembling the lightning ! kulu om ! One having no flesh ! *kaṭa kaṭa* ! Wearing the ornament of *gonasa* (a kind of gem) ! Cili cili ! One who wears the garland of dead bodies ! Drive away. *Om* ! One having a terrible form ! One who is clad in raw hide ! (You) gape ! Om ! Dance O goddess wielding the creeper-like sword ! One whose side glances have been hot with anger. One having the third eye ! One whose body has been besmeared with marrow and fat !

Kaha kaha om. Laugh. Be angry. *Om.* One possessing the colour of a blue cloud ! One who has made the garland of cloud as the ornament ! Shine ! *Om.* One having the body strewn by the sound of the bell ! *Om* ! One who rides the lion ! One of light-red complexion ! *Om hrām hrīm hrūm.* One of terrible form ! *Hrūm hrīm klīm om hrīm hrūm om.* Attract. Shake. *Om he haḥ khaū.* One who wields the club ! *Hūm kṣūm kṣām.* One who has the form of wrath ! Inflame. *Om.* Terribly frightening one ! Break. *Om.* One having a big body ! Cut. *Om.* One having a dreadful form ! Burrow. The mother of great goblins ! One who wards off all the wicked ! Victorious one ! *Om.* Victorious one ! *Om.* One who conquers the three worlds ! *Hūm phaṭ* oblations. One should propitiate the goddess of blue complexion, remaining on dead bodies and possessing twenty arms for (gaining) victory. After having located on the five parts of the body, red flowers should be offered (to the goddess). There would be routing of the (enemy) forces in the battle by the repetition of the formula (known as) conquering three worlds. *Om.* (Obeisance) to (the god of) manifold forms. Paralyse. *Om.* Stupefy. *Om.* Scatter away all enemies. *Om.* Attract (lord) Brahmā. Attract (lord) Viṣṇu. Attract (lord) Maheśvara (Śiva). *Om.* Make (the god) Indra tremble. *Om.* Make the mountains move. *Om.* Dry up seven oceans. *Om.* Cut through. Cut through. Obeisance to (the god) of manifold forms. One should then meditate (while pronouncing this formula) that the enemy is present in an image of a serpent made up of earth.

CHAPTER ONE HUNDRED AND THIRTYFIVE

Formula for success in battle

The lord said :

1. I shall describe the garland of words of the formula that gives victory in the battle. *Oṁ hrīm* (Goddess) Cāmuṇḍā (having a terrific form) ! One who dwells in the cremation ground ! One who holds in hand the club with a skull at the top !

One who is riding the terrific dead body (or the body in the form of universe at the time of deluge) ! One who is surrounded by the great vehicle in the form of the decaying universe ! The dark night at the destruction of universe ! One who is surrounded by the great attendant gods ! Goddess with a great mouth ! Possessing several hands ! (One who holds) the bell, the little drum and the small bell ! One who has a terrific laughter ! *Kili kili om hūm phaṭ.* One who makes (the world) dark by her fierce teeth ! One who makes many kinds of sounds ! One who is clad in the hide of an elephant ! One who is besmeared with flesh ! One whose terrific tongue is licking ! The great demoness ! One having the terrible teeth ! One who has frightening roar of laughter ! One who has the splendour of shining lightning ! Move. Move. *Om.* One who has the eyes like the *Cakora*[1] (bird) ! *Cili. Cili. Om.* One who has a lustrous tongue ! *Oṁ bhīm.* One who has a frown on the face ! One who frightens by uttering the syllable *hum* ! One who wears the moon on the crown on her matted hair surrounded by the garland of skulls ! One who has the terrific laughter ! *Kili kili oṁ hrūm.* One who makes (the world) dark by her frightening teeth ! One who destroys all obstacles ! (Youṁ) accomplish this act. *Om.* Do it quickly. *Om phaṭ om* subjugate with (your) mace. Enter. *Om* Dance. Dance .Shake. *Om.* Make (the enemies) move. *Om.* One who is fond of blood, flesh and intoxicating drink ! Kill. *Om* trample. *Om* cut. *Om* kill. *Om* chase *Om* make the strong body (of the enemy) fall down. *Om.* Enter into the beings of three worlds whether wicked or not wicked, taken possession or not. *Om* dance. *Om* extol. One who has sunken eyes ! One having erect hairs ! One having the face of an owl ! One who holds skull (in the hand) ! *Om.* One who wears a garland of skulls ! Burn. *Om.* Cook. Cook. *Om.* Seize. *Om.* Enter into the middle of the circle (of the enemies). *Om.* Why do you delay ? Overwhelm (them) with the strength of (lords) Brahmā, Viṣṇu and Rudra and the strength of sages. *Om Kili kili om khili khili vili vili om.* One who displays an ugly form ! One whose body is enveloped by a black serpent ! One who subjugates all planets ! One who has a long lip ! One whose nose rests on the frowning eyes ! One who is

1. A fabulous bird supposed to live on the ambrosia of the Moon.

having a frightful face ! One having tawny matted hair ! Brāhmi ! Break. One whose mouth emits flames ! Yell. *Om.* Make (the enemies) fall down. *Om.* One having red eyes ! Roll the earth. Make (them) fall. *Om.* Catch hold of the head. Close the eye. *Om.* Catch hold of the arms and feet. Split open the posture (of the hands). *Om phaṭ om.* Pierce open. *Om.* Cut with the trident. *Om* kill with the mace. *Om* strike with the stick. *Om.* Cut with the disc. *Om.* Break with the spear. Stake with the teeth. *Om.* Pierce with the middle finger. *Om.* Seize with the goad. *Om.* Release. Release the possessive spirits like the Ḍākinī and Skanda and also the fevers occurring every day, second day , third day and fourth day (and the diseases of) the head and eyes. *Om.* Cook. *Om.* Destroy. *Om.* Make them fall to the ground. Om. Brahmāṇī ![1] Come. *Om* (goddess) Māheśvarī ! Come. *Om* Kaumāri ! Come. *Om* Vaiṣṇavi ! Come. *Om* Vārāhi ! Come. *Om* Aindri ! Come. *Om.* Cāmuṇḍā. Come. *Om* Revati ! Come. *Om.* Ākāśarevati. Come. *Om.* One who moves like the snow. Come. *Om.* One who has slain (the demon) Ruru ! One who annihilated the demons ! One who goes in heaven ! Bind. Bind with the noose. Pierce with the goad. Stand for the moment. *Om* enter the circle (of enemies) ! *Om.* Seize. Bind the face. *Om.* Bind the eyes, arms and feet. Bind the malefic planets. *Om.* Bind directions. Charm the cardinal points, the space below and all places. *Om.* Subjugate all with ashes or water or earth or mustard. *Om.* Make them fall. *Om.* (goddess) Cāmuṇḍā ! *Kili kili ām vicce hūm phaṭ* oblations. This is known as the garland of words that accomplishes all acts.

2-6. One gets victory in battle always by oblations, repetitions and reading of this formula. One has to contemplate (on the goddess) as having twenty-eight hands holding the sword, club, mace, stick, bow, arrow, clenched fist, hammer, conch, sword, banner, club, disc, axe, little drum, mirror, spear, dart, plough, mace, nose, an iron club, large drum, *paṇava* (a kind of musical instrument), conferring pose, clenched fist, threatening posture, killing the (demon in the form of a) buffalo in the pairs of hands. By making oblations one would conquer the enemies.

1. From Brahmāṇī to Cāmuṇḍā are the eight divine mothers.

The (above) oblations should be done with three sweet things (honey sugar and clarified butter). This incantation should not be disclosed to everyone.

CHAPTER ONE HUNDRED AND THIRTYSIX

The diagram of asterisms indicating the period for undertaking a journey

The Lord said :

1-6. I shall describe the diagram indicating good or bad results in journey undertaken. A diagram consisting of three columns should be drawn and (the asterisms) Aśvinī etc. should be represented therein (by their first letters). (The asterisms) Aśvinī, Ārdrā, Pūrvā (phālgunī), Uttaraphālgunī, Hasta, Jyeṣṭhā, Mūla, Vāruṇa (Śatabhiṣak) and Ajaikapāt (Pūrvabhādrapada) consist of first column. (The asterisms) Yāmya (Bharaṇī), Mṛgaśira, Puṣya, Bhāgya (Pūrvaphālgunī), Citrā, Maitra (Anurādhā), Āpya (Pūrvāṣāḍha), Vāsava (Jyeṣṭhā) and Ahirbudhnya (Uttarabhādrapada) (are located in the second column). (The asterisms) Kṛttikā, Rohiṇī, Ahiḥ (Āśleṣā) Citrā, Svātī, Viśākhā, Śravaṇa and Revatī are located in the third (column). One should know the good or bad results from the asterisms associated with three columns. This is known as the diagram of *phaṇīśvara* (lord of serpents) divided into three columns. The presence in Sun, Mars, Saturn and Rāhu (the ascending node) indicate bad luck and the rest good luck. The position is the same, such as the country or village, the brothers and wife indicate good. The twentyseven asterisms should be known as (represented by letters) *a*, *bha*, *kṛ*, *ro*, *mṛ*, *ā*, *pu*, *pu*, *ā*, *ma*, *pū*, *u*, *ha*, *ci*, *svā*, *vi*, *a*, *jye*, *mū*, *pū*, *u*, *śra*, *dha*, *śa*, *pū*, *u* and *re*.

CHAPTER ONE HUNDRED AND THIRTYSEVEN

Description of the formula known as Mahāmārī

The Lord said :

1. I shall describe the formula known as Mahāmārī (that which brings death) that routs the enemies. *Oṁ hrīm* Mahāmārī ! One having red eyes ! One having black complexion ! O One who commands the god of death ! One who destroys all beings ! Kill such and such a person. Kill. *Om* burn, hum. *Om* cook, cook. *Om* pierce, pierce. *Om* kill, kill. *Om* annihilate, annihilate. *Om* one who charms all good (beings) ! One who grants all desires ! *Hum phaṭ* oblations. *Om* Māri ! Obeisance to the heart. *Om Mahāmārī* ! Oblations to the head. *Om* Dreadful night (at the time of deluge) ! *Vauṣaṭ* to the tuft. *Om* possessing black complexion ! *Khaḥ* to the armour *hum*. *Om* one having starry eyes ! One having the tongue-like lightning ! One who frightens all beings ! Protect, protect in all my undertakings. *Hrām*. To the three-eyed *vaṣat*. *Om* Mahāmārī ! One who controls all beings ! Mahākāli ! To the weapons *hum phaṭ*. O Great goddess ! This is the rite of location to be performed by the votary.

2-3. After having collected from the dead body, the cloth of the shape of a square of three cubit's length, one should draw (the image of the goddess) of black complexion, having three faces and four hands, (and draw) on the cloth with different colours, (the weapons) bow, spear, scissor, staff with skull at its top and the eastern face having black colour.

4-6. By the fall of the sight (of this face) it would devour the man in front. The second (face) on the south (is) red-red-tongued, frightening, licking, dreadful and frightful with protruded lips through which a row of horrid teeth are visible. A look at this (face) is sure to devour the horses etc. (of the enemies). The third face of the goddess is of white colour and is the destroyer of the elephant etc. The western face (of the goddess) should be propitiated with incense, flower, honey and clarified butter etc.

7. By the remembrance of this sacred syllable the diseases of the eye, head and others (limbs) get destroyed. The *yakṣas*

(semi-divine beings) and demons come under one's control. The enemies get destroyed.

8. There is no doubt that by oblation made with the twigs of margosa tree mixed with the blood of a she-goat, the angry votary would kill (his enemies).

9. If the oblation is done for seven days in front of the army of the enemy, the army would be afflicted with diseases and the enemies get routed.

10. In whose name eight thousand oblations are made with (the same) twigs, he would die even if protected by Brahmā.

11. (If oblations are made) for three days with the twigs of *unmatta* (a kind of plant) with blood and poison for thousand times, the enemy would get destroyed together with his army.

12. One would rout the enemy by doing oblations of black mustard and salt for three days. The oblations made with the addition of the blood of an ass would make the enemy fly away.

13. The oblation made with the addition of the blood of a crow would cause annihilation of the enemy. Whatever (the votary) does as he wished for the destruction (of the enemy) (should be completed with an oblation performed with the same material).

14-18. Then at the time of battle the votary should ride an elephant accompanied by a couple of girls, his body having been sanctified by sacred syllables. He should then charm the musical instruments like the conch etc. at some distance (from the enemy) and should cut (the enemy forces) at the battle-field holding the cloth containing the figure of Mahā-māyā. He should show that great cloth against the army of the enemy. The girls should be fed therein and the lump (of food ?) should be carried round. The votary should then think that the army has become immobile like a stone, crest-fallen, broken and confused. This paralysing (formula) has been uttered by me. It should not be disclosed to everyone. The cloth described above (may also have the outlines of) Durgā, Bhairavī, Kubjikā, (different forms of the consort of Śiva), Rudra and Narasiṁha (man-lion) manifestation of Viṣṇu) besides those of (Mahā) māyā that conquers the three worlds.

CHAPTER ONE HUNDRED AND THIRTYEIGHT

The six accessory acts relating to all mantras

The Lord said :

1-5. I shall describe six acts (to be used) in all sacred syllables. Listen (to me). The *sādhya* (to be accomplished) should be written first being followed by the sacred syllable. This is known as the *pallava* (bud) and should be used in all incantations. First the sacred syllable (is written), then the *sādhya* and then the sacred syllable. This is known as the *yoga* (combination). This should be employed for the *utsādana* (extinction) of one's race. The sacred syllable is written first and the *sādhya* is added at the middle and again the sacred syllable at the end. This tradition is (known as) the *rodhaka* (that which arrests) and should be employed in *stambhana* (stupefying the faculties of the enemy). The *sādhya* should be added at the bottom and top, left, right and middle. This is known as the *sampuṭa* (casket) and should be employed in *vaśya* (subjugation) and *ākarṣa* (attraction).

6. When the letters composing any particular sacred syllable are of the category of *sādhya* letters, that sacred syllable is known to be the first class. It is capable of attracting and subjugating (another person).

7. Two of the letters constituting the sacred syllable are written first and one *sādhya* letter afterwards. This is known to be the *vidarbha* and should be made use of in attraction and subjugation.

8-10. The acts of *ākarṣaṇa* etc. as also (in subduing) high fever should be performed only in the spring. The term *svāhā* (oblations) is auspicious in attraction and subjugation. The term *namaskāra* (obeisance) should be employed for peace and prosperity. The term *vaṣaṭ* (should be made use of) for good health and in acts of attraction and subjugation. (The term) *phaṭ* would be (used) for creating dissension, causing death and to break an auspicious one. The term *vaṣaṭ* gives accomplishment in gains and initiation in sacred syllables.

11. You are Yama (god of death). You are the sovereign over the dead (Yamarāja). You are of the form of time. You

are the reign of righteousness. You quickly make dead this enemy offered by me.

12. The priest, who is the destroyer of the enemy, should say with pleased mind, "O Votary ! Be calm ! I shall kill (him) with (all my) efforts."

13-14. This gets accomplished after worshipping the god of death in white lotus and making oblations contemplating himself as Bhairava and Kuleśvarī (as remaining) at the centre. (The votary) would know in the night the result (of the incantation) on himself and the person (concerned). One would become the killer of his enemy by propitiating the (goddess) Durgā with the formula "O (goddess) Durgā ! Durgā ! You are the guardian !" One should kill the enemy by the repetition of letters "*ha, sa, kṣa, ma, la, va, ra* and *ya*" sacred to (the goddess) Bhairavī.

CHAPTER ONE HUNDRED AND THIRTYNINE

The names of sixty years of Hindu cycle and the good or bad results from them

The lord said :

1. Listen ! I shall describe the names of sixty years and the good or bad results from them. Sacrificial rites (would be done) in *Prabhava*. The people would be comfortable in *Vibhava*.

2. All grains (grow well) in *Śukla*. (People) rejoice in *Pramoda* (*Pramodāt*). There would be increase (of articles of comforts) in *Prajāpati* (*Prajotpatti*). (The year) *Aṅgirā* (*Āṅgīrasa*) would increase comforts.

3. The people (population) increase in *Śrīmukha*. Thoughts flourish well in *Bhāva* (*Bhava*). (In the year) *Yuva* the life essence gets filled up. *Dhātā* makes the herbs sprout well.

4. *Īśvara* (gives) welfare and health. *Bahudāna* gives prosperity. In *Pramāthī* (there would be) moderate rains. There would be plenty of grains in *Vikrama*.

5. *Vṛṣa* (*Viṣu*) makes all things thrive. *Citrabhānu* sees many

wonderful events. *Svarbhānu* (gives) prosperity and health. The clouds are favourable in *Tāraṇa.*

6. (There would be) abundance of rains in *Pārthiva. Jaya* (*Vijaya*) (indicates) excessive rains. *Sarvajit* (indicates) good showers. *Sarvadhātrī* gives prosperity.

7. *Virodhī* destroys clouds. (*Vikṛti*) causes panic. Men become chivalrous in *Khara*. The people rejoice in *Nandana.*

8-9. *Vijaya* kills enemies. (*Jaya*) annihilates enemies and diseases. People suffer from fever in *Manmatha.* People become wicked in the cruel *Durmukha*. There will not be prosperity in *Hemalamba.* O great goddess ! the year *Vilamba* gives prosperity.

10. *Vikārī* causes the wrath of enemies. O Victorious one ! (The year) *Sarvadā* (*Śārvarī*) gives comforts to all. Water inundates (the earth) in *Plava.* O Good-natured one ! The people do auspicious things in *Śubhakṛt*[1].

11. The people (become) cruel in *Rākṣasa.* In *Ānala* (*Nala*) (there would be plenty of) different kinds of grains. (There would be) good showers in *Piṅgala* and destruction of wealth in *Kālayukti.*

12. All things are accomplished in *Siddhārtha* (*Siddhārthi*). Dreadful events take place in *Raudra* (*Raudrī*). (There would be) moderate rains in *Durmati. Dundubhi* causes welfare and (plenty of) grains.

13. It rains well in *Rudhirodgārī. Raktākṣa* and *Krodhana* (give) victory. In *Kṣaya* (*Akṣaya*) people get reduced to poverty. These are the sixty years.

CHAPTER ONE HUNDRED AND FORTY

Description of herbs used in charms

The Lord said :

1-3. I shall describe (drugs) used in charms. These should be written in eight squares. They are *bhṛṅgarāja, saha-*

1. The text then omits the names of 12 years and continues from *Rākṣasa,* the 49th year.

devī, mayūraśikhā, putrañjīva, kṛtāñjali, adhaḥpuṣpā, rudantikā, kumārī, rudrajaṭā, viṣṇukrāntā, white *arka, lajjālukā, mohalatā,* black *dhattūra, gorakṣa, karkaṭī, meṣaśṛṅgī* and *snuhī.*

4-5. The symbolical numbers of herbs are *ṛtvijaḥ* (priests) (16), *vahnayaḥ* (fires) (3), *nāgāḥ* (elephants) (8), *pakṣau* (wings) (2), *muni* (sage) (3), *Manu* (14), *Śiva* (11), *vasavaḥ* (vasus) (8) *dik* (directions) (10), *rasāḥ* (tastes) (6), *vedāḥ* (4), *grahāḥ* (planets) (9), *ṛtavaḥ* (seasons) (6), *Ravi* (Sun) (12), *Candramāḥ* (Moon) (1) and *tithayaḥ* (phases of the Moon) (15). The first four (of the above-said herbs) should be used to fumigate (the body of the votary) or in the burning sticks.

6. Collyrium should be made out of the third (in the list). Bathing should be done with the fourth. The unguent of four kinds should be made with the *bhṛṅgarāja* and the one following it (in the list).

7-8. (The herbs represented symbolically by) *muni* in the list should be used in unguent for the right side, by *yuga* for the left side, by *bhujaga* for the foot and *īśvara* for the head. Fumigation of the centre should be done with *arka* (12) and *śaśi* (1), in all acts. A body besmeared with these would be worshipped even by the celestials.

9. Incense sticks made of the sixteenth (herb in the list) should be burnt and taken round the house. (The herbs standing as) the fourth should be used in the collyrium and those (standing as) the fifth should be used in bathing.

10. (The herbs denoted by the number) eleven should be used for eating and fifteen for drinking. A mark on the forehead with (the herbs denoted by the numbers) *ṛtvik* (16), *veda* (4), *ṛtu* (6), *nayana* (2) captivates the world.

11. A lady being besmeared with (the herbs denoted by) *sūrya* (12), *tridaśa* (13), *pakṣa* (2) and *śaila* (7) gets captivated. Women get captivated by besmearing their genital organ with (herbs denoted by) *candra* (1), *Indra* (1), *phaṇi* (8) and *rudra* (11).

12. A pill made of (herbs denoted by) *tithi* (15), *dik* (8), *yuga* (4), and *bāṇa* (5) can subjugate. This pill should be given in eatables, food and drink as a charm.

13. (The herbs denoted by) *ṛtvik* (16), *graha* (9), *akṣi* (2) and *śaila* (7) if had on the face (are effective) in paralysing weapons. One can remain in waters by besmearing limbs

with (the herbs denoted by) *śaila* (7) *Indra* (1), *veda* (4) and *randhra* (9).

14. A pill of (the herbs denoted by) *bāṇa* (5), *akṣi* (2), *manu* (14) and *rudra* (11) removes hunger and thirst. A miserable woman would be made happy by besmearing with (herbs denoted by) *tri* (3), *ṣoḍaśa* (16), *dik* (8) and *bāṇa* (5).

15. One would (be able to) play with serpents by besmearing with (herbs denoted by) *tri* (3), *daśa* (10), *akṣi* (2), *dik* (8) and *netra* (2). A woman delivers a child comfortably by an application of the unguent of (the herbs represented by) *tri* (3), *daśa* (10), *akṣi* (2), *īśa* (11) and *bhujaga* (8).

16. One is sure to win in dice (by wearing) a cloth besmeared with (the herbs represented by) *sapta* (7), *dik* (8), *muni* (3) and *randhra* (9). Male child (would be born) by besmearing the penis with (the herbs denoted by) *tri* (3), *daśa* (10), *akṣa* (2), *abdhi* (7) and *muni* (3) before coition.

17. A pill made (of the herbs represented by) *graha* (9), *abdhi* (7), *sarpya* (8), *tri* (3) and *daśa* (10) would be able to charm. The efficacy of the herbs in the sixteen places has been explained.

CHAPTER ONE HUNDRED AND FORTYONE

Description of herbs used in charms, medicines etc.

The Lord said :

1. I shall describe the effect of the herbs arranged in 36 squares which were used by lords Brahmā, Rudra and Indra and which if used make men immortals.

2-5. (They are)—*harītakī*, *akṣi*, *dhātri*, *marica*, *pippalī*, *śilphā*, *vahni*, *śuṇṭhī*, *pippalī*, *guḍūcī*, *vacā*, *nimba*, *vāsaka*, *śatamūli*, *saindhava*, *sindhu-vāraka*, *kaṇṭakārī*, *gokṣurakā*, *bilva*, *paunarnavā*, *balā*, *eraṇḍamuṇḍī*, *rucaka*, *bhṛṅga*, *kṣāra*, *parpaṭa*, *dhanyāka*, *jīraka*, *śatapuṣpī*, *javānikā*, *viḍaṅga*, *khadira*, *kṛtamāla*, *haridrā*, and *siddhārtha* located in the 36 squares.

6-10. The herbs duly counted from one and placed in all squares are highly efficacious in curing ailments, making (men) immortal and cure wrinkles and baldness. Their crushed powder compounded and treated with mercury and used as an electuary with pieces of jaggery, honey or ghee or as an astringent or through the medium of ghee or oil taken by all would save their lives. One can take half a *karṣa*[1] or one *karṣa* or half a *pala*[2] or one *pala* and may live for 300 years although he may be pursuing an indisciplined way of life. There is no other combination more (efficacious) than this remedy reviving the dead.

11. One gets free from all diseases by the combination of the first nine (herbs). One gets free from aches by (the use of) second, third and fourth (herbs).

12. So also (one gets free from all diseases by the use of) six herbs from first to sixth as well as ninth.

13. One gets free from wind (affecting the body) by (the use of herbs) one to eight and from biles by *agni* (third) *bhāskara* (twelfth), twenty-sixth and twenty-seventh.

14. One gets cured of (deranged) phlegm by (the use of herbs) *bāṇa* (fifth), *ṛtu* (sixth), *śaila* (seventh) *vasu* (eighth) and *tithi* (fifteenth). (Herbs denoted by) *veda* (four), *agni* (three), *bāṇa* (five) and six would be (efficacions) against (diseases caused by) charm.

15. One would get freed from (all afflictions due to) planets and being possessed (by goblins) by (the due use of herbs denoted by) one, two, three, six, seven, eight, nine and eleven.

16. There is no doubt that (they would also be cured by herbs denoted) by thirty-two, fifteen and twelve. This knowledge relating to thirty-six places should not be imparted to everyone.

---

1. One *karṣa* is equal to 16 *māṣas* where *māṣa* stands for the weight of a kind of grain.

2. One *pala* is equal to 4 *karṣas*.

CHAPTER ONE HUNDRED AND FORTYTWO

Description of medicinal incantations

The Lord said :

1-2. I shall describe the medicinal incantations and diagrams which yield all (desires). The number of letters composing the name of a thief should be doubled (and added to) the number of its syllables multiplied by four. (The total thus obtained) should be divided by (the number of letters in) the name (of a person) and if there be any remainder (he should be reckoned as) a thief. I shall describe (the process of reckoning) the birth (of a child). If there are odd numbers of letters in the question (put to the soothsayer), it indicates that the child in the womb would be a male.

3-4. (The child would be born) blind in the left eye if the letters in the name are even and in the right eye if the letters are odd. The number of letters composing the names of both the male and female should be multiplied by the number of their syllables and divided by four. (The quotient), if even, (would indicate the birth of) a female child and if odd, a male child. If there is no remainder, (it indicates) the death of the woman.

5. If there is no remainder in the former, (it indicates) the death of the husband first. In hoary science one should take the subtle *akṣara* in all divisions.

6-7. I shall describe the diagram of Saturn. One should avoid the aspect of that (Saturn) (at all times). (The Saturn in) its house has one hundred and fourteen (units) aspect at the seventh. It has one-fourth its aspect in the first, second, eighth and twelfth (places). One should avoid them. The lord of the day governs one eighth part of a day. The others govern half a *yāma* (three hours).

8-10a. One should avoid the period of Saturn during the battle. I shall describe the rule of Rāhu (the ascending node) on a day. It (lies) always at the east on Sunday, at south-east on Saturday, at the south on Thursday, at the north-west on Friday, at the south-east on Tuesday, and at the north on Wednesday, while the *Phaṇirāhu* lies enclosing at the north-east, south-east, south-west and north-west and kills one who sets on a journey against it.

10b.-13. I shall describe the position of Rāhu on different days of a month. Rāhu kills the enemy facing it on the full moon day at the south-east and on new moon day at the north-west. Rāhu will lie facing on the days represented by (the letters) *ka* to *ja* and, in the south on (the days of) *sa* to *da*, in the east on (the days of) *dha* to *ma* and in the north on (the days of) *ya* to *ha* and one should avoid those associated with Mars in the bright (fortnight). Three lines towards the east and three lines towards the south (should be written) and then one should write from *Sūryarāśi* onwards in the main division. (If battle is made) in the *rāśi* aspected by Rāhu there will be defeat and victory if otherwise.

14-18a. I shall describe the *viṣṭirāhu*. Eight lines should be drawn. The Rāhu, the great, moves with the *viṣṭi* (hell) from the north-east to the south, south to the north-west, from the north-west to the east, from the east to the west, from the south-west to the north, from the north to the south-east and then to the west and from the west to the north-east. The Rāhu kills the enemies on the third day (of a lunar month) in the north-east, on the seventh day in the south and so also in the dark and bright fortnights in the north-west. (One has to propitiate), Indra and others, Bhairava and others, brahmin and others and planets numbering eight in each class in the east and other (directions) and the *vāta-yoginī* (the presiding goddess) in (the directions) south and others. One should kill the enemy in that direction in which the wind blows.

18b-19. I shall describe (the rite) that strengthens one. (The herb known as) *śarapuṅkhikā* if worn on the neck, arm etc. on (a day ruled by the asterism) Puṣya would prevent the (enemy's weapon) striking at the neck. *Aparājitā* and *Pāṭhā*, the two (herbs) in the same manner would ward off the sword. (The following is the *mantra* to be used) :—*Om*. Obeisance. Goddess Vajraśṛṅkhalā ! Kill. Kill. *Om*. Devour. Devour. *Om*. Eat. *Ām*. Eḥ. Drink the blood with the skull O Red-eyed one ! One having the red cloth ! One having the body besmeared with ashes ! One wielding the weapon of mace ! One who is covered by the action of the mace ! Close, close the eastern direction. *Om*. Close, close the southern direction. *Om*, Close, close the western direction. *Om*. Close, close the northern direction. Bind, bind the serpents. Bind, bind the wives of the serpents. *Om*. Bind, bind the demons. *Om*. Bind, bind the Yakṣas, demons and goblins. *Om*. Guard, guard (me) from the dead, goblins and *Gandharvas*, whoever troubles me. *Om*. Guard, guard above. *Om*. Guard, guard below. *Om*. Bind, bind the knife. *Om*. Burn. One of great strength ! Ghaṭi *ghaṭoi*: *Om Moṭi moṭi saṭāvali*. Fiery mace ! One who strikes with the mace ! *Him phaṭ hrīm hrūm śrīm phaṭ hrim haḥ phūm phem phaū*. From all planets, from all diseases from all wicked afflictions, *hrīm* from all things guard, guard me. One should employ this in all acts such as those relating to the planets, fevers and goblins.

CHAPTER ONE HUNDRED AND FORTYTHREE

Mode of worship of Goddess Kubjikā

The Lord said :

1. I shall describe the mode of worship of (goddess) Kubjikā that accomplishes all comforts. (It is only by such worship) the celestials had conquered the demons together with their weapons and kingdom.

2-3. One should locate the *māyābīja* (the secret basic *mantra* of the goddess) at the secret organ and the six (syllables) of the weapons on the hand. (One should say) Kālī, Kālī (and touch) the heart and Duṣṭacāṇḍālikā (vicious Cāṇḍālikā) (and touch) the head. "*Hrīm sphem ha sa kha ka cha ḍa* syllable *om* Bhairava" (is the *mantra* to be said to touch) the tuft. Bhelakī (for) the *kavaca* (armour) and Dūtī and Raktacaṇḍikā (for) the eyes.

4-5. (Then one should say) *guhya* Kubjikā (and touch) the weapon. One should worship (goddess Kubjikā) in the lotus at the centre and the seat at the south-east, the head at the north-east, the tuft at the south-west, the armour at the west, the eyes at the centre and the weapons in all directions of the circle in the thirty-two petals. The principal *mantra* (for the goddess Kubjikā is) *ha, sa, kṣa, ma, la, na, va, vaṣaḍ*."

6. (The eight goddesses) Brahmāṇī, Māheśī, Kaumārī,

Vaiṣṇavī, Vārāhī, Māhendrī, Cāmuṇḍā and Caṇḍikā (should be worshipped) in the directions east onwards.

7-8. One has to (locate and) worship (the subtle letters) *ra*, *va*, *la*, *ka*, *sa*, and *ha* at the (petals at the) north-east, east, south-east, south, south-west and west. A garland of flowers and the five mountains such as Uḍḍiyāna, Jālandhara, Pūrṇagiri and Kāmarūpa should be worshipped at the north-west, north-east, south-east and south-west and (goddess) Kubjikā at the centre.

9-10. The five Vimalas such as Anādivimala, Sarvajña-vimala, Prasiddhavimala, Saṁyogavimala and Samayavimala (should be worshipped at the tips (of the petals) at the north-west, north-east, south-west, south-east and north.

11-14. Khiṅkhiṇī, Ṣaṣṭhā, Sopamā, Susthirā and Ratna-sundarī (should be worshipped) in the north-east corner for (the worship of) Kubjikā. The eight Ādināthas—Mitra, Oḍīśa, Ṣaṣṭhi, Varṣa etc. (constituting) the jewels of heaven (should be worshipped) in the south-east, west and north-west and the *kavacaratna* (the excellent *mantras* serving as armour) in the west. (The syllable) '*brum*' (should be worshipped) in the north-west, north-east and south-east together with the five basic letters. The five gems (the divine mothers) (should be located and worshipped) at the south and south-east. Among these, the three, Jyeṣṭhā, Raudrī and Antikā are very old. They and other god-desses and others (should be worshipped) with the five *praṇavas* (syllable *om*). The worship is of two kinds—twentyseven and twentyeight.

15-17. Then (the god) Gaṇapati (lord of the attendant gods on Śiva and son of the latter) of the form of *praṇava* and a boy should be worshipped duly with (the *mantra om em gūm*. Gaṇapati should be worshipped in a square diagram on the south. The Vaṭuka (form of Gaṇapati) (should be worshipped) on the left. The sixteen preceptors—*nāthas* (tāntrik preceptors) and eighteen *nāthas* should be worshipped in the north-west and other (directions). Then the gods Brahmā and others (should be worshipped) around in the six angular points. At the centre the nine gods (should be worshipped). This is always the mode of worship of (goddesses) Kubjikā, Kulaṭā etc.

CHAPTER ONE HUNDRED AND FORTYFOUR

Mode of worship of goddess Kubjikā

The Lord said :

1. I shall describe the worship of glorious Kubjikā who grants righteousness, wealth and victory. One should worship her together with her attendants with the basic *mantra* : *Om aim hraum śrīm khaim hrem ha, sa, kṣa, ma, la, va, ra, ya, ūm* Goddess ! Mother ! *Hrāṁ hrīṁ kṣrīm, kṣauṁ kṣūm krīṁ Kubjikā* ! *Hrīm om ṅa*, ña, *na*, *ṇa*, ma Aghoramukhi ! *Vāṁ chrām chīm kili kili kṣraum vicce khyoṁ śrīṁ krom oṁ hroṁ aiṁ* Vajrakubjini ! *Strīṁ* Trailokyākarṣiṇi (One who subjugates the three worlds) ! *Hrīm* Kāmāṅgadrāviṇi (one who melts away the god of love) ! *Hrīṁ strīm* Mahākṣobhakāriṇi (the great agitator) ! *Aiṁ hrīṁ kṣraum aiṁ hrīṁ śrīm pheṁ kṣaum* obeisance. O Goddess ! *Kṣaum Kubjikā* ! *hrīṁ kraiṁ ṅa, ña, ṇa, na, ma* Aghoramukhi ! *Chrām chām vicce om kili kili.*

2-4a. After locating the *mantras* on the hand and the body, one should perform the worship of twilight (addressed to the goddesses) Vāmā, Jyeṣṭhā and Raudrī. (The following is the *mantra*)—May we know you as Kulavāgīśi. Let me contemplate on (the goddess) Mahākālī. May (goddess) Kaulī impel us to the same. There are five *mantras* such as *praṇava* etc. (The votary should say) "I am worshipping the sandals." The name (should be) at the middle, ending with (the term) obeisance with eighteen *bīja* (letters). Then (the name of the goddess) in the sixth (declensional) case with (the term) 'obeisance' and the end. I shall describe all of them to be known.

4b-12. Kaulīśanātha, Sukalā, Kubjikā from the birth, Śrīkaṇṭhanātha, Kauleśa, Gaganānandanātha, Caṭulādevī, Maitrīśī, Karālī, Tūrṇanāthaka, Ataladevī, Śrīcandrādevī are their names. (These should be invoked) as stupefying the attendants of Śiva and the sandals should be worshipped. Then the sandal endowed with gems that excel the bliss in the world should be worshipped. Brahmajñānā, Kamalā and Paramā together with Vidyā (should also be worshipped). I shall describe the threefold purifications of *vidyā* (knowledge), Devī (goddess) and *guru* (preceptor). By means of the *ṣoḍānyāsa* (six ways of touching the body with mystical letters) the following deities should be located in the body—Gagana, Caṭulī, Ātmā, Padmānanda, Maṇī, Kalā, Kamalā, Māṇikyakaṇṭha, Gagana, Kumuda, Śrī, Padma, Bhairava, Ānanda, Deva, Kamala, Śiva, Bhava, Kṛṣṇa, the nine and then sixteen *siddhas*—Candrapaūra, Gulma, Śubha, Kāma, Atimuktaka, Viraktaka, Prayoga, Kuśala, Devabhoga, Viśvedeva, Khaḍgadeva, Rudra, Asidhanya, Mudrāsphoṭa, Vaṁśapūra and Bhoja.

13-14. After having put flowers on the circle, the circles (of the deities) should be worshipped. Then one should worship Ananta, Mahānanta, sandals of Śiva, *mahāvyāpti* (the great pervading force), the void circle consisting of five principles, sandals of Śrīkaṇṭhanātha and Śaṅkara and Ananta.

15. One should worship within the circle Sadāśiva, Piṅgala, Bhṛgvānanda, Nāthaka, Rāṅgūlānanda and Saṁvarta.

16-18. Śrīmahākāla, Pinākī, Mahendraka, Khaḍga, Bhujaṅga, Bāṇa, Aghāsi, Śabdaka, Vaśa, Ājñārūpa and Nandarūpa should be worshipped in the south-west after making the offering (victim) (with the following *mantra*)—*Hroṁ khaṁ khaṁ hūṁ saum* (obeisance) to (god) Vaṭuka. *Aru aru* (you) accept, accept *argha* (water offered as token of respect), flower, incense, lamp, perfumes and *bali* (offering). Obeisance to you. *Oṁ hrāṁ hriṁ hrūṁ kṣem* (obeisance) to the guardian of the ground. (You) descend, descend. One bearing the great grown matted hair ! One having a face shining with the flames in the three eyes ! (You) come. Come. Accept, accept worship with perfumes, flowers and *bali* (offering). *Khaḥ, khaḥ, oṁ kaḥ, oṁ laḥ om* oblations to the lord of great *ḍāmara* (uproar). The *trikūṭa* (the three groups) should be worshipped with (the syllables) *hrīṁ hrūṁ hāṁ śrīm* and the offering of the remnant of *bali* in the left, right and middle. The sandals of Niśānātha (are worshipped) in the south, Tandrinātha on the right and Kālānala in the front.

19-24. The mountains Uḍḍiyāṇa, Jālandhara, Pūrṇa and Kāmarūpa and the five gems Gaganānandadeva, Svargānanda, Paramānandadeva, the sandals of Satyānanda and Nāgānanda (should be worshipped) in the north. One should worship the six—the sandal of Suranātha (Indra), Śrīsamayakoṭīśa, Vidyākoṭīśvara, Koṭīśa, Bindukoṭīśa and Siddhakoṭīśvara in the north-east. The *siddhacatuṣka* (four *siddhas*)—Amarīśeśvara, Cakrīśanātha, Kuraṅgeśa, Vṛtreśa and Candranāthaka should be worshipped in the south-east with perfumes etc. The *Vimalapañcaka* (five Vimalas)—Anādivimala, Sarvajñavimala, Yogīśavimala, Siddha (vimala) and Samaya (vimala) (should be worshipped) in the south.

25. One should worship the four gods Kandarpanātha and others, all the female energies already described and the sandals of (goddess) Kubjikā.

26. (The votary) should always worship the thousand-eyed and blemishless (god) Viṣṇu and (god) Śiva with the *mantra* of nine syllables or five *praṇava* (*mantras*).

27-37. Brahmā and other gods (should be worshipped) from the east to the north-east. (The goddesses) Brahmāṇī, Māheśvarī, Kaumārī, Vaiṣṇavī, Vārāhī, Indrāṇī, Cāmuṇḍā and Mahālakṣmī should be worshipped from the east to the north-east. (The goddesses) Ḍākinī, Rākiṇī, Kākinī, Śākinī and Yākinī should be worshipped in the six directions (commencing) from the north-west. The goddess composed of thirty-two letters should be worshipped with five *praṇavas* or syllable *hrīm*. She should be contemplated upon as of dark complexion like the petals of blue lotus, having six faces, of six kinds, as eighteen kinds of *cicchakti* (faculties of the mind), possessing twelve arms, seated comfortably on the throne, remaining on the lotus of absolute dead (of primordial matter), and shining with the splendour of multitudes of *kulas*. She should also be contemplated as having Karkoṭaka (one of the eight principal cobras) as the girdle, Takṣaka (a cobra) above, Vāsuki (a cobra) as a garland on the neck, Kulika (a cobra) on the ears, the tortoise as the ear-stud, (the serpents) Padma and Mahāpadma forming the eye-brows, and having skull, a serpent, rosary, a club with a skull at the top, a conch and a look in her left (hand) and a trident, a mirror, a sword, a garland of gems, dart and a bow in the right (hand). The upper front face of the goddess (should be contemplated) as having a white complexion and elevated, the eastern face pale, the southern one angry, the western face of black colour, and the northern one of the colour of snow and jasmine. Moreover, Brahmā (should be imagined to be) as remaining at the foot, Viṣṇu at the buttocks, Rudra at the heart, Īśvara at the neck, Sadāśiva at the forehead, Śiva as remaining above her. Kubjikā should thus be contemplated as whirling in all acts of worship.

CHAPTER ONE HUNDRED AND FORTYFIVE

Different kinds of mantras and the rites of locating them

The Lord said :

1. I shall describe different kinds of *mantras* preceded by *ṣoḍhānyāsa* (the six ways of touching the body with the *mantras*). There are three kinds of *ṣoḍhānyāsa*—the *śākta*, *Śāmbhava* and *yāmala* devoted to the goddess, lord Śiva and both).

2-3. In the *śāmbhava* (rite), the six terms would have sixteen knots. The three kinds of knowables are related to the *nyāsa* of this kind. It connotes the principles. The fourth (*nyāsa*) is of the *vanamālā* of twelve *ślokas* (letters). The fifth (*nyāsa*) (is known as) the *Ratnapañcātmā* (comprising the five gems) and the sixth one is said to be the *Navātmā* (comprising nine).

4-17. In the case of *śākta* (*nyāsa*), (the first one is) Mālinī (*nyāsa*) the second one (is) *trividyā*, the next one (third is the *nyāsa* of) the eight *aghoris*. The fourth one (is on) the twelve parts (of the body). The fifth one is (of) six parts. (The sixth one) is of the *astracaṇḍikā* of the form of *śakti* (goddess). *Krīṁ hrauṁ klīṁ śrīṁ krūm phaṭ* (are the *mantras* in the above) three, known as the fourth accomplishing everything. The *mālinī* would be from *na* to *pha*. The *nādinī* is known to be the tuft. The *agrasani* would be on the head. (The letter) *śa* (should be) like a garland around the head. (The letter) *ṭa* (representing) peace be (on) the head. (Goddess) Cāmuṇḍā (be) on the three eyes. (The letter) *ḍha* (denoting) pleasing look (should be) on the two eyes. (The goddess) Guhyaśaktinī (should be) on the nostrils. (The letter) *na* (standing for) (goddess) Nārāyaṇī (should be) on the two ears. (The letter) *ta* that stupefied (should be) on the right ear. (The letter) *ja* (representing) wisdom (should) remain on the left ear. (Goddess) Vajriṇī is known to be on the face. (The letter) *ka* (representing) (the goddess) Karālī (of horrible features) (should be on) the right tooth. (The letter) *kha* (representing) (the goddess) Kapālinī (bedecked with human skulls) (should be on) the left shoulder. (The letter) *ga* (representing the goddess) Śivā be (on) the upper tooth. (The letter) *gha* (representing the goddess) Ghorā (should be on the left tooth. (The letter) *u* (denoting the goddess) Śikhā has her place on the tooth. (The letter) *ī* (representing the goddess) Māyā is represented by the tongue. (The letter) *a* should be (located) as (the goddess) Nāgeśvarī in the words. (The letter) *va* (representing the goddess) Śikhivāhinī (having peacock as the vehicle) (is located) in the throat. (The letter) *bha* (representing the goddess) *Bhīṣaṇī* (frightening) (is located) on the right shoulder. The letter *ma* (representing the goddess) Vāyuvegā (swift as the wind) (should be located) on the left (shoulder). (The letter) *ḍa* (denoting) *Nāmā* (should be located) in the right arm. (The letter) *ḍha* (representing the goddess) Vināyakā (remover of obstacles) on the left arm. (The letter) *pa* (denoting) Pūrṇimā (the full moon) (be located) on the two hands. The syllable *om* etc. should be (located) on the ring fingers. (The letter) *am* (be represented by) Darśanī (one who exhibits) on the finger of the left (hand). (The letter) *aḥ* be (located) on the hand (representing) Sañjīvanī (the vitalising force). (The letter) *ṭa* (be located on) the skull (representing) Kapālinī (the goddess wearing garland of skulls). (The letter) *ta* (representing) Dīpanī (the goddess who illuminates) (be located) on the staff of the spear. (The letter) *ca* (representing) *Jayantī* (the goddess who is victorious) be (located) on the trident. (The letter) *ya* is remembered to be Sādhanī (one who accomplishes) (as representing) the process of growth. (The letter) *sa* known to be Paramā (the Supreme goddess) be (located) in the soul. (The letter) *ha* remembered to be (representing) Ambikā (the mother goddess) be (located) in the vital principle of life. (The letter) *cha* (representing) Śarīrā (the goddess with a visible body) (be located) on the right breast. (The letter) *na* (representing) Pūtanā (the demoness) (be located) on the left breast. (The letter) *za* (be looked upon as permeating) the breast milk. (The letter) *ā* (representing) the crushing Lambodarī (the big-bellied goddess) (be located) in the belly. (The letter) *kṣa* representing Saṁhārikā (the goddess of destruction) may be (located) on the navel. Mahākālī (the most ferocious goddess) (be located) at the buttocks. (The letter) *sa* representing) Kusumamālā (the goddess wearing garland of flowers) (be located) in the arms. (The letter) *ṣa* (representing) Śukradevikā (the goddess of fertility (be located) in the semen. (The letter) *ta* (representing) Tārā may be (located) on the two thighs. (The letter) *da* (signifying) Jñānā (the goddess of knowledge) (be located) on the right knee. (The letter) *au* (representing) *u* Kriyāśakti (the energy of activity) may be (located) in the left (knee). The letter *ro* (denoting) Gāyatrī (the personification of the *mantra* of that name) be located in the groins. (The letter) o (representing goddess) Sāvitrī (be located) on the left groin. (The letter) *do* (representing) (goddess) Dohinī (be located) on the right (groin).

18-31. (The letter) *pha* (representing the goddess) Phetkārī (should be located) at the left foot. I shall describe the rite relating) to the *Mālinī-mantra* of nine parts. (It is as follows). (The letter) *a* (denoting the god) Śrīkaṇṭha be (located) on the tuft. (The letter) *ā* (representing the god) Ananta be (located) on the face. (The letter) *i* (standing for the god) Sūkṣma be (located) on the right eye. (The letter) *ī* (signifying the lord) Trimūrti (of three forms) (be located) at the left (eye). (The letter) *u* (representing) Amarīśa (the lord of celestials) (be located) at the right ear. (The letter) *ū* representing Ardhāṁśaka[1] (one who has assumed half of the divine form) (be located) at the other ear (left ear). (The letter) *ṛ* (denoting) Bhāvabhūti (the lord of ensuing fortune) (be located) at the tip of the nose. (The letter) *ṛ* (denoting) Tithīśa (the lord of the day) (be located) on the left nostril. (The letter) l (representing) Sthāṇu (of the form of a pillar) should be (located) at the right cheek. (The letter) *ī* (signifying lord) Hara (should be located) at the left cheek. (The letter) *o* (standing for) Kaṭīśa (be located) at the rows of teeth. (The letter) *ai* (representing) Bhūtīśa (the lord of fortunes) (should be located) at the upper (row of) teeth. (The letter) *o* (denoting) Sadyojāta (one of the five forms of Śiva) (should be located) on the lower lip. (The letter) *au* (standing for) Anugrahīśa (one who confers blessing) (should be located) at the upper lips. (The

1. This may denote one half of either the combined form of Śiva and Viṣṇu. or that of Śiva and his consort.

letter) *aṁ* (denoting) Krūra (the cruel one) be (located) at the back of the neck. (The letter) *aḥ* (signifying) Mahāsena (the lord of huge army) (be located) in the tongue. (The letters) *ka, kha, ga, gha, ṅa, ca, cha, ja, jha, ña, ṭa, ṭha, ḍa, ḍha, ṇa, ta, tha, da, dha, na, pa, pha, ba, bha, ma, ya, ra, la, va, śa, ṣa, sa, ha and kṣa respectively* denoting *Krodhīśa* (lord of wrath), Caṇḍīśa (consort of Caṇḍī), Pañcāntaka (the destroyer of the five elements), Śikhī (tufted), Ekapāda (onefooted), Kūrmakā (manifest as the tortoise), Ekanetra (one-eyed), Caturvaktra (having four faces), Rājasa (possessing the quality of *rajas*—passion) Sārvakāmada (one who confers all desires), Someśa (lord of moon), Dakṣa (Able), Lāṅgalī (wielder of the plough), Dāruka (lord of woods), Ardhajaleśvara (lord of half the watery region), Umākānta (consort of Umā (Pārvatī)). Āṣāḍhī (holding a kind of wood), Daṇḍī (holding a stick), Bhida (one who breaks), Mīna (of the form of the fish), Meṣa (of the form of the ram), Lohita (of red complexion), Śikhī (tufted), Galaṇḍa(?),Dviraṇḍaka(?) Mahākāla (the great god of darkness at the time of deluge), Vāṇīśa (the god of speech), Bhujaṅgeśa (the lord of serpents), Pinākī (the wielder of the bow *pināka*), Khaḍgeśa (the lord of the sword), Baka, Śveta (Śiva's manifestation as the sage), Bhṛgu (a sage), Nakulīśa (a manifestation of Śiva) and Saṁvarta (lord of destruction) (may be respectively) (located) on the right shoulder, arms, elbow, right wrist, fingers, left shoulder, arms, elbow, wrist, fingers, buttocks, right thigh, right knee, leg from the ankle to the knee, fingers, buttocks, left thigh, left knee, left leg from the ankle to the knee, toes, right belly, left belly, the back bone, navel, heart, memory, blood, flesh, one's own self (soul), bones, marrow, semen, life force and sheaths (of human organism). One would get all things by the worship of the energy of Rudra with the syllable *hrīm*.

CHAPTER ONE HUNDRED AND FORTYSIX

Names of different goddesses

The lord said :

1. I shall describe the three parts (of mantras) relating to (the gods) Brahmā, Viṣṇu and Maheśvara. *Om* obeisance to the lord Rudra. Obeisance. Obeisance to Cāmuṇḍā. Obeisance to the (divine) mothers in the ethereal region who accomplish all the desired materials, who have unobstructed movement everywhere, who transform their forms, who are engaged in doing all deeds of *sattva, vaśīkaraṇa, utsādana* and *unmūlana* (pacification, attraction, destruction and eradication). The secret (*mantra*) of all the divine mothers, the most accomplished one which nullifies the incantations of others and accomplishes the supreme (thing) ! (The following) one hundred and twenty-one (terms) are in the section of Brahmā. They are as follows : Om obeisance. Cāmuṇḍā (a terrific form of Durgā) ! Brahmāṇī (consort of Brahmā) ! Aghorā (not terrific) ! Amoghā (infallible) ! Varadā (conferer of boons) ! Viccā (one who shines) ! Oblations. Om obeisance. O Cāmuṇḍā ! Māheśvarī (consort of Lord Śiva) ! Aghorā ! Amoghā ! Varadā ! Viccā ! Oblations. *Om* obeisance. O Cāmuṇḍā ! (one having a maiden-form) ! Aghora ! Amoghā ! Varadā ! Viccā ! Oblations. *Om* obeisance. O Cāmuṇḍā ! Vaiṣṇavī (relating to Viṣṇu) ! Aghorā ! Amoghā ! Varadā ! Viccā ! Oblations. *Om* obeisance. O Cāmuṇḍā ! Vārāhī (the *śakti* of Viṣṇu in the form of the boar) ! Aghorā ! Amoghā ! Varadā ! Viccā ! Oblations. *Om* obeisance. O Cāmuṇḍā ! Indrāṇī (the consort of Indra) ! Aghorā ! Amoghā ! Varadā ! Viccā ! Oblations. *Om* obeisance. O Cāmuṇḍā ! Caṇḍī ! (name of Durgā) ! Aghorā ! Amoghā ! Varadā ! Viccā ! Oblations. *Om* obeisance. O Cāmuṇḍā ! Īśānī (related to the Īśāna form of Śiva) ! Aghorā ! Amoghā ! Varadā) ! Viccā ! Oblations.

2. The second part relating to Viṣṇu has equal number of terms (as follows). Om obeisance. O Cāmuṇḍā ! One who has erect hairs (on the head) ! One who has flames on her head ! One whose tongue is like lightning ! One whose eyes are sparkling like stars ! One who has tawny brows ! One who has uneven teeth ! The Angry one ! *Om*, One who is fond

of flesh, blood, wine and spirituous liquor ! (You) laugh, laugh. *Om* dance, dance. *Om* yawn, yawn. *Om* bind, bind, *Om* to all those thousands of sorceres who change the form of three worlds by their incantations ! *Om* thrash, thrash. *Om ciri ciri. Om hiri hiri. Om bhiri bhiri.* One who frightens and frightens. One who whirls round and whirls round. One who makes (something else) melt and melt. One who agitates and agitates. One who kills and kills. One who revives and revives. *Heri heri geri geri gheri gheri om muri muri om* obeisance to the mothers. Obeisance. Obeisance. Viccā. (There are) thirtyone terms for Śambhu (Śiva) and the syllables (are) one hundred and seventy-one.

3-21. One should repeat *trikhaṇḍī* (*mantra*) (*mantra* of three parts) (with the syllables) *he* and *ghaum* preceded and followed by the five *praṇavas* (*oṁkāras*) and worship. The sacred secret *mantra he ghaum* of (the goddess) Kubjikā should be added in between the terms. It should be in the middle of the three *akulādi*, the three *kulādi*, the three *madhyama* and the *piṇḍa* at the foot. It must have one and a half vowels and *praṇava* etc. (at the) tuft of Śivā. *Om kṣrauṁ* obeisance to Śikhābhairava. *Skhīm Skhīm Skhem* the three letters with the *bīja* (basic) mantra). *Hrām hrīm hraim* without the *bīja*, the three waters and the supreme thritytwo letters. The letters *kṣa, ka* are the *akula* (*mantras*) according to the order of Kula. (The goddesses of energy are) Śaśinī (goddess in the moon), Bhānavī (the energy in the sun), Pāvanī (the purifier), Śivā, Gāndhārī (whose essence is the letter) *ṇa*, Piṇḍākṣī (of round eyes), Capalā (fickle-minded), Gajajihvikā (tongue like that of an elephant). (The letter) *ma* represents (the goddesses) Mṛṣā (untruth) and Bhayasāra (the essence of fear). (The letter) *pha* (represents) (goddesses) Madhyamā (the middle one), Ajarā (without aging). (The letter) *na* represents (goddesses) Kumārī (maiden), Kālarātrī (dreadful night at the time of deluge). (The letters) *da* and *dha* respectively represent (goddesses) Saṅkaṭā (diffiiculty) and *Kālikā* (of dark complexion). (The letter) *pha* (represents) Śivā (consort of Śiva), *ṇa*—Bhavaghorā (the frightening god of the cycle of existence), *ṭha*—Bībhatsā (disgusting one), *ta*—Vidyutā (the goddess in the form of the lightning), *ṭha*—Viśvambharā (the sustainer of the universe). (The letter) *ḍha* (is the representation) of Śaṁsinī (the goddess of doubt), Jvālāmālā (garland of flames), Karālī (ugliness), Durjayā (invincible), Raṅgī (sportive), Vāmā (beautiful), Jyeṣṭhā (the eldest) and Raudrī (terrible). (The letter) *kha* (represents) Kālī (the goddess of time), *ka*—Kulālambī (goddess regulating succession of events), *da*—Anulomā (of descending order) and Piṇḍinī (regulating the three primordial forces), *ā*—Vedinī (of the form of pain), *i* —Śāntimūrti (of the form of peace) and Kalākulā (embodying the arts), *ṛ*—Khaḍginī (the sword-wielding goddess), *u*—Balitā (strong), *l*—kulā (belonging to the *kula* class), *l*—Subhagā (fortunate), Vedanā (pains), ṛ—Karālī (dreadful), *aṁ*—Madhyamā (middle one) and *aḥ*—Apetarayā (unimpetuous). These goddesses of energy should be duly worshipped on the altar. *Skhāṁ skhīṁ skhaum* obeisance to the great Bhairava. (The (goddesses) Akṣodyā (uncrushable), Akṣakarṇī (eyes reaching up to the ear), Rākṣasī (demoness), Kṣapaṇakṣayā (indestructible), Piṅgākṣī (having tawny coloured eyes), Akṣayā (undecaying), Kṣemā (of the form of welfare), and Brahmāṇī (energy relating to Brahmā) are the eight (belonging to the group of Brahmāṇī). (The goddesses) Ilā (representing the earth), ṛilāvatī (sportive), Nīlā (blue-coloured), Laṅkā, Laṅkeśvarī, Lālasā (extreme desire), Vimalā (spotless) constitute the group of Māheśvarī (relating to Śiva). (The goddesses) Hutāśanā (fire), Viśālākṣī (large-eyed), Hrūṅkārī (of the form of syllable *hrūṁ*) Vaḍavāmukhī (having volkanic fires in the mouth) Hāhāravā (having wailing sound), Krūrā (cruel), Krodhā (angry), Bālā (graceful) and Kharānanā (having the face of an ass) had their origin from the body of (the goddess) Kaumārī (virginity). (They are) accomplishers of all things when worshipped. (The goddesses) Sarvajñā (omniscient), Taralā (tremulous), Tārā (shining), Ṛgvedā (the goddess of the Ṛgveda), Hayānanā (horse-faced), Sārā (essence), Sārasvayaṁgrāhā (one who herself absorbs the essence) and Śāśvatī (eternal one) (had their origin) in the family of (goddess) Vaiṣṇavī (relating to Viṣṇu). (The goddesses) Tālujihvā (of the form of a crocodile), Raktākṣī (red-eyed), Vidyujjihvā (lightning like tongue), Karaṅkiṇī (having the skull), Meghanādā (sounding like the cloud), Pracaṇḍogrā (terribly ferocious), Kālakarṇī (representing misfortune) and Kalipriyā (fond of strife) were born of the family of (the goddess) Vārāhī (relating to the boar form). They should be worshipped by those who seek victory.

(The goddesses) Campā, Campāvatī, Pracampā, Jvalitānanā (having flaming face), Piśācī (of the form of a demoness), Picuvaktrā and Lolupā (ardently longing) are born of (the goddess) Aindrī (relating to Indra). (The goddesses) Pāvanī, Yācanī, Vāmanī, Dāmanī, Binduvelā, Bṛhatkukṣī, Vidyutānanā Viśvarūpiṇī born in the family of goddess Cāmuṇḍā should be worshipped in the circle of victory. (The goddesses) Yamajihvā (frightening tongue), Jayantī (victorious), Durjayā (unconquerable), Yamāntikā (one who subdues the god of death), Biḍālī (a female cat), Revatī, Jayā (victorious) and Vijayā (victorious) were born in the class of (goddess) Mahālakṣmī. Thus the eight (goddesses) in the eight groups of (goddesses) have been explained.

CHAPTER ONE HUNDRED AND FORTYSEVEN

Mode of worshipping the goddess Tvaritā and others

The Lord said :

1-2. *Om* Guhyakubjikā (Goddess Kubjikā of secret powers) ! *Hum phaṭ*. You destroy and destroy all my miseries and also whatever incantations of the form of *yantra* (written on a plate), *mantra* (repetition of some syllables), *tantra* (use of mystic syllables) and *cūrṇa* (powders) done or made to do by some one, or being done, or would be done or would be made to do. O One possessing frightening teeth ! *Hraiṁ hrīṁ hum* oblations to Guhyakubjikā. *Hrauṁ oṁ khe voṁ* obeisance to Guhyakubjikā. *Hrīm*. One who subjugates all people ! One who attracts the people ! *Om kheṁ khyaṁ*. One who attracts all people be the stupefier of the people. *Om khyauṁ*. One who paralyses all people ! *aiṁ khaṁ khrāṁ*. Agitator. *Aiṁ* the basic syllable comprising the three principles, that which is excellent in the *kula* (system). The five-syllabled *mantra*. *Phaṁ śrīṁ kṣīṁ śrīṁ hrīṁ kṣeṁ O Jacchā ! kṣe kṣe hrūṁ phaṭ hrīṁ* obeisance. *Oṁ hrāṁ kṣe* Vaccā *kṣe kṣo hrīṁ phaṭ*. Thus the *tvaritā mantras* are of nine kinds. They must be known and they confer victory if propitiated.

3. The seat should be (offered) with (the *mantra*) *hrauṁ* to the lioness. (The *mantra*) *hrīṁ kṣe* is said to be the heart. Vacchā ! Oblations to the head. This (*mantra*) of Tvaritā is remembered in the tuft.

4. *Kṣeṁ hrīṁ vauṣaṭ* be (the *mantra*) for the tuft. *Kṣeṁ huṁ* would be for the armour. *Hrūṁ vauṣaṭ* (be) for the three eyes ending with *hrīm* and *phaṭ*.

5. (The names of) the nine (goddesses of) energy (are) Hrīṁkārī, Khecarī, Caṇḍā, Chedanī, Kṣobhaṇī, Kriyā, Kṣemakārī, Hrīṁkārī and Phaṭkārī.

6-8. Now, I shall describe the envoys (companions) of the goddess Tvaritā), to be worshipped in the directions east and others. *Hrīṁ* Nalā ! possessing thick lips and who moves in the sky. *Hrīṁ* Khecarā (one whose region of movement is the sky) ! Embodied as glowing flames ! Burn, *kha khe cha che*. Frightening like the dead body ! *Ca che* O Caṇḍā (fierce) ! Chedanī (one who breaks) ! Karāli (dreadful) ! *kha khe che khe*. One whose physical constituents are (the letters) *kha*, *ra* and *ha*. *Hrīm kṣe va kṣe* O Kapilā (tawny-coloured) ! *Ha kṣe hrūṁ kuṁ* Jejovati (resplendant) ! Raudri (one in rage) ! O Mother ! *Hrīṁ uhe ve phe phe* Vakrā (crooked one) ! Varī *phe puṭi puṭi* ghore (frightening one) ! *Hrūṁ phaṭ* Brahmavetāli ! Middle one ! I shall again describe the secret *mantras* and principles relating to (the goddess) Tvaritā. *Hraiṁ hraṁ haḥ* are said to be (located) at the heart. *Haruṁ* and *ha* are remembered to be (for) the head. *Phāṁ* sparkle sparkle (is for) the tuft. *Vara ilā hraṁ huṁ kroṁ kṣūṁ śrīṁ* is said (to be for) the eye. *Kṣauṁ* (is) for the weapon. Or (the *mantras*) *phaṭ huṁ khe vacche kṣeḥ hrīṁ kṣeṁ huṁ phaṭ* (is said) then. O *Huṁ* for the head must be in the middle. *Khe* at the beginning. O Sadāśivā (ever benevolent one). *Va* (for) *Īśaḥ*, *che* (for) Manonmanī, *ma* and *kṣe* (for) the Garuḍa, *hrauṁ* for Mādhava, *kṣeṁ* (for) Brahmā, *huṁ* (for) Āditya. The (*mantra*) *phaṭ hrauṁ* is always remembered as cruel.

CHAPTER ONE HUNDRED AND FORTYEIGHT

Mode of worship for success in the battle

The Lord said :

1-7. *Oṁ ḍe kha khyāṁ*. Obeisance to Sun, the victorious in the battle, *hrāṁ, hrīṁ, hrūṁ, hreṁ, hroṁ, hraḥ*. These are the six *mantras* for the Sun, who confers success in the battle. *Oṁ haṁ khaṁ* oblations to Khakholka. *Sphūṁ hrūṁ huṁ krūṁ śrīṁ hoṁ kreṁ*. The eight attributes *prabhūta* (plenty), *vimala* (spotless), *sāra* (essence), *ārādhya* (to be worshipped), *parama* (supreme), *sukha* (happiness), *dharmajñāna* (knowledge of righteousness) and *vairāgya* (firm resolve) should be worshipped. Then the seats *anantāsana* (having ananta, the serpent as the seat), *siṁhāsana* (the lion seat), *padmāsana* (lotus seat) (should be worshipped). Then the pericarps *N* (of the mystic diagram) consisting of the spheres of sun, moon and fire such as Dīptā (luminous), Sūkṣmā (subtle), Jayā (victorious), Bhadrā ! (conferring safety), Vibhāti (fortune), Vimalā (spotless), Amoghā (infallible), Vidyutā (lightning) and Sarvatomukhī (having face every side), the ninth one, should be worshipped. Then one should worship (the qualities) *sattva, rajas* and *tamas, prakṛti* (the source of the material world) and *puruṣa* (the soul), one's soul, one's inner soul and the supreme soul. All the endowed with the *bindu* and *māyānila*. One should worship Uṣā (dawn), Prabhā (lustre), Sandhyā (twilight), Sāyam (evening), Māyā (mysterious), Balā (strong), Bindu (dot) and endowed with Viṣṇu. The eight attendant gods at the entrance such as Sūrya, Caṇḍa, pracaṇḍa and others should be worshipped with perfumes etc. One would be victorious in the battle etc. by the worship, meditation and oblation.

CHAPTER ONE HUNDRED AND FORTYNINE

Mode of performing lakṣa and koṭihoma

The Lord said :

1. A *homa* (oblation) performed after having practised the

prāṇāyāma (control of breath) hundred times and purifying with the rite of *kṛcchra*, confers victory in battle, gets kingdom and destroys obstacles.

2-5. After having repeated *gāyatrī* (*mantra*) (remaining) in the water, one should perform *prāṇāyāma* sixteen times. Oblation of *havis* (clarified butter) should be made into fire in the forenoon. One should eat only that which has been procured after begging or eat only fruits and roots. One should take only single morsel of food such as milk or flour or ghee. O Pārvatī ! as soon as the (rite of a) lakh of oblations concludes, one should give cows, clothes and gold as fees. (The oblation should be done) by fifteen brahmins in the case of all disasters that befall. There is no disaster in the world that does not get warded off by this oblation.

6-10. There is no such benevolent (rite) that could excel this (rite). A king, whosoever, arranges to do the rite of *koṭi-homa* (making a crore oblations) as before (employing) the brahmins, his enemies cannot face him in battle any time. There cannot also be any disease in his country that would kill him. (By its virtue) excessive rainfall, deficient rainfall, mice, crickets, parrots demons and others get controlled. So also the enemies (get controlled) in the battle. One should employ twenty or a hundred or a thousand brahmins for the performance of *koṭihoma*. One would get fortunes as much as one desired. A brahmin or a king or a tradesman, whoever may perform the *koṭihoma*, would get whatever was desired by him. (Moreover) he would go to heaven with his mortal frame.

11.15. By the performance of this *homa* with the *gāyatrī* (*mantra*), or the *mantras* of planets, or those used in the (rite known as) *kuṣmāṇḍa* or those addressed to the Fire God or the gods of directions east, west, north-west, south and south-east or the *mantras* relating to (lord) Viṣṇu or the goddesses or Śambhu (Śiva) or Sun, one would get lesser benefits (if it is done) for ten thousand times. One who does *homa* a lakh times would be able to get rid of all distress. The all-yielding *koṭihoma* (is done) for the destruction of all aflictions. The following materials should be used for oblations—barley, paddy, sesamum, milk, ghee, *kuśa*, *prasātikā* (a variety of rice), petals of lotus, *uśīra* (the fragrant root of a plant) and *bilva*. In the *koṭihoma* the fire-pit should measure eight cubits. Half its measure is laid down in the oblation for a lakh times. Thus the mode of performance of oblation ten thousand lakh and crore times have been explained.

CHAPTER ONE HUNDRED AND FIFTY

Names of different Manus, different sages and others during their periods

The Fire-god said :

1-5. I shall describe the Manu periods. Svāyambhuva is (the name of) the first Manu. Agnīdhra and others (were) his sons. The celestials (were) known as Yama[1]. Indra (was a performer of) hundred sacrifices. In the period of (the second Manu) Svārociṣa, the seven sages (were) Aurva and others. Indra (was) Vipaścit. Pārāvatas and Tuṣitas (were) the celestials. Urja, Stambha and others (were) the brahmins. Caitra, Kimpuruṣa and others (were) the sons. The third Manu (was) Uttama. Indra (was) Suśānti. Sudhāma and others born in the family of Vasiṣṭha (were) the seven sages. Aja and others (were) their sons. Tāmasa Manu was the fourth. Svarūpa and others (were) the celestials. Śikhi[2], Jyotirddhāma and others (were) the sages and Navakhyāti and others his sons.

6. In the (period of the fifth Manu) Raivata, Vitatha[3] (was) the Indra, Amitābhas were the celestials, Hiraṇya[4]-romā and others were the sages and Balabandha and others were his sons.

7. In the (period of the sixth Manu), Cākṣuṣa, Manojava (was) the Indra. Svāti and others (were) the celestials, Sumedhā and others (were) the sages and Puru and others (were) the sons.

8-15. Śrāddhadeva, son of Vivasvān (Sun) (was) the next Manu. Ādityas, Vasus and Rudras (were) the celestials. Purandara (was) the Indra. Vasiṣṭha, Kāśyapa, Atri,

1. For their different names see *Vi.P.* I,vii. 7-21 and III. i-ii.
2. *Vi.P. III.* i. 17 reads Śibi.
3. *Vi.P.* III.i. 20 reads Vibhu.
4. *Vi.P.* III.i. 23 reads Balabandhu.

Jamadagni, Gautama, Viśvāmitra and Bharadvāja (were) the seven sages. Ikṣvāku and others (were his sons). Lord Viṣṇu was manifest with a part (of his energy in each one of these periods). He was born as Mānasa in the (period of) Svāyambhuva and Ajita in the next one (that of Svārociṣa). Then (he was born as) Satya, Hari, Devavara, Vaikuṇṭha and Vāmana (in the respective Manu periods which followed). The eighth Manu would be born as the son of Sūrya and Chāyā. As he would be a cognate of his predecessor, this eighth Manu to come (would be known as) Sāvarṇi. Sutapā and others (would be) the clans of celestials. Dīptimān Drauṇi (Aśvatthāmā) and others (would be) the sages. Bali (would be) the Indra. Viraja and others (would be) the sons. The ninth (Manu would be) Dakṣasāvarṇi. Pāra and others (would be) the celestials. Adbhuta (would be) the Indra. Savana and others (would be) the sages. Dhṛtaketu and others (would be) (his) sons. The next (Manu would be) Brahmasāvarṇi. Sukha and others (would be) celestials. Śānti (would be) their Indra. Haviṣya and others (would be) the sages. Sukṣetra and others (would be) the sons of that (Manu).

16-19. (The eleventh Manu would be) Dharmasāvarṇi. Vihaṅga and others (would be) the celestials then. The Indra (would be Vṛṣa)[1]. Niścara[2] and others (would be) the sages. The sons of Manu (would be) Sarvatraga and others. Rudra Sāvarṇi would be (the twelfth) Manu. Ṛtadhāmā (would be) the Indra and Harita and others (would be) the celestials. Tapas and others (would be) the seven sages. Devavān and others (would be) the sons. The thirteenth Manu (would be) Raucya. Sutrāmaṇa and others (would be) the celestials. Divaspati (would be) their Indra who routs the demons etc. Nirmoha and others (would be) the seven sages. Citrasena and others (would be) the sons.

20-22. The fourteenth Manu (would be) Bhautya. Śuci would be the Indra. Cākṣuṣa and others (would be) the celestials. Agnibāhu and others (would be) the sages. Uru and others (would be) the sons of Bhautya, the fourteenth Manu. The seven sages (would descend) to the world from the heavens

1. Cf. *Vi.P.* III. ii.29.
2. *Vi.P.* III.ii.30 reads Nissvara.

and propagate the *Vedas*. Then (the respective) celestials would partake the oblations of sacrifices and the earth would be protected by the sons (of Manus). O Brahmin ! Fourteen Manus (will reign) in the course of a day of Brahmā.

23. Lord Hari (Viṣṇu), who preceded the Manus, divided the *Veda* at the end of the *dvāpara*[1] (*yuga*). The first *Veda* had four parts consisting of a lakh (of verses).

24-26. The *Yajurveda* originally a single work was divided into four. The sage (arranged) the office of an *adhvaryu*[2] priest (to be done) with the *Yajurveda*), the *hotra*[3] with the *Ṛks*, the *audgātra*[4] with the *Sāmans* and *brahmatva*[5] (relating to omissions and antedotes) with the *Atharvan*. Paila, the disciple of Vyāsa and proficient in the *Ṛgveda* imparted the first (*Veda*) to Indrapramiti and the *saṁhitā* (part) to Bāṣkala. He also (divided) that *saṁhitā* into four parts and gave it to Bauddhya and others.

27-30. The great man of intellect Vaiśampāyana, the disciple of Vyāsa, divided the tree of *Yajurveda* into seven branches. The Kāṇvas, Vājasaneyas and others are known to be (the branches founded) by Yājñavalkya and others. Jaimini, the disciple of Vyāsa, divided the tree of *Sāmaveda* into branches and Sumantu and Sukarmā received one part of the *saṁhitā*. Sukarmā had received one thousand *saṁhitā* text. Sumantu, the disciple of Vyāsa, divided the tree of *Atharvaveda*. He imparted it to thousands of Paippalāda, his disciples. Sūta made the *Purāṇa-saṁhitā* by the grace of Vyāsa.

CHAPTER ONE HUNDRED AND FIFTYONE

Description of duties laid down for different castes

The Fire-god said :

1. Puṣkara narrated to Paraśurāma the duties which the

1. The third among the four *yuga* periods of time, equal to 8,64,000 years of men.
2. The priest of the *Yajurveda* who attends to the needs of the sacrifice.
3. The priest of the *Ṛgveda* who does the oblation.
4. The priest of the *Sāmaveda* who sings the *sāman* melodies.
5. The priest of the *Atharvaveda*.

Manus practiced and had enjoyment and emancipation as described by lord Varuṇa to him.

Puṣkara said :

2. I shall describe the laws of conduct relating to the castes, stages of life etc. spoken by the Manus and others, that would give all (benefits) and please (lord) Vāsudeva (name of Viṣṇu in his manifestation as Kṛṣṇa) and others.

3-9. O Excellent one among Bhṛgus ! abstaining from killing, truthfulness, compassion, kindness towards all beings, visiting sacred places, munificence, celibacy, not jealous, doing service to god, brahmins, preceptors and others, listening to all laws of conduct, worship of the manes, veneration towards the king, sustained interest in good scriptures, mercy, forbearance and theism are the general good and bad conduct for all castes and stages of life. The duties of a brahmin should be pointed out as performing religious rites, officiating as priests at the sacrifices, munificence, imparting vedic knowledge, accepting gifts and engaging in the study. The duties of a *kṣatriya* (warrior class) and the *vaiśya* (tradesman) are said to be munificence, engaging in the study and perform sacrificial rites as laid down. Protection and suppression of the wicked are special (duties enjoined) on a *kṣatriya*. Agriculture, protecting the cows and trade are spoken to be (the duties) of a *vaiśya*. (The duties) of a *śūdra* (the fourth class of men) (are) to serve the brahmins or (to practise) handicrafts.

10. Since the binding of the girdle of the muñja grass (at the time of investiture of the sacred thread), the brahmins and others (are supposed to) take a second birth. One's caste is decided from that of the mother in the natural order of castes.

11. Contrary to the natural order the son of a brahmin woman through a *śūdra* (is known as) *Caṇḍāla*, from a *kṣatriya* (as) *sūta* and from a *vaiśya* (as) *devala*.

12. A son born to a *kṣatriya* woman and a *śūdra* contrary to the natural order would be (known as) *pukkasa*. Similarly (a son born to a *kṣatriya* woman) and a *vaiśya* would be *māgadha* and from a *śūdra* as *āyogava*.

13. There are thousands of *pratilomas* (born to higher caste woman and lower caste man) among the *vaiśyas* from the order contrary to natural one. Therefore a marriage (should be done)

only between (members of) the same class and (should not be) with (members of) either the higher or the lower class.

14. The killing of those condemned to death by law and living by means of women are laid down as the duty of a *caṇḍāla*. (The duty) of a *vaidehaka* is said to be their protection.

15-18. To be a charioteer (is the duty) of the *sūtas*, and hunting (is the duty) of the *pukkasas*. (The duty) of the *māgadhas* is singing panegyrics. (The duty) of an *āyogava* is said to be the profession of an actor and living by handicrafts. It is laid down that a *caṇḍāla* should live outside the village, wear the clothes of the dead and should not be touched by others. One, who belongs to any one of the other community, discards his life for the sake of a brahmin or a cow or a woman or child in distress, gets accomplished. The mixed castes should be known from the work done by the father or mother.

CHAPTER ONE HUNDRED AND FIFTYTWO

Duties of a householder

Puṣkara said :

1. A brahmin should live following the code of conduct laid down for him or those of the *kṣatriya* or *vaiśya* or *śūdra*. But he should never live by doing such acts exclusively (laid down) for a *śūdra*.

2. A brahmin may engage himself in agriculture, trade, keeping cows and usury. But he should abstain from taking milk, jaggery, salt and meat and using red-dye.

3. One gets purified from the sin accruing from ploughing the earth and cutting the plants and killing insects and ants by doing a sacrifice. The cultivator (gets free from the sin) by worshipping the god.

4. A virtuous man (should yoke) eight bullocks, one who lives by any means six bullocks, wicked men four bullocks and those who have transgressed rightful living two bullocks.

5. One should live by picking grains in the field and on alms got without solicitation. (One may live) on alms got by solici-

tation or got without solicitation a second time. Otherwise (one may live) by truth and false (i.e., trade). But (one should never (live) on servitude.

CHAPTER ONE HUNDRED AND FIFTYTHREE

Duties of a Student

Puṣkara said :

1-6. Listen ! I shall describe the righteous (way of living for those in (different) stages (of life), which yields enjoyment and emancipation. The mensus flow for women lasts for sixteen nights. Among these the first three are censured. One who desires for a male child should cohabit on even (nights). When the conception is explicitly known, the rite favouring conception is prescribed. The rite to be performed with the intention to get a male child is done even before the embryo (in the womb) begins to move. The (rite of) parting of the hair (should be done) in the sixth or eighth (month). The asterism relating to the name should be such that it confers a child (good) and is auspicious. (The rite known as) the *jātakarma* (performed soon after the birth of a child) should be done by wise men before the separation of the umbilical cord. The rite of naming the child should be done after the period of pollution is over. The name of the child of a brahmin is said to end with (the word) *śarmā*, of the warrior class to end with (the word) *varmā*, of the tradesmen and *śūdra* with (the words) *gupta* and *dāsa* respectively. (After the birth of a child) the child should be brought to the father (of the child by the other) with (the words) "This is your son".

7-10. The tonsure ceremony (is laid down) according to one's family (custom). *Upanayana* (the rite of investiture of sacred thread) should be done in the eighth year from that of the conception or in the eighth year of the child for a brahmin. (The same is to be done) in the eleventh year from that of pregnancy for the warrior class and in the twelfth year from that of pregnancy for a tradesman. It should never be done after the sixteenth year (for any one). The *mauñjya* (the girdle to be worn after the above rite) is known to be (made) of *muñja* (grass) or bark. The hides of deer, tiger or goat (should be worn) by those in the student life. The sticks are said to be from the *parṇa* (*palāśa*), *pippala* (fig) and *bilva* tree. They should be (long enough to reach) upto the hair, forehead and face respectively (for the three classes). All the sticks should be having the barks and should not be having bends or be burnt ones.

11-12. The sacred thread (should be made of) cotton, silk or wool respectively (for the three classes). The three classes are indicated by the (repetition of the word) *bhavati* (address to the housewife) at the beginning, middle or end while begging food. One should seek food first at such a place where one would be certain about getting food. The above rites are performed without (the repetition of) *mantra* in the case of female children. But the marriage (should be done) with (the repetition of) *mantra*.

13. After investiture of the sacred thread, the preceptor should instruct his pupil first with cleanliness and then with codes of conduct, the worship of fire and the worship of twilight.

14. Eating facing the eastern direction is conducive to (one's) longevity, the southern direction brings fame. Eating facing the western direction gives wealth. Eating facing the northern direction gets rightful living.

15. Offering to fire should be made in the morning and in the evening. (One should) not (offer) impure things or with separated hands. One should abstain from (drinking) intoxicants, (eating) flesh, singing and dancing with men.

16. (One should also eschew) violence, spreading scandal about others and especially speaking unpleasant words. (The student), whose stick (and other things) get damaged, should throw them in water and have another.

17. (He) should learn the scripture (from the preceptor), pay fees to the preceptor and perform the bathing (ceremony marking the completion of one's study). But the *naiṣṭika brahmacārī* (one who has taken a vow of life-long abstinence) should remain with the preceptor till his (own) death.

CHAPTER ONE HUNDRED AND FIFTYFOUR

Rules of Marriage

Puṣkara said :

1. The brahmin should marry four wives, the warrior class three wives, the tradesmen two wives as they desire. The last class should marry only one wife.

2-3. All the righteous acts should not be done in the company of women not belonging to one's own community. One should marry only from his own community. (At the time of marriage) the warrior class should hold the arrow, the tradesmen should bear the toad and then the last community the fringe of a garment. A girl should be given (in marriage) only once. One who abducts such a girl deserves the same punishment as for a thief.

4-7. No atonement is laid down for one who sells his children. Marriage is said to consist of four kinds of acts such as *kanyādāna* (giving the girl as a gift), *śacīyāga* (rite relating to the wife of Indra), marriage and *caturthikā* (the fourth one). Women are allowed to have another husband in the following five adversities—if (the first husband is) lost, dead, has become an ascetic, impotent or fallen morally. If (the husband) is dead, (she) should be given to the brother (of the deceased). In the absence (of a brother) (she should be given) as one wished. The three *pūrvas* (*pūrvā*, *pūrvāṣāḍhā*, *pūrvaproṣṭapadi*), *āgneya* (*kṛttikā*), *vāyavya* (*svāti*), the three *uttarās* (*uttarā*, *uttarāṣāḍhā*, *uttarāproṣṭapadi*) and *rohiṇī* are the asterisms always commended for copulation.

8-11. O Bhārgava (Paraśurāma) ! One should not choose (the bride) from the same *gotra* or born in the line of same sage. (One may choose) from (descendants of) more than seven (generations) on the paternal side and more than five (generations) on the maternal side. Having invited a person endowed with good conduct and belonging to a good family and giving a girl as a gift is known as *brāhma* (type of marriage). The lustre due to the offering of a girl as a gift always elevates men. Then the marriage accompanied by the offer of the gift of a pair of cows is spoken to be the *ārṣa* (variety of marriage). The offer made to one after solicitation (is known to be) *prājā-*

patya (variety of marriage) for the purpose of righteousness. It is *āsura* (type of marriage in which the girl is offered) along with the purchase money. (It is considered as) the lowest. The marriage by mutual consent (is known as) *gāndharva*. (Marriage) by abduction after a battle (is known as) *rākṣasa* (variety of marriage). (It is known as) the *paiśāca* (variety) if the girl is married after deceiving her.

12. An image of Indrāṇī (wife of Indra) should be made with potter's earth on the marriage day. She (that image) should be worshipped at a pond and (then) the bride should be taken inside the house accompanied by music.

13-14. The marriage should not be done when lord Keśava (Viṣṇu) sleeps[1] and also in (the months of) *Pauṣa* (December-January) and *Caitra* (April-May), on Tuesday and on the days of *riktā*[2] and *viṣṭi*.[3] (The marriage should also) never (be done) when Venus and Jupiter are not to be visible and the Moon has been eclipsed. (So also it should not be done) in asterisms ruled by (the planets Sun, Saturn and Mars and days afflicted by *vyatipāta*.[4]

15. The asterisms (suitable) for (the performance of) a marriage (are) *Mṛgaśirṣa*, *Maghā*, *Svāti*, *Hasta*, *Rohiṇī*, the three *Uttaras* (*Uttara*, *Uttarāṣāḍhā* and *Uttaraproṣṭapadi*), *Mūla*, *Anurādhā* and *Revatī*.

16-19. The ascendant and the *aṁśa* (subdivision of the stellar house) relating to a mortal are auspicious. (The planets) Sun, Saturn and Mercury in the third, sixth, tenth, eleventh and eighth (houses) are commendable. Mars in the eighth (is) not (commendable). All the other planets are commendable in the seventh, twelfth and eighth (houses). Even among them, Venus in the sixth from the sixth house is not commendable. (Just as the worship of Indrāṇi is done) in the asterism on the marriage day, the *caturthikā* (the rite on the fourth day of the marriage) should also be done in the asterism of the marriage. The marriage should not be performed if four planets are in the

1. The four month period commencing with the eleventh day of the bright half of the month of Āṣāḍha (June-July).
2. The fourth, ninth and fourteenth days of a lunar fortnight.
3. An adverse period.
4. The day of the new Moon occurring on a Sunday and when the Moon is in a particular asterism.

same house. One should cohabit his wife only on days other than the *parva* (days) (the eighth and fourteenth days as well as the full-moon and newmoon days). When a truthful (girl) is given in marriage (there would be) pleasure always.

CHAPTER ONE HUNDRED AND FIFTYFIVE

The code of conduct

Puṣkara said :

1-12. After getting up in the *brāhma muhūrta* (about 48 minutes prior to sunrise), one should contemplate on the gods Viṣṇu and others. One should pass both urine and stools facing the north during the day time, facing the south during the night and as in the day during the two twilight periods. One should not do on the roads, water, streets and on the grassy surface. After having purified oneself with earth, one should sip water three times and then cleanse the teeth. Bathing is said to be six kinds such as daily, casual, performed with some desire, part of a purificatory rite, removing the bodily dirt and at the time of obsequies. The religious act done without bathing yields no result. Hence one should bathe in the morning. Among the waters of a sacred place, a river, a tank, flowing water, water present in the well and water drawn (from the well), the preceding one is more meritorious than the succeeding one in order. The waters of (the river) Ganges are always meritorious. After having cleansed the impurities (on the body), one should remain submerged in (the waters of) the tank. After having touched waters one should sprinkle them (on his body) three times with the (repetition of the *mantra*) *hiraṇyavarṇā*[1], then with (the *mantra*) *śanno devī*[2], three times with *āpo hi ṣṭhā*[3], and then with *idam āpa*[4]. Then one should remain in the water of the tank and mutter (sacred syllables) (remaining) in the water. One should

1. ṚV. 5.87.1a.
2. *Śrīsūkta*. *ṚV*. 10.9.4a.
3. *ṚV*. 10.9.1a.
4. *ṚV*. 1.23.22a.

either recite the *aghamarṣaṇa*[1] hymn or the *drupadā*[2] or *yuñjate mana*[3] or the *puruṣasūkta*[4]. The *gāyatrī* (*mantra*) should be recited especially. *Bhāvavṛtta* is the deity, Aghamarṣaṇa is the sage and *anuṣṭubh* is the metre for the *aghamarṣaṇa* hymn. Lord Hari (Viṣṇu) is remembered to be Bhāvavṛtta. After squeezing the garment (one should) offer (respectful) waters of oblation to the gods and manes. One should offer waters of homage with the palms with the recitation of the *puruṣasūkta*. Then one should offer oblation to fire and make gifts befitting one's capacity.

13-14. Then one should worship lord (Śiva) for the sake of one's prosperity. One's seat, bed, vehicle, wife, children and water-vessel are pure for one's self. (But they) are not pure for others. Even preceptors should leave way for pregnant women afflicted by the weight.

15. One should not look at the rising or setting Sun or in the waters. One should not look at naked woman. One should not peep into the well and look at a dog, or drinking house and a sinner.

16. One should not tread on cotton, bones, ashes and that which is despised. (One should not enter) the apartments of women or treasury. One should not go as an emissary of another person.

17. One should not board an uneven boat, or (climb) a tree or a mountain. One should then be interested in sciences relating to acquisition of wealth.

18. One who tramples on clod of earth, one who cuts the grass and one who eats the nail would perish. One should not desire to raise sounds with the mouth. One should not stir out in the night without a lamp.

19. One should not enter a house not having a door. One should not change the colour of the face. One should not interrupt in the midst of a conversation. One should not wear other's garments.

20. One should always say good. One should never utter that which does not please others. Seat made of *palāśa* (wood) is prohibited. One should move in the shade of gods etc.

---

1. *ṚV.* 10.190.
2. *AV.* 6.115.3a.
3. *ṚV.* 5.81.1a.
4. *ṚV.* 10.90.

21. One should not go in between revered people. One should not look at the broken (and falling) asterism. One should not utter the name of another river (while standing) in one river. One should not gargle with two hands.

22. One should not cross the river without propitiating the forefathers and gods. One should not throw impurities like feces in the waters. One should not bathe remaining naked.

23. Then one should worship lord Īśvara (Śiva) for the sake of welfare and prosperity. One should not remove one's garland oneself. One should avoid the dust of an ass and other animals.

24. One should not ridicule mean (people). One should not go (with them) and live with them. One should not also reside at a place devoid of a physician, a king and a river, a place ruled by other races, women and many men.

25. One should not converse with women in their monthly menstrual courses or otherwise fallen. One should contemplate on lord Keśava (Viṣṇu) (if happened to converse with the above). One should not laugh, yawn and sneeze without covering the mouth.

26. A wiseman should avoid disrespect shown to his master and his own self. One should guard the words of one's self and his master. One should not yield to (the dictates of) his organs. One should not control the natural impulses of the body.

27. O Bhārgava ! One should not ignore a disease like an insignificant enemy. One should always sip waters (for purification) whenever one goes in the street. One should not carry water and fire.

28. One should not utter *hum* to a good and venerable person. One should not tread over one foot with the other. One should not speak something unpleasant to someone either in his presence or his absence.

29. One should refrain from abusing the scriptures, king, sages and gods. One should not envy women and one should avoid having faith in them.

30. One should hear righteous things, have devotion to gods and adhere to righteous path. One should worship Soma (moon) as well as gods and brahmins in the natal star.

31. One should avoid bathing with the application of oil on the sixth, eighth and fourteenth (days of the fortnight). (One should pass) urine and stools far away from the house. One should not have enmity with great men.

CHAPTER ONE HUNDRED AND FIFTYSIX

Purification of things

Puṣkara said :

1-2. I shall describe the (mode of) purification of things. Earthen vessel made impure by contact with urine or feces would become pure by heating again. A copper and gold vessel similarly made impure (may be made pure) by melting or the copper one by water or acid. (The vessels made) of bell-metal and copper (may be purified) with acid. (Those made) of pearls (get purified) by washing.

3-5. Lotuses, vessels made of iron, vegetables, ropes, roots, fruits and cane (could be made pure by washing). The sacrificial vessels (are made pure) by sprinkling (water) with hand at the sacrificial work. Those made of oily things (such as wax) could be purified with hot water being sprinkled in the house. Muddy water may be purified by straining it through a cloth, or by sprinkling on many cloth. Wooden (things) get purified that moment (by sprinkling with water).

6-7. Liquid materials which have become solidified (would become pure) by sprinkling or by leaping up. A bed, seat, vehicle, winnowing basket and cart would become purified by sprinkling (water), as also in the case of straw and fuel. (Things made) of the horn and tusk (may be purified) by a paste of white mustard.

8. A vessel (containing) flesh (may be purified) with cow's tail. Bones have to be (purified) as in the case of horns. Molasses of jaggery and solution of salt (may be purified) by drying.

9. Safflower, flowers, wool and cotton (may be purified) in the same manner. The flowing water of a river is pure. So also the water that remains spreads out.

10-15. A cow is pure except in its mouth. The mouths of a horse and goat are impure. The mouths of women, calves of cows, birds and of dogs (are pure). While hunting a dog dripping water from its mouth is always pure. One should sip (water thrice for purification) after eating, sneezing, sleeping, drinking (water), having had a dip in the water, walking on the street and having changed the dress worn. The cat is pure because it moves (here and there). A women in her menstrual courses (becomes pure) after bathing on the fourth day. She becomes eligible (to take part) in rites relating to gods and manes. (In impurity) due to the *apāna* (one of the airs in the body) five parts of mud (should be used), fifteen parts in purification after urine and seventeen parts in impurity due to feces. One should apply one part of mud to the penis and three times two parts (of mud) on both hands. For the *brahmacārins* (students), the foresters and ascetics (it is laid) as four times. Silken cloth (are purified) with *śrīphala* (emblic myrabolan), white cloth with white mustard. It is said that the hairs of animals would be purified by sprinkling water. Flowers, fruits etc. would get purified by sprinkling water.

CHAPTER ONE HUNDRED AND FIFTYSEVEN

Pollution and Purification

Puṣkara said :

1. I shall describe purification after death and after the birth (of a child). The pollution due to the death of a *sapiṇḍa*[1] is prescribed for ten days.

2-7. O Excellent among Bhṛgus (descendants of Bhṛgu) ! So also purification (from pollution) is after birth in the case of brahmins, after twelve days for the warrior class, after fifteen days for the tradesmen, and after a month for *śūdra* (fourth class). If the dead belongs to the higher class, the pollution for the servant (of the lower class) would be as for

1. A kinsman connected by offering the funeral rice-ball to the manes of certain relatives.

the master. A brahmin or a person of the warrior class who had his birth through the warrior, tradesman or *śūdra* gets purified after six or three or one day in order. O *Paraśurāma* ! if born of a tradesman and *śūdra* purification would be after six or three nights (respectively) and if born of a *śūdra* and tradesman purification would be) after six (nights). (If one's child dies) before the formation of teeth, one become pure at once, (if it dies) before tonsure, (the parent) has pollution for a night, if before the *vratabandha* (vow relating to investiture of thread) pollution lasts for three nights, and ten nights if afterwards. If a *śūdra* dies at less than three years of age, the purification should be after five days. If aged more than three, purification would be after twelve days, if aged six years, the purification would be after a month.

8-9. If a female (child) (dies) before tonsure, the purification would be after a night. Similarly, the relatives of female children dying after tonsure get purified in three days. No pollution is laid down for the parental side if (a female dies after marriage. If a woman delivers a child in her parent's house, the relatives get purified after a night.

10-14. A woman after childbirth gets purified after ten days) and not otherwise. There is no doubt that if a married girl dies in her father's house, the relatives get purified after three nights. If two pollutions take place and the second one is equal or inferior to the first one, the pollution ends with the first one, and ends with the second one if the second is not equal. These are the words of Dharmarāja[1]. One who lives abroad happening to hear (the news about) the death of his kinsmen would be impure only for the remaining part of the ten days (of impurity). (If it is known) after ten days, impurity would last for three days. Then if one year had elapsed, one would become pure after bathing. (One has to do as before) if either the maternal grandfather or the preceptor dies.

15-16. One gets purified after abortion after the same number of nights proportionate to the months (period) of pregnancy. O Bhārgava (son of Bhṛgu)[2] whoever of a *sapiṇḍa*[3] of a brahmin caste may die the pollution ends after ten days for all with-

1. The lord of righteous living; may mean any upholder of a code.
2. Denotes Paraśurāma.
3. See 157. fn 1.

out any distinction. So also for a warrior (class) (it would end) after twelve days, the tradesmen after fifteen days and the *śūdras* after a month.

17. A ball should be made and offered from the remnants of the ceremony and placed in front. One who does the deed should then declare the name and clan of that person (dead).

18-24. After the excellent brahmins had partaken food, were well honoured with gifts and had blessed with unbroken rice and water with the recitation of the name and clan (of the doer), one should dug up three pits of four cubits breadth and depth and of twelve cubits length. Near the pits one should kindle three fires. O Rāma (Paraśurāma) one should offer oblations to Soma, Agni (Fire god) and Yama four (handfuls) three times each. Balls of rice should be offered separately (in each one of these)as before. One should fill (pits) with cooked rice, curd, honey and flesh. If an inter-calary month occurs this should be done in addition. Or (this ceremony) should be completed in twelve days. If an inter-calary month occurs in the middle of the year, then there would be extra rites at (the time of doing) the twelfth ceremony. After the completion of one year the ceremony should be done as the annual ceremony.

25. If one dies balls of rice should be offered to the ancestors of the three past generations. Likewise the fourth is brought together.

26. O Bhārgava ! After having worshipped and offering (ball of rice) with (the recitation of syllables) *pṛthvī samānā*[1], the ball of rice (intended) for the dead should be united with those (intended) for the other (ancestors).

27. So also the vessel for the dead should be united with the vessels (for the ancestors). This rite of uniting the vessels should be done one by one.

28. This rite is laid down without (the recitation of) syllables for the *śūdra*. The rite of *sapiṇḍīkaraṇa*[2] should be done in the same way for women.

29-30. If one dies, a potful of cooked rice should be offered for a year and the ceremony should be done every year. One

1. *cf. pṛthvī samā HG.* 2-11-4.

2. The rite of uniting the ball of rice for the dead with those for the ancestors.

may be able to count the sand particles in the Ganges or the rain drops as Indra rains. But one may not be able to count in this world the past ancestors. In the ever-moving time there is no permanence. Hence, one should do the deeds.

31-32. The dead would get the results of ceremony whether (they are) in heaven (or) in hell. No benefit would accrue to the dead if one is only mourning (the death). There is no pollution due to the death of a person by (falling from) a cliff, (burnt) by fire, in a trap, by (drowning in) the water or by suicide. (There is no pollution on account of the death) of those fallen (from their caste) and those killed by lightning and weapons.

33. Ascetics, those who have undertaken vows, student-celibates, kings, sculptors and those initiated for religious ceremonies and those under the command of the king should bathe, if they had followed the dead body.

34. Immediate bathing is laid down after copulation and (coming across) smoke from (a burning) dead body. A *śūdra* should never carry the dead body of a brahmin.

35. So also a brahmin should not carry (the dead body) of a *śūdra*. There would arise sin from these. One would reach heaven by carrying the dead body of a destitute brahmin.

36-41. One who gifts fuel for burning the (dead body of a) destitute person would get victory in battle. (One who performs the cremation of the dead) should solemnly vow that he is a relative and then circumambulate the funeral pyre in the anti-clock direction. (After the completion of cremation rite) all should get out and bathe with their clothes. Then handful of water should be offered thrice for the dead. After that one should enter the house after placing the foot on a stone at the entrance (to the house). Unbroken rice should be offered to the fire and margosa leaves should be eaten. All should sleep separately on the floor. One should eat light food that has been bought. The learned one who offered the ball of rice becomes pure after shaving, bathing with white mustard and sesamum and wearing different clothes on the tenth day. Neither cremation with fire, nor the rites of offering waters should be done in the case of the death of children who had not grown teeth and in the case of abortion. The gathering of the bones (of the cremated) should be done on the fourth day. It is laid down that one may touch (the polluted person) after (the rites of) gathering of bones have been done.

CHAPTER ONE HUNDRED AND FIFTYEIGHT

Kinds of pollution

Puṣkara said :

1-4. I shall describe the pollution due to abortion accepted by Manu and others. In the case of abortion (pollution lasts) so many nights proportionate to the period of pregnancy (for the mother). If the abortion is after four months (the pollution lasts) for three days, after five months for ten days. It lasts for four nights in the case of royal people, and for five days in the case of tradesmen. It lasts for eight days in the case of *Śūdra* and for twelve days in the case of others. Purification has been prescribed for women. But the father (of the abortive) (becomes pure) by bathing alone. No bathing has been laid down for those who are *sapiṇḍas*. (If the abortion) occurs in the seventh or eighth (month), (pollution lasts) for three nights. In the case of the death of a child after the appearance of the teeth, the *sapiṇḍas* become purified immediately.

5-7. (If the death of a child occurs) before the tonsure, the pollution is for a night, and before the undertaking of the vow (for the investiture of sacred thread) (it lasts) for three nights (for *sapiṇḍas*). For the mother and father (the pollution) lasts for ten nights. (For those who are not *sapiṇḍas*), if the child dies before the appearance of the teeth, or after the tonsure, (the pollution) lasts for three nights. If the child dies before it is three years old, one becomes pure after a night. In the case of a warrior class purity is after two days, and three days in that of the tradesman. A *Śūdra* becomes pure after five days. (If the death occurs) before marriage, (the pollution lasts) for twelve days.

8. In the circumstances in which the pollution for brahmins is noted as three nights, in such cases a *Śūdra* (would have)

for twelve days and the warrior class and tradesmen (would have) for six and nine (days respectively).

9. If (a child) dies (when) two years old no cremation (be done). It should be buried in the ground. No water of libation need be given even if it had been named. Or it should be done if the child had grown teeth. (If death occurs) after the investiture of sacred thread (one has pollution) for ten (days). A brahmin who propitiates the fire and is well versed in the scriptures becomes pure after a day.

10. (The pollution) lasts for three or four days if one is inferior or still less inferior in his (learning).

11. One who has neglected the worship of fire (would become pure) after five days. One who has neglected the duties of a brahmin (would become pure) after ten days.

12. A warrior gets pure after nine days and a brahmin possessing qualities after seven days. A tradesman possessing qualities (becomes pure) after ten days. A *śūdra* (gets pure) after twenty days.

13. (The normal period of pollution) would be ten days for a brahmin, twelve days for the warrior class, fifteen days for the tradesman and one month for the *śūdra*.

14. If there be excellent qualities (the normal pollution) for ten days would become three days, for three days would become a day, for one day would become immediate purity. One has to infer in this way in all the cases.

15. The pollution for the servant, pupil, hired servant and disciple, residents of same place will be as that of their masters. But the pollution for the death would be separate.

16. In the case of pollution due to the death of a person who performs sacrifices etc., the obsequial rites should be commenced after doing purification before the cremation is done.

17. One may touch a person (polluted) after one-third (of the period of pollution) is over in the case of all the castes. (The period after which) one may touch (the polluted) is three, four, five and ten days for the (four) castes respectively.

18. The gathering (and immersion) of the bones should be done on the fourth, fifth, seventh and ninth day (after the death) for the (four) castes in the successive order.

19. (Pollution) would be for a day in (the death of) girls not given in marriage and three days in (the death of) girls

after marriage. A night and two days enclosing it has been laid down (as the period of pollution) in the (death of) married sisters and others.

20. The *gotra* for the unmarried girls would be that of the father, and for the married girls that of their husbands. The water of libation (should be offered) to the father on both sides in the case of the married.

21. (The pollution) for the parents (would be) for three days after ten days in (the case of) the death of the daughter. O Brahmin ! the *sapiṇḍas* would become pure immediately in (the death of the boy) before the tonsure is done.

22. (The pollution would be) for one day in (the death of a girl) before the marriage (had been done) and three days after the girl had been given in marriage. (The pollution lasts) for a night and two days enclosing it in (the death of) the brother's son and immediately for the *sapiṇḍas*.

23. A brahmin becomes pure after ten days in the death or birth through the brahmin woman. So also (a brahmin becomes pure in the death or birth) through the warrior, tradesman and *śūdra* respectively after six or three days or one day.

24-27. This should be known as (applicable) to the *sapiṇḍas*. I shall describe (the pollution) in (the case of the death of) illegitimate (children). It is said that there would be purity after three days in (the case of the death of) the illegitimate children adulterous wives and women who had former husbands. No water of libation (need be given) for those born in the mixed castes and, those gone abroad and those committing suicide. Pollution for those having one mother and two fathers and brothers having illegitimate wives; would be one day for birth and two days in (the case of) death. (I have described) the pollution for *sapiṇḍas*. I shall describe (the pollution) for those having relationship by the libation of waters.

28. One becomes pure after bathing with the dress worn at the death of a person who is not a *sapiṇḍa*, whether the dead be a boy or has died abroad.

29. But *sapiṇḍas* would become pure only after ten days in the case of both birth and death. The members of the same family (distant relatives) (would become pure) after three nights. Those belonging to the same clan would become pure after bath.

30. The relationship of *sapiṇḍa* would cease after the seventh (generation) in the case of males. The status of being eligible for waters of libation would cease after the fourteenth generation.

31-33. If details about one's birth are not remembered he is said to belong to another clan. One who hears about the death of a person abroad within ten days after the death, pollution would last only for the remaining period of the days. (If it is heard) ten days after (the death) pollution would be for three days. (If one hears) after one year had elapsed, one becomes pure after touching waters. (The pollution lasts) for a night enclosed by two days (in case of death) of the maternal uncle, a night (in case of death) of the pupil, priest and relatives.

34. Only bathing is laid down in (case of) the death of son-in-law, daughter's son, nephew (sister's son), brother-in-law and the son of the latter.

35-38. (The pollution would last) for three days in (case of) the death of maternal grand-mother, preceptor and maternal grand-father. It is laid down that one becomes pure (in the following cases): (Death at the time of) a famine, the decadence of kingdom, a calamity has befallen, in case of death due to misfortune (or at the time of eclipse), in the death of) knower of brahman by means of fire, (in case of the death of) one who constantly performs sacrifice, one who observes a vow, a celibate, in (case of death at) battle and national calamity, while gift is being made, a sacrifice is being performed and the marriage is being conducted. An atonement in the form (of discarding life) by entering fire or water has been laid for those who kill a brahmin, a cow, and the king as also those who (attempt to) commit suicide, and one who has an incurable disease and one who is incapable of doing *svādhyāya*[1].

39-41. If a woman or a man dies by hanging one's self on account of disgrace, anger, affection and insult, somehow he (or she) would live for a lakh (of years) in an impure hell. If an old man who has neglected the ritual enjoined by the scriptures and code books, discards his life, (the period of) pollution is for three days. The collection of bones (after cremation) is done on the second day. Water of libation is to be done on the

1. Study of one's own branch of the *Veda*.

third day. The *śrāddha* (annual ceremony for the dead) should be done on the fourth day.

42. In the death of people struck by lightning or by fire, pollution lasts for three days for the *sapiṇḍas*. Women who had taken to heretic path and those who had killed their husbands are not eligible for water of libation.

43. If one's father or mother had died (in the above described manner), one should wear wet clothes, and fast. After one year had gone, the obsequies should be done as laid down.

44. If one, who is an *asapiṇḍa*[1], carried the dead body, he becomes pure after bathing with the dress, touching the fire and taking ghee.

45. If one eats food from them, he becomes pure only after ten days. If not eaten food there, he becomes pure that day itself. Then one should not stay in that house.

46. The brahmins who carry the dead body of a destitute brahmin, get the benefits of a sacrifice at their each step and would become pure after bathing alone.

47-49. A brahmin who accompanies the dead body of a *śūdra* becomes pure after three days. After having mourned the death of a person along with the relatives, one should avoid making any gifts or doing *śrāddha* etc. will-fully for a day. If a *śūdra* woman delivers (a child) or dies in one's house, the vessels should be discarded and one becomes pure after three days by sweeping the floor (of the house with water). The dead brahmin should not be made to be carried by a *śūdra* when the same (caste men) are available.

50. After bathing the dead body, it should be cremated after being worshipped with flowers. Never should the (dead) body be cremated naked. A part (of the body) should be left (uncovered).

51-53. One who is born in the same clan should lift and place (the dead body)on the funeral pyre. A brahmin who had consecrated the sacred fire should be appropriately cremated with the three fires[2]. One who has not consecrated the sacred

1. Not a *sapiṇḍa*.

2. Sacrificial fire of three kinds *gārhapatya*, *āhavanīya* and *dakṣiṇa*—the fire perpetually maintained in the house, a consecrated fire taken from the previous, the sacred fire lit on the south.

fire (should be cremated) with one (among these three fires). The others (should be cremated) with the ordinary (fire). The son should place the fire at the face with the words, "You were born from this. May this be born from you again. This is for the heaven". The relatives (should utter) the name and clan (of the dead) and sprinkle water once.

54. The water of libation (should be done) in this way in the death of the maternal grand-father, and the preceptor. The water of libation is optional in (the case of) the death of the girl friend, sister's son, father-in-law and priest.

55-56. The son should offer the water of libation for ten days (with the syllable) *apo naḥ śośucad.*[1] Ten balls of rice should be offered (at the death) of a brahmin. Twelve (balls of rice) are remembered (to be offered) for a warrior. Fifteen (balls) are spoken to be for a tradesman. It is said that thirty (balls) (should be offered) for a *śūdra.* A son or daughter or anybody else may offer the balls of rice like the son.

57-59. After biting the margosa leaves, becoming self-controlled and sipping water at the entrance to the house, all should touch fire, water, cowdung, white mustard and place foot slowly on a stone and enter (the house). Till the pollution goes pungeant and saline food should not be taken. Flesh should not be eaten and all should sleep on the floor. After bathing, food bought from outside should be eaten. The same person, who did the first day rite, should do rites for ten days. In the absence (of that person), a brahmacāri may offer the balls of rice and waters of libation

60. Just as the pollution for the *sapiṇḍas* at the death (of their relatives) has been laid down, so also it would be in regard to birth for those who desire for purification.

61. The pollution due to death is applicable to all. But the pollution due to birth is only for the father and mother. Pollution would be for the mother only and the father would become pure after touching water.

62. If it had been decided that *śrāddha* should be done on the day of birth of the (dead) son, cow, gold and dress should be given as gift on that day.

63. The pollution due to death (goes) with (another)

1. *ṚV.* I.97.1a.

pollution. The pollution due to birth (goes) with (another) pollution. Even between them one gets pure with that which occurs first.

64. If a pollution due to death occurs while there is pollution due to birth and vice-versa, the pollution is based on that of death only and not on that of birth.

65. If one pollution occurs when there is already another pollution, if the two are equal or the latter is less equal then the pollution should be completed with the former. If the two are unequal, it should be completed with the second according to the words of Dharmarāja.

66. If death occurs at the end of another death, there is purification after the end of first pollution. The greater one always affects the lighter one. But the lighter one never affects the greater one.

67. If the pollution due to death or birth occurs in the midnight when there is already a pollution due to death or birth, all would become pure with the remaining part of pollution. That is that part of the night added to two days.

68. If the pollution occurs in the morning, one becomes pure after three days. In both cases one should not eat food from that family.

69. One should refrain from making any gifts. If one happened to die, he should do rites of atonement. There is no sin if it is done unknowingly in the former. Otherwise, it would be for a day for the one who dines.

CHAPTER ONE HUNDRED AND FIFTYNINE

The merits of the offer of libation and the performance of good deeds

Puṣkara said :

1. One would reach heaven whether the cremation is done or not done if Lord Viṣṇu is remembered. The dead gets redemption if the bones are immersed in the waters of the Ganges.

2-4. One remains in heaven till (the period) his bones remain in the waters of the Ganges. No cremation (is laid down) for those committing suicide and those fallen (from righteous living). Even for them it is beneficial to drop their bones in the waters of the Ganges. The waters and food offered for them would be absorbed in the sky. The (rite of) *Nārāyaṇabali*[1] should be done with great compassion for the dead fallen (from righteousness). Hence, that person would enjoy favour.

5. The lotus-eyed (Viṣṇu) is without decay. That which is offered there will not perish. Lord Janārdana (Viṣṇu) is the vessel because that protects from falling.

6. It is certain that (Lord) Hari (Viṣṇu) is the only (god) who confers enjoyment, emancipation etc. for the fallen. Seeing the people dying one should do the helpful righteous deeds.

7. Even after the death (of a person), the relatives would not be able to follow the dead person. The path of death is different for all others except the wife.

8-15. Only the deeds accompany one wherever one may go. One should do today the work of tomorrow and in the forenoon that of the afternoon. The death does not wait to see whether (the work) has been done or not done. One who is attached to the plot, market and house and has his mind drawn towards something else, death takes him and goes away like the she-wolf seizes the ram. No one is dear, nor one is an enemy of time. When the life (period) and one's work are over, (it) endures and takes away the people. Even if pierced with hundred arrows one does not die at the inopportune time. One does not live if the destined time has come even if he has been touched only by the tip of *kuśa* (grass). Medicines and sacred syllables and others cannot save one who is destined to die. Certainly one's past actions find the doer like (the cow finding its) calf. That which precedes one's birth and that which succeeds one's death is not explicit. Only that which is in between is explicit in this world. Just as we have the boyhood etc. for the body, so also another body is got. Just as the body wears another new dress, so also the soul (gets another body). (The soul) is always indestructible. Hence one should discard grief.

---

1. A particular funeral ceremony.

CHAPTER ONE HUNDRED AND SIXTY

Duties of a brahmin leading life in the forest

Puṣkara said :

1-2. Listen to me ! I shall describe the duties of an anchorite leading life in the forest. He should have matted hair, worship fire, sleep on the ground and wear the hide of an antelope. He should live in the forest. He should maintain his life with milk, roots, *nivāra* (rice growing uncultivated) and fruits. He should not take alms. He should bathe thrice a day. He should observe celibacy.

3. The duty of an anchorite is to worship gods and guests. A householder after having seen the grandchild should resort to the forest.

4-5. The third part of one's life (should be spent in the forest) either alone or with the wife. One should do severe penance in the midst of five fires in the summer, under the clouds as the shelter in the rainy season, with wet dress in the winter. One should resort to a life of not expecting (any thing from anybody) and go on straight in (different) directions.

CHAPTER ONE HUNDRED AND SIXTYONE

Duties of an ascetic

Puṣkara said :

1. I shall describe the duties of an ascetic which confer knowledge and release (from cycles of birth and death). When one reaches the fourth part of his life, he should renounce contact (with men).

2-3. One should renounce on that very day when he gets disinterested (in worldly activities). A brahmin should leave the house after performing the *Prājāpatya*[1] rite, worship of

1. Giving away the whole of one's property before entering the life of an ascetic.

all gods along with the (appropriate) fee and invoking fires in one's own self. One should move alone daily. One should resort (to the village) only for a morsel of food.

4-5. The ascetic should be indifferent and should not acquire wealth. A bowl, roots of a tree, tattered clothes and equanimity towards everything are the characteristics of a liberated soul. One should neither welcome death nor life.

6-8. One should await only the time just like a servant (waiting for) the command. One should set his foot (at a place) purified by his look, drink water purified with a cloth, utter words purified by truth, do (things) (that are considered to be) purified by the mind. A vessel made of gourd or wood or earth or burnt ashes (are the symbols) of an ascetic. An ascetic should seek alms daily (from the house) when the smoke has ceased, the pestle has been set aside, the charcoal has been put out, the inmates have eaten, the food vessel has been kept inverted after eating.

9. Begging is of five kinds—collected from different places like a bee, unintended (not already fixed), that has already been fixed, temporary (arranged just when the ascetics seek alms) and (food) made ready and brought (to him).

10. (The alms) may be (received) in the vessel in the hand or transferred from the vessel to the vessel. He has to examine the state of men (from whom alms are received) due to their discreditable conduct.

11. One should pursue righteousness entertaining purity of thought in whichever order of life he may be interested. He should treat all beings equally. The cause of righteousness does not lie in the symbol (associated with the different orders of life).

12. Although the fruit of the *kataka* tree purifies the water, the water cannot become pure by the mere mention of its name.

13. An honest person, eunuch, lame, blind and deaf person associated with the wicked on account of ignorance get liberated by pious men.

14. If an ascetic kills any being unknowingly during the day or night he should bathe for purification and do the *prāṇāyāma* six time

15-16. (The ascetic) should discard his body having bones as the pillar, united with sinews, besmeared with flesh and blood, covered with skin, full of foul smell of urine and feces, subject to old age and grief. (It is also) the abode of diseases and afflictions, emotional and non-eternal.

17. Firmness, forgiveness, self-restraint, not-stealing, purity, control of senses, modesty, learning, truthfulness and absence of anger are the ten characteristics of righteousness.

18. The ascetics are of four types—*kuṭīcaka*, *bahūdaka*, *haṁsa* and *paramahaṁsa*. Each succeeding one is superior.

19-26. An ascetic would be liberated, whether he is an *ekadaṇḍin* (holder of one stave) or *tridaṇḍin* (holder of three long staves tied (together). Abstaining from killing, truthfulness, not stealing, celibate life, and non-possession of things are the five moral observances for an ascetic. Purity, gratifying, penance, study of vedic texts of one's school and worship of the deity are the (five) self-imposed moral observances. The *padmaka*[1] and others are the postures. The *prāṇāyāma* (the controlled breathing) is of two types—*sagarbha* and *agarbha*. The *garbha* type is that associated with the repetition and contemplation (of a sacred syllable) and *agarbha* is the opposite. Each one of these is again of three kinds—inhalation (filling), retention and exhalation (emptying). The breath is said to be filling as it fills up, retention as there is no movement, and emptying on account of emptying. It is also of three kinds on account of difference in the (period of) measure, such as twelve, twenty-four and thirtysix *mātrā* respectively. One *mātrā* is the time (taken) for (pronouncing) a short vowel. One should repeat syllables like the *praṇava* (*oṁ*) slowly. The *pratyāhāra* (restraining the organs) is (only) for those who repeat (sacred syllable). *Dhyāna* is the contemplation on god. The firmness of mind is the *dhāraṇā*. *Samādhi* is the state of continuous existence in *brahman*. This self is the supreme *brahman* (of the form of) truth, knowledge and bliss. I am that supreme *brahman*, effulgent self, the (lord) Vāmadeva (Śiva) liberated *oṁ*.

27-28. (I am) devoid of a body, sense organs, mind, intellect, life and ego. (I am) free from (the states of) waking, dreaming and deep sleep, (and I am) the *brahman* of the fourth (state). (I am) eternally pure, realised, liberated, truth, bliss and without

1. The posture of sitting erect with crossed legs, the right foot resting on the left loin and the left foot on the right loin.

a second. I am the *brahman*, the supreme effulgence, undecaying (and) all-pervading lord Hari (Viṣṇu).

29. That person who (is in the) Sun, that I am, the undivided, *oṁ*. (I am) one who is devoid of all beginnings, equal towards grief and pleasure and having forbearance.

30-31. A person would become *brahman* being pure in one's thought and after having pierced the primordial egg. One should perform the vow of *cāturmāsya*[1] on the full moon day of *āṣāḍha* (June-July). Then one should move out on the ninth day etc. One should have the shave at the junction of two seasons. The atonement for ascetics are contemplation, (doing) *prāṇāyāma* and (the practice of) *yama*, (moral observances).

CHAPTER ONE HUNDRED AND SIXTYTWO

The code of laws

Puṣkara said :

1-2. I shall describe concisely the code of laws as narrated by Manu, Viṣṇu, Yājñavalkya, Hārīta, Atri, Yama, Aṅgiras, Vasiṣṭha, Dakṣa, Saṁvarta, Śātātapa, Parāśara, Āpastamba, Uśanas, Vyāsa, Kātyāyana, Bṛhaspati, Gautama, Śaṅkha and Likhita. You listen to that which would yield you enjoyment and emancipation. The path of action adhering to the Vedas is of two kinds—taking active part in worldly life (*pravṛtta*) and abstaining from worldly acts (*nivṛtta*).

3-5. An act performed for (getting) particular object would be taking active part in worldly life. Abstaining from worldly acts is preceded by true knowledge. The study of the *Vedas*, penance, knowledge, control of senses, non-injury and service to the preceptor all confer extreme pleasure. But the knowledge of one's own self is the most superior to all.

6-7. It is the leading one among all knowledge. One gets ambrosia from that. A learned man who studies his own self

1. A period of four months during which an ascetic has to stay at the same place.

and sees equally his own self in all beings and all beings in his own self attains identification of his own self with the *brahman.* One should make equal efforts in (the acquisition of) knowledge about self and in the study of *Veda.*

8-10. This is the same for all the twice-borns and it is specially (laid down) for brahmins. One who knows the scriptures and sciences and their import is set for becoming identical with brahman even as he is living in this world and remaining in different stages of life. The commencement of vedic study of one's own school should be in the month of *śrāvaṇa* (July-August) in the (asterism) *śravaṇa.* (It can also be done) in the (asterism) *hasta* or Monday or fifth day (of the lunar fortnight) in the (month) of *śrāvaṇa,* or in the (asterism) *rohiṇī* in the month *pauṣa* (January-February), or in the *aṣṭakā* (the three days 7th to 9th).

11-18. The study of *Veda* should be commenced as laid down outside on the banks of a tank. There would be cessation of vedic study for three days at the death of the pupil or the officiating priest or the preceptor or the relative. So also (there would be cessation of vedic study) at the beginning and conclusion of the vedic study if a person well-versed in one's own branch of *Vedas* (dies). If there is thunder at the (time of) twilight or a hurricane or earthquake or fall of meteor (cessation of study is laid down). Even if the study has been completed and the ceaseless study has been made in the forest (there would be cessation of study). So also (there would be cessation of study) on the fifteenth, fourteenth and eighth days of a lunar fortnight, at the time of eclipse (of the sun or moon), at the junctions of seasons, after having dined at a *śrāddha* and after having received a gift. (There would be cessation of study) for a day and night if a hare or frog or mongoose or dog or serpent or cat or pig goes in between (the preceptor and the pupil). It is the same if there is lightning or rising of planets. If the sounds of a dog or a jackal or ass or owl (are heard) once, five times or six times or at a place impure, or associated with a corpse, *śūdra,* or an *antya* (the fifth caste), cremation ground or a person fallen from righteous living, (there is cessation of study). (So also there is cessation of study) in evil asterism, and when there is lightning, thunder and floods. (So also there is no study) after eating, with wet hands, remaining in waters, at midnight, (and on the days when there is) excess of wind, dust storm, morbid heat, the fall of snow and at the time of twilight and while having other fears. (So also there is no study) while running or being disturbed by animals or when a great person has come home or while climbing a mule, camel, vehicle, elephant, horse, boat and tree. These are known to be the thirtyseven temporary (instances) of cessation of the vedic study.

CHAPTER ONE HUNDRED AND SIXTYTHREE

Mode of performance of a śrāddha

Puṣkara said :

1-2. Listen to me. I shall describe the procedure for (the performance of) annual ceremony that yields enjoyment and liberation. After having invited brahmins the previous day, they should be welcomed in the afternoon, worshipped and seated on the seat. Two (brahmins are invited) in the ceremony intended for gods and one by one in the ceremony intended for departed forefathers. They (are made to sit) facing the east in the ceremony for the gods. There may be three or one (brahmin) in the ceremony for forefathers.

3-7. The same (procedure is followed) in regard to the ceremonies) of the maternal forefathers also. (I shall describe the procedure for) the *vaiśvadeva*[1]. After having given (waters) for washing hands and *kuśa* (grass) for the sake of seat and having obtained permission (from brahmins) (all gods) should be invoked with the syllables, *viśvedevāsaḥ*[2]. After having spread the barley then, and pouring water in the vessel containing *pavitraka* (the purifying *kuśa*) with (the syllables) *śanno devi*[3] and then the barley with (the syllables) *yavo'si*[4], the

1. An offering made to gods.
2. ĀpŚ. S. 3-10-1 d.
3. ṚV. 1ú.9.4a.
4. ĀpŚ. S. 7.9.10.

libation is placed on the hand with the sacred syllables *yā divyā*[1]. Then, after having offered waters, fragrance, flowers, incense and lamp, and shifted the sacred thread to (rest on) the right (shoulder), the forefathers should be circumambulated. The forefathers should be invoked with the syllables *uśantastvā*[2] extending two *kuśa* (grass). After having been permitted by them, one should recite (the syllable) *ā yantu naḥ*[3].

8-15. Sesamum should be used in the place of barley. Respectful offering of water should be made as before. After having done it, the remains of libation should be collected in a vessel as laid down and the vessel is turned upside down with the (syllable) *pitṛbhyaḥ sthānamasi*[4]. Then the cooked rice covered with ghee should be taken (in hand) and asked, "shall I offer it to the fire ?". Being permitted (to do so saying) "Do it", one should offer it to the fire as in the ceremony (done) for the manes. The remnants of offering should be given with devotion in vessels secured according to one's status or especially in silver (vessels). After having offered food the vessel should be consecrated with (the sacred syllable) *pṛthivīpātraṁ*[5]. Then the thumb of the brahmin should be placed therein with (the recitation of the sacred syllable) *idaṁ viṣṇuḥ*[6]. After reciting *gāyatri*[7] together with the *vyāhṛtis*[8] and the hymn *madhuvātā*[9] it should be stated "(eat) comfortably". They should also eat controlling their speech. They should be served the cooked rice and the clarified butter after the repetition of (sacred syllable) of purification. Then cooked rice should be taken (and shown and enquired) : "Are you satisfied ?". The remaining cooked rice should be scattered on the ground and water should be sprinkled one by one. The cooked rice (that was scattered) should be gathered together with sesamum and as in the case of the ceremony for the manes the balls of rice should be offered

---

1. ĀpŚ.S. 22.28.13.
2. ĀpŚ.S.8.14.18.
3. *cf. ā yantu naḥ* V. Sam. 19.58 a.
4. Y.Dh. 1.234.
5. Y.Dh. 1.237.
6. Y.Dh. 1.237. Āp.Ś. 2-6-1.
7. *Oṁ bhūrbhuvassuvaḥ tatsaviturvareṇyaṁ* etc.
8. *Oṁ bhūḥ* etc.
9. ĀpŚ.S. 16-25-1. ṚV. 1-90-6a.

remaining facing the south in the proximity of the place where the food was eaten (by the brahmins).

16-20. (It is done) in the same way for the maternal forefathers also. Then water for sipping is offered. Then the words of benediction should be uttered. So also the undecaying waters (should be offered). After having paid fees befitting one's capacity, the syllable *svadhā* should be pronounced. After-having been permitted to say, (the words) *svapitṛbhyaḥ svadhā*[1] (*svadhā* to my forefathers) should be said. When (the brahmin) says let *svadhā* be (repeated), it should be done so. Then water should be sprinkled on the ground. Water should be offered with the (repetition of the syllables) *priyantāṁ*[2] or *viśve devaḥ.*[3] After having said "Let our donors, the *Vedas* and the progeny flourish. Let not our earnestness dwindle. Let us have plenty to give"[4] and uttering sweet words (the brahmins) should be allowed to go. The satisfied manes should be bade adieu after (repeating the syllable) *vāje vāje*[5] .

21-23. The vessel in which the remnants of libation had been poured earlier, that vessel of the manes should be made upright and the brahmins should be bade adieu after following them in such a way as circumambulating. After having eaten (remnants of) the food partaken by the forefathers, one should observe continence that night in the company of brahmins. After having done the circumambulation of the manes in the *nāndi*[6] in connection with the impurity caused by the birth of a child, they should be worshipped with the balls of barley mixed with curd and (fruit of) jujube.

24. The *ekoddiṣṭa*[7] (ceremony) (is done) without (the worship of) (Viśve)devas. There would be only one libation and one purificatory rite. The (offering should be made) in the

---

1. MS. 1.6.1.45.
2. MS. 11.9.2.
3. See p. 457, vv 3-7.
4. Y.Dh. 1.245.
5. ṚV. 1.30.7b.
6. The ceremony performed in memory of the manes, preliminary to any festive occasion such as marriage etc.
7. The rite performed for one individual deceased not including other ancestors.

āvāhana fire without the instrumental (syllable) with the sacred thread lying on the right shoulder.

25.. One should say 'let you get up' in place of 'imperishable' and 'may you be satisfied' in place of bidding adieu to the manes (in the former). They should say "We are satisfied"

26-27. Four vessels containing fragrant waters and sesamum should be kept apart, the vessel of the dead person should be sprinkled with (waters), the waters of libation from the vessels of the forefathers with the two (sacred syllables) beginning with) *ye samānā*[1]. The remaining (acts) should be done as before. When this *ekoddiṣṭa*[2] becomes the *sapiṇḍikaraṇa*[3] (it should be done adding the (dead) woman also.

28. If the *sapiṇḍikaraṇa* has to be performed for a (dead) person within a year (after death), the food for him should be given to a brahmin the whole year together with a vessel filled with water.

29. The ceremony should be done on the day of death for every month in a year and should be done for every year as the food (offered) every month.

30-31. (The forefathers would be satisfied for) a month with cooked rice and a year with *pāyasa* (sweet liquid made with flour, rice, sago etc.). The forefathers get pleased by a month more with (the offer of) flesh of the fish, deer, ram, bird, sheep, spotted antelope, black antelope, *ruru* deer, boar and hare in the succeeding order.

32-33. The offer of any one of the following—the flesh of a buffalo, of a kind of sea crab, cooked rice with honey, the flesh of the red goat, *kālaśāka*, the flesh of a rhinoceros while at Gayā would (please the manes) immensely. So also (the offer made) on the thirteenth day in the asterism of *maghā* in the rainy season (would) no doubt (please the manes).

34-35. One who does the (annual) ceremony always makes grow the prosperity of his daughter, progeny, attendants, animals, chief among the sons, ghee, agriculture, trade, animals-cloven-footed and not cloven-footed, sons possessing the lustre of *brah-*

1. ĀpŚ. S. 1.9.12 a; T. Dh. 1.253.
2. See p. 453. fn. 7.
3. The rite performed to merge the soul of the dead person with the ancestors.

man, gold, silver and the excellence of the relatives. He will also get his desires fulfilled.

36. The ceremony is to be done on all days from the first lunar day except the fourteenth day. (The ceremony) is to be done on that day (fourteenth) for the sake of those who were killed by weapons.

37-39. One who does the ceremony as laid down gets heaven, progeny, radiance, valour, land, strength, excellence of sons, progeny with prosperity, importance, sons, unimpeded sovereignty, trade, lordship, unimpaired health, fame, absence of grief, excellent state, wealth, learning, the accomplishment of a physician, silver, cows, small cattle, horses and long life.

40-41. (If the ceremony) is done in the asterisms commencing with *Kṛittikā* and ending with *bharaṇi* one gets all these desires fulfilled. The Vasus, Rudras, Ādityas, the deities in the form of manes get pleased with the men who satisfy the manes with (the performance of) ceremony. The forefathers being pleased confer on men long life, progeny, wealth, learning, heaven, liberation and comforts.

CHAPTER ONE HUNDRED AND SIXTYFOUR

The propitiatory rite for the planets

Puṣkara said :

1. One should commence the propitiatory rite for the planets if one desires for prosperity or appeasement (of planets) or rains, long life, or nourishment or exorcising for malevolent purposes.

2-3. Sun, Moon, Mars, Mercury, Jupiter, Venus, Saturn, Rāhu and Ketu (the ascending and descending nodes of Moon referred to as planets) are known to be planets. (The images of) these planets should be made of copper, crystal, red sandal, gold, silver, iron and lead respectively.

4-7. Otherwise (the images may be made) of gold and worshipped. Or their figures may be drawn in the circles drawn with fragrant materials. The dress and flowers should be offered matching their respective colours. Lines made of perfumes and *guggulu* as the incense should be offered. *Caru*[1] should be offered to each god along with the sacred syllables (as follows) :*ā kṛṣṇena*[2] *imaṁ devā*[3], *agnirmūrddhā divaḥ kakut*[4] and *udbudhyasva*[5] are said to be the syllables in order. *Bṛhaspate atiyadaryaḥ*[6], *annāt parisrutaḥ*[7], *śaṁ no devī*[8], *kāṇḍāt*[9] and *ketum kṛṇvan*[10] are the (syllables).

8-9. The *arka*, *khadira*, *apāmārga*, *pippala*, *udumbara*, *śamī*, *dūrvā* and *kuśa* are the twigs in order. Each one of these should be offered to fire one hundred and eight times or twenty-eight times together with honey, clarified butter and curd.

10-12. Rice boiled with coarse sugar, rice boiled with milk or water, cooked food, dish of liquid rice and milk, curd rice, ghee, small round cakes made of flour, flesh and rice mixed with coconut and other things should be offered to the planets in the respective order. A wiseman should feed the brahmins according to one's capacity after having worshipped them as laid down according to one's knowledge. Cow, conch, ox, gold, dress, horse, black cow, iron and goat are the things to be given as gifts in order.

13-14. One should worship a planet with great effort if that planet remains in a bad house at that time for that person. They were blessed by lord Brahmā (that they should be) worshipped (by the people). The rise and fall of the people are subject to the planets. They are the existence and the non-existence of the world. Hence the planets ought to be worshipped.

---

1. An oblation of rice, barley and pulse boiled.
2. Y.Dh. 1.299.
3. Y.Dh. 1.299.
4. ĀPŚ. S. 5.28.11.
5. ĀPŚ. S. 3.13.1.
6. ĀPŚ. S. 17.21.7.
7. V. Saṁ. 19.75a.
8. Y.Dh. 1.300. ṚV. 10.9.4a...
9. ĀPŚ. S. 16.24.1.
10. ĀPŚ. S. 20.16.3. ṚV. 1.6.3a.

CHAPTER ONE HUNDRED AND SIXTYFIVE

Code of conduct

Fire-god said :

1. One should contemplate the soul, the lord that remains in the heart like a lamp, having his mind, intellect, memory and the senses not resting on any other object.

2. One should give things got from a cow, curd, ghee, and milk. Saffron, *masūra* (a kind of pulse), *vārtāku* (egg-plant) and *kodrava* (a species of grain) should not (be given).

3. When the son of *Siṁhikā* (Ketu) swallows the Sun (that is, there is an eclipse of the Sun due to the descending node of the Moon) at the junctions of the lunar fortnights, it is known to be *hasticchāyā*. The ceremony and gift made then (yield) undiminishing (benefits).

4. When the Moon is in (the asterism) *paitrya* (*maghā*) and Sun in (the asterism) *kara* (*hasta*), the day is known as *Vaivasvatī* and the shadow is that of *kuñjara*.

5. The remnant of that offered unto the fire should not be given in the (rite of) *vaiśvadeva*. The fees should be paid on the hand of the brahmin in the absence of fire.

6-9. A woman is not defiled by a paramour and also a brahmin (who has defaulted) from vedic rites. A woman enjoyed by employing force or fallen into the hands of an enemy should be abandoned. She becomes pure after the menstrual period. Earlier, women were enjoyed by the celestials such as the Moon, *Gandharvas* and Fire. The men enjoy them later. (Hence) they do not get defiled by any one. If a woman is impregnated by one not belonging to the same caste, that woman becomes impure till the extraneous matter is not discharged. When the extraneous matter had come out, she then becomes pure by her menstrual flow.

10-12. Whoever does not see another as different from his own self, becomes here the *brahman* itself. One who rejoices in his own self is (said to be) free from impurity. Some describe union as the union of objects and senses. Verily unrighteousness has been taken as righteous view by those ignorant (people). Others (say) that the union of the soul and mind as the union.

13. After having restrained the mental activity and unifying one's soul with the Supreme Being, one gets released from bondage. This union (is said to be) the outstanding one.

14. It is a collection of five family members. The sixth one is extremely great. It cannot be conquered by the celestials or demons or mortals.

15. All those (the senses) which look externally should be made (to look) inward. The collection of senses (should lie) in the mind. The mind should be united in the soul.

16. One's soul that is free from all feelings should be fixed in the *brahman*. This is the knowledge and meditation. Everything else that remains would be elaborating the text.

17. That matter which (one thinks) as non-existent in all the worlds is spoken to be as present. That which is spoken (as being present) does not remain in the heart of another (other than a *yogi*).

18. As a virgin (does not know) the happiness of a woman so also that *brahman* is really unknowable. One who is not a *yogin* never knows it just as a born-blind person (does not know) the pot.

19. Having seen a renouncing brahmin, the Sun moves from his position (thinking that) "This person would pierce my orb and reach the Supreme Brahman".

20. (One would get as) a fruit of that what one would get by fasting, vow, bathing, sacred spots, the fruit of penance and the gaining of a brahmin.

21. Supreme Brahman is the single letter. The control of breath is the supreme penance. There is nothing more purifying than the (sacred syllable) Sāvitrī (addressed to the Sun-god).

22. One who eats even from an outcaste would get pure by contemplation. The meditator is the soul, the meditation is the mind, the object of meditation is lord Viṣṇu and the fruit is lord Hari.

23-28. Just as the *Paṅktipāvana*[1] purifies in a ceremony so also the ascetic (gets) imperishable worlds (for others). I do not find an atonement that purifies a brahmin if he slips after entering the state of abstinence. He is the killer of (his) soul.

---

1. One who purifies a party of diners by his presence. He would be a learned person and follower of codes of conduct.

Those who are the progenitors through their wives after having renounced, (their progeny) become outcastes known as *bindulā*. There is no doubt. An eagle dies after hundred (years). A dog (lives) for twelve (years). A vulture (lives) for twenty years. Then the pig (dies) after ten (years). A tree without flowers becomes fruitless and is surrounded by thorns. Then having been burnt by forest fire it becomes a dry trunk on a peak. Then it remains a lifeless matter for eight hundred years. After one thousand years are over it becomes a *brahmarākṣasa* (spirit of a brahmin indulging in sinful deeds). One gets liberation from this either by deluge or the annihilation of the family. One should always resort to (the practice of) *yoga*. There is no other sacred syllable that removes sin.

CHAPTER ONE HUNDRED AND SIXTYSIX

Duties of different castes

Puṣkara said :

1-5. I shall describe the codes of conduct (laid down) by the scriptures and codes of law. (The codes of conduct) are of five kinds. That is known to be the codes of conduct of the castes in which the authority rests on the caste alone. A thing that is laid down resting on the stages of life is said to be the code of conduct of the stages of life. The codes of (the above) both which are made prevalent by a motive is known to be *naimittika* (occasional or produced by a cause) like the codes of atonement. O King ! the student, the householder, the forester and an ascetic are said to be the codes of conduct of stages of life. The fourth one is the practical code and the fifth one is the metaphysical code. It is said to be the practical code which has its say in the six qualities.

6. This is of three kinds. According to Manu *mantra* (mystic syllable) and *yāga* sacrifice (are) metaphysical codes. Those which belong to the two classes are justice and administration of justice.

7. Even for the same kind of things it is said that there would

be option due to *yāga* (sacrifice). The same duty is laid down in the codes also as in the scriptures.

8. Followers of Manu (declare) that the code brings forth repetition for the purpose of the work undertaken. Otherwise the repetition is specially for the quality of limitation.

9. Followers of Manu (state) that this (repetition) is only a special practical code for the result. One would reach the world of Brahmā by doing the forty-eight purificatory rites.

10-19. (They are) the impregnation[1], causing the birth of a male child[2], the parting of the hair[3], rites done at the birth of a child, naming the child, the first rice-feeding of the child[4] the tonsure[5], investiture of the sacred thread, the collection of four vedic observances—the completion of one's studies, marriage, the collection of five devotional acts—towards the gods, manes, mortals, beings and sages, seven simple domestic sacrifices—the *aṣṭakā* and *pūrvaṇasrāddha*, *śrāvaṇī*, *agrahāyaṇī*, *caitrī*, and *āśvayujī*, then the *haviryajñas* (such as) the *agnyādheya*, *agnihotra*, *darśapaurṇamāsa*, *cāturmāsya*, *āgrahāyaṇyeṣṭi*, *nirūḍhapaśubandhaka* and the *sautrāmaṇi*, the seven *somasaṁsthās*—commencing with *agniṣṭoma*—*atyagniṣṭoma*, *uktha*, *ṣoḍaśī*, *vājapeyaka*, *atirātra* etc. and the eight basic human qualities—compassion, forbearance, freedom from malice, absence of exertion, propitiation, charity and absence of desire. Whoever possesses these attains the supreme. One should observe silence in the six (acts)—evacuation of bowels, copulation, passing urine, cleaning the teeth, bathing and eating. One should avoid making a gift again (of an article received as a gift) drinking separately the ghee and milk in the night, removal of teeth and hotness in the seven (kinds of) flours. One should not gather flowers without bathing. It is said to be unfit for the (worship of) gods.

20. If a person not belonging to the same *gotra* and not related does the cremation of a dead person, he has to complete ten day rites by offering balls of rice and water.

1. Is done when the conception is known.
2. Is done before the embryo begins to move.
3. Is done in the eighth month after pregnancy.
4. Is done in the six months after the birth of a child.
5. Is done in the third y ear of a child.

21. If one has to dine with unequal persons there is no defiling of the row if (the two) are separated by water or grass or ashes or door or pathway.

22. The five oblations to the (five breaths) (at the commencement of taking food) should be done with the union of the ring-finger and the thumb.

CHAPTER ONE HUNDRED AND SIXTYSEVEN

Propitiatory rite for the planets

Fire-god said :

1. I shall again describe (the mode of performing) the propitiation of the planets for the sake of prosperity, peace and success. The propitiation of planets is of three kinds—oblations ten thousand times, lakh times and crore times.

2-7. After having invoked planets in a circle at the north-east of the fire-pit with the sacred syllables, Jupiter (should be located) at the north (of that circle), Mercury at the north-east, Venus at the east, Moon at the south-east, Mars at the south and the Sun in the middle. Saturn (should be located) at the west, Rāhu, the ascending node at the south-west and Ketu, the descending node at the north-west. Iśa (lord Śiva), Umā, Guha, Viṣṇu, Brahmā, Indra, Yama (god of death), Kālaka and Citragupta[1] are the presiding deities (of the places where the planets have been located). The fire, water, earth, Hari (lord Viṣṇu), Indra, the presiding deity of the east, Prajeśa (the lord of men), Serpent (god) and Brahmā are the subordinate deities respectively. Gaṇeśa, Durgā (the consort of Śiva), wind, sky and Aśvinī gods (are also the gods). They should be worshipped with their respective basic vedic syllables. The twigs of *arka*, *palāśa*, *khadira*, *apāmārga*, *pippala*, *udumbara*, *śamī*, *dūrvā* and *kuśa* should duly be offered in the fire mixed with honey, clarified butter and curd one hundred and eight times.

1. An inmate of the world of Yama recording the vices and virtues of mankind.

8. After having filled one, eight and four pitchers, the final oblation (should be made). Then the *vasordhārā*[1] should be offered and the fees paid.

9-10. The sacrificer should be anointed with (the waters of) the four (pitchers) along with sacred syllables. (The following benediction should be made)—"May the celestials—Brahmā, Viṣṇu, Maheśvara, Vāsudeva, Jagannātha, lord Saṅkarṣaṇa Pradyumna and Aniruddha be for your victory."

11-13. May Indra, Fire-god, Yama, Nairṛta, Varuṇa, Pavana (wind), Kubera (lord of wealth), Śiva, Śeṣa (the lord of serpents) along with Brahmā and the gods of the directions always protect you all. May the (divine) mothers, the chaste wives Kīrti, Lakṣmī, Dhṛti, Medhā, Puṣṭi, Śraddhā, Kriyā, Mati, Buddhi, Lajjā, Vapus, Śānti, Tuṣṭi and Kānti who have gathered here anoint you.

14. The planets Sun, Moon, Mars, Mercury, Jupiter, Venus, Saturn, Rāhu and Ketu, who have been appeased, anoint you.

15-18. May the celestials, demons, *gandharvas*, *yakṣas*, *rākṣasas*, serpents, sages, Manus, cows, the divine mothers, the wives of gods, trees, serpents, progeny of Diti, heavenly nymphs, attendant gods, weapons, scriptures, kings, vehicles, herbs, gems, the constituents of time, rivers, oceans, mountains, holy waters (places), clouds and the west-flowing rivers all these anoint you for the attainment of all desires. After having adorned, one should then give gold, cow, food, earth etc.

19. O Rohiṇī ! The Tawny-coloured ! You are to be worshipped by all gods and hence you are made up of all holy spots and gods. Hence you give me tranquillity.

20. O Conch ! You are the meritorious among all merits, auspicious among all auspiciousness. You are borne by lord Viṣṇu always. Hence (you) give me tranquillity.

21. O Righteousness ! You make the universe rejoice in the form of the bull. You are the location of eight forms.[2] Hence you give me tranquillity.

---

1. A profuse oblation of ghee offered in the fire through a long bamboo or plough.

2. Relating to Śiva, being the five elements, sun, moon and the sacrificer.

22. O Golden embryo of the Fire god or Sun that is lying imbedded inside the golden egg ! You give me appeasement that yields limitless meritorious fruits.

23. The pair of yellow cloth is the favourite of lord Vāsudeva. Hence lord Viṣṇu (would be pleased) by making a gift of the same. Hence give me tranquillity.

24. You are lord Viṣṇu in the form of Fish from which the nectar has come. You have the moon and the sun as the vehicle always. Hence you get me tranquillity.

25. O Cow of the colour of (lord) Keśava (Viṣṇu), on account of the fact that you are the entire earth that always removes the sin, you give me tranquillity.

26. (O Iron) On account of (the fact that) all deeds as well as weapons such as the plough are always subject to your control, you get me tranquillity.

27. On account of (the fact that) you are always the origin of fire and remain as a constituent of all sacrifices, you get me tranquillity.

28. Because the fourteen worlds remain in the limbs of the cow, let me have good in this world as well as in the next.

29. On account of the fact that the beds of Keśava and Śiva are not empty let my bed also be not empty in every birth being given (now).

30. Just as the celestials are established in all gems so also let the celestials get me tranquillity by my gift of gems.

31. Just as the other gifts are not equal to one-sixteenth (of the merit) of making a gift of land, may I have peace by the gift of the land.

32-41. (The performance of) sacrifice (to appease) the planets with ten thousand oblations with the payment of the fee (secures) victory in battle. At the time of marriage, festivities, sacrifices, rites for the installation and for the fulfilment of desires, it is said (that one should do) the two—the oblations a lakh times and crore times. In the (oblation) ten thousand times a pit of one cubit length and another pit having a girdle and hole (should be made ready) at (the exact spot for building) the house and pavilion. (There should be) four sacrificial priests. In the (oblation for a) lakh times there may be the self alone. These are ten times meritorious. (The pit may be a square of) four cubits or two cubits (long). Here Tārkṣya (the bird vehicle of lord Viṣṇu) should be worshipped more. (He should be addressed as) "You are the vehicle of highly adorable god and your body is composed of the sound of *sāman* (melodies). You are always the remover of things. Hence you get me tranquillity. As before the sacrificial pit should be sanctified and the oblation lakh times performed. The *vasordhārā*[1] should be given then. (Then) bed, ornaments and other things should be offered (as gift). There may be ten or eight sacrificial priests in the performance of oblations lakh times. (By the performance of this) one would get sons, food, kingdom, conquest, enjoyment and liberation. One who performs oblation a crore times after making different gifts, would kill his enemy as a result of it. The sacrificial pit (may be a square) of four or eight cubits and there may be twelve sacrificial priests. (There may be) twentyfive or sixteen (priests) and four (?)[2] on a cloth at the entrance. One who does oblation crore times gets the desired things and reaches the world of lord Viṣṇu. The oblation (may be done) with the sacred syllables of planets, or the *gāyatrī* or those of Viṣṇu, or those addressed to the fire god or those of Śiva or the well-known vedic (hymns). One gets the benefit of (doing) *aśvamedha* (sacrifice) by (making oblations with) sesamum, barley, ghee and grains.

42-44. (In the oblations intended) to cause enmity or sorcery the sacrificial pit should be a triangular one. The twigs (should be offered) with the left hand together with bones of the eagle and fire by (those) who contemplate evil for their enemy and who have red dress and untied hair. "Let the person who hates have enemies. *Hum phaṭ*". This is the (sacred syllable). The image (of the enemy) made of flour should be cut with a knife and the enemy should be killed. Or one ball of rice should be offered. One who does so would go to heaven.

---

1. See p. 468 fn. 1.
2. The text is cryptic. The exact significance is not known.

CHAPTER ONE HUNDRED AND SIXTYEIGHT

Kinds of major sins

Puṣkara said :

1. The king should punish the men who do not perform atonement (for their own misdeeds). One should perform atonement (irrespective of the fact that the misdeed was done) with one's wilful desire or not.

2. One should never eat (food) from intoxicated, angry and sick men. (One should not eat food) touched by great sinners and that touched by a woman in her courses.

3-9. (One should) also (not take) food (prepared) for a group of persons, food from the courtezan, an usurer, a singer, a cursed person, an eunuch, a (woman) having a paramour in the house, a washerman, a noxious person, a panegyrist, a cheat, a false ascetic, a thief, one who has undergone a punishment, one who is born to an adulterine, one who is born to a widow, one who is controlled by a woman, one who sells scriptures, an actor, a weaver, and food from an ungrateful person. One should avoid food from the blacksmith, hunter, washerman of sarees, falsely renounced person, a harlot, an oilman, one who had ridden (on a horse etc.) and fallen and one's enemies. So also (one should not eat food) from a brahmin, being not invited by that brahmin. So also a *śūdra* should not eat food from a brahmin even if invited. If one happens to eat unknowingly from the other among these, one has to fast for three days. After having eaten knowingly one should observe the *kṛcchra*.[1] One who had eaten food from a Caṇḍāla and śvapaca and the semen, feces and urine, should observe the *cāndrāyaṇa*.[2]

10-11. One should observe *taptakṛcchra* after having eaten food within ten days of pollution, food intended for the dead or that is smelt by a cow or the remnant of that eaten by a *śūdra* or a dog and the food from a fallen person. (When the food has been taken) at the time of pollution one should observe *kṛcchra*. Whoever eats food from a person having pollution also becomes impure.

---

1. A simple expiation of fasting etc.
2. Fast regulated according to the phases of the moon.

12. An excellent brahmin who had drunk water from a well into which a five-nailed dead animal (had fallen) or containing feces, should observe fast for three days.

13-21. In all the cases the *śūdra*, *vaiśya* and *bhūmipa* (the ruling class) (would have fasting) one fourth, half and three-fourth (of days prescribed for the brahmins). A brahmin who has partaken the urine and excreta of a bird, boar, mule, camel, jackal, monkey and crow should observe *cāndrāyaṇa*.[1] One gets purified by (observing) *taptakṛcchra*[2] after having eaten dry flesh, food (intended) for the dead, (flesh of) *karaka* (a species of bird) (and also after eating the flesh) of a carnivorous animal, boar, camel, jackal, monkey, crow, cow, man, horse (and) camel and after having eaten mushroom, the village cock as well as the flesh of an elephant. So also a *brahmacārī* having eaten at the *āmaśrāddha*[3] and consumed honey or garlic or onion etc. get purified by (doing) *prājāpatya*[4] etc. So also one should do *cāndrāyaṇa*[5] after having eaten flesh made ready (cooked) by himself. So also *pelugavya*[6] and *peyūṣa*[7] which cause excess of phlegm and *vṛtā-kṛsarasaṁyāva*[8], *pāyasa*[9], cakes, fried eatables made of flour, flesh of animal not prepared for a sacrifice, food intended for the gods, oblations and all (kinds of) milks except (those) of cows, she-buffaloes and goats are prohibited as well as their waters ten days old. The hare, porcupine, *godhā* (a kind of an alligator), rhinoceros and tortoise are (those among) the (animals having) five nails (whose flesh) could be eaten. The remaining ones are prohibited. One may eat fish such as the *pāṭhīna* (a kind of sheat-fish), *rohita* and lion-faced fish.

---

1. See note 2 on p. 471.
2. Drinking water with milk and ghee once in three days for twelve days.
3. An ancestral rite in which uncooked food is offered.
4. A kind of fast for 12 days, eating food in the morning for the first three days, in the evening for the next three days, only if given as alms the next three days and a plenary fast the rest of the days.
5. See note 2 on p. 471 above.
6. The exact meaning is not known.
7. The milk of the cow within seven days after calving.
8. Food consisting of wheat flour, rice and sesamum not prepared for any religious purpose.
9. Rice boiled with milk or sugar.

22-23. (Having eaten) all (eatables) made of barley and wheat and (all) transformations of milk, *vāgaṣādgavacakra* (?) and others, that which is oily and (the food) kept overnight, a brahmin should do the *agnihotra*[1], kindle the fire and as desired observe *cāndrāyaṇa*[2] for a month. The posture of *vīrāsana*[3] is said to be conducive.

24-25. The killing of a brahmin, drinking of wine, stealing and copulating with preceptor's wife are said to be great sins. The association with them, pleasure in untruth, miserliness in a king, speaking ill of the preceptor are equivalent to the killing of a brahmin.

26. Neglecting the *Vedas*, censuring the *Vedas*, bearing false witness, killing of a friend, eating forbidden food and clarified butter are the six equivalents to the drinking of wine.

27. The stealing of the entrusted such as a man, horse, silver, land, gems like diamond are remembered to be equivalent to the stealing of gold.

28. Cohabiting with consanguineous girls, (women) of low caste, wife etc. of the son of a friend are known to be equivalent to cohabiting with the wife of the preceptor.

29-40. Killing of a cow, doing a sacrifice for an outcaste, adultery, selling oneself, forsaking the preceptor, mother, and father as well as one's vedic study, the fire-worship and the son, marrying before the marriage of one's elder brother, getting one's daughter married to a person whose elder brother is unmarried, conducting a sacrifice for them,seducing a girl, practising usury, breaking of a vow, selling a tank, garden, wife and son, becoming an outcaste by the non-performance of the religious rites, forsaking the relatives, teaching the servant taking instruction from a servant, selling of things prohibited for sale, exercising control over all the mines, instituting a potent amulet, destroying herbs, living by means of a woman, disregarding one's work, felling of unwithered trees for fuel, taking many wives, associating with those who despise women, commencing some action for the benefit of one's own self, eating of censured food, not invoking the

1. A daily oblation to the fire.
2. See note 2 on p. 471.
3. Posture of squatting on the thighs, the lower leg being crossed over each other.

sacrificial fires, indulging in stealing, not discharging the debts, studying of false scriptures, bad conduct, (doing) deeds harmful (to others), stealing grains, metal and cow, cohabiting woman fond of drinking, killing a woman, a *śūdra*, a *vaiśya*, or a *kṣatriya* and atheism are all minor sins. Causing injury to a brahmin, the act of smelling something that should not be smelt or the wine, deceitfulness, and cohabiting with men are known to be the acts to make one an outcaste. The killing of a dog, mule, camel, lion, goat, ewe, fish, snake and mongoose are known to be *saṅkīrṇakaraṇa* (mixed acts). Getting money from the defamed, doing trade, serving a *śūdra*, and speaking untruth are known to be *apātrikaraṇa* (doing unworthy acts). The killing of insects, worms and birds, taking food followed by drinking wine, stealing fruits, fuel and flowers and cowardice are also defiling (acts).

CHAPTER ONE HUNDRED AND SIXTYNINE

Atonements for various offences

Puṣkara said :

1-4. (I) shall describe the atonements for the sins described so far. A killer of a brahmin should live in a forest for twelve years in a hut. For the sake of one's purity one should seek alms carrying the skull of the dead person on a staff. Or one should throw oneself in the kindled fire thrice with head downwards. Otherwise one should do the *aśvamedha*, *svarjit* or *gosava*. Or one should recite one of the *Vedas* and walk one hundred *yojanas*[1]. Otherwise one should give away all (his wealth) to a brahmin, learned in the *Vedas*. The impurity due to the great sins gets destroyed by these observances.

5-10. One who is possessed of minor sins (such as) killer of the cow should drink (only water along with) barley. After having had a shave he should live in the cowshed covering himself with the hide of that (cow killed by him). He should

1. A *yojana* is equal to eight or nine miles.

eat a little without alkaline things and salt in the fourth part (of the day). He should bathe in cow's urine for two months controlling his senses. He should follow the cows during the day and consume the dust rising (from their feet) standing with raised (face). After having taken and observing a vow, he should make a gift of eleven bulls and a cow. In the absence of these one should make a gift of all his possessions to those learned in the scriptures. Having caused obstruction to the movement (of a cow) one should do a fourth (of the above atonements) and two-fourth if (he had) kept (the animal) bound. It would be a fourth less (i.e., three-fourth) if yoked and in full if (a cow) has been killed. If some mishap has occurred (to the cow) in the forests, mountains, inaccessible (terrain) and (due to) sickness, one fourth (of the atonement) is laid. If it dies on account of the tying of the bell or ornament, half the above (atonement) should be prescribed.

11. A quarter less (of the above expiation) should be observed if (the cow or ox) dies on account of taming (goading) or chaining or confining or yoking to a cart or (while being tied) to the pillar, chain or rope.

12-15. When the horn or the bone (of a cow) has been broken or the tail has been cut off, one has to drink barley (water) till the cow becomes healthy. One should repeat the *gomati-vidyā*[1] and the hymn on the cow and contemplate on the *gomati* (*vidyā*). If a herd of cows has been killed accidently, one fourth (atonement) should be practised separately for every killing. There will not be any sin if any mishap occurs when some help is rendered (with good intention). Those subject to minor sins except those who have violated the vow of continence should observe this vow or the *cāndrāyaṇa*.

16-18. One who has broken the vow of continence should worship Nirṛti in the night at the cross-road with the performance of *pākayajña* (a domestic sacrifice) with a black ass. After having kindled the fire as laid down, a wiseman should offer oblation to the Moon, Indra, Jupiter, Fire-god and others with twigs, vedic hymns and clarified butter. Otherwise one should wear the hide of an ass and roam about in the world. One should

1. A vedic hymn to be repeated while observing an expiation for having killed a cow.

observe the vow for killing a brahmin after having killed an ass unknowingly.

19. Having drunk wine, through ignorance, a brahmin should drink wine of the colour of fire, or cow's urine of the colour of fire or water alone.

20-21. A brahmin, who has stolen gold should approach the king and confess his act and say, "Let you punish me". The king should take the club and kill with one stroke the person who had himself come. The expiation for the thief is by death. A brahmin (gets purified) by doing penance.

22-24. Having violated one's preceptor's bed, one should cut off the penis and testicles himself, hold (them) in the folded palms and move towards the south-west until he does not fall down. Then he should observe *cāndrāyaṇa* for three months controlling his senses. After having done wilfully one of the acts making one an outcaste, one should practise the *sāntapana*[1]. The expiation (known as) the *prājāpatya* (is laid down for the same done) unwillingly. For acts causing mixture of castes, the expiation of *cāndrāyaṇa* (should be observed) for a month.

25-29. Foı acts which defile one (drinking of) boiled barley (water) for three days would be (the expiation). A fourth part (of the expiation) for the killing of a brahmin is prescribed for killing of a warrior class, an eighth part (for killing) a tradesman and a sixteenth part (for killing) the fourth class. Having killed a cat, a mongoose, a blue jay, a frog, a dog, *godhā* (a kind of allegator), an owl, and a crow one should practise the expiation as for killing the *śūdra*. For having killed an unsteady woman belonging to any one of the four castes and for having killed a woman unintentionally one should observe the expiation as for killing the fourth class. Doing breath-control is the expiation for killing all (beings) not having bones. One should practise the expiation *sāntapana* for having stolen things of little value from another's house. One becomes pure after completing the vow.

30. The five products got from a cow are the purification

1. The expiation in which cow's urine, cowdung, milk, curd, clarified butter or water with *kuśa* is taken and fasting is observed for one night.

for the stealing of eatables, food, vehicle, bed, seat, flowers, roots and fruits.

31. Fasting for three nights would be (the expiation) for (having stolen)grass, log of wood, tree, rice in the husk, molasses, saree, hide and flesh.

32. One should be eating a small quantity of food for twelve days (having stolen) gems, pearls, corals, copper and silver.

33. (One who had stolen) the cotton or silk or woollen rope of cloven-hoofed or whole-hoofed (animal), a bird, perfume and herb (shall take) only milk for three days.

34. One who had cohabited with a woman related by blood or with the woman, or daughter of the son of a friend as well as a woman belonging to the low caste should practise the expiation for that of violating the bed of his preceptor.

35. One should practise *cāndrāyaṇa* for having cohabited father's sister's daughter, (one's) sister, mother's sister's daughter or (the daughter) of mother's brother or a friend.

36. One should practise the *kṛcchra sāntapana* for having (emitted semen) in an unnatural way or (having gone) to a menses woman or having emitted semen in the water.

37. A brahmin who had intercourse with a woman in the bullock-cart or in the water or during the day should bathe together with his dress.

38. A brahmin cohabiting a woman of the *caṇḍāla* or the low caste and having eaten (food therein) and having received a gift (from them) unknowingly gets defiled. But (done) knowingly becomes in par (with them).

39. The husband should keep the woman defiled by a brahmin confined in a room. That which a male should observe for having cohabited other's wives, the same vow should be made to be practised by her.

40. If she is defiled again being advised by a person of the same (character), only *kṛcchra cāndrāyaṇa* is remembered to be the purification for her.

41. That which a brahmin does in one night by resorting to a low-caste woman, gets rid of it by eating only that collected

as alms and by repeating (the sacred syllables) daily for three years.

CHAPTER ONE HUNDRED AND SEVENTY

The description of expiations for association with major sinners

Puṣkara said :

1. I shall describe the expiations (to be practised) by those who associate with major sinners. A man having associated with a degraded person for a year would himself be degraded.

2-3. A person who officiates as a priest or teaches or has marital relationship or travels in the same vehicle or eats together or shares a seat and has thus association with a degraded person should do that vow (relating to that act) for the purification from such an association. The water of libation should be offered (for that person) in the company of *sapiṇḍas*[1] and relatives.

4-9. On the day of degradation, a servant (of that person) should throw around a pot with water in the presence of the relatives, priest and preceptor at evening (time) as if he was dead. One should fast the whole day and observe pollution along with the relatives. (The relatives) should cease to talk with him and seize the share (of the paternal property) as the eldest. The share of the property as the eldest would be got by the younger brother excelling him in moral qualities. After the expiation has been done (the relatives) should bathe in the sacred waters of a tank and fill a new pot with water and drink water along with the degraded person. The same procedure has to be followed in the case of degraded women also. They should be supplied with dress, food and drinks and they should live near the houses (of their husbands). The hymn of Sāvitrī[2] of those brahmins (who officiate as priests for the degraded) become degenerated. (A brahmin who) has officiated so should practise

1. Those eligible to have the same rice-ball offering.
2. The *gāyatrī mantra* is called so as it is addressed to the Sun god.

three *kṛcchra*[1] (observances) and as laid down should be invested with the brahminhood. (Those brahmins) who do not practise the rites enjoined on them become outcastes and the same procedure is to be prescribed also for them.

10. One gets free (from the sin) of accepting a gift from a vile person by repeating the *sāvitrī* (*mantra*) for three thousand times and drinking milk at the cow-shed for a month.

11. For having forsaken a person who had sought refuge and having violated the *Veda*, a brahmin gets rid of that sin by taking limited food for a month.

12. One who has been bitten by a dog, jackal, mule or carnivorous village animals, or a man, camel or horse or pig gets pure by doing *prāṇāyāma*.

13-19. In the (case of) breaking the vow of *snātaka*[2] and neglecting) his duty (one should) fast. Having uttered the syllable of *huṁ* to a brahmin and (having made) familiar address to the elder, one should bathe and abstain from food the rest of the day and appease (the offended person) after prostration. One should practise *kṛcchra* and *atikṛcchra*[3] respectively for having assaulted and assaulted fatally (a brahmin). One should observe *kṛcchrāti-kṛcchra*[4] for having caused blood to come out from a brahmin. If a *cāṇḍāla* and others happen to stand at the house (of a person) unknowingly, purification should be done from the time it was known explicitly, *Cāndrāyaṇa* or *parāka*[5] are the purificatory (rites) for a brahmin. *Prājāpatya* is (laid down for the fourth class of men. The rest follow this. If the jaggery or flower (safflower) or salt or grains etc. (get polluted) they should be kept in the house and at the entrance and they should be put into the fire. It is laid down that (the polluted) earthen vessel should be discarded.

---

1. Consists of taking urine or dung or milk or curd or butter of a cow or the *kuśa* immersed water and fasting for a night.

2. The observance marking the completion of one's study.

3. A kind of severe penance to be finished in 12 nights.

4. Eating for nine days the quantity of water one can hold in the hand and fasting for three days. But compare the explanation given in the next chapter.

5. Fasting for twelve days.

20-29. Purification of the materials is laid down in the case of materials which are remnants. Those who have become polluted by drinking (water) from the same well and by touch get pure by fasting or by the five things got from a cow. A brahmin who eats as desired after having touched a *caṇḍāla*, should do the *cāndrāyaṇa* or the *taptakṛcchra*. One becomes pure after six nights after having eaten or drunk from a vessel in a melee defiled by *caṇḍāla* and others of vile (caste). Those of the twice-born communities after having eaten the remnants (of food) eaten by the low-castes should do the vow of *cāndrāyaṇa* and a *śūdra* (should do it) for three nights. A brahmin who had unknowingly drunk water from a well or pot (used by) a *caṇḍāla* should do the *sāntapana*[1] and a *śūdra* should fast for a day. A brahmin who drinks water after having been touched by a *caṇḍāla* (should fast) for three days and a *śūdra* should fast for that day. A brahmin who has been touched by a dog, a *śūdra* or by the remnants (of food) becomes pure after fasting a night and by taking the five products obtained from a cow, and (if touched) by a tradesman or a warrior should bathe (that) night. A brahmin beginning a journey and discharging urine at a forest where there is no water holding cooked food on his lap without placing it anywhere should cleanse himself, sprinkle (water on the food) and show it to the sun and fire.

30-32. I shall describe the mode of purification for travellers for having taken food both permitted and prohibited in a place habited by aliens and robbers. After having returned to one's native place (one should do) in the natural order of the castes. At the end of the *kṛcchra* a brahmin is again to be given the *saṁskāra* (purificatory rite). A warrior (class) (gets purified) after three-fourths (of the above rite), a tradesman after half of it and the fourth class after doing a quarter and gets purified after making a gift.

33. A woman in her courses touched by another woman in her courses belonging to the same caste no doubt gets purified by bathing that day itself.

34. A woman in her courses having been touched by a

1. Drinking milk, ghee or water heated once every three days.

woman of the lower caste should not eat until she gets pure. She gets pure by the purificatory bath.

35. A man having discharged urine passing through a road and drinking water forgetfully becomes pure after fasting a day and night and by taking the five products got from a cow.

36. A brahmin having discharged urine and eaten forgetfully without having cleansed himself becomes pure after drinking barley (water) for three nights.

37-38. I shall now describe the mode of purification for the brahmins who have renounced the life of a mendicant and the life of detachment. They have to do three *kṛcchras*[1] or *cāndrāyaṇa*.[2] Then they should be purified by purificatory rites such as the *jātakarman*[3] and others.

39. One whose face comes into contact with the sandal or impure thing, the means of purification for him are the earth, cow-dung or the five things got from a cow.

40. A brahmin who had shaved or sold or wears blue coloured cloth etc. for the purpose of austerity becomes pure by (doing) three *kṛcchras*.

41. A woman in her courses having been touched by a low caste or a *caṇḍāla* becomes pure on the fourth day. She has to observe (a vow for) three nights.

42. One who has touched a *caṇḍāla* or *śvapaca* or the discharge from a delivered woman or a dead body or a person who has touched it (dead body) becomes pure immediately after bathing.

43-45. A brahmin gets purified by bathing with oil after touching the bone of a man. One who had a vomitting or purging becomes pure after (smearing) with street mud and water below the navel, bathing and taking ghee. One who had done the shaving (gets pure) by bathing, One who eats food at the time of an eclipse (gets purified) by doing the *kṛcchra*. One who has eaten food with an outcaste (becomes pure) after taking (the five) things got from a cow. One who has been bitten by a dog, one who has been bitten by an insect and one who commits suicide (gets purified) by (doing) *kṛcchra*,

1. A kind of simple expiation.
2. See note 2 on p. 471.
3. Rite performed immediately after the birth of a child.

repetition (of *mantras*) and (offering) oblations. All sinners get purified by repentance and by doing oblation etc.

CHAPTER ONE HUNDRED AND SEVENTYONE

Description of certain subtle expiations

Puṣkara said :

1. I shall describe certain subtle expiations which are highly purificatory. One's sins would get destroyed by the repetition of the *puruṣasūkta*[1] for a month.

2. By the repetition of the *aghamarṣaṇa*[2] thrice one gets free from all sins. The repetition of the vedic (*mantras*) such as the (hymns of) *vāyu*, *yama* and *gāyatrī* and the observance of the vow destroys all sins.

3-7. In all the (expiations called) *kṛcchras* (there would be) shaving, bathing, offering of oblations and worship of Hari (Viṣṇu). After getting up, one should stand during the day and sit during the night (when practising the expiations). This is said to be the *vīrāsana*. One who does the *kṛcchra* in that (posture) gets rid of sins. (Eating) eight morsels (of food) everyday is known as *yati-cāndrāyaṇa*. (Eating) four (morsels) in the morning and in the evening is known to be *śiśucāndrāyaṇa*. Eating two hundred and forty balls (of food) in any manner in a month is *suracāndrāyaṇa*. One should drink hot water for three days and hot milk for the (next) three days. (Then) drinking hot ghee for three days, one should be consuming (only) wind for three days. This is said to be *taptakṛcchra*. It is said to be *śīta* (*kṛcchra*) by the (use of) cold (things).

8-10. *Kṛcchrātikṛcchra* (is that of maintaining) with water for twentyone days. (Drinking) cow's urine, cow dung, milk, curd, clarified butter and water with *kuśa* (for a day) and fasting one night is known to be the expiation *sāntapana*. The same if practised every day is known to be *māhāsāntapana*. If each

1. ṚV. X. 90. 1a.
2. ṚV. X. 190.

one of these is taken for three days, it is known to be *atisāntapana*. The expiation known as *parāka* would be (the practice of) fasting for twelve days.

11-14. Practising eating (food) once a day for three days and (eating food obtained) unsolicited in the night (is known to be) *prājāpatya*. A quarter (of the *kṛcchra*) is the *pādakṛcchra*. (Maintaining) with fruits for a month (is known to be) *phala* (*kṛcchra*) and with *bilva*, is said to be *śrī-kṛcchra*. (Similarly, one may maintain) with lotus seeds and myrabolans. (Maintaining) with flowers (is known to be) *puṣpakṛcchra*. *Patrakṛcchra* (would be) with leaves, *toyakṛcchra* with water, and *mūlakṛcchra* with roots. (So also one may maintain) with curd, milk and butter-milk. It would be *vāyavyakṛcchra* if one eats food (every day) for a month that he can hold in the hand. The expiation (known as) *āgneyakṛcchra* (is) by (the eating of) sesamum for twelve nights. It destroys one's disease.

15-16. (Eating) a handful of fried grain (every day) for fifteen days would be *brahmakūrcca*. One should fast on the fourteenth day and then eat the five things got from a cow on the full-moon day and twice-cooked food thereafter. A person who does so twice in a month gets free from all sins.

17. One who desires to be prosperous and wealthy and one who wishes to attain heaven and to have all sins destroyed should be intent on propitiating god. One who performs the expiations would get all things.

CHAPTER ONE HUNDRED AND SEVENTYTWO

The hymn which destroys sins

Puṣkara said :

1. When the minds of men indulge in (coveting) other's wives or other's property or in doing harm (to others) the expiation for that is the extollation (of the god).

2. Obeisance to that all-pervasive (four times repeated) always. I salute the All-pervasive who resides in the mind, and that lord Hari (Viṣṇu) who is the sense of my ego.

3. (Obeisance to) that lord who remains in the mind and who is unmanifest, endless and unconquered. (I salute) lord Viṣṇu (all-pervasive), the adorable by one and all, one without an origin, endless and lord of all.

4-5. Let my sin get destroyed by my contemplation on that only lord Viṣṇu, who remains in my mind, intellect and ego and that lord Viṣṇu, who is well-established in me and who makes the immovable and movable beings as made of their acts.

6. I (bow) to that Upendra[1], (lord) Viṣṇu and (lord) Hari that removes the distress of the worshipper, and who removes the sin seen in one's dream or due to imagination.

7. I salute that supreme lord Viṣṇu who is the supporting hand for one who is sinking down in the supportless dark world.

8. O Lord of all lords ! Lord of all ! Supreme soul ! One who has under him the thunderbolt ! O Lord of the senses ! (repeated three times) (My) obeisance to you.

9. O Man-lion-formed ! Endless one ! Cow-herdsman ! An Efficient cause of all beings ! One having handsome hair ! (My) obeisance to you ! You subdue the sin, the wicked (words) spoken, wicked (deeds) done and (wicked) thoughts.

10. O Keśava (one having handsome hair) ! You put down the wicked thoughts of mine under the influence of the mind and that very fierce and unworthy (act of mine).

11. The Sacred god ! Cowherdsman ! Devoted to the sublime truth ! The Lord of the universe ! The creator of the world ! O Decayless one ! Subdue (my) sin.

12-13. Let my sins done in the forenoon, midday, afternoon and night with the body, mind or speech unknowingly or knowingly or in dream get destroyed by the repetition of the three names—O Hṛṣīkeśa (lord of the senses) ! Lotus-eyed ! Consort of Lakṣmī !

14. O Lord of the senses ! Lotus-eyed ! Consort of Lakṣmī ! You destroy my sins done by my body or speech. O Consort of Lakṣmī !

15-16. Whatever sin I have committed while eating, sleeping, standing, going and remaining awake by my body, mind

1. Viṣṇu in his manifestation as the dwarf was known to be the brother of Indra and was called as Upendra.

or speech, whether little or big which brings forth a wretched birth or stay in hell, let all that be subdued by the pronunciation of the word Vāsudeva[1].

17. That which is the Supreme Brahman, the Supreme Abode, the Holiest, the Supreme, when that Lord Viṣṇu is praised let my sin get destroyed.

18. Let that position of Viṣṇu reaching which the learned never return and which is devoid of smell, touch and other (qualities), subdue all my sins.

19-21. Whoever either reads or hears this hymn, which destroys the sins, would become free from sins done by the bodies, minds and speeches. One reaches the supreme place of lord Viṣṇu (released) from all evil planets. Hence one should repeat this hymn that destroys the sin when a sin has been done. This hymn is an expiation for multitude of sins. This is the excellent one for a person practising a vow. Sin gets destroyed by expiations, repetition of hymns and vows. Then one has to do them for the sake of perfection and for enjoyment and emancipation.

CHAPTER ONE HUNDRED AND SEVENTYTHREE

Different expiations for different sins

The Fire-god said :

1. I shall describe the expiation as told by Brahmā that would alleviate the sin. That action which results in the separation of the soul from the body (death) is known to be killing.

2. One who kills a brahmin on account of anger, hate or by one's own or other's fault, would become a killer of a brahmin.

3. If one is a killer among many who are engaged in the same act and who bear weapons, all of them are considered to be killers.

4. If a brahmin dies on account of being censured or beaten or is hurt by means of wealth that person (who caused death) is said to be the killer of that person.

1. An appellation of Lord Viṣṇu in his manifestation as lord Kṛṣṇa, son of Vasudeva.

5. When some help is rendered such as (the supply of) medicine there is no sin if the recipient dies. There is no sin when the son or pupil or wife dies when chastised.

6. One should examine carefully the place, time, age, ability and sin and lay down expiation when no expiation has been indicated.

7. One should give up his life at once for the sake of a cow or a brahmin. One gets free from (the sin of) killing a brahmin by throwing himself into the fire.

8. One who kills a brahmin should hold the skull on the banner and seek alms proclaiming the act (done by him) for twelve days, eating moderately. He would become pure.

9. A man who had killed a brahmin becomes pure by doing good deeds for six years. Twofold (expiation) is laid down for a motivated action as that of an unmotivated one.

10-12. The expiation would be for three years in the (case of a brahmin) who has attempted to kill. If a warrior kills a person (the expiation would be) twofold. A tradesman or the person of the last class (doing that crime has to observe) thrice that twofold (expiation). In the case of a brahmin (causing the death) of a warrior (the expiation) would be a fourth less (of that prescribed for the death of a brahmin), and half a quarter in the case of (causing the death of) a tradesman. In the death of a warrior caused by a warrior and (the death) of an old man, woman, child and sick it would be one fourth of that for killing a brahmin. In (the death of) a tradesman (it would be) one-eighth part (of that) and it would be known to be one-sixteenth in commencing (to kill) the last caste.

13-20. One should practice the vow (prescribed) for killing the last caste for having killed a woman not wicked. A killer of a cow should drink five things got from a cow and have (the senses) subdued for a month. (He) should lie down in a cowshed, follow a cow and he becomes purified by giving a cow as a gift. It will be a quarter less in the *kṛcchra* or *atikṛcchra* for the kings and others. A brahmin who has killed a very old or very emaciated or very young or sickly cow should practice half the vow as mentioned above. He should feed the brahmins according to his ability and should give away gold, sesamum etc. It should be declared as killing a cow if the cow had been struck with clenched fist or by the elbow or the horn had been broken or had been struck with the club or stick. In the event of the death of a cow while being subdued or chained or yoked to a cart etc. or (being tied) to a post, chain or rope, one should do three-fourth (expiation of the above). One should practise *sāntapana* (if the death is due) to a log of wood, *prājāpatya* (if due) to a lump of earth, *taptakṛcchra* (if due) to a stone and *atikṛcchra* (if due) to a weapon. One who has killed a cat or an alligator or a mongoose or a frog or a dog or a bird should drink milk for three days and practise expiation (called) *cāndrāyaṇa*. (If the sin has been done) in secret, the expiation (should be done) in secrecy and (if done) explicitly, (expiation should be done) explicitly.

21-25. One should do hundred *prāṇāyāma*[1] for dispelling all sins. Beverages, grape juice, date juice, palm juice, sugar-cane juice, spirituous liquor got from the flower of *madhūka*, *ṭaṅkamādhvīka* (a kind of liquor), *maireya* (a kind of intoxicating drink) and coconut juice are not (classified as) intoxicating drinks although (they are) intoxicating. Only those which are mainly made of flours are known to be *surā* (wine). Drinking (of wine) is prohibited for the three castes. After drinking so one should do penance and become pure (by drinking) water. Then he may eat small quantity of food for a year or oil-cake once in the night. For dispelling (the sin due to) drinking of wine one should wear woollen dress, have matted hair and hold a staff. Having eaten unknowingly the excreta or urine or something which has come into contact with wine, the three castes of twice-borns require to be purified again by the performance of rites. One who has drunk water kept in the vessel for wine should observe a vow for seven days.

26. One who has drunk water belonging to a *caṇḍāla* should practise a vow for six days. One should practise *sāntapana* for having drunk water from the well or vessel belonging to a *cāṇḍāla*.

27-28. A brahmin (becomes pure by eating) the five things got from a cow for three nights for having drunk the water belonging to the last caste. (One who has eaten) fish, thorn, snail, conch-shell, shell and a small shell and has drunk fresh water becomes pure by (taking) five things got from a cow. One

1. Breathing regulated by the repetition of *gāyatrī mantra* and the *vyāhṛtis*.

gets pure after three nights after having drunk water from a well having a dead body.

29. One should practise *cāndrāyaṇa* for having eaten food from a man belonging to the lowest caste. (If one had eaten food) at the house of a *śūdra* at the time of distress, he becomes pure by means of repentance.

30-31. A brahmin eating from the vessel of a *śūdra* (gets purified) by (eating) the five things got from a cow and fasting. That which is cooked in an oven, cooked in oil, oil, curd and flour as well as jaggery, milk and juices from a *śūdra* are not prohibited (items). One who eats without bathing gets pure by fasting and repeating (sacred syllables) at the end of the day.

32-34. One who had eaten food after discharging urine without getting purified becomes pure after three nights. One who had eaten food into which hair or worm had fallen, knowingly touched by the foot, seen by one who causes abortion, or touched by a woman in her courses, licked by a crow and other (birds), touched by a dog, and smelt by cow etc. should fast for three days. One who eats the semen, excreta or urine should practise the *prājāpatya*.

35-36. It is opined that *cāndrāyaṇa* (should be done) at (the time of) *navaśrāddha*[1], *parāka* at the *māsika* (monthly rites for the dead). *Atikṛcchra* would be (in the ceremony) after three fortnights and *kṛcchra* at the six-monthly (rite). *Pādakṛcchra* would be (done) at the annual (ceremony) and one day (rite) at the second annual (ceremony). The annual ceremony will be on the preceding day and the second annual ceremony on the next day.

37. The expiation for having eaten the prohibited food is fasting. One should do the *śiśuka* expiation (*śiśucāndrāyaṇa*) for having eaten *bhūstṛṇa* (a kind of fragrant grass) and garlic.

38. One who has eaten prohibited food and remnant of food eaten by women and a *śūdra* and prohibited flesh should drink milk for seven nights.

39. If a *brahmacārī* (student) or an ascetic or one who has undertaken a vow (drinks) wine and eats flesh while he is impure due to the death (of a person) or birth (of a child), he should do the expiation (known as) *prājāpatya*.

1. The first series of ceremonies collectively offered on the 1st, 3rd, 5th, 7th, 9th and 11th days after the death of a person.

40-41. Taking away another's (belongings) by illegitimate means is said to be stealing. One who has stolen gold gets purified if the king beats him to death with a club. Otherwise he should lie down on the floor, bear matted hair, eat leaf, root and fruit and eat well only once a day. He gets purified after twelve years.

42. A person who had stolen gold or drunk wine or killed a brahmin or cohabited the wife of the preceptor or committed theft or drunk wine should practise *kṛcchra* for a year.

43. (One who steals) gems, pearls and corals, copper, silver, iron, bronze and stones should eat little quantity of food for twelve days.

44. The expiation for abduction of men or women or taking possession of lands or houses or wells or tanks is said to be *cāndrāyaṇa*.

45. The five things got from a cow are the purification for the stealing of eatables, food, vehicle, bed, seat, flowers, roots and fruits.

46. One should not take food for three nights (for having stolen) the grass, wood, tree, dry food, jaggery, dress, hide and flesh.

47-54. One who cohabits his mother, sister, the daughter of his preceptor, the wife of the preceptor and his own daughter should be deemed to have violated his teacher's bed. He should be declared as having violated his teacher's bed and made to embrace a heated and glowing iron image (of a woman) and he becomes purified by death. Otherwise a person who has violated the bed of his teacher should practise *cāndrāyaṇa* for three months. One should follow the same procedure for having cohabited even fallen women. One should perform that vow for such (women) which a person would perform for others' wives. It is laid down that one should end his life for having cohabited girls, *caṇḍāla* women, daughters and wives of one's *sapiṇḍa*. (The sin) which a brahmin commits in a night by cohabiting a women of the lowest caste is got removed by him in three years by eating (the food) got after seeking alms and daily repetition (of sacred syllables). One has to practise *cāndrāyaṇa* for having cohabited the wife of the paternal uncle, wife of one's brother, woman of the lowest caste, a woman of the *pukkasa*[1] caste, one's daughter-in-law, sister, friend, sisters of the mother and father, a woman who has been entrusted to one's care, a woman who has sought refuge, wife of maternal uncle, one's sister, a woman belonging to the same clan, a woman who desires another person, the wife of one's pupil and the wife of one's teacher.

CHAPTER ONE HUNDRED AND SEVENTYFOUR

Expiations for discontinuing the worship of gods

Fire-god said :

1-3. (I shall describe) the expiation for omission in the worship of gods and orders. One should repeat one hundred and eight times and worship twice for omission in worship. After having made oblations with the five upaniṣadic sacred syllables brahmins should be fed. One should repeat hundred times if (the idol of) the deity has been touched by a woman who has delivered a child, a woman of the lowest caste and a woman in her courses. (One should do) worship with the five upaniṣadic (sacred syllables) and two times bathing. When there is omission in the oblations brahmins should be fed. (Then one should do) oblation, bathing and worship.

4-5. When the materials for the oblation have been eaten by rats, etc., or abound with worms, that part alone should be rejected, sprinkled (with water) and the deities worshipped. When it is broken or damaged to the extent of a sprout it should be rejected. When it has been touched by an untouchable it should be transferred to another vessel.

6. If the sacred syllable or the materials get altered at the time of worship or in destroying the impediments due to the gods and mortals one should mutter the basic (syllable) and repeat again.

7. (One should) repeat one hundred times if the pot is lost. If (the image of) the deity has fallen from the hand and got

1. A kind of mixed caste.

broken or lost there will be welfare only after fasting and (doing) oblations hundred times.

8. For a man who repents after doing a sin, the best expiation is to remember lord Hari.

9. The practice of *cāndrāyaṇa* or *parāka* or *prājāpatya* destroys the sin. The repetition of the sacred syllables of the Sun, Īśa (lord Śiva), Śakti (consort of lord Śiva), Śrīśa (lord Viṣṇu) and others would destroy the sin.

10-11. The repetition of *gāyatrī*, *praṇava* (*oṁ*), hymns and sacred syllables destroy sins. The sacred syllables of the Sun, Īśa, Śakti and Śrīśa beginning with the (letters) '*ka*' etc. and their basic syllables and ending with the respective letters are separately more than a crore. (The sacred syllables) such as *oṁ*, *hrīṁ* etc. and ending with (the name) in the fourth case and (the word) 'salutation' are capable of yielding all desires.

12. The sacred syllables of (lord) Nṛsiṁha (man-lion form of lord Viṣṇu) consisting of twelve and eight letters etc. destroy sin. The reading and hearing etc. of *Āgneyapurāṇa* (would also be expiation to remove all sins).

13-16. Lord Viṣṇu is of two forms of *Vidyā*[1]. He is praised in the form of fire. The supreme lord is praised in all scriptures as the face of the celestials. He is worshipped as the conferer of enjoyment and emancipation in taking active part in worldly life as well as in inactivity. The oblations, contemplation, worship, repetition (of sacred syllables), hymns and obeisance made to lord Viṣṇu of the form of Fire (god) would destroy sins relating to one's body. Making a gift of ten gold (things), twelve (kinds) of grains, sixteen great gifts such as making a gift of something equal to one's own weight and other great gifts such as giving food remove all sins.

17. Practising vows on the phases of the moon, weeks, asterisms, movement (of planets from one constellation to another), good periods of the day and period of Manu for the Sun, Īśa, Śakti and others would destroy sins.

18-19. The sacred places such as Ganges, Gayā, Prayāga, Kāśī, Ayodhyā, Avantikā, Kurukṣetra, Puṣkara, Naimiṣa, Puruṣottama (Purī), Śālagrāma, Prabhāsa and others

1. *Vidyā*, knowledge, is of two kinds : *aparā* and *parā*, standing respectively for the *vedas* etc. and for the knowledge about supreme Brahman.

also destroy sins. The contemplation that 'I am the brahman, the supreme effulgence' would destroy sins.

20-24. The *Brahmapurāṇa* and the *Āgneyapurāṇa*, (lords) Brahmā, Viṣṇu, Maheśvara, the manifestations (of the god), all kinds of worship, the installation of the images (of deities) etc. (also remove one's sins). The science of astrology, *Purāṇas*, codes of law, penance, vow, the science of politics, *sarga*[1] etc., the medical lore, the science of archery, phonetics, metrics, grammar, etymology, lexicon, manual of rituals, logic, *mīmāṁsā* (the science investigating the vedic texts) and all other things are the lord Hari (himself). The sins of others get destroyed by seeing one who has got the knowledge about the single lord without the second from which (all are produced) and in which (all repose) and who is everything. He is verily the lord Hari. Lord Hari remains in the form of eighteen *vidyās*[2]. He is subtle and gross. He is the most supreme. He is the effulgence and the sentient, immutable, brahman, supreme, omni-present and blemishless.

CHAPTER ONE HUNDRED AND SEVENTYFIVE

Rules and regulations relating to the vows

Fire-god said :

1. Listen O Vasiṣṭha ! I shall describe the vows for men and women (to be observed) in order on the phases of the moon, weeks, asterisms, particular day (of a week), month, season, year and the entry of the Sun (from one constellation into another).

2. The *vrata* (vow) is a restraint as told in the scriptures. It is known to be a penance. The special observances of *dama* (subduing) etc. are for the vow.

1. The primary and secondary creation, genealogy of gods and sages, periods of Manus and accounts of royal genealogy.

2. The four Vedas, the six accessory texts, *mīmāṁsā*, *nyāya*, *dharmaśāstra*, *purāṇa*, *āyurveda*, *dhanurveda*, *gāndharvaveda* and *arthaśāstra*.

3. A vow is designated as a penance because it causes mortification of the body for the doer. It is said to be a restraint as it controls the collection of senses.

4-9. O brahmin ! Those brahmins who do not worship fire get prosperity by vows, fasting, restraints and many kinds of gifts. The gods etc. who confer enjoyment and emancipation become pleased. One who has turned back from sins and lives with qualities it is known as *upavāsa* (fasting). It is devoid of all enjoyments. One who is fasting should reject bellmetal, flesh, *masūra* (a kind of pulse), chick-pea, *koradūṣaka* (a species of grain), vegetable, wine, food from others, (association with) a woman, flowers, ornaments and dress, incense, perfume and unguent. (People) do not commend the cleaning of teeth and (use of) collyrium. The five things got from a cow should be used in the place of the toothstick in the morning and the vow commenced. Fasting gets vitiated by frequent drinking of water, the chewing of betels, dreaming and having intercourse during the day.

10-17. Forbearance, truth, compassion, charity, cleanliness, control of the senses, worship of gods, making oblation to fire, happiness and not stealing are remembered to be the ten general virtues (to be practised) in all vows. Befitting one's capacity one should repeat the sacred hymns and offer oblations (to fire). One should bathe daily, eat moderately and worship preceptors, gods and brahmins. One should avoid taking alkaline substances, honey, salt, wine and meat. Among the grains (all the grains) except sesamum and *mudga* (a kind of kidney-bean) are commendable. Wheat, *kodrava* (a species of grain), *cīnaka* (a kind of paddy), *devadhānya*, leguminous grain, sugar, *śitadhānya* (barley or white paddy ?), roots from the market are deemed to be alkaline things. Rice, *ṣaṣṭika* (a kind of rice), *mudga* (a kind of kidney bean), sesamum, barley, *śyāmāka* (a kind of corn), rice grown without cultivation and wheat etc. are conducive to vows. One should avoid taking pumpkin, bottle-gourd, brinjal, *uālaṅkī* (?) and *pūtikā* (a kind of herb). Sweet porridge, the flour of barley, pāṭā-herb, curd, ghee, milk, *śyāmāka* (a kind of corn), rice, rice growing without cultivation, *mūlataṇḍula* are conducive as *haviṣya* (fit to be offered as oblation) at the time of vows (in general) and *nakta* (*vrata*) (eating food only in the night) in the rites of offering made to fire. Except wine and meat, the other things are said to be conferring good in a vow.

18. A brahmin who observes the *prājāpatya* should eat in the morning for three days, in the evening for three days, without seeking alms for three days, and should not eat the next three days.

19. A brahmin who is practising the *atikṛcchra* should eat one morsel a day for three days three times as before and fast for three days at the end.

20. The expiation *sāntapana* is known to be (that of taking) cow's urine, cowdung, milk, curd, clarified butter and water with the *kuśa* and fasting for a night.

21. Maintaining with the (six) materials used in the *sāntapana*, each one for a day for six days together with fasting in seven days is known to be *mahāsāntapana*, which removes the sin.

22. *Parāka* is fasting for twelve days and it destroys all sins. If it is three-fold (of above) it is said to be *mahāparāka*.

23-30. Commencing with fifteen morsels (of food) on full-moon day, reducing one morsel a day and no food on new-moon day and then increasing a morsel a day is (known to be) *cāndrāyaṇa*. Or one *pala* (a measure of weight) of urine of a tawny cow, cowdung of half the volume of a thumb, seven *palas* of milk, two *palas* of curd, ghee one *pala*, one *pala* of water (in which *kuśa* has been dipped) should be collected. Among these, urine of cow should be gathered with the syllable *gāyatrī*[1], cowdung with *gandhadvāra*[2], milk with *āpyāyasva*[3], curd with *dadhikrāvṇa*[4] clarified butter with *tejo asi*[5], and water in which *kuśa* has been dipped with *devasya*[6]. It is *brahmakūrca* by doing as above. Then one should repeat the hymn *āpo hi ṣṭhā*[7]. They all should be mixed with the (repetition of the) hymn *aghamarṣaṇa*[8] or the *praṇava* (syllable *oṁ*). After drinking (the mixture) one gets free from all sins and reaches the world of Viṣṇu after fasting. A person who

1. The *mantra* addressed to the deity in the orb of the Sun.
2. ṚVKh. 5.87.9a.
3. ṚV. 1.91.16a.
4. ṚV. 4.39. 6a.
5. TS. 1.1.10.3.
6. TS. 1.3.1.1.
7. ṚV. 10.9.1a.
8. ṚV. 10.190.

fasts, eats only in the evening, an ascetic, and one who eats only in the sixth part of the day, avoids (eating) meat, performs the *aśvamedha* (sacrifice) and speaks truth would reach heaven. The maintenance of sacred fire, the installation (of images of deities), (the performance of) sacrifices, (making) gifts and (practice of) vows, observance of religious vow, the rite of letting out a bull, tonsure, (the investiture with) the girdle and the auspicious bathing should be avoided in the *malamāsa* (a solar month in which two new moons occur).

31. The lunar (month) would be from the new moon to the new moon. The *sāvana* (month) (would be of) thirty days. The solar month (would be reckoned) from the movement (of the sun from one constellation to another). An astral (month) is from (one) revolution of an asterism.

32. Solar month (should be taken) for the marriage etc., and *sāvana* for sacrifices etc. Lunar month is recommended for the annual ceremony and ancestral rites.

33. The fifth one would be that which concludes with the-(month of) *āṣāḍha* (July-August). One may perform the ceremony (for the ancestors) at that time whether the Sun moves into the constellation Virgo or not.

34. Whenever a lunar day occurs twice in a month in a year, there the second one is known to be the excellent one and the first one would be bad.

35. One should fast in an asterism when the Sun sets in that. The lunar days are meritorious during the day. They are auspicious in the night in the rite observed in the night.

36-37. The combination of the lunar days—second and third, fourth and fifth, sixth and seventh, eighth and ninth, eleventh and twelfth, fourteenth and full moon, the first and the new moon is of great consequence. This is individually very bad and destroys the meritorious act done previously.

38. It has been stated that (there would be) immediate purity for the kings, ministers and ascetics in (the case of) calamity at the time of marriage etc. as also in the forest path or some danger or in the assembly.

39-41. A king should not obstruct the vow of those who had undertaken a prolonged penance or of a woman. If a pregnant woman or a woman who has delivered a child or a girl who is in her monthly course becomes impure after beginning a long vow she may arrange always to do the same by someone else. If the vow is broken on account of anger or mistake or greed, one should not eat for three days. Otherwise, one should shave his head. If a person who practises a vow is unable to continue, his wife or son may be made to continue it.

42. A worship that has been begun should not be discontinued when (a pollution is caused) by the birth (of a child) or by the death (of some relative). A person observing a vow falling into a swoon should be brought back to his senses by the preceptor by (giving him) milk and other drinks.

43. Water, roots, fruits, milk, clarified butter, the desire of a brahmin, the words of the preceptor and herb are the eight (things) which do not vitiate a vow.

44-58. (One should resolve as follows) : "O Lord of vows ! I am doing this vow for the furtherance of fame, progeny, learning, prosperity, and health and for purity, enjoyment and emancipation. I have taken this excellent vow in your presence. O Lord of the Universe ! Let it come to fruition without impediment by your grace. After taking this excellent vow if I happen to die when it is not completed, let all that be complete when you, the lord of beings, are pleased. I invoke the embodied image of the vow, the prosperity of the world for all accomplishments. My obeisance to you. O Lord Keśava (one having beautiful hair) ! Be manifest. I bathe you with the five nectars, the five things got from a cow and good water mentally arranged with devotion. You become the remover of my sin. O Lord of libation ! (Here is) the auspicious libation mixed with fragrance, flower and water. Accept waters for washing (the feet), for sipping. Make me always fit to offer libation. O Lord of dress ! Accept the meritorious dress and O Good lord of vows ! Make me always covered by good dress, ornaments etc. O Embodiment of fragrance ! Accept the spotless fragrant perfume. You make me have good fragrance and (make me) free from smell of sin. Accept the flower and make me always abundant with flowers. The spotless fragrance of the flower is for the furtherance of longevity and health. Accept the incense (stick) made of ten (fragrant) ingredients, the *guggulu* and ghee. O good lord of incense ! You make me fragrant with perfumes. O Embodied form of the lamp ! You accept the lamp having upward flames and which makes everything shine. (You) make (me) endowed with lustre and elevated movement always. O Good Lord of food ! Accept the offerings such as food etc. (You) make (me) abundant with food and as a giver of food and all (things). O lord ! whatever my omission in the sacred syllable, in the act and devotion, and the worship offered to you may all that be complete for me. O lord of vows ! Give me virtue. Give me wealth, prosperity, continuous flow of qualities and fame. Give me learning. Give me longevity, heaven and emancipation. O Lord of vows ! Accepting this worship you may go now only to come again, to confer boons, O Lord !

59-62. In all the vows the embodied golden images of vows should be worshipped by the person practising a vow after bathing (according) to his means. He should sleep on the floor. (He should do) repetition (of sacred syllables), (offer) oblation and (make) gifts at the end of a vow in general. Twentyfour or twelve or five or three or one brahmin should be worshipped. The preceptors should be fed. The fee (such as) cows, gold etc., sandals, shoe, water vessel, food vessel, earth, umbrella, seat, bed, pair of dress and pots should be paid according to (one's) means to every one. The rules and regulations have thus been described.

CHAPTER ONE HUNDRED AND SEVENTYSIX

Vows observed on the first lunar day

Fire-god said :

1. I shall describe the vows for the first lunar day which would confer on you everything. The first lunar day of *kārttika* (November-December), *āśvayuji* (October-November) and *caitra* (April-May) are the days of (lord) Brahmā.

2. After having had no food on the fifteenth (lunar) day, one should worship (lord) Aja (Brahmā, the unborn) on the first lunar day (with the words) *Oṁ tatsat* obeisance to (lord) Brahmā or with *gāyatrī* for a year.

3. A golden (image of lord) Brahmā (carrying) a rosary and ladle in the right (hand) and a *kamaṇḍalu* (a wooden or earthen water-pot) and a small ladle in the left (hand) and (having) a long beard and matted hair should be worshipped.

4. According to one's means one should offer milk, (to lord Brahmā stating) that let (lord) Brahmā be pleased. A brahmin would become stainless, enjoyer of pleasures in heaven as well as on earth and wealthy.

5-6. I shall describe an excellent vow (by practising which) an unfortunate one would become fortunate. After having fasted and offering oblations on the night of the first lunar day of *mārgaśirṣa* (December-January), one would get all (things) by worshipping fire (stating) 'Obeisance to fire'. Eating food once on the first lunar day and giving a tawny (cow) at the conclusion one reaches the place of lord fire. This is known to be *śikhivrata* (vow dedicated to fire).

CHAPTER ONE HUNDRED AND SEVENTYSEVEN

Vows observed on the second lunar day

Fire-god said :

1-8. I shall describe vows (performed) on the second lunar day which would confer enjoyment, emancipation etc. Eating flower one should worship Aśvins the celestials. One who practises vow for a year would get good fortune and reach heaven. One should worship the god of Death on the second day of the bright fortnight in (the month of) *kārttika* (November-December). A practiser of the vow fasting for a year would reach heaven and (would) not (go to) hell. I shall describe the vow (called) *aśūnyaśayana* (the bed that has not become empty) which would confer (the fruit of) not becoming a widow. This should be practised on the second lunar day in the dark fortnight in (the month of) *śrāvaṇa* (August-September). "O Bearer of *śrīvatsa* (a mark on the chest of lord Viṣṇu) ! Consort of Śrī ! (Lakṣmī) ! Abode of Śrī (Lakṣmī) ! Consort of Śrī ! Immutable ! May not my life of a householder get destroyed. Let it be the conferer of virtue, materials and desire. Let not the (sacred) fires be destroyed. Let not the deities be destroyed. Let not my ancestors be destroyed on account of my married life being shattered. Just as you the lord never get separated from (Goddess) Lakṣmī, so also O lord ! let not my association with my wife get separated. O Conferer of boons, O Lord ! Just as your bed does not become devoid of (Goddess) Lakṣmī, O Slayer of (demon) Madhu ! let my bed also be not empty. One should worship (Goddess) Lakṣmī and (Lord) Viṣṇu for a year and bed and fruits should be given away (as gift).

9-12. Libation should be offered to Soma (moon) every month with the (recitation of) sacred syllables. One who lights up the courtyard of the sky ! One who is born from the churning of the milky ocean ! Enjoyer of the starry quarters of heaven ! Younger brother of Lakṣmī ! Obeisance to you. *Oṁ śrīṁ* obeisance to the Sustainer of Śrī ! One should worship lord Hari of the form of the Moon. *Dhaṁ*, *ḍhaṁ*, *bhaṁ*, *haṁ* obeisance to Śrī ! to the great soul of ten forms ! Oblation (should be made) in the night with ghee. A bed may be given to a brahmin. A pot with water and an image of the deity together with a lamp, food vessel, umbrella, shoe, seat and a vessel (may be given) then.

13-14. One who does so in the company of his wife would get enjoyment and emancipation. I shall describe the *kāntivrata* (the vow that makes one shining). It should be done in the white (fortnight) of (the month of) *kārttika* (November-December). Taking food only in the night on the second lunar day, one should worship Bala(rāma) (brother of Viṣṇu in his manifestation as Kṛṣṇa) and Keśava for a year. One gets shining (body), long life and health etc.

15-20. Then I shall describe the *Viṣṇuvrata* which gets the mentally desired (fruits), after doing it for four days in the second lunar day in the white (fortnight) of (the month of) *pauṣa* (January—February) etc. One should bathe on the first (day) with white mustard, then with black sesamum the second day) and with *vacā* (aconis calamus) on the third day and with all herbs on the fourth (day). *Murāmāṁsi*, *Vacā*, *kuṣṭha*, *uṣṭha śaileya* (bitumen), the two (kinds of) *rajanī*, *śaṭī*, *campaka* and *musta* are remembered to be the collection of herbs. One should worship with (the repetition of) the names Kṛṣṇa, Acyuta (unslipping), Ananta (endless), *Hṛṣikeśa* (the lord of the senses) with flowers duly at the foot, navel, eye and head. Libation (should be made) to Moon with the (repetition of the) names *śaśi, candra, śaśāṅka* and *indu*. The person (who does the vow should eat in the night before the moon sets. (By the practice of) this purifying (vow) for a year and a half, the performer would get all things. This vow was practised by the kings and women in the past.

CHAPTER ONE HUNDRED AND SEVENTYEIGHT

Vows observed on the third lunar day

Fire-god said :

1. I shall describe the vows (to be practised) on the third lunar day which would confer enjoyment and emancipation. Listen to me. (I shall describe) the *mūlagaurīvrata* for the (goddess) Lalitā (a form of consort of Śiva) (to be done) on the third lunar day.

2-23. Goddess Gaurī was married by Hara (Śiva) on the third day of the bright (fortnight) in (the month of) *caitra* (April-May). (Then on that day) one should bathe with sesamum and worship Śambhu (Śiva) in the company of Gaurī with golden fruits etc. "Obeisance to Pāṭalā" (saying so one should worship) the feet of the goddess and Śiva. One should worship ankles for Jayā after saying "to Śiva". (One should worship) the two shanks (by saying obeisance) to the destroyer of the three cities, to Rudra, to Bhavānī, the two knees (by saying obeisance) to Śiva, to Rudra, to Īśvara (the lord) and to Vijayā (the victorious), the hip (by saying obeisance) to Īśa for the goddess and to Śaṅkara for Śaṅkara. The two bellys (should be worshipped by saying obeisance) to Koṭavyā and the Śūlin (lord Śiva) (by saying obeisance) to the one having trident in the hand. The stomach should be worshipped (by saying) obeisance to you, Maṅgalā (the auspicious). Rudra (should be worshipped by saying) obeisance to the soul of all beings, the two breasts (by saying obeisance) to Īśānī. Similarly (lord) Śiva should be worshipped (by saying) (obeisance) to Hlādinī. Lord Śiva (should be worshipped by the words obeisance) to the great lord and the two hands (by saying obeisance) to Anantā. (Lord) Hara (should be worshipped with the words obeisance) to the three-eyed one and the arm (with the words obeisance) to the consort of the destructive fire at the end. The ornaments should be worshipped (by saying obeisance) to Saubhāgyā (the fortunate) and the great lord. The lips (should be worshipped by saying obeisance) to the (goddess) dwelling in the honey of *aśoka* (flowers) and to the lord. The face (should be worshipped) by saying obeisance to the consort of the four-faced one and to Hara and the immovable one. Obeisance to lord Hara, the lord of the man-woman form and the nose (should be worshipped) (by saying obeisance) to measured limbs. The lord of the universe (should be worshipped by saying) obeisance to the fierce one and then the two eyes (saying obeisance) to Lalitā. The destroyer of the cities (should be worshipped saying obeisance) to Sarva (all) and the palate (with the words obeisance) to Vāsantī (the one belonging to the spring), Obeisance to the consort of Śrīkaṇṭha (one having the auspicious mark on the throat) and the hair (saying obeisance) to Śitikaṇṭha (having black mark on the throat). (Obeisance) to fierce one and (the goddess) of good form and (worship) the head (by saying) obeisance to the soul of all beings. The (following) flowers should be used in order in the respective months—jasmine, *aśoka*, lotus, jasmine, *tagara*, *mālatī*, *kadamba*, *karavīra*, *bāṇa*, *mlāna*, *kuṅkuma* and *sindhuvāra* After having worshipped (goddess) Umā and (lord) Maheśvara, the (following) eight auspicious things should be placed in front : ghee, *niṣpāva*, *kusumbha*, *kṣīrajīvaka*, *tarurāja*, *ikṣu*, *lavaṇa* and *kustumburu*. One should take *śṛṅgodaka* in (the month of) Caitra (April-May) and sleep in front of the god and goddess. One should bathe in the morning, worship (the god and goddess) and worship the brahmin couple. The above (mentioned) eight (things) should be given to the brahmin. (He should then say) "Let (the goddess) *lalitā* (consort of Śiva) be pleased (by this gift of) mine. *Śṛṅgodaka*, cow-dung, *mandāra*, *bilva* leaf, water with *kuśa*, curd and milk are the things and ghee mixed with coagulated milk (are the things offered) in (the month of) *kārttika* (November-December). Cow's urine, clarified butter, black sesamum and the five things got from a cow (are the) food to be eaten duly. "(Goddesses) Lalitā, Vijayā, Bhadrā, Bhavānī, Kumudā, Śivā, Vāsudevī, Gaurī, Maṅgalā, Kamalā and Satī be pleased." Thus one should say at the time of making a gift in (the months of) Caitra (April-May) etc. He should then offer one *pala* (a measure of weight) of the purifying clarified butter and a bed should be given at the end of the vow, A golden (image of) Umāmaheśvara, (Śiva and his consort), a bull and a cow (should also be given). The performer would get enjoyment and emancipation by (offering) clothes etc. and worshipping the teacher couple. (One would get) fortune, health, beauty and longevity from the (performance of the) vow *saubhāgyaśayana.* One should perform the vow in the (month of) *nabhas* (*śrāvaṇa*—July-August) or *vaiśākha* (June-July) or *mārgaśira* (December-January) on the third lunar day in the bright fortnight. One should worship (saying) "Obeisance to (goddess) Lalitā". After having worshipped in every fortnight and having worshipped twentyfour couples at the end of the vow by (giving) clothes etc , the performer gets enjoyment and emancipation.

24-28. Thus a second way (of performance of the vow) has been told. I shall describe the *saubhāgyavrata* (the vow which confers fortune). One should avoid salt on the third lunar day in the (month of) *phālguna* (March-April). When (the vow) is completed he should give a bed and a house with household things after having worshipped a brahmin couple (by saying) "Let (goddess) Bhavānī be pleased". The vow on the third lunar day for the sake of (getting) fortune has been told. (Goddess) Gaurī confers heaven etc. So also (one would get) by doing the vow on the lunar day in (the months of) *māgha* (February-March), *bhādra*(*pada*) (September-October) and *vaiśākha* (May-June) A person who performs (the vow of) *damanakatṛtīyā* should worship with *damanaka* (fragrant leaf used for worship) in (the month of) *caitra* (April-May). (The third lunar day) in (the month of) *mārga* (*śirṣa*) (December-January) (is k.nown as) *ātmatṛtīyā* (the third lunar day relating to the soul). One who worships by giving the goddesses) Gaurī, Kālī, Umā, Bhadrā, Durgā, Kānti, Sarasvatī, Vaiṣṇavi, Lakṣmī, Prakṛti, Śivā and Nārāyaṇī duly commencing from the third lunar day in (the month of) *mārga* (*śirṣa*) (December-January), (by giving) the desired things, food etc would get fortune and gold.

CHAPTER ONE HUNDRED AND SEVENTYNINE

Vows observed on the fourth lunar day

Fire-god said :

1-5. I shall describe now the vows (to be performed) on the fourth lunar day which would yield enjoyment and emancipation. On the fourth lunar day in the bright (fortnight) in (the month of) *māgha* (February-March), one should fast and worship *gaṇapati* (the lord of attendants). One who gives sesamum rice on the fifth lunar day for a year will be happy without obstacles. *Gaṁ* oblations is the chief mystic syllable. (The syllables) commencing with *gāṁ* are the heart etc. (of the mystic syllable). Having invoked (god) (saying), "come (obeisance) to *ulka* (the fiery)". The permission (for the deity) to go (would be by saying) "Go away (obeisance) to *ulka* (the fiery)". One should worship commencing with '*ga*' and '*gam*' and ending with *ulka* by (offering) *modaka* (sweet ball) etc. (The sacred syllable would be)—"*Oṁ* we know the great fiery (god), we meditate on the (god) with the curved trunk, let that god having the tusk impel us". One who performs the vow on the fourth lunar day in the month of *bhādrapada* (September-October) would reach (lord) Śiva. One would get (all desired things) by worshipping the lord of attendants on the fourth lunar day on Tuesday. It is known to be *avighnā caturthī* (the fourth lunar day without any obstacle) on the night of the fourth lunar day in (the month of) *phālguna* (March-April). One who worships (the lord of) attendants on the fourth lunar day in (the month of) *caitra* (April-May) with *damana* would be happy.

CHAPTER ONE HUNDRED AND EIGHTY

Vows observed on the fifth lunar day

Fire-god said :

1-2. I shall describe the vow (performed) on the fifth lunar day which would confer health, heaven and emancipation. The serpents Vāsuki, Takṣaka, Kālīya, Maṇibhadraka, Airāvata, Dhṛtarāṣṭra, Karkoṭaka and Dhanañjaya should be worshipped (on the fifth lunar-day) in the bright fortnight in (the month of) *nabhas* (August-September), *nabhasya* (September-October), *āśvina* (October-November) and *kārttika* (November-December). These would confer protection from fear, longevity, learning, fame and wealth.

CHAPTER ONE HUNDRED AND EIGHTYONE

Vows observed on the sixth lunar day

Fire-god said :

1-2. I shall describe vows (to be performed) on the sixth lunar day. It should be done in (the months of) *kārttika* (November-December) etc. One who eats fruits and offers libation etc. on the sixth lunar day gets enjoyment and emancipation. The *skandaṣaṣṭī* vow (done) on the sixth lunar day in (the month of) *bhādra(pada)* (September-October) is said to (confer) undiminishing (benefits). I shall describe the *kṛṣṇa-ṣaṣṭīvrata* that should be done in (the month of (*mārgaśirṣa*) (December-January) remaining without food for a year. One would get enjoyment and emancipation (by that).

CHAPTER ONE HUNDRED AND EIGHTYTWO

Vows observed on the seventh lunar day

Fire-god said :

1-4. I shall describe vows (performed) on the seventh lunar day that would yield enjoyment and emancipation. One would be free from grief by worshipping Sun in the white lotus in the month of *māgha* (February-March). One would get everything by the worship of Sun on the seventh lunar day in the month of *bhādra(pada)* (September-October). The worship of Sun in the bright (fortnight) in the month of *pauṣa* (January-February) without taking food would destroy the sin. The seventh lunar day in the dark fortnight (in the month) of *māgha* (February-March) would confer everything. The seventh lunar day in the bright fortnight in (the month of) *phālguna* (March-April) (is known as) *nandāsaptamī*. (It confers benefit) by the worship of Sun. The seventh lunar day in the bright (fortnight) in (the month of) *mārgaśirṣa* (December-January (is known as) *aparājita* (unconquered). (It would make one so) by worshipping (Sun then). Women (who worship) on the seventh lunar day in the bright (fortnight) in (the month of *mārgaśirṣa* (December-January) and for a year would get female children.

CHAPTER ONE HUNDRED AND EIGHTYTHREE

Vows observed on the eighth lunar day

Fire-god said :

1-2. I shall describe the vows (to be performed) on the eighth lunar day. Lord Kṛṣṇa (one of the ten manifestations of lord Viṣṇu) was born in (the asterism) to *rohiṇī* on the eighth lunar day in the month of *bhādrapada* (September-October) at midnight. Hence the eighth lunar day would be victorious. By fasting on that day one would become free from sins committed in seven generations.

3. Fasting on the eighth lunar day in the dark fortnight in (the month of) *bhādrapada* (September-October) marked by (the asterism) *rohiṇī* one should worship lord Kṛṣṇa, the bestower of enjoyment and emancipation.

4-17. I invoke (the gods) Kṛṣṇa and Balabhadra (brother of the former) and Devakī (mother of the former), Vasudeva (father of the former), Yaśodā (the cowherdess who brought up

Kṛṣṇa in his childhood) and the cows. I worship them. "Obeisance to you. Obeisance (repeated) to the communion, the master of the communion and the lord of the communion. Obeisance (repeated) to the one who grazes the cows and the one who is born of communion." (Water for) bathing should be given and the libation should be made with this (utterance). Obeisance to the sacrifice, the lord of the sacrifice and the master of sacrifices. O Lord ! Accept the fragrant flowers dear to you. O Lord ! Saluted by the celestials ! Be the bestower of all my desires. O Perfumed by the incense ! You being incensed accept the incense (offered) by me. O Lord Hari ! You make me always profusely perfumed. You accept the great lamp that is lighted and offered by me and be always conferer of the light of the lamp. Make me going upwards. Obeisance (repeated) to the universe, master of the universe and lord of the universe. It has been made known to the one born of the universe etc. and the cowherdsman. Obeisance (repeated) to virtue, master of virtue, lord of virtue and to the one born of virtue etc. O cowherdsman ! You lie down. Obeisance (repeated) to one who is everything, to the master of everything, to the lord of everything and to the one born of everything. And to the cowherdsman, the purification. O The one born of the milky ocean ! The one born of the eye of (the sage) Atri ! O One having the spots resembling the hare ! Accept libations of mine in the company of *rohiṇī* (the asterism, referred to as the wife of the moon). The lord should be established on the altar. Rohiṇī together with the moon should be worshipped. (In the same way) one should worship Devakī, Vasudeva, Yaśodā, Nandaka (foster father of Kṛṣṇa) and Bala(bhadra). Showers of milk together with molasses and clarified butter should be made to fall (on the image) in the midnight. Clothes, gold etc. should be given (to brahmins). The person who practises the vow should feed the brahmins. One who does the vow of *janmāṣṭami* (the eighth lunar day, the birth-day of Kṛṣṇa) would have children and attain the world of Viṣṇu. One who does it every year seeking progeny does not know any fear. "Give me children. Give me riches, longevity, health, progeny, virtue, desire, fortune, heaven and emancipation.

CHAPTER ONE HUNDRED AND EIGHTYFOUR

Vows observed on the eighth lunar day

Fire-god said :

1. Since (the gods) Brahmā and others worshipped the (divine) mothers one should repeat (their names) on the eighth, lunar day of the group of (divine) mothers. One would get wealth by the worship of (lord) Kṛṣṇa on the dark fortnight in the month of *caitra* (April-May) and for a year.

2-10. I shall describe the *kṛṣṇāṣṭamī vrata* (the vow practised on the eighth lunar day of the dark fortnight). It should be performed in the month of *mārgaśira* (December-January). Having (fasted) in the night and becoming pure one should drink cow's urine in the night. The doer of the vow should lie on the (bare) floor in the night and worship (lord) Śaṅkara (Śiva). (One should worship) lord *Śambhu* (Śiva) in (the month of) *pauṣa* (January-February) after taking ghee lord Maheśvara (the great lord, Śiva) in (the month of) *māgha* (February-March) (taking) milk and lord Mahādeva (the great god, Śiva) in (the month of) *phālguna* (March-April) after fasting and taking sesamum. One should worship lord Sthāṇu (firm as the pillar, Śiva) in (the month of) *caitra*(April-May) taking barley and lord Śiva in (the month of) *vaiśākha* (May-June) taking water with *kuśa* and lord Paśupati (lord of the flock) in (the month of) *jyaiṣṭha* (June-July) taking *śṛṅgodaka*. One (should worship) lord Ugra (the fierce, a form of Śiva) in (the month of) *āṣāḍha* (July-August) eating cow-dung, (lord) Sarva (a form of Śiva) in (the month of) *śrāvaṇa* (August-September) eating the *arka* (the sun-plant), lord Tryambaka (three-eyed) in (the month of) *bhādrapada* (September-October) eating *bilva* leaf in the night, lord Īśa (a form of Śiva) in (the month of) *āśvayuji* (October-November) eating rice and lord Rudra in (the month of) *kārttika* (November-December) taking curd. Oblations should be made and worship should be offered in a circle at the end of the year. Cow, clothes and gold should be given to the preceptor. After having requested the brahmins thus and after feeding them one would get enjoyment and emancipation. One should eat only in the night on the eight lunar days. One who gives a cow at the end of the year would get the place of Indra (the lord of celestials). *Svargativrata* (the vow that conveys one to heaven) is described. When the eight lunar day (falls) on a Wednesday in both fortnights, then the vow should be practised. Otherwise one who eats (food) with molasses and observes discipline on that (day) would never have his fortune affected.

11-12. Eight times fist full of rice less the quantity that would rest on two fingers should be cooked and kept on mango leaves knit together and spread on the *kuśa* and (the goddess) Ambikā with her retinue and benevolent attendants should be worshipped. (The food) should then be eaten while the anecdotes (relating to the goddess) are being heard. Fees should be paid according to one's means. (One should also give) *karkaṭī* (a sort of cucumber) together with rice.

13-23. (The following is the anecdote related to the vow): (There was) a brahmin (by name) Dhīra. His wife (was) Rambhā, son Kauśika and daughter Vijayā. The bestower of wealth for that Dhīra was a bull. Kauśika took that and was grazing it in the company of cowherds. When he was bathing in the river Ganges, the bull was driven away by thieves. After bathing and not finding the bull he started searching for that in the company of his sister Vijayā. He then found a group of divine damsels in a tank and asked them to give (him) food. The group of damsels told him "You do the vow and hence (be) our guest and eat". (Accordingly) after performing the vow he ate (the food) and got (the position of) the guardianship of the forest. He then came to Dhīra with the bull and Vijayā. Vijayā was given by Dhīra to the God of Death and the father died (afterwards). On account of the merits of the vow Kauśika became the king of Ayodhyā. Seeing the parents in hell Vijayā (felt) grief-stricken. She went to the God of Death (and) implored him to show them mercy). (Finding Dhīra) come for hunting (the next day) she asked him how he got freed from hell. The God of Death said that it was after getting the two vows which Kauśika had given. The two parents reached heaven as a fruit of the two eight lunar days on Wednesday. Vijayā rejoiced and practised the vow for accomplishing enjoyment and emancipation. Those who drink eight buds of *aśoka* in the (asterism) *punarvasu* in the month of *caitra* (April-May) on the eighth lunar day of a white (fortnight) would never get grief. (The following is the prayer made to *aśoka*): "O Aśoka ! Dear to Lord Hara (Śiva) ! One produced in the month of *madhu* (January-February) ! Being tormented by grief I am drinking you. You always make me free from grief. One who worships (divine) mothers in (the month of) *caitra* (April-May) on the eighth lunar day would conquer his enemies.

CHAPTER ONE HUNDRED AND EIGHTYFIVE

Vows observed on the ninth lunar day

Fire-god said :

1. I shall describe the vow (performed) on the ninth lunar day which would accomplish enjoyment, emancipation etc. The goddess should be worshipped in the bright (fortnight) in (the month of) *āśvina* (October-November). It is known as the *gaurīnavamīvrata*.

2-4. The ninth lunar day known as the *piṣṭaka* (cake made of the flour of any grain) (is called so) on account of eating the cake and worshipping the goddess. On the eighth lunar day in the bright (fortnight) in (the month of) *āśvina* (October-November) when the sun is in the (constellation) Virgo in the asterism *mūla* is said to be the great *navamī* (ninth lunar day) which destroys the sin always. (Goddess) Durgā (a form of the consort of Śiva) should be worshipped as housed in nine places or as stationed in one place having eighteen hands. The rest (of the images) (should have) sixteen hands. The collyrium and *ḍamaru* (little drum) (should be held in two hands).

5-10. (The forms of the goddess) to be worshipped (are) Rudracaṇḍā, Pracaṇḍā, Caṇḍogrā, Caṇḍanāyikā, Caṇḍā, Caṇḍavati, Caṇḍarūpā, Aticaṇḍikā and Ugracaṇḍā (otherwise known as) Durgā, the killer of the buffalo (demon) in order at the centre. The ten-syllabled mystic formula is *Oṁ* Durgā ! Durgā ! The protector ! Oblations ! It begins with the long letter ā, has nine eyes and ends with 'obeisance'. Obeisance, *svadhā*, *vaṣaṭkāra* and *hṛt* etc. occupy six places. After having assigned the limbs in the toes to the little finger, (goddess) Śivā should be chanted. One who repeats thus the secret (syllable) would not be affected by anybody. One should worship (the goddess) as holding human skull, *kheṭaka* (club), bell, mirror, threatening posture, bow, banner, little drum and noose in left hands. One should worship (her as holding) the weapons spear, club, pike, thunderbolt, sword, dart, conch, disc and stick (in right hands).

11-15. After having repeated (the name) Kāli (twice) (a form of consort of Śiva), the animal (that is to be offered to her) should be killed with a sword. "O Kāli ! Kāli ! Vajreśvari (the goddess with the thunderbolt) ! Obeisance to the one having the metal rod ! " (is the formula). The blood and flesh got from that (killing) (should be offered) to Pūtanā (a demonness) on the south-west, to Pāparākṣasī (the demoness representing sin) on the north-west, to Caraki (a form of the goddess) on the north-east, to Vidārikā on the south-east and Mahākauśika (should be worshipped) for the fire. The king should bathe in front of that and kill the (form of the) enemy made of the cake. Offerings should be made to Skanda and Viśākha (the progeny of Śiva and Pārvatı). (The goddesses) Brāhmī and others should be worshipped in the night. Obeisance to you O Jayantī (victorious) ! Maṅgalā (auspicious) ! Kālī (dreadful) ! Bhadrakālī (Benevolent Kālī) ! Kapālinī (the bearer of (the skull) ! Durgā (difficult to reach) ! Śivā (auspicious) ! Kṣamā (forbearance) ! Dhātrī (supporter) ! Svāhā and Svadhā (the two syllables used at the time of oblations made into fire). After having bathed the goddess with the five sweet things, she should be worshipped with veneration etc. One who carries the goddess in a chariot with banner etc. and offers a victim would get all benefits.

CHAPTER ONE HUNDRED AND EIGHTYSIX

Vow observed on the tenth lunar day

Fire-god said :

1. I shall describe the vow (to be performed) on the tenth lunar day that would confer virtue, desire etc. One should

eat once on the tenth lunar day and give ten cows as gift at the end. Land and gold should be given. One would become a lord of the brahmins.

CHAPTER ONE HUNDRED AND EIGHTYSEVEN

Vows observed on the eleventh Lunar day

Fire-god said :

1-9. I shall describe the vow (to be performed on the) eleventh (lunar) day that would yield enjoyment and emancipation. One should take restricted food, avoid (eating) flesh and copulation. He should not take food on the eleventh day in both the lunar fortnights. When there is a conjunction of the eleventh and twelfth (lunar) days (lord) Hari (Viṣṇu) is present therein. One gets the merit of doing hundred sacrifices by (such fasting and) taking food on the thirteenth (lunar) day. When a part of the eleventh day exists followed by the twelfth day (if one fasts) and takes food on the thirteenth day one gets the merit of (doing) hundred sacrifices. One should never eat at the junction of tenth and eleventh (lunar) days. It would confer hell. One should fast on the eleventh day and take food the next day (and say) "O lotus-eyed ! I am eating. O The unchanging one ! (You) become my refuge". When the asterism *puṣya* rules over the eleventh day of a bright fortnight one is said to get undiminishing benefit. It is known to be destroyer of sins. If the (asterism) *śravaṇa* marks the conjunction of the eleventh and twelfth (lunar) days, it is said to be victorious. It confers victory on the votaries. The same in the month of *phālguna* (March-April) and endowed with the (asterism) *puṣya* it is said to be victorious by pious men. (It is said to be of) crores and crores of virtues. One should worship lord Viṣṇu on the eleventh day. It confers all good, (makes one) wealthy and begets progeny in this world. It makes him honoured in the world of lord Viṣṇu.

CHAPTER ONE HUNDRED AND EIGHTYEIGHT

Vows observed on the twelfth lunar day

The Fire-god said :

1-14. I shall describe the vows (to be observed) on the twelfth (lunar) day that would confer enjoyment and emancipation. The person practising the vow should eat once in the course of the day food that has been got without seeking alms, or fast or eat food obtained after seeking alms. One who practises the vow of *Madanadvādaśī* should worship lord Hari and the God of love on the twelfth day in the bright fortnight inthe month of *caitra* (April-May), if he desires enjoyment and emancipation. One who practises *Bhīmadvādaśī* on the twelfth day in the bright (fortnight) of (the month of) *māgha* (February-March) should worship (lord) Viṣṇu (repeating) "Obeisance to lord Nārāyaṇa (attribute of Viṣṇu)". He gets all things. One who practises *Govindadvādaśī* (should worship) in the bright fortnight of *phālguna* (March-April). One who performs the *Viśokadvādaśī* should worship lord Hari in the (month of) *āśvayuja* (October-November). One who gives salt on the twelfth day of a bright (fortnight) in the (month of) *mārgaśirṣa* (December-January) after worshipping lord Kṛṣṇa, is deemed to have given all niceties (of food). One who observes the vow of *Govatsadvādaśī* should worship a calf in the (month of) *bhādra-(pada)* (September-October). When the (month of) *māgha* (February-March) is over and if the twelfth (lunar) day is marked by the (asterism) *śravaṇa* in the dark (fortnight), it is said to be *Tiladvādaśī*. Bathing and oblation are done with sesamum. Sesamum balls are the offering. A lamp (should be lit) with the sesamum oil. Then water of libation should be given together with sesamum. Sesamum should be given to brahmins. One gets the fruit by doing oblation and fasting. One should worship (with the sacred syllable) *Oṁ*. Obeisance to lord Vāsudeva. One who practises the vow of *Tiladvādaśī* reaches heaven with his family. One who performs *Manorathadvādaśī* should worship in the bright (fortnight) in (the month of) *phālguna* (March-April). One who practises the vow of *Nāmadvādaśī* should worship lord Hari for a year with (the recitation of) names Keśava and others. That person would reach heaven and not hell. One becomes the performer of the vow of

Sumatadvādaśī by the worship (of the lord) in the bright (fortnight) in (the month of) *phālguna* (March-April) and the performer of the vow of *Anantadvādaśī* in the bright (fortnight) in the month of *bhādrapada* (September-October). A person who performs *Tiladvādaśī* should do oblations with sesamum and worship (the lord saying) "Obeisance to (lord) Kṛṣṇa" in the asterisms of *āśleṣā* or *mūlā* in (the month of) *māgha* (February-March). The performer (of the vow) of *Sugatidvādaśī* should worship (the lord) in the bright (fortnight) in (the month of) *phālguna* (March-April). (One should worship the lord) for a year (on the twelfth days) (saying) "O Victorious Kṛṣṇa ! Obeisance to you" to get enjoyment and emancipation. One is (known to be) the performer of *Samprāptidvādaśī* (by the worship of the lord) on the twelfth day in the bright (fortnight) of *pauṣa* (January-February).

CHAPTER ONE HUNDRED AND EIGHTYNINE

Rules of observing Śrāvaṇadvādaśī vrata

Fire-god said :

1-2. I shall describe the (mode of performance of) *Śrāvaṇadvādaśī*. Fasting (on the twelfth day) in the bright (fortnight) in the month of *bhādrapada* (September-October) marked with (the asterism) *śravaṇa* is highly meritorious. One would get the benefits of the *Śrāvaṇadvādaśī* by bathing at the confluence of rivers. (The twelfth day) marked by (the asterism) *śravaṇa* and a Wednesday is extremely meritorious for making gifts.

3-15. One should do even that which is prohibited. One should eat after the fast on the thirteenth (lunar) day. One should fast on the twelfth (lunar) day (saying) "I am worshipping Vāmana" and invoke the golden (image) (of Vāmana) in a water-pot (saying) "I am invoking Vāmana, (a form, of) Viṣṇu bearing the conch and disc. I am bathing lord Viṣṇu with waters such as the five sweet things and others in the pitcher covered by a pair of white cloth (and provided with) good umbrella and sandals. (I worship lord) *Viṣṇu* holding an umbrella and staff. Obeisance to Vāmana. O Lord of the celestials

I offer you libation. Being worshipped always with good libation and others you make me endowed with enjoyment, emancipation, progeny, fame and all fortune. Obeisance to Vāmana." With this (sacred syllable), perfume (is offered)and oblations hundred (times are made). "*Oṁ*, Obeisance to Vāsudeva." The head of lord Hari is worshipped. Similarly the face (is worshipped with the syllable obeisance) to *Śrīdhara*, and on the neck (with) "Obeisance to Kṛṣṇa", the chest (with) "Obeisance to the consort of Śrī (Lakṣmī, the arms (with obeisance)" to the wielder of all weapons", the navel (with) "Obeisance to the omnipresent", the hip (with) "Obeisance to Vāmana, the male organ with (obeisance) "to the Creator of the three worlds". The shank of lord Hari should be worshipped (with Obeisance)" to the lord of everything". The feet of Viṣṇu (are worshipped with) "Obeisance to the lord of all beings" . Offering prepared in ghee as well as pitchers with curd rice should be made. After having remained awake in the night and bathed in the morning at the confluence (of rivers) and worshipped with perfumes, flowers and other things, one should say "This handful of flowers (is offered)" "Obeisance to you, O Govinda ! One who is named as (the planet) Mercury and (asterism) *śravaṇa* ! You destroy the floods of sins and become the conferer of all happiness. O Lord ! Lord of celestials ! Be pleased with me always O Janārdana !" Vāmana is the bestower of wisdom. Vāmana himself is stationed in the materials. Vāmana accepts the gift and Vāmana also confers on me. Vāmana is always stationed in the materials. Obeisance to Vāmana". After having given fees to the brahmins and fed them, (the performer) himself should take food.

CHAPTER ONE HUNDRED AND NINETY

Mode of practising Akhaṇḍadvādaśī vrata

Fire-god said :

1-6. I shall describe the (mode of performing) *Akhaṇḍadvādaśī vrata* (unbroken twelfth day), that is complementary to all vows. The performer should worship lord Viṣṇu on the twelfth day in the bright (fortnight) in the (month of) *mārgaśirṣa* (December-January) after fasting and bathing in water mixed with five things got from a cow and drinking the same. He should give to a brahmin a vessel with barley and rice on the twelfth day. "O Lord ! that vow which has been broken by me in the (past) seven births let it now get complete for me by your grace. O Excellent Being ! Just as you are the unbroken entire world, in the same way let all my vows get completed." It is laid down for every month in the same way for four months. Otherwise (it may be practised) in the months of *caitra* (April-May) etc. Vessel (filled) with flour should be given as a gift. If the vow is begun in the (months of) *śrāvaṇa* (August-September) etc., one should break it at the end of *kārttika* (November-December). The deficiency in the vows (practised) in the seven (past) births gets fruitful by the performance (of this). One would get long life, health, fortune, kingdom and pleasures.

CHAPTER ONE HUNDRED AND NINETYONE

Mode of practising vows on the thirteenth lunar day

Fire-god said :

1-10. I shall describe vows (to be practised) on the thirteenth day that gives all (things). I shall describe *Anaṅga-trayodaśī* (the thirteenth day of God of love) that was done at first by the God of love. Lord Hara (Śiva) (of the form of) God of love should be worshipped on the thirteenth day in the bright (fortnight) in (the month of) *mārgaśirṣa* (December-January). One should take honey in the night and do oblation with ghee, sesamum and unbroken rice. One who worships Yogeśvara (Lord of *Yogas*) (on the thirteenth day of the bright fortnight) in (the month of) *pauṣa* (January-February) after using sandal and offering oblations and one who worships Maheśvara (the great lord Śiva) in (the month of) *māgha* (February-March) (on a similar day) after using pearls would reach heaven. One who practises the vow should take water and raven and worship (on a similar day) in (the month of) *phālguna* (March-April) and consume camphor and worship (lord Śiva) of his own form in (the month of) *caitra* (April-May). (By those) one would become fortunate. One should worship Mahārūpa (the lord of the great form) in (the month of) *vaiśākha* (May-June) eating fruits of nutmeg. One who practises vow should worship (lord) Pradyumna (one of the five forms of Viṣṇu) on (a similar) day in (the month of) *jyaiṣṭha* (June-July) eating cloves. One should worship the consort of Umā (Śiva) in (the month of) *āṣāḍha* (July-August) taking sesamum water. One should worship the bearer of trident in the hand (Śiva) in (the month of) *śrāvaṇa* (August-September) consuming fragrant water. (The practiser of vow) should worship Sadyojāta (one of the five forms of Śiva) in (the month of) *bhādrapada* (September-October) consuming agallochum. One should worship Indra (the lord of thirty-three celestials) in (the month of) *āśvina* (October-November) taking gold (immersed) water. The person practising vow should worship Vighneśvara (lord of obstacles, son of Śiva) in (the month of) *kārttika* (November-December) eating *madana*. The golden (image of) Śiva should be covered with mango leaves and a cow (covered and) worshipped and bed, umbrella, pitcher, sandals and vessel for edibles should be given to a brahmin at the end of the year. One should contemplate on (lord Śiva) causing delight to Rati (wife of God of love) on the thirteenth day in the bright (fortnight) in (the month of) *caitra* (April-May) and should draw *aśoka* tree with red-lead and turmeric. One who seeks pleasure should worship for a year and practice the vow of *Kāmatrayodaśī*.

CHAPTER ONE HUNDRED AND NINETYTWO

Vows to be observed on the fourteenth day

Fire-god said :

1-10. I shall describe the vow (to be practised) on the fourteenth (lunar) day that would confer enjoyment and emancipation. One should fast on the fourteenth day in (the month of) *kārttika* (November-December) and worship (lord) Śiva. One who performs (the worship of) Śiva (on) the fourteenth day would get all pleasures through the year, wealth and long life. One should take the vow of an ascetic on the eighth or third or twelfth or fourteenth day in the bright (fortnight) in (the month of) *mārgaśīrṣa* (December-January), eat fruit (only) and worship the lord. Then one should leave (taking fruits) and give fruits as gifts practising the vow of *Phalacaturdaśī*. One should worship (lord) Śambhu (Śiva) on the eighth and fourteenth days in both the dark and bright fortnights without eating. (One who practises the vow) on both the fortnights would reach heaven. One who eats food only in the night on the eighth and fourteenth days of the dark (fortnight) would get all pleasures in this world and good position in the other (world). One who bathes on the fourteenth day in the dark (fortnight) in (the month of) *kārttika* (November-December) (would be) happy, when he worships Mahendra in flagstaffs in the form of the banner. One should worship Ananta (endless), (a form of) Hari on fourteenth day of the bright (fortnight). After having made a water-vessel out of *darbha*, one should prepare cakes from the flour of a *prastha* (a measure) of rice. He should give one half (of that) to a brahmin and enjoy the other half himself. (This vow) should be done near the river and after the narration of the anecdotes of (lord) Hari. "O (lord) Vāsudeva ! Lift us drowned in the great ocean of endless mundane existence and put in the limitless form. Obeisance to you of the limitless form". After having worshipped with these (words) and bound the consecrated thread on his own hand or the neck, the performer of the *Anantavrata* becomes happy.

CHAPTER ONE HUNDRED AND NINETYTHREE

Description of Śivarātrivrata

Fire-god said :

1-6. Listen ! I shall describe the vow of Śiva's night that confers enjoyment and emancipation. The fourteenth day in the dark (fortnight) in between (the months of) *māgha* (February-March) and *phālguna* (March-April) is endowed with *kāma* (pleasure). One who practises the vow should fast, keep awake (and resolve) "I shall do *Śivarātrivrata* fasting on the fourteenth day and worship lord Śiva after remaining awake and undertaking the vow. I invoke lord Śambhu (Śiva), the conferer of enjoyment and emancipation and the boat that rescues from the ocean of hell. Obeisance to you. Obeisance to lord Śiva, the tranquil person, the bestower of progeny and kingdom, the giver of fortune, health, knowledge, material prosperity and the pathway to heaven. Give me righteousness. Give me riches. Give me fulfilment of desires and enjoyment. Give me the happiness of good quality and fame. Get me also heaven and emancipation. (By the practice of this vow) the greedy sinner Sundarasena acquired merit.

CHAPTER ONE HUNDRED AND NINETYFOUR

Details relating to the vows of Aśoka-pūrṇimā

Fire-god said :

1-7. I shall describe the (vow of) *Aśokapūrṇimā*. One should worship Bhūdhara (the supporter of the universe) and the earth on the bright fortnight in (the month of) *phālguna* (March-April). One would get the whole year enjoyment and emancipation. After having set free a bull in (the month of) *kārttika* (November-December) one should do the *nakta* (*vrata*) (eating food only in the night). One would reach the place of lord Śiva. This *Vṛṣa vrata* (vow of letting lose the bull) is an excellent one. The offering made to the fore-fathers on the new-moon day relating to the forefathers has undiminishing (benefits). After fasting the whole year and worshipping the forefathers one becomes free from sin and reaches heaven. One who worships the birthless deity (Brahmā) on the fifteenth (lunar day) (new moon) in (the month of) *māgha* (February-March), would get all (things). I shall describe the new-moon day (known as) the Sāvitrī, that is auspicious and bestows enjoyment and emancipation. A woman should practise vow on the fifteenth day (new moon) in (the month of) *jyeṣṭha* (June-July) and worship the great chaste woman (Sāvitrī) at the foot of the banyan tree with seven (kinds of) grains after fasting three nights. Women should deeply embrace the banyan tree (besmearing) with saffron etc. doing dancing and singing in the night and worship (Satyavān and Sāvitrī) in the morning (saying) "Obeisance to Sāvitrī and Satyavān". The offering should be gifted to a brahmin. After reaching the house one should feed brahmins and eat oneself and request them to go (saying) "May the goddess Sāvitrī be pleased and let (me) get fortune etc."

CHAPTER ONE HUNDRED NINETYFIVE

Vows relating to the week-days

Fire-god said :

1-5. I shall describe vows relating to the week-days that would confer enjoyment and emancipation. (The asterism) *punarvasu* on the Sunday is the hand (of Sun). Bathing with all herbs is auspicious (on that day). One who performs the ancestral rite on a Sunday would be free from disease for seven births. A Sunday (occurring) on the *saṅkrānti* (Sun's entry from one constellation into another) is the auspicious heart of the Sun. One who eats in the night on a Sunday (occurring) in (the asterism *hasta*) for a year would get everything. One who practises a vow on Mondays (occurring) in (the asterism) *citrā* seven times would be happy. One who undertakes to do the vow of eating only in the night on a Tuesday (occurring) in (the asterism) *svāti* seven times would be free from difficulties. One who takes the vow of eating only in the night on Wednesday (occurring) in (the asterism) *viśākhā* seven times would get rid of afflictions due to planets. One who eats only in the night on Thursday in (the asterism) *anurādhā* seven times would destroy all afflictions due to planets. One who undertakes to practise eating only on Friday in (the asterism *jyeṣṭhā* for seven nights would get rid of all afflictions due to planets. One who resolves to practise eating only seven nights on Saturday in (the asterism *mūla* would destroy all afflictions due to planets.

CHAPTER ONE HUNDRED AND NINETYSIX

Vows relating to different asterisms

Fire-god said :

1-7. I shall describe (the practice) of vows in (different) asterisms, Lord Hari worshipped in the asterism gives material prosperity. Lord Hari in the form of asterisms should be first worshipped in the month of *caitra* (April-May). The legs should be worshipped in (the asterism) *mūla*. The shanks of lord Hari should be worshipped in (the asterism) *rohiṇī*, the knee in the combination of *aśvinī*, the two thighs in the *āṣāḍha*, the male organ in the *pūrva* and *uttara*, the hip in the *kṛttikā*, the two sides in the *bhādrapada*, the belly in the *revatī*, breasts in the *anurādhā*, the backside in the *dhaniṣṭhā*. The arms should be worshipped in the *viśākhā*, the fingers in the *punarvasu*. Having worshipped nails in the *āśleṣā*, the neck should be worshipped in the *jyeṣṭhā*. The two ears of lord Viṣṇu should be worshipped in the *śravaṇa* and the face in the *puṣya*. The tip of the tooth should be worshipped in the *svāti*, the face in the *śatabhiṣak*, the nose in the *maghā*, the eyes in the *mṛgaśirṣa*, the forehead in the *citrā* and the hair in the *Ārdrā*. A golden image of lord Hari should be worshipped in a pot filled with molasses at the end of a year and bed, cow and materials (should be given) as fees.

8-22. Lord Viṣṇu should be worshipped in the form of the asterisms and in the form of lord Śiva. One who practises the vow (known as), *Sāmbhavāyanīya* should worship lord Hari in the asterisms of every month, in the *kṛttikās* in the (month of) *kārttika*, in the *mṛgaśirṣa* in the *mṛgāsyaka* (*māgha*), with the names, such as Keśava etc. or (with the words) "Obeisance to Acyuta (one without a loss)". One should worship lord Hari of the form of the asterisms on the day of (the asterism) *kṛttikā* in the (month of) *kārttika*. (One should resolve that) "I shall do the vow (known as the) *Sāmbhavāyanīya*, that confers enjoyment and emancipation. I am invoking the lord of great forms such as Keśava etc., that bestows everything and furthers longevity and health". Food together with a pool (should be offered) for four months commencing with *kārttika*. Rice and pulse boiled with spices (should be offered for four months) beginning with *phālguna* and sweet gruel from *āṣāḍha*. Offering should be made to the lord and brahmins in the night. One becomes pure after bathing in water (mixed with) the five things got from a cow and drinking the same. Whichever material is offered before allowing the invoked deity to go is told as offering. When lord Jagannātha (the lord of the world) is allowed to go it becomes the remains of the offering in a moment. "O Acyuta (one without a loss) ! Obeisance to you. Let my sin get destroyed and (my) merits grow. Let all my fortune, wealth etc. be without decay. Let not my progeny get destroyed. Just as you are decayless, greater than the greatest, that Supreme soul who has become the Brahman, in the same way, you make that desired by me as without a loss. O Immeasurable one ! You take away the sin done by me. One without a loss ! Limitless ! One who protects the cows ! You grace me with the desired things. O Immeasurable being ! You make me without a loss, O Excellent among beings !" After having worshipped for seven years one would get enjoyment and emancipation. I shall describe the vow (known as) *Ananta*, (endless) among the vows relating to asterisms, that would yield wealth. One should worship lord Hari in the (asterism) *mṛgaśira* in (the month of) *mārgasirṣa* drinking cow's urine. Lord Ananta (the limitless) confers endless fruits for all desires and also the same endless (fruits) in the next birth. This great vow makes one acquire a limitless acquisition of merits. It would make one get the desired objects without loss. After having worshipped the feet etc., one should eat without oil in the night. Oblation should be made for four months for the sake of Ananta with ghee. Oblation (should be made) with rice (for four months) commencing with *caitra* and with milk in (the four months) beginning with *śrāvaṇa*. Māndhātā was born as the son of Yuvanāśva as a result of (doing) *Anantavrata*.

CHAPTER ONE HUNDRED AND NINETYSEVEN

Vows performed on certain days

Fire-god said :

1-6. I shall describe the vows to be performed on certain days. I shall first explain the *Dhenuvrata* (vow of giving a cow as a gift). One who gives as a gift a cow delivering a calf together with plenty of gold and observes the *payovrata* (drinking milk oozing from the udders of a cow), reaches the exalted position. After practising *payovrata* for three days and giving a golden (replica of) *kalpapādapa* (the celestial tree that yields the desired object), one reaches the place of lord Brahmā. This is known as the *kalpavṛkṣavrata*. One should give as gift golden (replica of) earth (weighing) more than twenty *palas* and practise *payovrata* that day. That person would reach (the world of) Rudra. One who eats food only once a day for three days in every fortnight would get enormous wealth. One who observes the *trirātravrata* (vow for three nights) every day in every month eating only once (in the nights) for three nights in every month would get the place of Gaṇeśa. One who practises the *trirātravrata* intended for lord Janārdana (a form of Viṣṇu) would reach the abode of lord Hari taking with him hundreds of his own family.

7-11. One who practises the vow called *trirātravrata* should begin it on the ninth day in the bright fortnight in (the month of) *mārgaśirṣa*. One should repeat, "*Oṁ*, obeisance to Vāsudeva", a thousand or hundred times. One should eat once on the eighth, day, fast for three days worship lord Viṣṇu on the twelfth day and practise the vow in *kārttika*. After having fed the brahmins, one should give clothes, beds, seats, umbrellas, sacred threads and vessels. He should then request brahmins "Whatever has become incomplete for me in this difficult vow, let it become complete being permitted by you". One who practises the *trirātravrata* would attain lord Viṣṇu after having enjoyed all comforts.

12-16. I shall describe the *kārttikavrata* that would confer enjoyment and emancipation. One who partakes five things got from a cow on the tenth day, fasts on the eleventh day and worships lord Viṣṇu in the bright fortnight in *kārttika* would reach him by the celestial vehicle. One who eats for three nights in *caitra* and gives five goats would be happy. Drinking milk for three nights and fasting for three days on the sixth day etc. of the bright fortnight in *kārttika* is said to be the expiation *māhendra*. After having drunk milk for five nights, fasting, taking only curd, on the eleventh day in *kārttika* is (known to be) the expiation Bhāskara, that confers wealth. Taking gruel made of barley and rice, curd, milk, ghee and water on the fifth day etc. in the bright fortnight is known to be expiation *sāntapana*.

CHAPTER ONE HUNDRED AND NINETYEIGHT

Vows performed in different months

Fire-god said :

1-2. I shall describe vows (to be performed) in different months, that would yield enjoyment and emancipation. A wise man should avoid bathing with oil for four months commencing with *āṣāḍha*. One who abstains (from using) flower and salt and gives a cow (as a gift) in *vaiśākha* would become a king. One who gives a cow and fasts a month is said to practise a terrible vow and is deemed to be lord Hari.

3-4. One who bathes (daily) early in the morning for four months commencing with *āṣāḍha* would reach lord Viṣṇu. One who gives molasses and cow in the month of *māgha* or *caitra* on the third day would be the great performer of the *guḍavrata* (vow of giving away molasses) and he would get (an identical form of) consort of Gaurī. One who eats food only in the night in the months of *mārgaśīrṣa* etc. would attain the world of lord Viṣṇu.

5-7. So also one who eats only once a day and observes the twelfth day vow would do. One who rejects fruit for four months commencing with *śrāvaṇa* and gives (the fruits) as gift would get everything. One should fast on the eleventh day in the bright fortnight in *āṣāḍha* and prepare to do the vows lasting for four months. One should worship lord Hari in the *āṣāḍha* at the entry of the Sun (into a constellation) in *karkaṭa*.

8-10. "O lord ! This vow has been undertaken by me in your presence. O Keśava ! When you are pleased let it be accomplished without impediment. O lord ! If I die after taking this vow and the vow becomes incomplete, let it become completed by your grace, O Janārdana !" One should avoid eating flesh and a brahmin should refrain from (the use of) oil and worship lord Hari. One who fasts on alternate days and for three nights would reach the world of lord Viṣṇu.

11. One who practises the *cāndrāyaṇa* would reach the world of Viṣṇu, the vow of silence would be fit for liberation, the vow of *prājāpatya* eating the flour of barley would reach heaven.

12-15. One who takes milk etc. and one who takes five things got from a cow would reach heaven. A person eating vegetables, roots and fruits would reach the world of Viṣṇu. One who avoids flesh and tasty food and takes barley would reach lord Hari. I shall describe the *Kaumudavrata*. Having observed a fast on the twelfth day in *kārttika* one should besmear lord Viṣṇu (with sandal) and worship (him) with lotuses and blue lotuses and offer a lamp lit by ghee and sesamum oil. "*Oṁ* obeisance to Vāsudeva." One should worship him with a garland of *mālatī* (flowers). One who practises the *kaumuda-vrata* would get piety, pleasure, wealth and liberation. One who practises the vow of fasting in the months (specified) and worships lord Hari would get everything.

CHAPTER ONE HUNDRED AND NINETYNINE

Vows relating to different seasons

Fire-god said :

1-3. I shall describe the vows relating to the seasons that would bestow enjoyment and emancipation. A brahmin who gives away fuel in the four seasons beginning with the rainy season and gives ghee and cow at the end would become *agni-vratī*. Maintaining silence at the twilight and giving a pitcher with ghee at the end of the month as well as sesamum, bell and clothes one would be happy. (He is known to be) the performer of *Sārasvatavrata*. One who bathes with the five sweet things for a year and gives away a cow would become a king.

4-5. Eating only in the night on the eleventh day in *caitra* food should be offered to (lord Viṣṇu). That person who practises the *Viṣṇu-madvrata* would reach the golden feet of lord Viṣṇu at the end of the month. One who eats sweet gruel and offers a pair of cows as a gift would get fortune. He would be (known as) the performer of *Devīvrata*. One who offers to the *pitṛdevas* (the dead ancestors) and eats (the food) would become a king.

6-8. I have described the *Varṣavratas* (the vows relating to rainy season). I shall describe the vows relating to the movement (of the Sun). A person who keeps awake in the night at the time of the movement (of the Sun from one constellation into another) would go to heaven. Similarly worship of Śiva in the form of the Sun at the time of the new-moon and Sun's movement (would get the same result). Bathing (the image of) Keśava with a *prastha* (a kind of measure) of clarified butter of thirty-two *pala* measures one gets free from all sins. One who bathes (the lord) with ghee, milk etc. at the time of the equinox etc. (would get the same fruits).

9-10. The *Umāvrata* done on the third day and the eighth days confers fortune on women. One who worships (goddess) Gaurī and lord Maheśvara would get all fortunes. After worshipping Umāmaheśvara one gets non-separation. The main performer of the vow in the *Umeśavrata* is the woman. A woman who is devoted to the Sun would certainly become a male.

CHAPTER TWO HUNDRED

Vow of giving a gift of lamp

Fire-god said :

1-5. I shall describe the vow of making a gift of a lamp that would yield enjoyment and emancipation. One who gives a lamp to the abode of a deity or a house of a brahmin is rewarded with everything for a year. (One who does so) for four months would reach the world of Viṣṇu, and (giving) in *kārttika* would reach heaven. There is nothing greater than the gift of a lamp, neither there was, nor there would be. One gets longevity, eyesight, fortune and progeny etc. by giving a lamp. One who gives a lamp enjoys in heaven after getting fortune. Lalitā, the daughter of the king of Vidarbha, the beautiful and faithful spouse of a king became the foremost among hundreds of wives (of the king) by giving a lamp. That chaste lady used to give thousand lamps to the temple of Viṣṇu. When enquired about the greatness of the lamp she said to her co-wives as follows:

Lalitā said :

6-18. In olden days Maitreya was the priest of the king of Sauvīra. He caused a temple to be built for lord Viṣṇu on the banks of Devikā. He gave a lamp (for that temple) in *kārttika*. (The lamp) which was about to be extinguished was kindled with the wick by me as a mouse with my mouth (taking shelter there) on account of being afraid of a cat. After the death I was born as the daughter of a king and became a queen among the hundred (of the king's wives). The fruit of that act of kindling the lamp of the temple of Viṣṇu, even though not resolved, is enjoyed by me. Because I remember my past birth. I give lamps day and night. One who gives a lamp on the eleventh day rejoices in heaven in a vehicle. One who steals a lamp would become dumb or dull or fall into the dark hell difficult to be crossed. Seeing the crying men, the servant of the God of Death said to them :

"Enough of your wailing. What use of your wailing over misdeeds wantonly done by you before ? One is born as a man after a cycle of thousand births. O Extremely stupid fellow ! Why do you run after pleasures even in that (life) ? The result of enjoying according to one's desire is that of coming here and wailing. You are enjoying the fruits of your past deed. Why have you not thought about it ? The embrace of the breasts of other women for your pleasure has given you grief. The worldly enjoyment for a while causes grief many crores of years. O Seducer of other's wives ! Why do you cry "O Mother ! ? What would be very heavy (to bear) when the name of Hari is repeated with the tongue ? Fire can be had always with a wick and oil at low cost. The lamp has been stolen by you not showing inclination for giving. That is the cause of your grief. What use in wailing now? You bear that which has happened.

Fire-god said :

19. After hearing what was told by Lalitā, (the other wives) reached heaven after giving a lamp. Hence there would be great benefit by the gift of a lamp.

CHAPTER TWO HUNDRED AND ONE

Mode of worshipping Viṣṇu in a figure of nine compartments

Fire-god said :

1-6. I shall describe the *navavyūhārcana* (worship in nine compartments) that was narrated by Hari to Nārada. The letter '*a*' with Vāsudeva should be worshipped at the centre of a lotus figure and the letter *ā* with Saṅkarṣaṇa and Pradyumna at the south, the letter *aḥ* and Aniruddha at the south-west, the letter *oṁ* and Nārāyaṇa at the west, (the words) *tat sat* and Brahmā at the north-west, (the letter) *huṁ* and Viṣṇu and (the letter) *kṣauṁ* and Nṛsiṁha at the north, and (the letter) *bhūḥ* and Varāha at the north-east. (The letters) *kaṁ*, *ṭaṁ*, *tam*, *śaṁ* and Garutmat (vehicle of Viṣṇu) (should be worshipped) at the western entrance (of that figure), (the letters) *khaṁ*, *chaṁ*, *vaṁ*, *huṁ*, *phaṭ* and the eastern face at the south, (the letters) *khaṁ*, *ṭhaṁ*, *phaṁ*, *śaṁ* and the mace at the north. (The letters) *baṁ*, *ṇaṁ*, *maṁ*, *kṣauṁ* and Īśāna should be worshipped at the north-east, (the letters) *dhaṁ*, *daṁ*, *bhaṁ*, *haṁ* and Śrī (Lakṣmī) at the south and (the letters) *gaṁ*, *ḍaṁ*, *vaṁ*, *śaṁ* and Puṣṭi. (The letters) *dhaṁ*, *vaṁ* (should be worshipped) and the garland of wild flowers at the west of the pedestal, the *śrīvatsa* (the mark on the chest of lord Viṣṇu) and (the letters) *saṁ*, *haṁ*, *laṁ* at the west and (the letters) *chaṁ*, *taṁ*, *yaṁ* and the *kaustubha* (the crest-jewel) to the west of it.

7-10. (After having worshipped with) "Obeisance to Ananta", worship should be made below in the order of the ten (forms) of Viṣṇu and the four pitchers representing Mahendra and others in the east and other directions in the above order of the ten forms (of Viṣṇu). The arches and canopy (should also be worshipped in the same way). After having contemplated the orbs of fire, wind and moon with (their respective) letters in order, one should worship the body and then bathe it. One should then contemplate on the subtle form of the self in the sky, submerged in the white nectar that flows from the disc of the moon. That is the eternal seed of one's self that has been consecrated by the flood. One should thus resolve the spirit that is being produced in the self.

11-16. Then one should do the location of twelve letters (after saying) "I am verily Viṣṇu produced (again)". The heart, head, tuft, armour and weapons should be located (respectively) on the chest, head, tuft, back and eyes. Then the weapons should be located on the two hands. Then one would have a divine body. One should do this location on the body of the disciple in the similar way (as it has been done) on one's self as well as the deity. The worship done for Hari on the heart is known to be *anirmālyā* (without remnant) and that done in a circle as *sanirmālyā* (together with remnant). The disciples with their eyes covered should throw the flower (on the images) (at the commencement of the worship). On which images the flower falls that name should be given to them. Then the disciples should be seated on the left and sesamum,rice and ghee should be offered (as oblation). After having made one hundred aud eight oblations, (one should do) thousand (oblations) for the purification of the body. One should do more than hundred (oblations) for the limbs of the images of the nine compartments. After having made the final (oblation) the preceptor should initiate them (the disciples). He has to be respected by them with riches etc.

CHAPTER TWO HUNDRED AND TWO

Different flowers used in Worship

Fire-god said :

1-2. Lord Hari gets pleased with flowers, perfumes, incense, lamps and offerings. I shall describe you flowers which are fit and unfit for the god. *Mālati* is the excellent flower. *Tamāla* (flower) confers enjoyment and emancipation. *Mallikā* (jasmine) destroys all sins. (The flower) *yūthikā* gets the world of Viṣṇu.

3. *Atimukta* will also get the same fruit. The *pāṭalā* (flower) conveys one to the world of Viṣṇu. One gets the world of Viṣṇu with the *karavīra* (flowers). One becomes fortunate with *japā* (flowers).

4. One would reach the world of Viṣṇu with the *pāvanti*, *kubjaka* and *tagara* (flowers). (One would reach) the world of Viṣṇu with the *karṇikāra*. There would be destruction of sin with *kuruṇṭha*.

5-6. One will have an excellent position with lotuses, *ketaki* and jasmine. One would reach the world of Hari with *bāṇa* flowers, *barbara* and *kṛṣṇā*. Similar result would be got by *aśoka*, *tilaka* and *aṭarūṣabhava*. The leaves of *bilva* would confer liberation. One will have the supreme position with the leaves of *śamī*.

7-11. One would reach the world of Viṣṇu with the *bhṛṅgarāja*. One would have same fruits with the leaves of *tamāla*. The black and white basil, white lotus, blue lotuses, lotus, red lotus are meritorious. Lord Hari (gets pleased) with a garland of hundred lotuses. One would get enjoyment and emancipation and destruction of sin with *nīpa*, *arjuna*, *kadamba*, *vakula*, fragrant *kiṁśuka*, *munipuṣpa*, *gokarṇa*, *nāgakarṇa*, *sandhyā* flower, *bilva*, *rañjani*, *ketaki*, *kūṣmāṇḍa*, *timira*, *kuśa*, *kāśa*, *śara*, *dyūta* etc., *maruvaka* leaves and other fragrant (leaves and flowers). The god would get pleased with all (that is offered) with devotion. A flower is more meritorious than a lakh of gold and a garland, more than a crore times.

12-15. It would be three times more meritorious with the forest flowers than with the flowers from one's own garden or another's garden. One should not worship lord Viṣṇu with withered or broken (flowers) or (flowers) having more than the usual parts. (One would reach) hell (by worshipping) with *kāñcanāra*, *unmatta*, *girikarṇikā*, *kuṭaja śālmalīyā* and *śiriṣa*. Lord Hari (is pleased) with *sugandha*, *brahma*, lotuses and blue lotuses. Lord Hara is worshipped with *arka mandāra* (and) *dhustūra* flowers. One should not offer *Kuṭaja*, *karkaṭi* flowers and *ketakī* for Śiva. (One should not use) *kūṣmāṇḍa*, *nimba* and wild flowers without fragrance (in worship).

16-18. One would get enjoyment and emancipation by worshipping gods with the eight flowers of gestures such as non-violence, conquest of senses, forbearance, knowledge, compassion and learning. Non-violence is the first flower. (The second) flower is the control of senses. Compassion for the beings is (said to be) all flowers. The flower of tranquility excells. Quietitude is a flower and penance is a flower. Meditation is the seventh flower. Truth is the eighth flower. Lord Keśava is pleased with these flowers.

19-23. When lord Hari is worshipped with these flowers, he certainly gets pleased. O Excellent among men ! There are other external flowers. When lord Viṣṇu is worshipped with devotion together with compassion, he gets pleased. Water is the flower for Varuṇa. Ghee, milk and curd (are the flowers) for Soma. Food etc. (are the flowers) for Prajāpati (Brahmā) and incense and lamp for Fire (god). The fifth flower is the fruits and flowers of the forest. The *kuśa*, roots etc. are the flowers of the earth. Fragrant sandal is that of the Wind (god). Earnestness is the flower for lord Viṣṇu. These are always the eight flowers. The seat, the form, the five limbs (such as the heart etc.) and Viṣṇu are the eight flowers. (Worship should be made with the names) Vāsudeva and others for Viṣṇu and Īśāna and others for Śiva.

CHAPTER TWO HUNDRED AND THREE

The nature of hell

Fire-god said :

1-5. I shall describe hells. One does not go to them if he worships lord Viṣṇu with flowers and other things. A man gets released from his life forces at the end of his life even though he does not wish for it. A man gets released from his life on account of some case such as water, fire, poison, weapon, hunger, illness and fall from a mountain. One takes another body to be experienced as a result of one's own acts. One who has committed a sin would experience grief and one who does good (deeds) would experience happiness. One is led to the God of Death by the dreadful messengers of God of Death through the southern gate if one has taken evil path. Pious men (would be taken) by the western and other (doors). (They are) cast into hells by the servants being ordered by the God of Death. On account of piety one is led to heaven according to the words of Vasiṣṭha.

6-9. The killer of a cow is tormented for a lakh of years in the *mahāvīcī* (one of the hells). The killer of a brahmin (would be tormented) in a well-heated copper pot (for the same period). One who steals the land would be slowly tormented in the *raurava* (hell) till the great deluge. One who kills a woman, child or the old (is tormented) in the dreadful *mahāraurava* (hell) till (the period of) fourteen Indras. One who sets fire to the house, ground etc. is burnt for a *kalpa* (432 million years of mortals). Thieves would fall into the *tāmisraka* hell. They would be pierced by the attendants of the God of Death with spears etc. for many *kalpa* periods. Then they would be tormented in the *mahatāmisraka* hell by serpents, leeches etc.

10-11. One who kills his mother would be struck by swords in the *asipatravana* (forest where the trees have leaves as sharp as swords) for many *kalpa* periods as long as the earth (remains). One who has burnt men would be burnt in muddy region with gravel etc. One who has eaten sweet food alone will suffer in *kākola* (hell) eating the excreta of insects.

12. One who has discontinued (doing) five sacrifices[1] (would suffer) in *kuṭṭala* hell eating urine and blood. One who has eaten the forbidden food would take blood in the filthy hell.

13. One who afflicts others would be tormented in the hell *tailapāka* like sesamum. One who kills a person who has sought refuge would be cooked in the *tailapāka*.

14. One who withholds gifts at the sacrifice and who sells wine would be thrown into the hell *nirucchvāsa*. Similarly,

1. To be performed by a householder—*brahmayajña*, *pitṛyajña*, *daiva-pitṛyajña*,, *bhūtayajña* and *nṛyajña* respectively denoting teaching, libation to manes, oblation to gods, offering made to spirits and feeding guests.

one who lies (would be thrown) into the great hell *vajrakavāṭa*.

15. Evil-minded persons (would suffer) in (the hell) *mahājvāla*; one who has cohabited the forbidden woman (would suffer) in (the hell) *krakaca*, the doer of mixed sins in (the hell); one who strikes at other's weakness would suffer in hells *guḍapāka* and *pratoda*.

16. The killer of an animal (would be thrown) into an alkaline lake. One who steals the land (would be placed) under a current as sharp as a razor. One who steals a cow or gold (would be thrown) into (the hell) *ambarīṣa*. One who cuts a tree (would be put) in (the hell) *vajraśastraka*.

17. One who steals wine would be put into *paritāpa* (hell) and one who steals other's wealth into *kālasūtra* (hell). One who eats flesh in excess (would be thrown) into *kaśmala* (hell). One who does not offer the rice-balls (for the manes) (would be put) into *ugragandha* hell.

18. One who receives a bribe (would be tormented) in (the hell) *durdhara*. One who cohabits women taken captive (would suffer) in the hell (called) *mañjūṣa*. One who censures scriptures (would be thrown) in the unstable hell *loha*.

19-20. One who bears false witness (would be put) in (the hell) *pūtivaktra*. One who steals wealth and one who kills a child, woman or the old and one who afflicts a brahmin would suffer in (the hell) *karāla*. A brahmin who drinks wine (would suffer) in (the hell) *vilepa*. Those who have caused breach (of friendship) (would be put) into (the hell) *mahātāmra*.

21. One who cohabits others' wives (would enter) (the hell) *śālmala* (and embrace) glowing iron or stone. Similarly, a woman cohabiting many men would do.

22-23. Those who cohabit their mothers and daughters, those who have cut the tongue (of others), those who have looked (at others' wives) with lustful eyes and those who have plucked the eyes would be thrown into a heap of charcoal. Thieves would be pierced with razors. One who eats flesh (would be made) to eat his own flesh. One who practises fasting for (the stipulated) months would not go to hell. So also one who practises the vow on the eleventh day and the *bhīṣmapañcakavrata*-(would not go to hell).

CHAPTER TWO HUNDRED AND FOUR

Mode of practising the vow of fasting for stipulated months

Fire-god said :

1-2. I shall describe the vow (known as) fasting for a month, that is the most excellent among (the vows). After having done the sacrifice relating to (lord) Viṣṇu and got the command of the preceptor and knowing one's own strength with (the practice of) *kṛcchra* etc., O Sage ! a forester or an ascetic or a woman or a widow should fast for a month.

3-5. One should undertake to observe this vow for thirty-two days after having fasted on the eleventh day of the dark fortnight of (the month of) *āśvina* (October-November). "O lord Viṣṇu ! Commencing from this day until you get up (from sleep) I shall worship you without taking food for thirty days. O Viṣṇu ! (this vow would be) till you get up in the (months of) *āśvina* and *kārttika*. Let not my vow be incomplete if I happen to die in the middle.".

6-9. (Lord Viṣṇu should be worshipped thrice with fragrant flowers after bathing thrice. The person practising the vow should repeat the songs of lord Viṣṇu and contemplate (on him). He should avoid vain discussion and should avoid desire for wealth. He should not touch someone who is not practising the vow. He should not enter into conversation with those addicted to vices. He should dwell in temple for thirty days. The observer of the vow should worship the brahmins on the twelfth day and feed them. After completing vow and paying fees, he should break the fast. One would get enjoyment and emancipation for thirteen *kalpas* (a *kalpa* is equal to 432 million years) by practising thus.

10-12. He should do the sacrifice relating to Viṣṇu and worship thirteen brahmins. He should give them as many pairs of clothes, vessels, seats, umbrellas, metal rings, pairs of sandals, upper cloth and sacred threads. All these things should also be given to another brahmin being permitted by them. After having worshipped golden lord Viṣṇu on the bed, he should worship his own form with clothes and other things.

13-15. Then he should tell brahmins, "O Brahmins ! I am going to the world of Viṣṇu being freed from all sins by the grace of lord Viṣṇu. I am becoming lord Viṣṇu himself". (The brahmins should say), "O One with divine wisdom ! You go to the faultless place of lord Viṣṇu by this vehicle and remain there spotless bearing the form of lord Viṣṇu". Then that bed should be offered to the preceptor. One who practises thus would elevate hundreds of his family and take them to the world of Viṣṇu.

16-18. That country in which there is a person observing fast for a month, would become spotless. What to speak about the family in which there is one who fasts for a month ! Seeing the person practising a vow fallen into a swoon, one should make him drink milk and clarified butter. These things would not nullify the vow. The ghee is allowed by the brahmins, and milk, water, roots are beneficial remedies (administered) by the preceptors. Lord Viṣṇu is the maker of all remedies. Hence he will make the vow complete.

CHAPTER TWO HUNDRED AND FIVE

Mode of performing the Bhīṣmapañcakavrata

Fire-god said :

1. I shall describe the *Bhīṣmapañcaka*,[1] that is the foremost among the vows and that which yields everything. It should be done on the eleventh day in the bright fortnight in *kārttika*.

2. (The observer of the vow) should bathe thrice (daily) for five days and satisfy gods and manes with five kinds of grains and sesamum. He should worship lord Hari silently.

3. Having bathed the deity with the five things got from a cow and with the five sweet things, sandal paste should be besmeared and *guggulu* should be burnt along with ghee.

1. The five days from the eleventh to the fifteenth of the bright half of *kārttika* said to be sacred to Bhīṣma. See chapter 205 below.

4. A lamp should be offered. Food offering should be made day and night. He should then repeat (the syllable) "*Oṁ* obeisance to Vāsudeva" one hundred and eight times.

5. The performer of the vow should then make oblations of sesamum and rice dipped in ghee with the sacred syllable of six letters along with the word 'oblations.'

6-8. He should worship the feet with lotuses (on the first day), the knee and thigh with the *bilva* leaves on the second day, the navel with the *bhṛṅgarāja* on the third day, with the *bāṇa*, *bilva* and *japā* (flowers) on the fourth day and with *mālatī* on the fifth day. The votary should lie down (only) on the (bare) floor. (He should use) cowdung on the eleventh day and cow's urine, curd and milk (on the subsequent days). (He should use) five things got from a cow on the fifth day. He should take food only in the night on the full moon day. The votary would get enjoyment and emancipation.

9. After having practised the (*Bhīṣmapañcaka*) Bhīṣma reached lord Hari. That is why (it is known as) *Bhīṣmapañcaka*. One should worship lord Brahmā and fast while practising the vow.

CHAPTER TWO HUNDRED AND SIX

Mode of offering water of libation to the venerable sage Agastya

Fire-god said :

1-4. (Sage) Agastya (is verily lord) Viṣṇu. After having worshipped him one would reach lord Viṣṇu. When the Sun has not entered (the constellation) Virgo one should offer libation to Agastya for three days and one-third part of a day after having fasted and worshipped him. An image of the sage (Agastya) made of the *kāśa* flower should be located in a pot at (the time of) nightfall and that image in the pot should be worshipped. He should then remain awake in the night. "O Agastya ! The foremost among sages ! A multitude of brilliance ! Great-minded person ! You accept with your wife this worship done by me" . After having invoked the presence (of (of the sage) with libation, he should worship him with sandal and other things.

5-13. After having led (the image) near the water tank in the morning libation should be offered. "O One having the colour of *kāśa* flower ! Born of Fire and Wind (gods) ! Son of Mitra and Varuṇa !-Born in the pitcher ![1] Obeisance be to you ! That Agastya by whom Ātāpi was eaten as also Vātāpi[2], the great demon and the ocean was dried, may he be present before me. I am praying to (the sage) Agastya with my deeds, mind and speech. Being desirous of attaining the other world, I shall pray to the son of Mitra, born in a different continent and most dear to the gods. Kindly accept the sandal that is the king among the trees. May you accept the garland, that is the destroyer of sins, the vessel of piety, wealth, desire and liberation and that which confers fortune, health and prosperity. O Lord ! Let the incense be accepted. You make my devotion steady. You confer on me the desired boon and also auspicious position in the next (place) (got) by the celestials and demons. O Excellent among the sages ! Conferer of all the desired fruits ! This libation has been offered by me together with clothes, rice, fruits and gold. I make known to (sage) Agastya that which I have raised with my mind. I offer libation with fruits. You accept libation, O Great Sage !" Agastya being thus excavated with the spades (gave) men the desired progeny and strength. (The sage) with fierce splendour along with his chaste wife nourished the two ears. He then conferred blessing on the celestials.

14. "O Daughter of a king ![3] Obeisance to you, the wife of the sage (Agastya) ! One who is a great devotee ! O Governess of the celestials ! Accept libation. O Lopāmudrā ! One who is famous !

15-16. Libation should be offered to Agastya together with a vessel containing five gems, gold and silver and enclosed by seven kinds of grains as well as curd and sandal. (The above libation should be done) by women and *Śūdras* without (the reci-

---

1. When the seed of Mitra and Varuṇa fell at the sight of the nymph Urvaśī, part of it fell into a jar and part into water. From the former arose Agastya, hence called 'born of the pitcher'.
2. They were brothers, both demons.
3. Daughter of the king of Vidarbha.

tation of) the sacred syllables. "O Agastya ! Foremost among the sages ! A multitude of splendour ! Bestower of all things !"

17. After having accepted this worship of mine you retreat in peace. One has to forego a kind of grain, a variety of fruit and a kind of taste for the sake of Agastya.

18. Then the brahmins should be given food (as well as) ghee, sweet gruel and sweet balls. Cows, clothes and gold should be given to them as fees.

19. That pitcher should be given to a brahmin together with gold and its mouth being covered by another vessel containing ghee and sweet gruel.

20. All would get all things by offering libation for seven years. A woman (would get) children and fortune and a girl (would get) a husband born to a king.

CHAPTER TWO HUNDRED AND SEVEN

Mode of performing Kaumudavrata

Fire-god said :

1. The Kaumudavrata, which has been described[1] by me, should be practised in the bright (fortnight) in *āśvayuji*. After fasting on the eleventh day, lord Hari should be worshipped for a month.

2. (One should resolve as follows): "I shall practise the *Kaumudavrata* taking food only once (daily) in the brightfort night in *āśvina* after repeating (the name of) Hari for a month, for the sake of enjoyment and emancipation".

3-4. After fasting, he should worship lord Viṣṇu, after having besmeared the lord with sandals, agallochum and saffron with lotus, blue lotus flowers or white lotuses or *mālatī* (flower). (He should offer) a lamp with oil silently. Offering of sweet gruel, cakes and sweet balls (should be made) day and night.

5. "*Oṁ* obeisance to Vāsudeva". Having made the offering (with this syllable) (the vow) should be completed. Food and other things should be given to a brahmin. The fast for a month would continue until the lord wakes up. (If it is continued) beyond that (it would get) greater benefit.

1. See Ch. 198 13-14.

CHAPTER TWO HUNDRED AND EIGHT

Rules and regulations relating to vows and gifts in general

Fire-god said :

1-3. I shall describe briefly the vows and gifts in general. Whichever vow or whichever gift or whichever article or the routines in whichever time such as the first lunar day and other days, on days such as the (Sunday), in asterisms such as the *kṛttikā*, in *viṣkumba* (a particular combination) etc., in the (constellations) aries etc. and at the time of the eclipses, lord Viṣṇu is the governing deity for all these materials, and time. Sun, Īśa, Brahmā, Lakṣmī and all others are the manifestations of lord Viṣṇu.

4-12. The vow, gift, worship and other acts done for him would yield all things. "O lord of the universe ! You come here. (Here are) seat, water for washing the feet, waters of libation, the sweet drink, water for sipping, bathing, clothes, perfumes, flower, incense, lamp and offerings. Obeisance to you." This is the common statement in worship, vow and giving gift. The statement for giving a gift is similar. Listen to me. "Today I offer this article dedicated to Viṣṇu to such and such a brahmin belonging to such and such a *gotra*. I offer this gift to you for the appeasement of all sins, for increasing the longevity and health, for increasing the fortune, for furthering the progeny in the *gotra*, for conquest, wealth, piety, desire for prosperity, the removal of that sin, and release from mundane existence. For the sake of the accomplishment of this gift I am giving to you only. May the lord, the master of the world, get permanently pleased with this. O Lord of sacrifice, gift and vow ! Give me knowledge, fame and other things. Give me piety, desire, wealth and emancipation, that which is wished by the mind". Whoever reads this collection of vow and gift daily, would get the desires fulfilled, would become pure and get enjoyment and emancipation. The vows which should be practised under the auspices of different lunar days, weekdays, casterisms, positions of the sun, astral combinations and Manu and the like should not be practised by worshipping god Vāsudeva in one and the same way.

CHAPTER TWO HUNDRED AND NINE

Rules relating to gifts

Fire-god said :

1. Listen to me. I shall describe the charities that would bestow enjoyment and emancipation. One who does acts of charity (such as digging wells etc.) would get all things.

2. (Digging) reservoirs, wells and tanks, (constructing) temples, giving food and (establishing) gardens are (known to be) *pūrtadharma*, that confers emancipation.

3. Performing *agnihotra* (a kind of sacrifice), penance, truth, protecting scriptures, serving guests, (doing) *vaiśvadeva* (an offering made to the gods Viśvedevas) are said to be *iṣṭa* that take one to heaven.

4. The gift (made) at the time of the eclipse of planets and (that offered) at the time of the entry of the Sun from one constellation to another, gift made on the twelfth lunar days etc. (are also) *pūrta*, which also take one to heaven.

5-7. A gift at the (proper) place, time and (to a proper) person would be of crore merits especially in the transit of the Sun on the tropics, on the equinox, at the (time of) *vyatipāta*, at the waning of the day, at different days beginning the cycles of period, at the transit of the Sun from one constellation to another, on the fourteenth days, on the eighth days, on the full-moon days, on the twelfth days, at the time of *aṣṭakas* (a collection of three days beginning from the seventh day after the full moon), at the time of sacrifices, festivals and marriages, at the Manu-periods, at the *vidhṛti* (*yoga*), on having had a bad dream and when a good brahmin has been got.

8-12. Otherwise it is desired that a gift (has to be bestowed) always upon those on whom one has the faith to do. Tropical (periods are) two, equinoxes (are) two making up four. The eightysix (auspicious periods are)—the four *viṣṇupadīs*[1]., the twelve transits of the Sun from one constellation to another (and) the transit of the Sun in virgo, gemini, pisces and sagittarious. The eightysix (periods) are said to have eightysix times merits (than ordinary periods). The two summer and winter solstices

1. . They are taurus, leo, scorpio and acquarious.

are meritorious when it has come and when it has not come i.e., thirty *nāḍīs*[1] in cancer and twenty in capricorn respectively. When the Sun stays in the libra or aries (it would be) ten (*nāḍīs*) in both. In the eightysix (periods) described already sixty *nāḍikās* (are auspicious after the Sun's entry). Among the auspicious periods of *viṣṇupadī* sixteen (*nāḍīs*) before and after (are auspicious).

13. It is said to be the *vyatīpāta* if the Sunday morning occurs in (the asterisms) *śravaṇa*, *aśvani*, *dhaniṣṭhā* and *āśleṣā*.

14-15. The *kṛta* (*yuga*) began on the ninth day in the bright fortnight in *kārttika*, the *tretā* (*yuga*) on the third day in the bright (fortnight) in *vaiśākha*, the *dvāpara* (*yuga*) on the new-moon day in the month of *māgha* and the *kali* (*yuga*) on the thirteenth day of the dark (fortnight) in *nabhasyaka* (*bhādrapada*). One has to know them thus. One should also know the periods of Manu and others thus.

16-19. Gifts made on the ninth day of the white (fortnight) in *aśvayuk*, the twelfth day in *kārttika*, the third day in *māgha* and *bhādrapada*, the new-moon day in *phālguna*, the eleventh day in *pauṣa*, the tenth day in *āṣāḍha*, the seventh day in the month of *māgha*, the eighth day of the dark (fortnight) in *śrāvaṇa*, the full-moon day in *āṣāḍha*, and similarly fifteenth day of *kārttika*, *phālguna* and *jyaiṣṭha*, the three *aṣṭakas*[2] in the later part of *āgrahāyaṇi* (December-January) and the eighth day known as the *aṣṭaka* confer undecaying benefits.

20. (In the same way one should give gifts in the auspicious periods) at sacred places like Gayā, (the river) Gaṅgā and Prayāga and temples etc. Gifts should be made without being requested. But knowledge, wealth and girls (should) not (be given as gifts thus).

21. Gift should be made facing the east and the gift should be received facing the north. (By this) the longevity of the giver increases and that of the recipient does not decrease.

22-26. (In general) (the name of) the *gotra* of the recipient and their own selves are repeated and the gift is made (by the givers). In the case of giving away a girl in marriage (the name of) the three (*gotras*) (should be repeated). Gift should be given after bathing and worshipping the deity (along) with (the reci-

1. One *nāḍī* is equal to 24 minutes.
2. The collection of seventh, eighth and ninth days after full-moon.

tation of) the *vyāhṛtis* (the syllables *bhū* etc. of the *gāyatrī mantra*) together with water. Gold, horse, sesamum, elephant, servant, chariot, earth, house, girl and tawny, cow are the ten great gifts. The money got by one's learning, valour, penance, means of a girl, by officiating as a priest and through the disciple is (said to be) *śulka* (fees, or bride's-price etc.). All the wealth acquired by following some trade or work is also (known as) *śulka*. All that which was got by usury, agriculture and trade and that obtained as a favour and the one got by gambling, dice, stealing etc. and similar heroic pursuits (are said to be acquired) by some device. The three kinds (of acquisition) have three different kinds (of fruits).

27. Woman's property is said to be of six kinds—*adhyagni* (gift made to a woman at the time of marriage), *adhyāvāhanika* (gift made to a woman at the time of leaving her father's house for her husband's house), gift made (by the husband) out of love or affection and gifts got from the brother, mother or father.

28. Brahmins, warriors and tradesmen (have their own) wealth. (But) a *śūdra* (will have) by their favour. One should not give as gift cow, house, bed and women to many.

29-30. If one promises to give a gift and does not give, it would kill hundred of generations. Whatever little merit one has acquired should be made to the gods, preceptors, mothers and fathers with one's effort. The wealth that has been given (as a gift) with a view to have something in return (would be) useless.

31-33. Piety is accomplished by faith. Even water given (to the thirsty gets) undiminishing (merit). One is said to be an excellent person (to receive a gift) if he is endowed with knowledge, good conduct and quality, avoids doing harm to others and protects and saves the ignorant. A gift made to the mother is hundred times (meritorious than the others), and that to the father is thousand times (meritorious). The gift given to the daughter (gets) endless (merits) and that to the sister (gets) undecaying (merits). A gift (given) to a creature (is) of equal merit and that (given) to a sinner (is) of great merit.

34-38. (A gift) to (a person of) the mixed caste (is) two times (meritorious), a gift to a *śūdra* (is) four times (meritorious), to a *vaiśya* (is) eight times (meritorious) and to a *kṣatriya* is sixteen times (meritorious). I shall describe (the merits of giving a gift) to a brahmin. (Gift made) to one who has [studied] the scriptures is hundred times (merit-worthy), to one who imparts the scriptures is of endless (merit). It is said that gift (given) to the priest and the officiating priest is of undecaying (merit). Gift given to those devoid of wealth and to a sacrificer would be of limitless (merit). A brahmin who does not do penances and study and has desire to accept gift would get drowned along with that just like a practitioner together with the stone in the floods. After bathing and touching (waters) properly one should accept the gift after becoming pure and restraining senses. The recipient of the gift should always repeat the *sāvitrī* (*gāyatrī*). Then the deity should be glorified together with the materials.

39-48. The recipient should utter the complimentary words loudly after having received from an excellent brahmin, (in a) soft (voice) (after receiving) from a *kṣatriya* (warrior), in a low voice (after receiving) from a *viśa* (tradesman) and mentally (after receiving) from a *śūdra*. (I shall describe the deities of different things). All (the gods) are the presiding deities for (the gift of) protection. Viṣṇu is the deity of the earth. Girl, servant and female servant are said to be governed by Prajāpati. An elephant is also governed by Prajāpati. The deity for the horse is Yama (god of Death). Similarly all the one-hoofed animals and the buffalo are governed by the God of Death. Nirṛti (is the presiding deity) of the camel, Śiva is that of a cow, Fire-god is that of a goat, Varuṇa is that of a ram, Hari is that of a boar, Wind-god is that of forest animals, Varuṇa for the tank, (Varuṇa) for vessels of water such as the pot etc. and gems got from the ocean, Fire-god for gold and iron, Prajāpati for food grains and cooked food, Gandharva for fragrant material, Bṛhaspati for dress, Wind-god for all birds, Brahmā for knowledge and its accessories, Sarasvatī for books etc., Viśvakarmā for sculpture, Vanaspati for the trees etc. The deities of the materials make up the body of Hari. Aṅgiras is said to be the deity of umbrella, antelope-skins, bed, chariot, seat, sandals and vehicle. All ammunitions, weapons, banners etc. (are governed) by all the gods. A house also (is governed) by all the gods. (Lord) Viṣṇu is the presiding deity of all things.

49-54. Or Śiva may be (the presiding deity) because there is no other article besides the above. One should mention the name of the material and say that "I am giving". Then water should be given on the hand. This is known to be the procedure in all gifts. (The receiver) should say "(Lord) Viṣṇu is the giver. (Lord) Viṣṇu is the materials. I am receiving." Wishing the welfare of the giver is the duty of the recipient (that confers) the two fruits of enjoyment and emancipation. One may accept gift from all for protecting the preceptors and servants and also to propitiate gods and manes. But he should not get satisfied with that. Money should not (be taken) from a *śūdra* for the sake of sacrifice. The benefit of that would reach the *śūdra*. Molasses, butter-milk and juices etc. may be accepted by an anchorite from a *śūdra*. A brahmin struggling for his existence may accept gift from all. If the brahmins are associated with fire and sun there cannot be any defect in teaching performing sacrifice or by accepting a gift from a prohibited person.

55. (A gift) is given in the *kṛtayuga* by approaching the person, is given in the *tretāyuga* after inviting (the person concerned). (A gift is made) in the *dvāparayuga* to one who seeks and in the *kaliyuga* to one who follows and begs.

56-63. Water should be poured on the ground after mentally resolving to give to a suitable person. The ocean has its limit. But there is no limit for the gift. (I shall give) to such and such a person belonging to such and such a *gotra*, who is a good soul, and a proper person who is learned in the *Vedas* and its accessories at the time of the eclipse of the Moon and Sun, at the entry of the Sun into a constellation, at the sacred places of great merit such as the Ganges, Gayā, Prayāga etc. "I make a gift of such and such an article for which Viṣṇu and Śiva and others, are the presiding deities for the sake of (getting) children, grand children, house, fortune, wife endowed with good qualities and for the increase of fame, learning, desire, fortune and health and for the destruction of all sins and for getting heaven, enjoyment and emancipation. I give this to you. May lord Hari (identical with) Śiva, the destroyer of spate of evils belonging to the heaven, sky and earth be pleased. May you be the conferer of the world of Brahmā on me for the sake of getting the piety, wealth and desire. I offer gold as fee to such and such a brahmin of such and, such a *gotra* for the sake of making this gift established". All gifts should be made with this sentence for giving a gift.

CHAPTER TWO HUNDRED AND TEN

Sixteen great gifts

Fire-god said:

1-4. I shall describe all the gifts. The great gifts (are) sixteen. (The gift known as) the *tulāpuruṣa*[1] is the first. (The others are) gift of *hiraṇyagarbha, brahmāṇḍa kalpavṛkṣa* (celestial tree). The fifth one (is the gift of) thousand cows. (The gift of) golden *kāmadhenu* (the celestial cow) (is the sixth one). The seventh one (is the gift of) golden horse. (The other gifts are) the golden horse and chariot and the golden elephant and horse. Then (the remaining gifts are) five ploughs and (the gift of) earth, *viśvacakra, kalpalatā,* the excellent seven oceans, *ratnadhenu* and *mahābhūtaghaṭa.* (The gift) should be given on an auspicious day.

5. Gift should be given to a brahmin after having worshipped gods in a circle in a shed. Listen to me. I shall describe ten gifts (known as) *merudāna* (heaps of different things).

6. The best gift is that of a thousand *droṇas* (a measure) of grains. The rest are successively half (the quantity) of the preceding ones. An excellent gift of a mountain of salt should be given (consisting of) sixteen *droṇas.*

7. An excellent (gift) of a mountain of molasses would be of ten *bhāras* (a measure). The rest (would be) successively half of the preceding ones. An excellent hill of gold would be of thousand *palas* (a measure of weight) and the rest as that (described above).

8. A hill of sesamum would be of ten *droṇas* (the rest being) duly five and three *droṇas.* The hill of cotton would be twenty, ten and five *bhāras* (respectively).

9. An excellent hill of ghee would be twenty pots of ghee. An excellent hill of silver (would be) ten thousand *palas.*

10-12. (An excellent) hill of sugar (would be) eight *bhāras* and the medium (would be) half that (and the inferior still half that. I shall describe the ten cows by giving which one would get enjoyment and emancipation. The first one would be the cow of molasses and the next one would be the cow of ghee. The third one is the cow of sesamum and the fourth one cow of

1. gold, jewel or other valuable things equal to a man's weight given to a Brāhmaṇa as a gift.

water. (The others are) cow of milk, cow of honey, cow of sugar, cow of curd and the cow of juices. The tenth one is the cow in its natural form. This is said to be the rule (governing the ten cows).

13-18. In the case of liquid materials given as the cow, they should be in the form of the pots. But they should be a heap in the case of other (materials). One should place a deer skin of four cubits (length) on the ground besmeared with cow dung with the neck (part) on the east. *Darbha* should be spread everywhere. Similarly (a seat) should be made for the calf with the tender skin of *eṇaka* (a kind of black antelope). The cow together with the calf should be arranged such as it faces the east and the feet point to the north. An excellent gift of cow of molasses would always be of four *bhāras* (out of which) the calf should be of one *bhāra*. The middle type is known to be of two *bhāras* (for the cow) and half a *bhāra* for the calf. The last type should be one *bhāra* (for the cow) and a quarter (*bhāra*) for the calf. Otherwise (the gift may be made) according to the molasses and wealth one may have. One *māṣa* (a measure) is five *kṛṣṇalakas* (seed of the *guñja* plant). One *suvarṇa* is equal to sixteen *māṣas*. One *pala* is equal to four *suvarṇas*. One *tulā* is known to be one hundred palas. A *bhāra* would be twenty *tulās*. One droṇa (is equal to) four *āḍhaka*.

19-22. The cow and the calf both made of the molasses should be covered by a thin white cloth. The ears (should be made of) pearl oyster, the feet of sugarcane and the eyes of pure pearls. The veins (should be made of) white thread, the woollen blankets (for spreading) of white wool, the backside with copper vases, the hairs with white chowrie, the two eye-brows with coral, the breast with butter, the tail with silken cloth, the milk pails made of bronze and the pupils with sapphire. The ornaments on the horns should be made of gold and the hoofs of silver. The teeth should be of different kinds of fruits and the nose of sandal.

23-29. O Brahmin ! After having made ready the cow, it should be worshipped with these sacred syllables. "That goddess who is the fortune of all beings and who remains in the celestials may in the form of the cow give me peace. The (goddess) Rudrāṇī is always dear to lord Śaṅkara and remains in the body, may that goddess in the form of the cow dispel my sin. That one who is on the chest of (lord) Viṣṇu and who is the *Svāhā* for the fire, who is the energy of the moon, sun and star, that is of the form of the cow O Goddess of Fortune ! May that cow which is the fortune of the four-faced one (Brahmā), the god of wealth and the guardian deity of the world, be the conferer on me. You are the *svadhā* (oblation of food) for all the manes and the *svāhā* for the partakers of sacrifices. Hence you are the cow that removes all sins. Hence you get me peace". The cow that has been sanctified thus should be given to a brahmin. The same procedure (holds good) for the (offerings) of all kinds of cows (mentioned already). After having obtained the benefits of all sacrifices one (would become) pure and get enjoyment and emancipation.

30-34. One should give as a gift a cow having golden horns, silvery hoofs, of good conduct and having udders with bronze, with milk and decked with cloth together with the fees. One who gives such a cow would stay in heaven for as many years as the number of hairs (on its body). If it is a tawny (cow) it would again elevate seven generations (of the giver). One who gives a cow having golden horns, silvery hoofs and bronze attached udders together with fees befitting one's capacity would get enjoyment and emancipation after giving. By giving a cow with a calf, i.e., a cow that is delivering a calf, one would reach heaven and stay there for so many years as the number of hairs (on the body of the cow). It should be given as laid down before. A cow and a calf should be given as a gift by one that is about to die as (laid down) before. (He should say) "There is the dark *Vaitaraṇī* river at the dreadful entrance to (the place of) the God of Death. I am giving this black cow in order to cross that Vaitaraṇī."

CHAPTER TWO HUNDRED AND ELEVEN

Different kinds of gifts

Fire-god said :

1. One who has ten cows should give one. One having hundred cows should give ten cows. A person having a thousand cows should give hundred. All yield the same benefit.

2. Those who give thousand cows (as gift) would go to a place where the mansions are golden, there would be flow of wealth and the *gandharvas* and celestial nymphs (dwell).

3. By giving hundred cows one becomes free from the ocean of hells. By giving a weaned calf one stays in comfort in the heaven.

4-6. By the gift of a cow one would get longevity, health, fortune and heaven. She is the auspicious queen of the guardian deities such as Indra and the like; may she be the bestower of all my desires by the greatness of the gift of the she-buffalo. That mother of the demon in the form of buffalo the children of which (woman) are established by the assistance of the Lord of Dharma, may be the bestower of wealth on me. One would get fortune by giving a she-buffalo and reach heaven by giving a bull.

7-11. The gift known as *saṁyuktahalapaṅkti* (attached with ten ploughs) confers all fruits. A collection of ten ploughs is said to be a *paṅkti*. They should be made of wood and yoked to bulls. One would stay in heaven by giving them bound with golden strips. The benefits of giving ten tawny cows at the Puṣkara (a sacred place) in (the month of) *jyeṣṭhā* is said to be undecaying. Similar benefit would accrue by releasing a bull. (One should say) "O Four-footed one ! You are the virtue. These four are dear to you. O lord of Viṣṇu ! One who nourishes the manes, beings and the sages ! Let me have the worlds free blemishes and undecaying when you are released. May I not have the debts due to the gods, beings, manes and mortals. You are the virtue. That fate which befalls one who resorts to you, let it be firm in me."

12-16. One should mark (the bull) with the circles and spears and let it go with these sacred syllables (described above). If a bull is released on the eleventh day of a dead person he would be freed from the world of the dead. (The same benefit would accrue if a bull is let loose) at the time of six-monthly ceremony and annual ceremony (for the dead). One who makes a gift of *gocarma* (a measure of surface) would get rid of his sins. A *nivarttana* would be of thirty *kuṇḍas*, each *kuṇḍa* being ten cubits. The ground extending to ten times (the *nivartana*) (is known to be) *gocarma*. One who gives deer's skin together with a cow, earth and gold would get united with lord Brahmā, even though he had done many sinful deeds. One may give vessels filled with sesamum, honey and black sesamum as well as a *prastha* (a particular measure) of long pepper. Having given a bed of good quality one may get enjoyment and emancipation.

17. After having made a golden image of the self and given (the same as a gift), (the giver could reach) heaven.

18. After having made a large house and giving it one would get enjoyment and emancipation. (One would reach) heaven by giving a house, a hut for an ascetic, hall and shelter. One who builds a cattle-shed and gifts it would be free from sin and reach heaven.

19-20. One who makes a gift of the buffalo (the vehicle) of the God of Death would be free from sin and would go to heaven. One who gives (as a gift the images of gods) Brahmā Hara (Śiva), Hari with the celestials and the messenger of the God of Death in their middle and (the god) Pāśī (Varuṇa) as cutting the head of the latter would reach heaven. A brahmin who accepts this gift known as the 'three-faced' would incur sin.

21. One should give to a brahmin a wheel made of silver together with gold after having placed it on (his own) lap. This is (known as) the 'wheel of time' of great merit.

22-27. One who makes a gift of iron equal to one's weight would not go to hell. One who gives an iron rod of fifty *palas* covered by a cloth to a brahmin would not get (the chastising) rod of the God of Death. One should give the root or fruit or other material collectively or separately for the Conqueror of Death for the increase of one's life. One should make (a figure of) a man with black sesamum, with the teeth (made) of silver, eye (made) of gold, wielding a sword in the hand, bedecked with *japā* flowers, wearing red cloth, adorned with a garland of conch-shells, the feet having a pair of sandals, the sides (covered) by black wool and holding a ball of flesh in his left (hand). He is (known as) the embodiment of time. After having worshipped that (image) with perfumes and other things, it should be given to a brahmin. (Such a giver) would be free from death and disease and become a monarch.

28. One who gives a gift of a cow and a bull to a brahmin

would get enjoyment and emancipation. One would not die by giving a golden hairy horse.

29-31. One who makes such a gift endowed with bells would also get enjoyment and emancipation. One who gives gold would get the desired things. When gold is given as gift, silver should be given as remuneration. Gold is the remuneration even in the case of other gifts. No remuneration (should be given) when gold, silver, copper, rice and other grains (are given as gift) or at the daily ceremony for the manes and at the worship of gods.

32-35. Silver (given) as remuneration at the ceremony for the manes is a means to get piety, pleasure and material comfort. A wiseman who gives land as a gift should also give gold, silver, copper, gems, pearls, wealth and all other things. One who makes a gift of land, that composed man satisfies the manes in their world and the gods in the world of gods. One who gives (as a gift) a market town or small town or village or field abound with grains or hundred *nivartana*[1] or half of that or a house etc. or only *gocarma*[2] extent of land would get all things.

36. Just as a drop of oil spreads on the waters so also the fruit of all gifts would follow the mortal in the next birth.

37. The benefit (of making a gift) of gold, land and an eight year old girl would follow (the giver) in his seven births. One who gives a girl (in marriage) would elevate twentyone generations of his family and attain the world of Brahmā.

38. Having given an elephant together with remuneration one becomes free from blemish and would attain heaven. Having given a horse one would get long and healthy life and fortune and ascend heaven.

39-40. One who gives a maid servant to an excellent brahmin would reach the world of nymphs. Having given a copper plate weighing five hundred *palas* (a measure of weight) or half the weight or a quarter of that weight or one-eighth of the weight would get enjoyment and emancipation. By giving a cart together with a bull one would go to heaven by means of a cart.

41. One who makes a gift of cloth would get longevity,

---

1. See verse 13 above.
2. See verse 14 above.

health and undecaying heaven. The giver of grains such as the wheat, *kalama* (rice sown in June and harvested in December), barley and other (grains) would attain heaven.

42-43. Having given (as a gift) a seat, metallic vessel, salt, fragrant sandal, incense, lamp, betel, iron, silver, gem and other rare materials, one would get enjoyment and emancipation. One would ascend heaven by giving sesamum and a vessel for keeping sesamum.

44-46. There is nothing superior to the gift of food. Neither there was nor there would be. The (merit of) gift of an elephant, horse, chariot, maid-servant, servant and house will not equal a sixteenth part (of the merit) of giving food. One who gives food after committing a great sin would become free from all sins and attain undecaying worlds. One who sets up a place for distributing water for drinking would get enjoyment and emancipation.

47. By giving fire and firewood (for travellers) on the way, one would get radiance etc. and would be served in the (celestial) vehicle in heaven by the celestials, *gandharvas* and women.

48. One would get all things by giving ghee, oil and salt. After having given umbrella, sandal and firewood etc. one would dwell in heaven happily.

49-52. A gift made after worshipping lords Hari, Hara, Brahmā and the guardian deities on the important lunar days like the first etc., on the combinations (known as) *viṣkambha* etc., in the (months) *caitra* and others, in the years and the (asterisms) *aśvinī* etc. is of great merit. One would get enjoyment and emancipation by providing shady trees, feeding places, (vehicles) to carry burden and for anointing the feet. There are three things which are of equal merits. (They are)—cows, land and imparting knowledge. By imparting knowledge one becomes blemishless and attains the world of Brahmā. One who imparts knowledge about the *brahman*, would be equal to one who gives earth consisting of seven continents.

53-54. One who gives refuge to all beings would get all things. One who copies and gives the *purāṇa* or *Bhārata* or *Rāmāyaṇa*, would get enjoyment and emancipation. One who teaches scriptures dancing and music would reach heaven.

55. Money should be given to the teacher and food etc. for the students. What more can be possibly given by one who does with a motive to acquire virtues and desires.

56. There is no doubt that one would get by imparting knowledge every benefit that he would get by (performing) a thousand *Vājapeya* sacrifices.

57. One who reads a book would be the giver of all gifts at the temples of (lords) Śiva, Viṣṇu and the Sun-god.

58. All the castes and the four institutions of life separately and all the gods such as Brahmā and others are established on the gift of knowledge.

59. Knowledge is the wish-yielding cow. It is the unsurpassing eye. One rejoices with the Gandharvas by giving the *Upavedas* (the secondary texts such as the *Āyurveda*).

60. One would attain heaven by giving the accessory texts of scriptures. One would rejoice with piety by giving the religious law books.

61. There is no doubt that one gets release (from the mundane existence) by giving the established texts (of any discipline). One would reap the same benefit by giving a book as he would by imparting knowledge.

62. One would get everything by giving sacred religious texts and *Purāṇas*. One would get the benefit of Puṇḍarīka[1] by imparting (knowledge to) the disciples.

63-65. There is not known to be any limit for the benefit accrued by one who gives that by which he lives. That which is the most excellent in the world and that which is liked by one should be given to the manes by one who desires to have them without depletion. One who gives materials for worship after having worshipped (lords) Viṣṇu, Rudra (Śiva), the Lotus-born (Brahmā), Goddess, Vighneśvara (lord of impediments) and others would get everything. One who causes (to construct) a temple and to make an image would get all things.

66. One would be free from blemishes by washing and cleaning the temple. One who draws the mystic diagrams would become the ruler of a province subsequently.

67-69. After having given perfumes, flowers, incense, lamp, food offering, circumambulation, bell, banner, canopy, (arran-

1. A unit of measurement.

ged) a show, musical instruments and music and clothes for the lord, one would get enjoyment and emancipation. One should give musk, benzoin, sandal wood, agallochum, camphor, *musta* (a kind of grass), *guggulu* (a fragrant resin) and *vijaya*. One who establishes light at the time of solstice and others with a *prastha* (a measure) of ghee would get everything.

70-71. Bathing is known to be with hundred *palas* (of materials), bathing with oil with twentyfive *palas*. A great bathing is said to be with a thousand *palas* (of materials). (By bathing) with water ten sins (are washed off), by bathing with thick milk hundred sins (are washed off), (by bathing) with milk a thousand (sins are washed off) and ten thousand (sins are washed off by bathing) with ghee.

72. One would get fortune and wealth and would go to heaven by giving a maid-servant, servant, ornaments, cow, land, horse and elephant and other things for the deity.

CHAPTER TWO HUNDRED AND TWELVE

Gifts granting the desired fruits

Fire-god said :

1. I shall describe gifts that confer the desired benefits. One should do daily worship each month and do the worship for (the accomplishment of one's) desires.

2-3. The undertaking of the vow, worship of the preceptor and the grand worship at the end of the year (are the routines). One who gives a horse and a lotus made of flour to lord Śiva after worship in *mārgaśīrṣa* would live in the world of Sun for a long time. (By giving) an elephant made of flour in *pauṣa*, one would lift twentyone generations.

4. By giving a horse and a chariot made of flour in *māgha*, one would not go to hell. One would become a monarch and would ascend heaven by giving a bull made of flour in *phālguna*.

5. Having given a cow made of sugarcane together with a servant and a female servant in *caitra*, one would remain in

heaven for a long time and would become a monarch at the end.

6. One would become verily (lord) Śiva himself by giving seven kinds of rice in *vaiśākha*. One would become (identical with lord) Śiva by making a circular altar in the *āṣāḍha*.

7. One would ascend heaven and also (become) a king by giving a vehicle made of flowers in *śrāvaṇa*. By giving two hundred fruits one would elevate his family (and become) a king.

8. One would become a king after ascending heaven by giving *guggulu* (gum resin) etc. in *bhādra*. Giving a vessel filled with milk and clarified butter in *āśvina* would convey one to heaven.

9. Having given pieces of jaggery and clarified butter in the *kārttika* one would go to heaven and then be a king. I shall describe the twelve varieties of gifts (known as) *merudāna* (heaps of things resembling the Meru mountain) that confers enjoyment and emancipation.

10-18. In the *meruvrata* one should give a *meru* (mountain) of gems to a brahmin in *kārttika*. Listen to me. (I shall describe) the measure (of things) in all (the gifts of) *Merus* duly. Only a *prastha* (a measure) of diamond, ruby, *mahānīla* (a kind of sapphire), sapphire, crystal, topaz, emerald and pearl are excellent. Half of that (measure) would be medium and a quarter of that (would be) inferior. One should avoid doing trickery knowingly. The Meru should be located in the pericarps presided by (the lords) Brahmā, Viṣṇu and Īśa. Mālyavān should be worshipped on the east and that is known as Bhadra still to its east. Aśvarakṣa is said to be the next. The Niṣadha, Hemakūṭa and Himavān, the three, should be (worshipped) on the south of Meru. The three (mountains) Nīla, Śveta and Śṛṅgī are (worshipped) on the north (of Meru). (The mountains) Gandhamādana, Vaikaṅka and Ketumāla would be on the west. Thus the Meru would be associated with the twelve (mountains). One should worship (lord) Viṣṇu or (lord) Śiva after fasting preceded by bathing. The Meru should be worshipped with the sacred syllables in front of the deity and given to a brahmin. (One should say) "I give this excellent material of (the shape of) Meru belonging to god Viṣṇu to a brahmin of such and such a *gotra* to become sinless and for the sake of enjoyment and emancipation." (One who does so) would be honoured by the celestials and would sport in the (divine) chariot in the worlds of Indra, Brahmā, Śiva and Viṣṇu after elevating his family. One should make the gift even at other times such as the entry of the Sun from one constellation into another.

19-22. One should offer the golden Meru of (the weight of) a thousand *palas*. It should have three peaks representing the (lords) Brahmā, Viṣṇu and Hara (Śiva). Each one of the mountains should be hundred (*palas*). Together with the Meru, the mountains are known to be thirteen. One who makes a gift of gold Meru to a brahmin at the time of solstices, eclipses etc., in the presence of (lord) Viṣṇu, after having worshipped lord Hari (Viṣṇu), would live in the world of Viṣṇu for a long time. One would be a king for such a long time as the infinitesimal particles (of the gift). One should resolve and give a silver Meru having twelve mountains.

23-26. It would have the aforesaid benefit. One should worship lord Viṣṇu and a brahmin and resolve (to give) *bhūmimeru* (land in the form of Meru) consisting of a circular orb or a village of one-eighth part. The other parts (carry) the same benefit as before. One who gives the Meru in the form of an elephant together with the twelve mountains and the three beings (gods) would get infinite benefit. Meru (in the form) of a horse (would be) fifteen horses together with twelve horses. Giving this (as a gift) after worshipping lords Viṣṇu and others one would enjoy comforts and become a king. One should give a Meru (in the form) of cow of the same number as the horse as before.

27. A gift of a Meru (in the form) of cloth would be a *bhāra* of silk cloth in the middle with the twelve cloth as mountains (around). By giving (this gift) (one will have) undiminishing benefit.

28-29. A mountain of clarified butter (would be) five thousand *palas* of ghee, each one (of the mountains being) five hundred. One should worship lord Hari in this mountain. Having offered it to a brahmin in the presence of (lord) Viṣṇu, one would get everything and reach lord Hari. One would get (the same fruit) by making a Meru of sugarcandy and giving in the same way.

30-35. The Meru of grains (should be) five *khāri* (a measure equal to 15 *droṇas*) and the other (mountains) of one *khāri* each. All should have golden peaks (denoting lords) Brahmā, Viṣṇu and Maheśvara. One would acquire special benefit by worshipping lord Viṣṇu in all of them. One should set up a Meru of sesamum in the same way measuring ten parts. The peaks should be as before for that (mountain) and other mountains. One who makes a gift of a Meru of sesamum would reach the world of Viṣṇu together with his relatives. "Obeisance to the form of Viṣṇu. Obeisance to (the mountain) Dharādhara. (Obeisance) to one having lords Brahmā, Viṣṇu and Īśa on the peaks, to one remaining at the navel of the earth, to the lord of twelve mountains, to the destroyer of all sins, to the devotee of lord Viṣṇu and to the calm person. You always protect me so that I may reach lord Viṣṇu together with my forefathers becoming sinless. *Oṁ*, obeisance. You are indeed lord Hari. I am lord Viṣṇu in the front of (lord) Hari. I shall inform lord Viṣṇu with devotion for the sake of enjoyment and emancipation.

CHAPTER TWO HUNDRED AND THIRTEEN

Mode of making a gift of earth and its benefits

Fire-god said :

1-4. I shall describe (the mode of) making a gift of the earth. The earth is known to be of three kinds (extending to) hundred crores of *yojanas* (containing) seven continents and the oceans. That earth upto the continent of Jambū is spoken as excellent. One should make an excellent one with five *bhāras* (measure of weight) of gold. The tortoise and lotus (supporting that) should be laid with half that (measure). The excellent earth is said to be (of the full measure). The middle one (is said to have) two parts. The last one (should be of) one-third part. The tortoise and lotus will be one-third. The wish-yielding (celestial) tree should be made (to weigh) a thousand *palas*.

5-9. The central stalk (of the tree) together with the leaves, fruits and flowers and having five branches should be got ready and the five should be given by a good man. One who makes this gift would rejoice in the world of Brahmā together with the manes for a long time. The celestial cow (should be made) with five hundred *palas* in front of lord Viṣṇu. The gods Brahmā, Viṣṇu, Maheśa and others are settled in the cow. The gift of a cow is the gift of all (things). It gives all (things) and also the world of Brahmā. Having given a tawny cow one would elevate all families. By giving a girl (in marriage) after decorating her, one would acquire the benefit of (doing the) horse sacrifice. One who gives a land in which all grains grow would get everyting. One who gives a village or a town or a hamlet would be comfortable. By setting free a bull in *kārttika* one would elevate the family.

CHAPTER TWO HUNDRED AND FOURTEEN

The system of veins in the body and their benefits

Fire-god said :

1-4. I shall describe the system of veins by knowing which one would know lord Hari. Fibre-like things spread out from the bulbous root below the navel. They are seventy-two thousand situated at the centre of the navel. They spread out and occupy everywhere across, above and below. They are situated like a wheel. Among these *iḍā, piṅgalā, suṣumnā, gāndhārī, hastijihvā, pṛthā, yaśā, alambuṣā, huhu* and *śaṅkhinī* are the ten principal veins.

5-14. These veins are said to be carrying the ten life forces—*prāṇa, apāna, samāna, udāna vyāna, nāga, kūrma, kṛkara, devadatta* and *dhanañjaya*. *Prāṇa* is the chief wind and is the lord of the ten. The *prāṇa* makes the life living from exhalation after the inhalation. Remaining in the chest of beings it fills up daily. The *prāṇa* gets united with life by exhalation, inhalation and coughing. Because it moves out from the life it is said to be *prāṇa*. *Apāna* pushes down the food in men. It is said to be *apāna* because it is the wind that carries the urine and semen. The wind known as *samāna* equalises the blood, biles, phlegm and wind in the body (caused by) drinking, eating and smelling.

The wind known as *udāna* agitates the vulnerable points and causes the quivering of lips, face and causes change in the complexion of the eye. (The wind) *vyāna* depresses the body and activates the disease. It is said to be *vyāna* because it returns from the throat and spreads out. The wind *nāga* (is known to be) in vomitting and *kūrma* remains in the opening. (The wind) *kṛkara* is in eating, *devadatta* in yawning, *dhanañjaya* in raising loud sound. They do not abandon even the dead. Thus goes the life cycle with the ten activities. Hence it is the cycle of veins.

15-20. The solstices, the equinoxes, day and night, the sun's passage north and south of the equator, intercalary month, debt, the incomplete night and wealth (are attributed to the different parts of the body and their functions). The incomplete night would be the hiccough and the intercalary mouth the yawning. The debt would be coughing. The exhalation is said to be wealth. The right side (of the body) is known to be the north and the left side is designated as the south. The equinoctical points are said to be in the middle line passing through the two parts while the solstice is that passing from its own nerve-centre to another centre. O Brahmin ! Suṣumnā is established in the middle of the body, the *iḍā* on the left and the *piṅgalā* on the right. The *prāṇa* above is remembered to be the day. In the same way *apāna* would be the night. One wind (exists) in ten forms. The expanse in the middle of the body is said to be the lunar eclipse. The expanse between the principles of the body is known to be the solar eclipse.

21. Filling the abdomen with wind as much as one desires is known to be the *prāṇāyāma* known as the *pūraka* because it fills up.

22. After covering all the holes, one should remain like a pot after filling (the abdomen with air) without exhalation and inhalation. That is the *kumbhaka* (variety of) *prāṇāyāma.*

23-26. One who knows the sacred syllable should push the wind upwards and let out in one breath. He should evacuate it upwards (to the region of the brain). Since (lord) Śiva residing in the body (of beings) himself utters (that) (the letter ha), that is said to be the repetition for those who know the principles. That master of *yoga* does the repetition twentyone thousand six hundred times in the course of a day and night. This *gāyatri* known as the *ajapā* is of the form of Brahmā, Viṣṇu and Maheśvara. There is no rebirth for one that repeats this *ajapā* (*mantra*).

27. The foremost *kuṇḍalinī* (the energy coiled in one of the psychometric centres) is considered to be associated with the moon, fire and sun. It is known to remain in the heart in the form. of a sprout.

28-32. The location of the creation should be therein because of its suspension from that. The foremost worshipper should contemplate therein the flowing ambrosia. The *sakala* (endowed with the parts) is known to be remaining in the body and the *niṣkala* (without the parts) as devoid of the body. That one who repeats *haṁsa* is the lord Sadāśiva (ever auspicious). That person remains in the body of the man both outside and inside just as oil in the sesamum and fragrance in the flowers. Lord *Brahmā* has his place in the heart. Lord Viṣṇu remains at the throat. Lord Rudra is situated in the middle of the cheeks. Lord Maheśvara is at the forehead. Lord Śiva should be known as the tip of the vital principle and the higher and the lower as its end. The *sakala* form is said to be of five kinds and *niṣkala* form as the contrary.

33-41. That person who produces the sound that is *prāsāda* (propitious) and repeats hundred times would no doubt get accomplished in six months endowed with *yoga*. There will be destruction of all sins because of the knowledge of the past and future events. One would get virtues such as *aṇimā* (the power to become minute as an atom) in six months. The *prāsāda* has been described by me as three: gross, subtle and foremost. *Prāsāda* is of three kinds—short, long and protracted. The short one burns sins. The long one would confer emancipation. The elongated one is in accomplishing things. It is adorned with a dot on its head. The syllable *phaṭ* is beneficial at the beginning and end of the short sound for the sake of destroying an enemy. The heart (*mantra*) at the beginning and end is stated to be useful in captivating (others' minds). One should repeat (the same) five lakhs time (standing facing) the southern face of the deity. After the repetition there should be oblation of ghee ten thousand times. With the sacred syllable having been accomplished thus one should do the repetition for captivating etc. It is void above, void in the middle and void below. It is devoid of blemishes. Whichever brahmin knows the three voids would certainly be released (from the mundane existence). One is said to be not a preceptor if he does not know the *prāsāda*, made of the five sacred syllables, endowed with thirtyeight parts. So also the preceptor knows the syllable *oṁ*, the *gāyatrī*, (lord) Rudra and others.

CHAPTER TWO HUNDRED AND FIFTEEN

Mode of reciting gāyatrī and its greatness

Fire-god said :

1-3. One who knows the syllable *oṁ* is verily a yogin and (the lord) Hari. Hence one should practise the syllable *oṁ*, that is the essence of all sacred syllables, and the giver of all things. The *praṇava* (*oṁ*) is known to be the first in the application of all the sacred syllables. Hence the act which becomes complete with that, will not get completed with any other (syllable). There are three great unmutilating *vyāhṛtis* (syllables) which are preceded by the syllable *oṁ*. The three-footed *sāvitrī* (*gāyatrī*) should be known as the face of (lord) Brahmā.

4. One who unweariedly repeats these everyday for three years, reaches the supreme brahman becoming the wind and embodying the sky.

5. The one syllable is the supreme brahman and *prāṇāyāma* (control of the birth) in the supreme penance. There is nothing greater than *sāvitrī*. Truthfulness excels silence.

6-7. The repetition (of *gāyatrī*) seven times would destroy one's sins and ten times would convey (the person) to heaven. That goddess repeated twenty times would convey him to the abode of (lord) *Īśvara* (Śiva). One would cross the ocean of mundane existence by repeating it hundred and eight times. The *Gāyatrī* excels the repetition of Rudra and Kūṣmāṇḍa (*mantras*) in its merit.

8-9. There is nothing excelling *Gāyatrī* for repetition. There is nothing equal to *vyāhṛtis* for doing oblations. A quarter of the hymn or a half of it or half the hymn or the whole hymn being repeated purifies one of the sins such as the killing of a brahmin, drinking of wine, stealing of gold and cohabiting the preceptor's wife.

10. On having committed a sin it is said that one should do oblations with sesamum repeating Gāyatrī. After repetition of Gāyatrī a thousand times and fasting one gets rid of his sin.

11-12. The killer of a cow, the patricide, the matricide, the killer of a brahmin, the defiler of the bed of preceptor, the person who has stolen gold and the drunkard get purified after repetition (of the *mantra*) a lakh number of times. Otherwise one should bathe and repeat hundred times remaining in the water. One would get rid of his sin by drinking water (consecrated by the repetition) of Gāyatrī hundred times.

13. The Gāyatrī repeated hundred times is remembered to destroy one's sins. That goddess repeated a thousand times would destroy the minor offences.

14-21. The repetition a crore times would yield the desired benefits and lead one to godhead and sovereignty. After having uttered the syllable *oṁ* first and (the syllables) *bhūḥ*, *bhuvaḥ* and *svaḥ* (the earth, sky and heaven) then, and the *praṇava* (*oṁ*) and Gāyatrī at the end is said to be (the mode) for repetition. *Viśvāmitra* is the sage, *gāyatrī* the metre and Savitā (Sun) the god (for the *mantra*) when it is used for appeasement (of gods), for repetition and for offering oblation. The gods who preside over different letters constituting the *mantra* are the Fire god, Wind god, Sun, Lightning, God of Death, lord of the water (ocean), Jupiter, God of rain, Indra, Gandharva, Pūṣan, Mitra, Varuṇa, Tvaṣṭṛ, Vasus, Maruts, Moon, Aṅgiras, Viśve (devas), *Nāsatya* (Aśvins), Ka, Rudra, Brahmā and Viṣṇu respectively who are said to destroy sins at the time of repetition of Gāyatrī. (They respectively protect) the toes, ankles, legs, knees, shanks, the male organ of generation, testicles, hip, navel, belly, breasts, heart, neck, face, cheek, nostrils, eyes, the centre of the eye-brows, forehead, front part of the face, the two sides on the right and left, head and the mouth in order.

22-24. Yellow, blue, tawny, green, colour of the fire, the golden colour of lightning, smoky, black, red, white, colour of the sapphire, crystal coloured, golden, white, red, all the lustre, golden, smoky, blood red, blue red, golden, white, dark green are the colours of Gāyatrī. It destroys sins at the time of repetition and confers all desires when used to offer oblation.

25-28. Oblations made with sesamum and Gāyatrī would destroy all sins. One who desires to appease should do with barley. One who desires life should do with ghee. For success in one's work (one should do) with white mustard. (One should do) with milk for spiritual splendour, with curd if one wishes to have children, with *sāli* (grains) if one desires to get grains. One (should do oblation) with twigs of *kṣīri* (milky) trees for the appeasement of affliction due to planets. Then one desiring for wealth (should do) with *bilva* (a kind of tree) and desiring for fortune (should do) with lotuses. (One should do) with *dūrvā* (a kind of grass) if he desires for health and the same if portents (are met with). (One should do) with *guggulu* (gum-resin) aspiring for prosperity and with sweet porridge if seeking knowledge.

29. There would be the indicated success with (oblation done) ten thousand times and the mentally desired (benefit) with a lakh times. One would be released from (the sin accrued) by killing a brahmin, be lord Hari and the elevator of the family with (oblations done) crore times.

30-31. One should invoke Gāyatrī at the commencement of oblations done for propitiating the planets or the one for ten thousand times or any other sacrifices. Then he should meditate on the syllable *oṁ*. After having remembered the syllable *oṁ* one should tie up the tuft with the Gāyatrī. Then after having sipped (three drops of water) one should touch the heart, navel and shoulders.

32. The sage is Brahmā, the metre is *gāyatrī* and the god is the Fire god for the *praṇava* (*oṁ*). It is the Supreme soul and it should be associated in all acts.

33-34. (She should be contemplated as) possessing white complexion, having fire as the mouth, divine, born in the *gotra* of Kātyāyana, encircling the three worlds, associated with the support of the earth, wearing the rosary, the goddess seated in the *padmāsana* (posture of sitting with legs crossed) and auspicious (with the following words): "*Oṁ* ! You are the lustre, the sacrifice, the strength, one of the seven Suns, the abode of the gods, the universe, the life of the universe, all beings and the life of all beings. *Oṁ* ! to the earth. O Goddess ! Bestower of boon ! You come ! The one to be repeated ! You be present before me !"

35-37. Prajāpati is the sage for all *vyāhṛtis* (the syllables *bhū* etc.). (They are used) separately and collectively with the letter *oṁ* of Brahmā. The sages (of the *vyāhṛtis* are) Viśvāmitra, Jamadagni, Bharadvāja, Gautama, Atri, Vasiṣṭha and Kaśyapa in order. Fire god, Wind god, Sun, Jupiter, Varuṇa, Indra, Viṣṇu are the (presiding) deities of *vyāhṛtis* in order.

38. Gāyatrī, Uṣṇik, Anuṣṭubh, Bṛhatī, Paṅkti, Triṣṭubh, and Jagatī are said to be metres (of these) respectively.

39-40. It is remembered that eight drops of water should be thrown upwards with the hymn *āpo hi ṣṭhā*[1] or *drupadāt*[2] or *hiraṇya-varṇāṁ*[3] or *pāvamānī*[4] at the end in the use of the *vyāhṛtis*, in the *prāṇāyāma* and in oblation. It destroys the sin done since the birth.

41. One should recite (the hymn) *ṛtaṁ ca*[5], the destroyer of sins, thrice in the water. Sindhudvīpa is the sage for the hymn *āpo hi ṣṭhā*.

42. The metre is *gāyatrī* and deity water for this (hymn) for *brahmasnāna* (bathing to get rid of sin). It should be used for sprinkling water on the body or at the time of bathing at the conclusion of a sacrifice.

43. Aghamarṣaṇa is the sage for this *aghamarṣaṇa* hymn. Anuṣṭubh would be the metre. Bhāvavṛtta is the deity.

44-49. (The *mantra*) *āpo jyotī raso*[6] is remembered to be the head of Gāyatrī. Prajāpati (Brahmā) is the sage for that because the *yajur* (*mantras*) are not metrical. Brahmā, Fire god, Wind god and Sun are said to be deities. The wind is generated from the suppression of breath. Fire is produced from wind. Water (is produced) from fire and then purity. Then one should rinse. It moves within beings, cavity and universal gods. The syllable *vaṣaṭ* is the sacrifice in the form of

1. ṚV.10.9.1.
2. AV. 6.115.3.
3. This is Śrīsūkta, ṚVkh. 5.87.1.
4. Designation of ṚV. 9.1.1 ff
5. ṚV.10.190. 1.
6. ṚV.10.9.

penance. Water is the lustrous sap of nectar. The sage of the hymn *udu tyam jātavedasaṁ*[1] is said to be Praskanna (?): *Gāyatrī* is stated to be the metre and Sun the deity. It is used in the *atirātra* (sacrifice) and the *agniṣṭoma* is the employer. Kautsa is stated to be the sage for the hymn *citraṁ devānām*[2]. *Triṣṭubh* is said to be the metre for this (hymn) and Sun the deity.

CHAPTER TWO HUNDRED AND SIXTEEN

Complete instruction relating to Gāyatrī

Fire-god said :

1-4. After having performed the twilight worship thus, one should recite *Gāyatrī*. It is known to be *Gāyatrī* because it saves disciples, wives and lives. It is known as the *Sāvitrī* because it illumines the Sun. It is (known as) *Sarasvatī* because it is the form of speech. It is known to be the *bharga*, the lustre, because it is the effulgence of supreme brahman. (The root) *bhā* denotes shining. It is also known that *bhrasj* denotes cooking. It ripens the herbs etc. (The root) *bhrājṛ* would denote shining. (The word) *Bharga* would be (denoting) shining. (In this sense) it has been used in the scriptures many times.

5-6. (It is said to be) most excellent because it has an exalted position than all the splendours. It is the one always desired by those who wish to attain heaven. As (the word) *vṛṇoti* means covering, (it signifies) an eternal, absolutely pure conscious, absolutely real and great god that is beyond (the states of) waking, dreaming and deep sleep.

7-10. I am that brahman, the supreme effulgence. I contemplate on that for the emancipation. That effulgence is lord Viṣṇu that is the cause of origin of the universe. Some read Śiva, some read a form of goddess, some Sun and some such as those learned in the scriptures and those propitiating fire, the fire (god). Lord Viṣṇu of the form of fire etc. is praised in the scriptures as the *brahman*. That most exalted place of lord Viṣṇu is known to be that of lord Savitā (Sun). That lord Hari, the self effulgent produces the (libations of) clarified butter.

1. ṚV.1.50. 1.
2. ṚV.1.115. 1.

(The same god) as the god of rain, the god of wind and the Sun would nourish (everything) by means of cold, heat etc.

11. Libations cast into the fire reach the Sun. Rains are produced from the Sun. Food grains (grow) from rain and then the people.

12-13. (The word) *dhīmahi* (may be) from the root *dhā* (to hold). (It means) "May we retain in our minds". The word *naḥ* (means) 'our' May that Bharga who is in the intellects of all beings prompt the intellects of those who enjoy in all their acts and results seen and unseen. He is of the form of Viṣṇu, Sun and Fire.

14. Being prompted by the lord one may reach heaven or the pit (of mundane existence). Everything is an abode of the lord. Lord Hari is verily (the worlds) such as the *mahat*.

15-16. "I am that lord who sports with the paradise and the like. That lord the universal being known as Bharga inside the Sun should be contemplated by those desiring for emancipation for the destruction of birth and death and the three kinds of griefs. This universal being should be beheld in the orb of the Sun.

17. You are that Supreme Being, the conscious *brahman* which is the exalted position of lord Viṣṇu. I am Bharga, the most exalted fourth place of lord Sun. I am the body and the like, the state of waking and that upto that *brahman*. I deem myself as the *brahman*. I am that absolute spirit in the Sun. I am the infinite. *Oṁ*. I am that one who always directs the knowledge in auspicious acts and the like.

CHAPTER TWO HUNDRED AND SEVENTEEN

Vasiṣṭha's hymn to lord Śiva

Fire-god said :

1. After having propitiated lord Śiva of the form of the *liṅga* with Gâyatrī, Vasiṣṭha obtained *yoga*. Moreover he

got the exalted *brahman* and emancipation from lord Śaṅkara (Śiva).

2. Obeisance to the golden *liṅga* and the *liṅga* in the form of scriptures. Obeisance to the supreme *liṅga* and the *liṅga* in the form of the sky.

3. Obeisance to the thousand *liṅga*-s and the *liṅga* in the form of the fire. Obeisance to the *liṅga* of the forms of the *Purāṇa* and the scriptures.

4. Obeisance to the *liṅga* in the form of the nether worlds and the *brahman*. Obeisance to the mysterious *liṅga* and the *liṅga* above the seven continents.

5. Obeisance to the *liṅga* as the soul of all beings and to the *liṅga* that is the limb of all people. Obeisance to the unmanifest *liṅga* and the *liṅga* of the form of the intellect.

6. Obeisance to the *liṅga* representing the ego and to the *liṅga* denoting the beings. Obeisance to the *liṅga* of the form of senses and the subtle principles.

7. Obeisance to the *liṅga* denoting the Supreme spirit and the sentiments. Obeisance to the *liṅga* above the (principle of) *rajas* and to the (principle) of *sattva*.

8. Obeisance to the *liṅga* of the form of becoming and of the form of the three qualities. Obeisance to the *liṅga* denoting future and the form of lustre.

9. Obeisance to the *liṅga* beyond the wind and of the form of the scriptures. Obeisance to the *liṅga* in the form of the (hymns of) *Atharva* (*veda*) and the *Sāma* (*veda*).

10. Obeisance to the *liṅga* that is the limb of the sacrifice and of the form of the sacrifice. Obeisance to the *liṅga* of the form of principles and to the *liṅga* of the form of the companion of the lord.

11. You impart me the excellent *yoga*. (Bless me) with a son equal to me. O Lord ! May I attain the imperishable *brahman*. O Lord (you also confer) tranquillity. May the progeny be without break and let them have an undiminishing interest in righteousness.

Fire-god said :

12. Once after having been propitiated by Vasiṣṭha on the Śrīparvata (mountain) thus, Śambhu (Śiva) granted the boon to Vasiṣṭha and disappeared there itself.

CHAPTER TWO HUNDRED AND EIGHTEEN

Mode of performing the coronation of a king

Fire-god said :

1. O Vasiṣṭha ! I shall describe now the duties of a king as told by Puṣkara to Rāma as the latter asked (him the same).

Puṣkara said :

2. I shall describe the duties of a king (foremost) among the host of other duties. The king should be the slayer of the enemy, protector of the subjects and administer justice properly.

3-6. He would look after the welfare of all those who are on the righteous path. He should practise this vow. He has to choose the astrologer, the brahmin priest, the ministers who had known the minds of the people and the queen endowed with righteous qualities. (After having practised the vow) for a year the king should have the anointment with all the regal paraphernalia at the proper moment. But there is no regulation about time for the same if the king has died (and a new king is installed). He should be bathed with sesamum and mustard and the astrologer and the priest should hail victory for the king. (Then the king) seated on the throne should proclaim protection (for all) and throw open (the gates of) the fortress for the provincial governors.

7-11. Before the anointment (is done), the priest should do the rite to appease Indra. After having fasted on the day of anointment, offerings should be made into the sacrificial fire for the Manus with the sacred syllables of lord Viṣṇu, Indra, Savitṛ (Sun), and the Viśvedevas and the sacred syllables that are auspicious, beneficial, conferring longevity and protection. The golden pitcher known as *aparājitā* (not defeated by anybody) containing the remnants of the sacrifice should be worshipped with perfumes and flowers on the right side of the fire. (The sacrificial) fire should have flames circling clockwise, having the colour of heated gold, should be like the moving chariot, be making sound like the cloud and without smoke. The flames in their natural form, fragrant, resembling the figure of a *svastika*[1], with clear and high flames and without sparks are benevolent.

1. Made up of two lines intersecting at right angles having perpendicular lines in the clock-wise direction at the ends of two lines.

12-17. Cats, deer and birds should not pass between (the king and the sacrificial fire). The king should cleanse his head with the mud (obtained) from the summit of a mountain, the ears with the mud from the top of an anthill, the face with that (mud) from the temple of (lord) Keśava, the neck with the mud from the temple of (lord) Indra, the heart (breast) with that (got) from the courtyard of the king (king's palace), the right arm with the mud dug up by the tusk of an elephant, the left arm with the mud dug up by the horns of a bull, the back with the mud from a tank, the abdomen with the mud from the confluence of rivers and the sides should be purified with the mud from both the banks of a river. It is laid down that the waist of a king should be cleansed with the mud (obtained) from the threshold of a courtesan, the thigh (with mud got) from the sacrificial place, the knees (with mud obtained) from the cow-shed, the shanks (with that got) from the stable, the feet with the mud from the wheel of a chariot. The head of the king seated on the throne (should be washed) with the five things got from a cow.

18-29. Four ministers (of the king) should anoint him with (waters from) the pitchers. A brahmin (minister should anoint him) with a golden pitcher filled with ghee from the east, a *kṣatriya* (minister) with a silver pitcher filled with milk from the south, a *vaiśya* (minister) with a copper pitcher (filled) with curd from the west and a *śūdra* minister with an earthen (pot) with water from the north. Then a brahmin priest reciting the *Ṛgveda* should anoint the king with honey and a priest of the *Sāmaveda* with waters along with the *kuśa*. O Fortunate one ! Then the (royal) priest should go towards the pitcher containing the residual offering , perform duly the protective amulet of the fire for the courtiers and give it (to the king) with those sacred syllables mentioned in connection with the coronation and with the recitations made by the brahmins. Then the priest should go to the foot of the sacrificial platform and anoint (the king) with a golden vessel having hundred holes. The head (of the king) should be touched with the herbs with (the recitation of the sacred syllables) *yā oṣadhī*[1],

1. ṚV. 10.97. 1.

with perfumes, with flowers with (the syllables) *puṣpavatī*[1], with seeds with (the syllables) *brāhmaṇa*[2], with gems with (the syllables) *āśuḥ śiśānaḥ*[3], with *kuśa* dipped in water with (the syllables) *ye devāḥ*[4] and a reciter of the *Yajurveda* or the *Atharvaveda* should touch the head and throat with *rocanā* with (the recitation of the syllables) *gandhadvārā*[5] and other brahmins with all the sacred waters. Then they should hold a pitcher filled with the herbs in front of the king to the accompaniment of singing and instrumental music and the (waving of) chowries and fans. The king also should see them as well as the auspicious things such as the mirror and ghee etc. Then the priest, seated on a bed covered with a tiger-skin, should worship (gods) Viṣṇu, Brahmā, Indra and others and the lords of planets and place the turban after having given the respectful offering of mixture of honey.

30-34. The crown of the king should be fixed with the hides of five animals. The king should place the hides of a bull, a cat, elephant, lion and tiger on that seat with (the recitation of the sacred syllables) *dhruvā dyauḥ*[6]. Then the door-keeper should present the ministers to the king. Then the king should give presents of cows, goats, sheep, houses and other gifts to the astrologers and priests. (The other) brahmins should be honoured by (giving gifts of) land, cows, food etc. Then (the king) should circumambulate the (sacrificial) fire and make obeisance to the preceptor. (He should then move) backwards, touch the bull and worship the cow and calf. Then he should ride the consecrated (royal) steed. Similarly, he should worship the royal elephant and mount it. He should then go round the royal path along with his army. Then he should enter the palace and send away all (those gathered) after pleasing them with gifts.

1. ṚV. 10.97.3.
2. AV. 5. 17. 9.
3. ṚV. 10.103. 1.
4. MS. 2. 6. 3.
5. ṚV Kh. 5. 87. 9.
6. ṚV. 10.173. 4.

CHAPTER TWO HUNDRED AND NINETEEN

Sacred syllables for coronation

Puṣkara said :

1. I shall describe the sacred syllables for the anointment of a king or god which would destroy sins. One would accomplish everything by sprinkling water from the pot with the *kuśa*.

2-6. (The sacred syllables are as follows) : "May the gods Brahmā, Viṣṇu, Maheśvara, Vāsudeva, Saṅkarṣaṇa, Pradyumna and Aniruddha install you. May the gods Indra and others occupying ten cardinal points confer victory on you. The lords of created beings such as Rudra, Dharma, Manu, Dakṣa, Ruci, Śraddhā, Bhṛgu, Atri, Vasiṣṭha, Sanaka, Sanandana, Sanatkumāra, Aṅgiras, Pulastya, Pulaha, Kratu, Marīci and Kaśyapa guard (you) always. May the God of Death, lustrous celestials, (the manes) Barhiṣadas, Agniṣvāttas Kravyādas, Upahūtas, Ājyapas and Sukālins guard you. May (the goddesses) Lakṣmī and others, the consorts of Dharma anoint you with fires.

7-13. May the consorts of Ādityas and others, the progeny of Kaśyapa, having many offspring, the wives of Kṛśāśva, the son of Agni, (the wives) of Ariṣṭanemi, Aśvinī and others, (the wives) of the Moon and the wives of Pulaha, namely, Bhūtā, Kapīśā, Daṁṣṭrī, Surasā, Saramā, Danu, Śyenī, Bhāsī, Krauñcī, Dhṛtarāṣṭrī and Śukī (install you). (May) Aruṇa, the charioteer of the Sun anoint you. May Āyati (future), Niyati (fate), Rātri (night) and Nidrā (sleep) who stabilise the world and support it as well as (the goddesses) Umā, (consort of Śiva), Menā (wife of Himavān), Śacī (wife of Indra) guard (you). May Dhūmrā, Ūrṇā and Nirṛti (confer) victory. May (the goddesses) Gaurī, Śivā, Ṛddhi, Velā, Naḍvalā, Asiknī and Jyotsnā, the consorts of the celestials and the presiding deity of the forest (confer victory). May the *mahākalpa* (greater cycle of time), *kalpa* (smaller cycle of time), *manvantara* (Manu periods), *yugas* (a certain long period of time), *saṁvatsara* (years), *varṣas* and the two half years (based on the movement of the sun) guard you. May the seasons, months, fortnights, night, day, twilight, *tithis* (lunar days), *muhūrtas* (period of 48 minutes), which are the constituents of the time personified (guard you).

14-41. May the planets such as the Sun as well as (the fourteen Manus) Svāyambhuva and other Manus guard you. Svāyambhuva, Svārociṣa, Auttami, Tāmasa, Raivata, Cākṣuṣa the sixth, Vaivasvata, Sāvarṇi, Brahmaputra, Dharmaputra, Rudraja, Dakṣaja, Raucya and Bhautya are the fourteen Manus. May the foremost celestials Viśvabhuk, Vipaścit, Sucitti, Śikhī, Vibhu, Manojava, Ojasvī, Bali, Adbhuta, Śānti, Vṛṣa, Ṛtadhāmā, Divaspṛk, Kavi, Indraka, Raivanta, Kumāra, Vatsaka, Vināyaka, Vīrabhadra, Nandī, Viśvakarmā and Purojava anoint you. May the celestial physicians Nāsatyā,[1] the eight Vasus Dhruva and others, the ten Aṅgirasas and the scriptures anoint you for gaining perfection. May the soul, duration of life, mind, mental power, egoism, life-breath, possessed of oblation, the most important, divine law and truth guard you. May Kratu, Dakṣa, Vasu, Satya, Kālakāma and Dhuri (lead you) to victory. May the Purūravas, Mādravas, Viśvedevas, Rocana, Aṅgāraka and others, Sūrya, Nirṛti and Yama, Ajaikapāt, Ahirbudhnya, Dhūmaketu, Rudrajas, Bharata, Mṛtyu, Kāpāli, Kiṅkiṇī, Bhavana and Bhāvana protect you with their children and wives, Kratuśravāḥ, Mūrddhā, Yājana, Abhyuśanāḥ, Prasava, Avyaya, Dakṣa, Bhṛgu, the celestials, Manaḥ Anumantā, Prāṇaḥ, Nava, Apāna, Vīryavān, Vītihotra, Naya, Sādhya, Haṁsa and Nārāyaṇa protect you. May the foremost among the celestials who are devoted to the welfare of universe such as Vibhu, Prabhu, and the twelve Suns Dhātā, Mitra, Aryamā, Pūṣā, Śakra, Varuṇa, Bhaga, Tvaṣṭā, Vivasvān, Savitā and Viṣṇu as well as Ekajyotis, Dvirjyotis, Trijyotis, Caturjyotis, Ekaśakra, Dviśakra, Triśakra, Mahābala and Indra command (saying) 'do not'. Then may Pratimākṛt, Mita, Sammita, Amita, Mahābala, Ṛtajit, Satyajit, Suṣeṇa, Senajit, Atimitra, Anumitra, Purumitra, Aparājita, Ṛta, Ṛtavāk, Dhātā, Vidhātā, Dhāraṇa, Dhruva and Vidhāraṇa, the mighty friend of Indra, Īdṛkṣa, Adṛkṣa, Etādṛk, Amitāśana, Krīḍita, Sadṛkṣa, Sarabha, Mahātapas, Dhartā, Dhurya, Dhuri, Bhīma, Abhimukta, Kṣapātsaha, Dhṛti, Vasu Anādhṛṣya, Rāma, Kāma, Jaya, Virāṭ, the forty-nine wind gods protect you. May the Gandharvas—Citrāṅgada, Citraratha, Citrasena, Kali, Ūrṇāyu, Ugrasena, Dhṛtarāṣṭra,

1. Literally means helpful, denotes the Aśvinī kumāras, the celestial physicians.

Nandaka, Hāhā, Hūhū, Nārada, Viśvāvasu and Tumburu anoint you for your victory. May the foremost among the priests and the divine group of damsels Anavadyā, Sukeśī, Menakā, Sahajanyā, Kratusthalā, Ghṛtācī, Viśvācī, Puñjikasthalā, Pramlocā, Ūrvaśī, Rambhā, Pañcacūḍā, Tilottamā, Citralekhā, Lakṣmaṇā, Puṇḍarīkā and Vāruṇī guard you. May the demons Prahlāda, Virocana, Bali and Bāṇa and their sons and other foremost demons Heti,Praheti, Vidyut, Sphūrjathu anoint you. (May) the Yakṣa, the accomplished soul-Maṇibhadra, Nandana, Piṅgākṣa, Dyutimān and Puṣpavanta bring forth victory. (May) the treasures *śaṅkha*(conch), *padma* (lotus), *makara* (fish), *kacchapa* (tortoise) (bring) victory.

42-46. May the ghosts Ūrdhvakeśa and others, the goblins who dwell on the earth, the (divine) mothers led by Mahākāla (form of Śiva at deluge) and Narasiṁha (man-lion form of Viṣṇu), Guha (son of Śiva), Skanda, Viśākha and Naigameya (other names of Guha) anoint you. May the female goblins and female attendants on God Śiva dwelling in the sky and on the earth and the principal birds such as the Garuḍa, Aruṇa and Sampāti guard you. May the great serpents Ananta, Vāsuki, Takṣaka, Airāvata, Mahāpadma, Kambala, Aśvatara, Śaṅkha, Karkoṭaka, Dhṛtarāṣṭra and Dhanañjaya, and the elephants Kumuda, Airāvaṇa, Padma, Puṣpadanta, Vāmana, Supratīka and Añjana protect you always from all evils.

47. May the swan, the bull, the lion and the buffalo, (respectively the vehicles) of Brahmā, Śaṅkara, Durgā and God of Death guard you.

48. (May) Uccaiḥśravas, the lord of the horses, (lord) Dhanvantari, Kaustubha, the foremost among the conches, always (proect) the mace, spear and the disc.

49. May Nandaka, Dharma, the governor of conduct, Citragupta, the wielder of the punishing rod, Piṅgala, Mṛtyu (death) and Kālaka (the regulator of time) protect the weapons.

50-51. May the sages Vālakhilyas and others and the foremost among the sages such as Vyāsa and Vālmīki, (the foremost among the kings of the past) Pṛthu, Dilīpa, Bharata, Duṣyanta, Śakrajit,Bali,Malla, Kakutstha, Anenas, Yuvanāśva, Jayadratha, Māndhātā, Mucukunda and Purūravas guard you.

52-53. May the presiding deities of the grounds and the twentyfive principles confer victory on you. (May) the golden earth, rocky soil, nether world, blue soil, yellowish red earth, white soil, Rasātala (a nether world), the earth, the terrestrial region and the foremost among the continents Jambū etc. (bring you) fortune.

54-55. May the Uttarakurus and the continents Ramya, Hiraṇyaka, Bhadrāśva, Ketumāla, Balāhaka, Harivarṣa, Kimpuruṣa, Indradvīpa, Kaśerumān, Tāmravarṇa, Gabhastimān, Nāgadvīpa and Saumyaka guard you.

56-72. Varuṇa, the ninth *gandharva*, the conferer of dominion protect you. The mountains Himavān. Hemakūṭa Niṣadha, Nīla, Śveta, Śṛṅgavān, Meru, Mālyavān, Gandhamādana, Mahendra, Malaya, Sahya, Śūktimān, Ṛkṣavān, Vindhya and Pāriyātra bestow peace upon you. May the *Ṛgveda* and the other (*Vedas*), the six accessory texts[1] *Itihāsa* and *Purāṇas*, medical science, science of music and archery, the accessory *Vedas* protect you. Phonetics, the texts laying down rules for sacrificial acts, grammar, etymology, astronomy and metrics, the (four) scriptural texts, *mīmāṁsā*[2], the science of logic, code of laws and *Purāṇa* are the fourteen branches of learning. (The schools of philosophy such as) the *Sāṅkhya* and *Yoga*, the *Pāśupata*[3], the Vedas and the *Pāñcarātra*[4] are the five dogmas. May (the goddesses) Gāyatrī, Śivā, Durgā, Vidyā and Gāndhārī protect you and confer peace on you. May the four oceans of salt, sugarcane juice, liquor, clarified butter, curd, milk and water and the different sacred spots protect you . (They are) Puṣkara, Prayāga, Prabhāsa, the excellent Naimiṣa, Gayāśīrṣa, Brahmaśira, Uttaramānasa, Kālodaka, Nandikuṇḍa, Pañcanadatīrtha, Bhṛgutīrtha, Prabhāsa, Amarakaṇṭaka, Jambūmārga, the spotless, the hermitage of Kapila, Gaṅgādvāra (Haridvāra), Kuśāvarta, Vindhyaka, Nīlaparvata, Varāhaparvata, Kanakhala, Kālañjara, Kedāra, Rudrakoṭi, Vārāṇasī, the great spot Badarikāśrama, Dvārakā, Śrīgiri, Puruṣottoma (Puri), Śālagrāma and Vāraha, the spots of confluence of the rivers with the ocean, Phalgutīrtha, Bindusara, Karavīrāśrama and the rivers Gaṅgā,

1. Phonetics, the texts laying down rules for sacrificial acts, grammar, etymology, metrics and astronomy.
2. The texts dealing with the interpretation of vedic texts.
3. Śaivite philosophical texts.
4. Vaiṣṇavite philosophical texts.

Sarasvatī, Śatadru, Gaṇḍakī, Acchodā, Vipāśā, Vitastā, Devikā, Kāverī, Varuṇā, Niścirā, Gomatī, Pārā, Carmaṇvatī, Rūpā, Mandākinī, Mahānadī, Tāpī, Payoṣṇī, Veṇā, Gaurī, Vaitaraṇī, Godāvarī, Bhīmarathī, Tuṅgabhadrā, Araṇī and Candrabhāgā (and the goddesses) Śivā (and) Gaurī anoint and protect you.

CHAPTER TWO HUNDRED AND TWENTY

Accomplishment of assistance to the king

Puṣkara said :

1-7. A foremost king thus crowned along with his ministers should conquer the enemies. A brahmin or a *kṣatriya* should be appointed by the king as the commander-in-chief. He should also be a descendant of a noble family and well-versed in ethics. The door-keeper (should be) learned in ethics. The emissary should be speaking sweet, strong and a matchless warrior. The betel-bearer (may be) a man or a woman devoted (to the king), capable of enduring fatigue and be affectionate. One who is proficient in the six expedients of royal policy[1] should be made the minister of foreign affairs. A guard should bear the sword. A charioteer should know the strength of (the hostile) army. The chief cook (should be) a beneficiary, learned and one living in the (royal) kitchen. The courtiers should be well-versed in righteousness. The (royal) scribe should be well versed in (the art of) writing. The door-keepers should know the appropriate time of call and bebeneficial. The treasurer should be a man well-acquainted with the gems and be beneficial in the acquisition of wealth. The royal physician should know the science of medicine. The superintendent of elephants should know (the science of) elephants. The rider of an elephant should be one who has conquered fatigue. The superintendent of horses should know equinology. The superintendents of forts should be beneficient and wise. The architects should be well-versed in the nature of the grounds.

1. Alliance, war, march, halt, seeking shelter and duplicity.

8. Persons (employed) to give instructions in (the use of) weapons, should be well-versed in the use of weapons projected by the machines or discharged by the hands or not discharged entirely or discharged and held back and fight with hands. He should be beneficial to the king.

9. The officer in the harem should be old, fifty years old if women and seventy years old if men. They should be engaged in all types of work.

10-15. (The man) in (charge) of the arsenal should be wakeful. A person is employed in a task after knowing (his ability). A king should employ foremost, medium and ordinary people after knowing the tasks as excellent, medium and ordinary. A king desirous of victory should bring beneficial accomplices. Righteous men (should be engaged) in righteous acts, valorous men in tasks like battle, clever men in acts yielding material gains and men of good conduct in all acts. Eunuchs should be employed in (matters relating to) women and cruel-(hearted men) in cruel deeds. Whomsoever the king knows to be of good conduct, that person should be employed (by the kings) in the acts of piety, acquisition of wealth and pleasure. Vile people (should be employed) in bad acts. The king should employ in appropriate task those people whose fidelity has been tested. The minister should engage properly men of the same kind to find the evil doers just as an elephant (is employed to control) the wild ones.

16-24. Experts should be employed in their own fields of specialization. The servants who have been serving since the time of the grandfather and father (of the king) should be engaged to do all tasks except in matters which are to be done by the heirs. In those acts, only those who have come (in that line should be employed). Men who have come from other kings (and) desiring protege should be given protection (irrespective of the fact) whether they are bad or good. If one is known to be bad, (the king) should not trust him and keep his livelihood under his control. Men who have come from a different country should be watched by (engaging) spies and then honoured (if they are found to be good). The enemies, fire, poison, serpent and the sword on one side and the trustworthy, distinguished servants (on the other side) should be known (as equal). So also the wicked servants on one side (equal the loyal servants) (?)

The king should have the spies as the eyes. He should always employ the spies. The spies should not be known to the people. They should be good and not known to each other. (He should employ the spies) in the guise of tradesmen, diplomats, astrologers, physicians and as ascetics knowing the strength and weakness (of the people). The king should not trust (the words of) a single person. He should believe the words of many. The king should make use of the likes, displeasures, merits and demerits of his servants and people, as well as the good and bad (deeds done by them) in order to control them. He should do only such acts which would attract them and desist from acts causing displeasure. The king would be adorned by the fortune of the pleasure of the people because of pleasing the people.

CHAPTER TWO HUNDRED AND TWENTYONE

Code of conduct for the servants

Puṣkara said :

1-5. The servant has to carry out the orders of the king, like a disciple, for the prosperity of the master. He should not disobey the commands of the king. He should speak only that which is good and dear to him. If an unpleasant news is beneficial (to the king), (the servant) should let him know in privacy. When he has been employed in some work he should not swindle the money. He should not do anything that would affect his dignity. He should not similarly put on the dress of the king and speak and act in the manner of the king. The superintendent of the attendants of the harem should not have any contact with those dismissed (by the king) and have become enemies. The servant should guard the secret of the king. After having done some act of ingenuity, (the servant) should ascribe it to the king. He should not give publicity to any of the secrets heard by him from the king. When some (superior person) orders him (to disclose) he should say, "what to do ?"

6-7. He should wear the dress, gems and ornaments given by the king. He should not enter the royal chamber without being asked (by the king). He should not see him at an improper place. He should avoid yawning, spitting, coughing, frowning based on depravity, raising the eyebrows and eructation near him.

8-14. One should engage others cleverly by making the king know about his qualities. Perfidy, avarice slandering, atheism, meanness and fickle-mindedness should always be avoided by one in the service of the king. A servant who thus associates his own self with the self by means of scriptural knowledge and manual work should then do the service to the king for the sake of the growth of fortune. He should always bow down to the sons, favourites and ministers of that person (the king). He need not gain the confidence of the ministers. He should do (such acts) which please the king. (The servant) should ignore those not liked by the king. One who knows the king should desire to earn his livelihood from those liked by the king. He should not speak anything when not asked by the king. He should do the desired when (he has) a misfortune. The king would be pleased with a person who gathers the words spoken. The king also would not suspect (that he would disclose) his secrets. (The duty of the servant is) to enquire about the health (of the king) and to make the seat ready (for him). (A servant) rejoices to hear the exploits of the king. He rejoices even after (hearing) an unpleasant (comment). He receives the small remuneration and remembers it on other occasion. Only such a servant should be employed. The services of others should be avoided.

CHAPTER TWO HUNDRED AND TWENTYTWO

Construction of Forts

Puṣkara said :

1-2. I shall describe the excellent fortification. The king should reside in the fort. It should abound with the traders and servants and sparsely with others. It should have few brahmins and plenty of artisans. A country not depending on rain-water and having plenty of water (for cultivation) is commended.

3. It should not be vulnerable for attack by others and should abound with flowers, fruits and grains. It should be impassable by foreign army and should be free from rogues and thieves.

4-5. The mighty king should build one of the following types of forts and live there. O Bhārgava (son of Bhṛgu; Paraśurāma) ! Fort guarded by archers, land, men, forest, water and hill (are the six kinds of forts). The excellent among these (forts) would be the fort protected by the hill. It is indestructible and it destroys others.

6. Such a fort should have the market place, temple and other things. A fort furnished with weapons and implements and surrounded by water is an excellent one.

7-9. I shall describe the means of protecting the king. The king has to be saved from poison. The *śirīṣa* well ground with (cow's) urine, (known as) *pañcāṅga* destroys poison. *Śatāvarī, chinnaruhā, viṣaghnī, taṇḍulīyaka, kośātakī, kalhārī, brāhmī, citrapaṭolikā, maṇḍūkaparṇī, vārāhī, dhātrī, ānandakaṁ, unmādinī, somarājī* and the gemstone destroying poison (are the antidotes for poison).

10. Residing in the fort possessing the characteristics of a dwelling place, (the king) should propitiate gods. (He) should protect the subjects, conquer the wicked and make gifts.

11. (The king) who takes away the articles (dedicated to) the god would dwell in hell for a *kalpa* (period). The king being devoted to the worship of gods should erect temples.

12-13. The temples should be protected and (images of) deities should be installed. A wooden one is meritorious than the earthen one, one made of bricks than the wooden one. One made of stone is meritorious than that of the (image) made of brick. One made of gold and gems (is meritorious) than that of the stone one. Even by the construction of a temple sportively one would get enjoyment and emancipation.

14. One who donates paintings, musical instruments and (arranges for) dramatic performances to be seen and who anoints the deity with oil, clarified butter, honey, milk and other things would go to heaven.

15-18. The king should worship and protect the brahmins. He should not take away the belongings of a brahmin. (The king) would reach hell and remain there till the inundation of beings (deluge) by taking away (a piece of) gold, a cow or an *aṅgula* breadth of a thumb) measure of land (from a brahmin). There is no other sin greater than the killing of a brahmin. The brahmins would make non-divine into divine and divine into non-divine. Brahmins are the most fortunate ones. They should always be respected. A brahmin woman who weeps would destroy the family, kingdom and subjects (of a king).

19-23. A righteous king should protect the chaste women. The women should engage happily and efficiently in the cores of household work. (She should be) decorating well the household articles and be frugal in her expenses. She should always do service to her husband to whom her father has given her (in marriage). The lady practising continence after the death of the husband goes to heaven. She should not have the desire (to live) in other's house and should not be quarrelsome. A widow as well as the wife of a man who has gone abroad, should not decorate her person. She should always be bent on the worship of god and the welfare of the husband. (A woman whose husband has gone abroad) should wear some ornaments for the welfare (of the husband). The woman (widow) who enters the (funeral) fire along with the (dead) husband would also reach heaven. (A householder) should worship the goddess of fortune and do the cleansing of the house etc. (He should worship lord) Viṣṇu on the twelfth day of *Kārttika* and then make a gift of a cow together with a calf. Her husband was saved by Sāvitrī (wife of Satyavān, king of Sālva) by practising truthfulness and good conduct. There need not be any doubt that a woman would have children by the worship of the Sun on the seventh day in the bright (fortnight) in (the month of) *mārgaśīrṣa* .

CHAPTER TWO HUNDRED AND TWENTYTHREE

Duties of a king

Puṣkara said :

1-4. A king should appoint a head for (every) village, for ten villages, for hundred villages, and then an over-all head. Their salaries would be in conformity with their duties. (The king) should watch them daily through (his) spies. Any irregularity that has arisen in the village should be controlled by the village head. If (he is) not able (to set it right) (he) should approach the head of ten villages and report him. The head of the ten villages also should take appropriate step after having heard the same. The king would get wealth etc. by protecting the state.

5-13. A wealthy man gets righteousness and enjoys the desires. All actions without (being supported by) wealth would be ephemeral just as the river in the summer. There is no difference between the fallen and the poor in the world. No one would take from the fallen. A poor man would not give. Even the wife of the poor would not lend him support. A king oppressing the country would dwell in hell for a long time. A king should do in the same way as a pregnant woman who would abandon her comforts and would attend to the welfare of the child in the womb. What (use) of the sacrifices or of the penance (for a king) whose subjects have not been protected. One whose subjects have been well protected, his house would be equal to heaven. One whose subjects have not been protected, his house would be the hell. The king collects one-sixth (of the income) of both the good and bad subjects. (The king) would acquire virtue by protecting (the subjects) and sin by not protecting them. The subjects should be protected (by the king) from the oppressions by thieves (in the guise of) the officers of the state, especially the writer-caste, just as a virtuous woman afraid of a villain (is protected). The subjects being protected from their fear (by the king) would be the subjects of the king. If not protected they become an easy prey for them. The wicked should be put down and the tax laid down in the codes should be taken.

14-17. Half (the amount collected) should be kept in the treasury and the other half should be given to brahmins daily. Having found a treasure a brahmin should take it in entirety.

The same having been found by a *kṣatriya*, a *vaiśya* or a *śūdra* it is enough if one-fourth or one-eighth or one-sixteenth part of the treasure is given (to the king) in order as per law. One who lies is punishable (with a fine) of one-eighth part of the treasure. The king should keep an unclaimed property in his custody for three years. (One who is able to establish his claim) after three years by saying that 'it is mine' should be given the property as laid down. On the contrary the king would forfeit the wealth.

18-21. The owner (of a property) deserves (to get) that property after furnishing (details about) its nature, dimension etc. The king should manage the property belonging to a minor till he (the minor) completes his study or crosses the state of childhood. The same (procedure) should be followed in the (case of the properties) belonging to widows with children and those not having the guardians. The righteous king should punish those relatives who seize (the properties) of faithful women (who have become) widows and weak, even as they are alive, with the punishment meted to the thief. In general the property stolen by a thief should be paid by the king himself.

22. The king should obtain from thieves and the officers in charge of the protection, the property taken by them. One who lies that he has been robbed when he has not been robbed should be punished and expelled (from the country).

23-29. The property that has been stolen by the inmates of the house need not be restored by the king. O Brahmin ! the king should take one twentieth of the value from the merchandise belonging to his country. The fees to be levied on goods from foreign countries should be determined after knowing the cost, the wear and tear and the profit got by the trader. (In this case) one twentieth of the profit should be taken. If not (paid) (the importer) should be punished. Freight should not be collected from women and mendicants. The ferryman should be made to repay by the king that which has been lost in transit on account of the fault of the ferryman. The king should take one sixth in the case of the grain *śūka* (barley) and one eighth in the case of the grain *śimbi* (a kind of kidney bean) as toll befitting the region and season. The king should take four and five parts respectively in the case of animals and gold. Only a sixth part should be collected in the case of perfumes, herbs, cereals, flowers, roots, fruits, leaves, vegetables, straw, bamboos hides, wicker works and vessels made of stone and all (other materials), honey, meat and clarified butter.

30-33. (The king) should not levy tax on the brahmins even in emergency. The king in whose realm a brahmin, well-versed in the scriptures, perishes on account of hunger, his kingdom gets ruined on account of diseases, famine and thieves. The king should ascertain the attainments and provide him an occupation. (The king) should always protect him just as the father (would protect) his son. The life of the king, the wealth and the kingdom would increase by the meritorious deeds of a person (brahmin) being protected by the king. The artisans of the king should work for a day in a month (without any remuneration). The other workers under him should (work without any remuneration) by taking food only.

CHAPTER TWO HUNDRED TWENTYFOUR

Duties of a king in the harem

Puṣkara said :

1-2. I shall describe the duties of the king in the harem. Virtues etc. (are) the purpose of life (for the king). The kings should entertain them without mutual conflict in the company of the women. Virtue is the root, worldly prosperity the bough and action or deed the great fruit. One who fosters this tree of the three objects of worldly existence, would realise the fruits.

3-9. O Rāma ! Women are subject to desire. Hence the gems are gathered for their sake. They should be entertained and also not much entertained by the king who desires for wealth. One should not indulge excessively in eating, sexual pleasure and sleep. It would cause disease. The king should share his bed only with his beloved women. A woman behaving badly, not rejoicing in (hearing his) exploits, associating with the enemies (of the king), feeling haughty and proud, wiping her face when kissed, not feeling grateful after accepting a present, sleeping before and getting up later after sleep, shaking the body when touched and preventing from touching the body on account of shyness, scarcely listening to pleasing words and keeping the face turned away, ignoring to look at things placed in front, concealing the loins, having a pale face when looked at, turning her face away from the friends, appearing as if a mediator in the (affairs of) other women loved (by the king) and not adorning her person even after knowing that it is time for adorning (should be rejected).

10-19. One who is disinterested should be rejected and one who is loving should be entertained. (The characteristics of a loving woman are as follows). She rejoices even at the sight (of her husband). When looked at she casts her eyes down. Being looked at she places her shaking glances elsewhere. Yet she would not be able to turn aside her look completely. O Bhārgava (son of Bhṛgu, Paraśurāma) ! She exhibits her concealed parts of body and covers up with effort the organs prohibited (from being displayed). She embraces and kisses him (immediately after) being seen. She always speaks only the truth. When being touched feels horripilation later manifesting as the sweat-drops (on the body). (O Rāma ! She asks for easy and simple things (from the husband). She gets great rejoice after getting even a little. She feels elated and favoured much by the mere pronunciation of her name. She sends fruits to her husband with the impressions of her nails. She holds those sent by her husband on the chest out of regard. She besmears the body as if with the ambrosia by her embraces. She sleeps after (the husband) had slept and would get up before (he gets up). She would wake him up from sleep by touching his thigh much. O Sage ! The clarified butter becomes fragrant by combination with the powders of *kapittha* and a column of curd as also with barley put in milk. This is the way by which an eatable thing should be dressed. Now I shall describe the mode of preparation of perfumes.

20-22. O Rāma ! Cleansing, gargling, vomitting, adorning (with flowers etc.), heating, burning (incense sticks) fumigation and perfuming are indicated to be the eight acts. Purification of a thing is by washing it with water containing the leaves of *Kapittha, bilva*, mango and *Karavīra*. In the absence of these, purification should be done with water saturated with musk.

23-29. The twenty-one herbs for fumigation are—*nakha*, *kuṣṭha*, *dhana*, *māṁsī*, *spṛkka*, *śaileyaja*, *jala*, saffron, shellac, sandal, agallochum, *nīrada*, *sarala*, *devakāṣṭha*, camphor, *kāntā*, *bāla*, *kunduruka*, *guggulu*, *śrīnivāsaka* and *sarjarasa*. Two of these should be taken and mixed with parts of resin from a *śāla* tree. They become fit for fumigation by being mixed with *nakha*, *piṇyāka*, *malaya* and honey and made as desired in the proper way. The bark, tubular part, fruit, oil, saffron, *granthiparvaka*, *śaileya*, *tagara*, *kāntā*, *cola*, camphor, *māṁsī*, *surā* and *kuṣṭha* are said to be the things (to be used) for bathing. One should bathe with any three (things) from these collected as one desires after mixing with the musk. This would increase the passion.

30. If one bathes with *tvak*, *murā* and *analada* in equal proportions added to half (the quantity) of *bālaka* with saffron and oil, one would have the fragrance of the lotus.

31. By adding a half of *tagara* (in the same), it will have the fragrance of the *jātī* flower. It gives a captivating fragrance of the *bakula* (flowers) with the *dhyāmaka* (grass).

32. One would get an auspicious fragrant oil by putting the *mañjiṣṭhā*, *tagara*, *cola*, *tvak*, *vyāghranakha*, *nakha* and *gandhapatra*.

33. O Rāma ! the oil extracted from the sesamum and scented with any of the flowers would certainly have the fragrance of the flower.

34. Cardamom, clove, *kakkola*, nutmeg and camphor mixed with the skin of the nutmeg would be able to make the mouth fragrant.

35-38. O Rāma ! a *kārṣika* (weight) of camphor, saffron *kāntā*, musk, *hareṇuka*, *kakkola*, cardamom, clove, *jātī*, *kośaka*, *tvakpatra*, *truṭi*, *musta*, *kastūrikā latā*, the thorns of clove, the fruit and skin of nutmeg and *kaṭuka* should be powdered and a fourth part of the essence of *khadira* that gives fragrance should be added. Then tablets should be made of them by (adding) mango juice. When kept in the mouth they give fragrance and destroy the diseases of the mouth.

39. Arecanut well washed with the waters of the leaves of five (trees) and made fragrant with the (above) things (used) for (making) the pills would make the mouth fragrant.

40. O Rāma ! (the herbs) *kaṭuka* and *dantakāṣṭha* soaked

in cow's urine for three days and perfumed as the arecanut would make the mouth fragrant.

41. Equal parts of *tvak* and *pathya* mixed with half (the quantity) of the camphor would give an attractive fragrance in the mouth similar to that of the *nāgavallī* (betel).

42. The king should always protect the women thus. He should not trust them, especially, the mother of children. He should never sleep in the night in the apartment of a woman. The faith (placed in them) should be feigned one.

CHAPTER TWO HUNDRED AND TWENTYFIVE

The duties of a king

Puṣkara said :

1-2. A king should protect the princess. He should instruct them in the sciences of virtue, polity, erotics, archery and fine arts through reliable persons. In the guise of protecting the body of the prince, guardians should be engaged (to guard from) those feigning to speak pleasant.

3. He should not be given (an opportunity) to associate with angry, greedy and dishonoured persons. If not able to inculcate virtue (in the prince, the king) should bind him with pleasures.

4. An obedient prince should be engaged in all posts of authority. The king should avoid hunting, drinking and dice (playing) that destroys the kingdom.

5-7. (He) should also avoid sleeping during the day-time, strolling about idly and scurrilous language. He should also leave off censuring, cruel infliction of punishment and extravagance. The destruction of mines, neglecting the care of the fort etc. and scattering wealth are said to be extravagance. A gift that is made to an unworthy person at an inappropriate place and time and engaging in unworthy acts are said to be extravagance.

8. One should avoid passion, anger, haughtiness, pride,

greed and arrogance. Then one should win (the love of) citizens after having controlled the servants.

9. Then (he) should subjugate his external enemies. The external enemies are of three kinds—those belonging to the same clan, those having enmity from the period of the ancestors and those who have enmity on account of some particular reason. Among these three each preceding one is greater than the succeeding one.

10. O Fortunate one! Friends are of three kinds—friend of the father and grandfather, feudatory under the enemy and artificial.

11. O Knower of virtue ! An empire is said to possess seven constituents—king, minister, subjects, fort, punishment, treasury and allies.

12-16. The central figure is the king. He should be protected and the kingdom is especially dependent on him. One who rebels against any of the above constituents of the kingdom should be killed. The king should be firm and liberal at (the appropriate) time. Thus there are two worlds (to be conquered by the king. The king should not cut jokes with the servants. The servants soon get an upper hand of the king whom they can persuade to laugh. In order to control people he should feign grief (in their misery). He should speak preceded by a gentle smile. He should make them feel delighted. It would certainly be detrimental to the work if the king is procrastinating. Procrastination is commended in the (following) acts—passion, arrogance, pride, quarrel, sinful acts and unpleasant things to be told. The king should hold secret counsel. There is no danger from secret counselling.

17-20. The acts relating to the state done (by a king holding such a counsel) is known from the deeds done and begun to be done. One's mind is known from the postures, gestures, gaits, action, speech and the changes in the eye and face. The king, should not keep his own counsel, nor consult a large number (of his ministers). The king mây have the counsel with many (ministers). But it (should be had) separately. (He should see that) none of his ministers would disclose his secret counsels. Men will always have trust in some one somewhere. In counsel decision must be made by one wise man.

21-22. A king would perish on account of immodesty and would acquire a kingdom on account of modesty. (A king should learn) the three sciences, the science of administration, metaphysics, science of wealth and business from the world. Only a person that has conquered his senses would be able to keep his subjects under his control.

23. The gods and all brahmins should always be worshipped and gifts should be given to them (brahmins). Gift made to a brahmin (would be) imperishable and the treasury cannot be destroyed by any of these.

24. Not retreating in the battle, protecting the subjects and giving gifts to the brahmins are the supreme good for a king.

25. (The king) should likewise arrange for the welfare and livelihood of the poor, destitute and old people, widows and women whose husbands have gone abroad.

26-33. (The king) should arrange for (the proper pursuit of) the orders of the *varṇa* (castes) and *āśrama* (stages of life). (He should) worship the ascetics. He should not trust everyone and trust only the ascetics. He should make (others) trust him adducing reason (to show that his words) are not impeachable. The king should think about the wealth like a crane, conquer like a lion, pounce (on the enemies) like a wolf, dart forth like a hare and strike firmly like a boar. The king should also be showing vanity like a peacock, faithful as a horse and be speaking pleasantly like a cuckoo. A king should always be suspicious as a crow while living in the residence of a stranger. A king should not partake of the food and touch a bed not tested before. He should not visit a woman whom he had not known before and not board an unfamiliar boat. One who oppresses his subjects would be deprived of the position and comforts of a sovereign. Just as a nourished bull gains strength and becomes fit for work, so also O Fortunate one ! the nourished sovereignty becomes fit for work. All these works are dependent on the providence and on one's efforts. Out of these two the providence is unthinkable and one's accomplishments depend on his effort. The kingdom and the wealth of the earth of a king belong to him by the good-will of the people.

TWO HUNDRED AND TWENTYSIX

The means of Conciliation

Puṣkara said :

1-4. One's own act that has been acquired from a previous existence of a person is known as the providence. Hence people declare that will-force is superior. So also an adverse providence can be nullified by one's efforts. One will accomplish by his previous deeds of virtue without providence. O Bhārgava (son of Bhṛgu) ! Effort yields fruit at the proper time by the grace of providence. The providence and effort are the two that yield fruit for a man. The fruits would be accomplished at the proper time by the combination of rain and ploughing. Along with virtuous deeds one should exert effort. One should neither be lazy nor be dependent on fate.

5-11. All the stratagems are accomplished by means of conciliation and other things. The seven means are conciliation, making gifts, creating dissent, punishment, stratagem, indifference and deceit. Conciliation is said to be of two kinds—true and untrue. Of these two the untrue (reconciliation) would be for the censure of the good people. Those who belong to good families, upright, always virtuous and have conquered their senses are conquerable by conciliatory words. Even demons are taken by false (conciliations). The description of the good services rendered by them (is conciliation). A dissension may be created between two who are inimical to each other, angry, afraid of each other and have been insulted by each other. He should instill fear in them. A king should give hopes to his own people (relatives). He should cause dissent in adversaries by holding out threats about which they are afraid. One who causes such dissents among such kinsmen should be protected by the king. The anger of the soldiers is external and those of the ministers, counsellors and princes etc. (are internal). The king should pacify the internal anger and conquer that of the enemies.

12-16. Paying money is the excellent expedient. By giving money one would get both the worlds There is no one for instance who is not influenced by the payment of money. Only (a king) who makes a gift of money would be able to cause dissent in the enemies who have become allies. A king should accomplish by (means of) punishment and service that which could not be accomplished by the other three. Everything rests on punishment which would destroy everything if improperly used. A king would be destroyed by punishing those unpunishable and not punishing those punishable. In the absence of punishment, the gods, demons, serpents, men, accomplished persons, goblins and birds would transgress their limits. The wisemen call 'the punishment' so because it controls the uncontrolled, punishes the unpunishable, controls and punishes.

17-20. The king like the sun cannot be looked at on account of his splendour. He should be like the moon to look at in order to please the people. The king is the wind-god since he spreads himself in the world by means of his spies. He becomes fire when he burns the wicked. When he makes the gift to the brahmins he is the lord of wealth (Kubera). Because he showers wealth he is known to be god Varuṇa among the celestials. The king would be the earth by supporting the universe with his forbearance. Then he is lord Hari (Viṣṇu) because he would protect the people with determination, incantation, strength etc.

CHAPTER TWO HUNDRED AND TWENTYSEVEN

The code of criminal laws

Puṣkara said :

1-8. I shall describe the criminal laws by (enforcing) which an elevated position is attained by a king. You know that (the weight of) three barley (grains) is (equal to) one berry seed. (The weight of) a black gram would be that of five berries. O Rāma ! It is said that sixty berries (make up) a half of one *karṣa* (weight). O Rāma ! A *suvarṇa* (weight) is said to be (equal to) sixteen blackgrams. Four *suvarṇas* make up one *niṣka* and ten *niṣkas* one *dharaṇa*. These are the measures of weight (used) in (weighing) copper, silver and gold. O Rāma ! *Kārṣika* is said to be *kārṣāpaṇa* by coppersmiths well-versed (with the same). Two hundred and fifty *paṇas* are remembered to be the *sāhasa* first. The middle one is known to be (equal to) five (hundred *paṇas*) and the foremost one as one thousand (*paṇas*). (These are the three kinds of punishments). If a person tells 'I have been robbed', when he has not been robbed by the thieves and is handed over to the king, such a person should be punished by making to pay the same amount. One who tells differently or falsely (about the exact amount robbed), both these should be levied double the punishment by the king. The men belonging to the three castes (other than brahmins) who bear false witness should be levied punishment. A brahmin (bearing false witness) should be expelled. The above punishment has not been prescribed (in that case). One who enjoys (a property) entrusted with him should be levied a fine of equal value.

9-11. O Righteous one ! (The same fine should be levied) in the case of clothes etc. (being used similarly). One would not swerve from righteousness by such an act. One who conceals the entrusted property and one who asks for restoration of things without having entrusted the same (to some one) should be punished like robbers or levied double the fine. One who sells away another's property unknowingly is free of fault. But (one who sells another's property) knowing (that it belongs to another) deserves punishment as for a robber. One who receives the price for a work and does not give goods, is indeed punishable.

12. The king should levy a fine of one *suvarṇa* for one who promises (to give something) and does not give. One who accepts payment and does not do the work should be levied a fine of eight *kṛṣṇalas*.

13-22. But (a master) dismissing a servant before (the end of) the term should be punished with the same fine. One who has a remorse after buying or selling something may return to its master or take from him within ten days (as the case may be). Neither one can receive nor return after ten days (in such a deal). Any person receiving or returning (such a property after that) should be levied a fine of six hundred (*paṇas*) by the king. One who solicits a girl for a bridegroom, should be levied a fine of two hundred (*paṇas*) by the king whether the marriage has been done or not. One who gives in marriage a girl who had already been married to another should be punished by a king.

The fine of *uttama sāhasa* (one thousand *paṇas*) (should be levied) in that case. One who enters into a solemn agreement (with a person for sale) and sells it to another person out of greed deserves to be punished with six hundred (*paṇas*). The keeper (of a cow-shed) not restoring the cow (to the owner) after receiving the charges for the upkeep should be punished by the king with one hundred (*paṇas*) and a *suvarṇa* if not taken proper care (of the entrusted animal). Land to the extent of one hundred *dhanus* (one *dhanu* is equal to four cubits) should be set apart around the village and twice or thrice as much around a city (for the grazing of the cows). It should be made in such a way that a camel would not be able to look over (the encircling wall). When the (stored) grains have not been enclosed and were lost there would be no punishment. One who frightens (the owner) of a house, tank, garden or land and takes the same should be punished with five hundred (*paṇas*). (If it is done) inadvertently the fine (would be) two hundred (*paṇas*). All those who break the boundaries should be punished with the first *sāhasa*[1].

23-25. O Rāma ! A *kṣatriya* censuring a brahmin deserves to be punished with (a fine of) one hundred *paṇas*, a *vaiśya*, two hundred *paṇas* and a *śūdra*, a capital punishment. A brahmin having censured a *kṣatriya* should be punished with (a fine of) fifty (*paṇas*), (having censured) a *vaiśya*, twentyfive (*paṇas*) and (having censured) a *śūdra*, twelve (*paṇas*). A *vaiśya* (having censured) a *kṣatriya* should get (punishment to pay) the first (class of) *sāhasa*. A *śūdra* having censured a *kṣatriya* should be getting (the punishment of) severing the tongue.

26-27. A *śūdra* giving moral instruction to brahmins is liable for punishment. One who preaches falsely the doctrines of scriptures should be levied (a fine of) twice the *sāhasa*. One who insults men of respect should be (meted the punishment of) *uttama sāhasa*. But the above described punishments should be half if the crimes have been done inadvertently or for fun.

28. One who accuses his mother or father or elder brother or father-in-law or the preceptor should be levied a fine of one hundred (*paṇas*). (The same punishment should be levied) for obstructing the pathway of the preceptor.

29. One of a lower caste should without enquiry be severed

1. See verse 4, pp. 588-589.

of the organ by which he had done harm to a member of the (three) higher castes.

30-31. The king should cause the lips to be cut off if a person spits on the ground with pride. Similarly, one passing urine or faeces on the body (of a brahmin) (should be punished by cutting the) penis and the anus respectively. If a member of a low caste had occupied the seat of a member of a higher caste, his lower organ (buttocks) should be cut. One who causes injury to any organ of another (should be punished by cutting the same organ (of the offender).

32. The killers of a cow, elephant, horse or camel should have their legs and hands cut off. One who would make a tree barren deserves the fine of a *suvarṇa*.

33-36. When the pathway or a boundary or the tank has been cut (by a person he) should be levied double the (above) fine. One who either wilfully or unintentionally takes away the articles of another should restore it to him to satisfy him and pay the fine to the king. One who steals the rope or the pot from the well and damages the channel should be punished for a month (with imprisonment). One should be punished (similarly) if he beats an animal. The punishment for stealing ten pitchers full of paddy is more than death. The punishment (for stealing) more than that (quantity) would be eleven times (the former). Capital punishment (should be ordered for stealing) gold, silver etc. (and for kidnapping) men and women.

37. The organ with which one would steal from others should be removed by the king for the sake of discipline.

38-39. A brahmin taking little (quantity of) vegetables and grains etc. (for his use without the knowledge of the owner) would not be a criminal. (Similarly) in the case of taking for the cows or gods (one would not be a criminal). One who attempts to kill another, should be killed.

40. One who seizes the house or field (belonging to another,) one who copulates with another's wife, one who is an incendiary and one who administers poison should be killed. So also in the case of one who attacks with a drawn weapon.

41-42. A king should kill those who cause the death of cattle by magic spells. One should not converse with another's wife and should never copulate with a forbidden (woman). A girl choosing her husband herself should not be punished by the king. A man of the lower caste holding incest with a woman of the higher caste deserves to be killed. The woman who breaks her faith in the husband, should be made to be bitten by dogs. A woman defiled by a man of her own caste should be made to live on a morsel of food (a day).

43-47. A woman defiled by one of the superior (caste) should have her head shaved. A brahmin copulating with a *vaiśya* woman and a *kṣatriya* going to a woman of the low caste (should be fined) with the first (variety of fine). A *kṣatriya* and a *vaiśya* are punishable for going to a *śūdra* woman. If a courtesan after having received a contract, goes to another on account of greed, she should pay (the first one), twice the contracted amount and (pay) twice the amount as fine. One's wife, sons, servants, pupil and brother having done an offence should be beaten with a rope or with a piece of bamboo A thief should be struck on the back but not on the forehead. One would acquire sin (by doing so) (by striking on the forehead). The officers in charge of protecting the people seizing very much should be banished (from the kingdom) after having seized all their (property).

48. Those who have been employed to do certain work if do not do the work of their employers, the king should make those shameless, cruel-minded to be penniless.

49. Likewise the king should banish the minister or justice after having taken the entire (property) for doing the work of another (king).

50. If one violates the bed of the preceptor, (mark of) female generative organ should be made (on the forehead), a pot of wine in case of drinking of wine, a dog in case of stealing and the head of a person in the case of killing a brahmin.

51. The king should kill (criminals belonging to) *śūdra* and other (communities) and banish the brahmin sinners. The wealth belonging to great sinners should be offered to (god) Varuṇa (God of righteousness).

52. (A king) should kill all those who offer shelter, food and wealth to thieves in the villages also.

53-54. The feudatory chiefs and the governors of provinces in the kingdom who are sinful should be killed. The king should place on the pike after having cut the arms of those thieves who commit theft in the night after having agreed (to show good conduct). The king should kill those who break tanks and temples.

55. One should be levied (a fine of) a *kārṣāpaṇa* for having committed nuisance on the thoroughfare when there was no adversity and be made to clean the impurity.

56-59. One who breaks his contract every month should pay (a fine of) five hundred (paṇas) to the party concerned (Merchants), dealing fraudulently with honest men in respect of the price (of a commodity), should be punished with the first or the middle (kind of) fine. The king should confiscate all goods from the obstructing merchants by (paying) small sum and punish them with the *uttama* (variety of) *sāhasa* separately. One who adulterates the materials and who sells imitation-articles should be given the middle (kind of) punishment. One who makes contraband goods (should be made to pay) *uttama* (*sāhasa*). One who insults in a quarrel should be given the punishment of twice that (amount).

60-64. A fine of *kṛṣṇala*[1] (should be collected) from a brahmin or a *śūdra* who eats the forbidden food. One who makes false balance and weight and those who make use of these should be levied the *uttama* (kind) of fine. The women who administers poison to her husband or preceptor, or a brahmin and children or sets fire to the house should be banished (from the country) with cows after having cut her ears, hands and nose. Those men who damage a land or house or village or forest and one who seduces the wife of the king should be burnt with the fire from the cremation ground. One who copies the royal edict omitting or adding (some sentences) and one who sets free an adulterer and a thief should be punished with the *uttama* (*sāhasa*) fine. The punishment for one who ascends the vehicle or the seat of the king is the *uttama sāhasa*.

65-66. If one thinks that he has not been defeated even though he has duly been defeated, (the king) should defeat him again and inflict double-fold punishment. One who summons a person that had not done any crime should be put to death. If an accused person escapes from the custody of the punisher on account of the latter's carelessness, that punisher should pay the fine.

---

1. See the first verse, p. 588.

CHAPTER TWO HUNDRED AND TWENTYEIGHT

Instructions relating to military expedition

Puṣkara said :

1. When a king is attacked by a strong enemy and he thinks "I have been attacked", he should undertake the military expedition.

2. If the (king thinks that the) warriors had been well-cared for and the servants well supported and he feels, "I have a strong army and I am capable of protecting the central (army)", he should go with them and move into the camp.

3-5. Otherwise one may invade (the country of) the enemy when it (the latter's country) is afflicted by natural calamities such as the appearance of the earthquake in that direction or the comet afflicting it or the army of the enemy king dislikes that king and awaits his ruin. One should enter the kingdom of the enemy when he has auspicious throbbing (of the muscles) of the body, has good dreams and good omens. One should employ an army consisting largely of infantry etc. and elephants in the rainy season.

6. In the early and advanced winter it should consist of chariots and cavalry, while it should consist of four divisions of an army (cavalry, infantry etc.) in the spring and autumn.

7. An army consisting of a large number of infantry would always win the enemies. The throbbing (of the muscles) on the right side (of the body) would be commendable.

8. So also the palpitation on the left back and the heart and mark of mole (on the left side) should be known as not commendable. While the contrary to what has been told on the left side would be auspicious for women.

CHAPTER TWO HUNDRED AND TWENTYNINE

The significance of dreams

Puṣkara said :

1-14. I shall describe the good and bad omens and the way to prevent bad dreams. The growth of grass and trees on one's body except the navel, the breaking of bronze on the head, the shaving (of the head), remaining nude, clad in torn dress, anointing with oil, besmearing with mud, falling from a great height, one's marriage, music, playing on the lute or any other stringed instrument, swinging in a hammock, gathering lotus and metals, killing of serpents, seeing red flowers and trees and a *cāṇḍāla*, riding a pig or dog or ass or camel, eating the flesh of birds, and the oil of kṛsara (?) entering the mother's womb, getting into the funeral pyre, the fall of the flag-post etc., the fall of the moon and the sun, seeing the divine beings of the terrestrial and celestial regions as well as a calamity (such as the earthquake), the wrath of the divine beings, brahmins, other beings and preceptors, dancing, laughing, marriage and singing, playing on stringed instruments other than the lute, drowning in a river, bathing in water mixed with cow-dung, or muddy water or water mixed with ink, embracing the unmarried girls, sexual union of men, injury to one's limbs, purging or vomiting, starting in the direction of the south, being afflicted by diseases, plucking of fruits, breaking of diseases, breaking of minerals, falling of buildings, sweeping the house, playing with goblins, flesh-eaters, monkeys and low-caste men, insult from others and feeling grief on account of that, wearing ochre robes and playing in that dress, immersion in oil and drinks anointing with red unguent are inauspicious omens and it is better not to describe them.

15-18. (After dreaming as above) one should continue to sleep, bathe, worship a brahmin, do oblations with sesamum, worship (gods) Hari (Viṣṇu), Brahmā, Śiva, Sun and Gaṇapati (Vināyaka). Then one should recite hymns (on gods) and repeat hymns such as the *Puruṣasūkta*[1]. The dreams dreamt in the first quarter of the night yield results within a year, the second (quarter), within six months, the third quarter of the

1. ṚV. 10.91.1.

night, within three months, the fourth (quarter), within a fortnight and within ten days (if dreamt) at (the time of) the sunrise. If (two dreams) either auspicious or inauspicious (were dreamt) on the same night, one should indicate the result of the dream dreamt later.

19-22. Hence, it is not commended to sleep after a good dream (has been dreamt). (Dreaming) as climbing a hill, mansion, elephant, horse or bull is beneficial. O Brahmin ! (Seeing) trees and white flowers in the sky (seeing) the navel as grown with trees, (seeing oneself) as having many arms and many heads, (seeing) the appearance of grey hair, bearing a garland of white (flowers), wearing white garment, the eclipses of the moon, sun and the stars, washing (oneself), embracing the flag-post and the raising of the banner (are good).

23-27. O Brahmin ! Seizing of land and stream of water, victory over the enemies, success in dispute, dice-play and battle, eating of raw meat and drinking of sweet porridge, seeing blood, bathing in blood, drinking of spirituous liquor, blood and wine, drinking of milk, making marks with the weapons on the earth, (seeing) the cleai sky, and sucking milk from cows, she-buffalos, lionesses, she-elephants and mares are commendable. O Brahmin ! The favour from the gods, brahmins and preceptors, the anointment with water and falling down from the horns of cow (are also commendable).

28-29. O Rāma ! (The dream) as falling down from the horns of a moon is known to be capable of bestowing kingdom. The installation as the sovereign, the cutting of one's head, the death, the destruction of one's house by fire, the gain of royal rewards and the play on stringed instruments (are auspicious).

30-31. The family of a person flourishes that sees an elephant or horse or gold or bull or cow. (Dreams of) riding a bull or an elephant, the climbing a peak or a tree, weeping, besmeared with ghee or excreta, copulating with a forbidden women, (seeing) a white cloth, clear waters, tree laden with fruits and clear sky (are good augury).

CHAPTER TWO HUNDRED AND THIRTY

The inauspicious auguries

Puṣkara said :

1-4. Mixtures of herbs and black cereals are inauspicious, Cotton, grass, dried cow-dung, wealth, charcoal, molasses and resin, one having a shaven head or one that has besmeared oil (for bathing) and one that is nude, iron, mud, hide and hair, a lunatic, an eunuch, a *cāṇḍāla*, a dog, an outcaste and others, men guarding the captives, a pregnant woman, widow and oil-cake, etc., dead (body), husk, ash, skull and bone and broken vessel are not commendable (to be seen). The sounds of musical instruments that are broken, frightening and harsh are also not commendable.

5. The sound 'come on', (heard) in front of the person undertaking a journey) is commendable, (while) that from behind is not (commendable).

6-7. The undesirable sounds (such as) "Where do you go", 'Stand', 'Do not go', 'What is there for you by going' are for death. So also (the appearance of) carnivorous animals, banners etc., the fall of vehicles etc., the breaking of weapons, dashing of the head against the door etc., and the fall of umbrella, dress etc., (are not commendable).

8. An inauspicious (augury) gets destroyed by the worship and invocation of lord Hari (Viṣṇu). If a second inauspicious augury is seen (while setting out) then one should re-enter the house.

9-13. White flowers are excellent augury. (So also) a pitcher full (of water) is greatly meritorious. Meat, fish, a distant sound, an old man, an animal, goat, cows, horses, elephants, (images of) gods, glowing flame, *dūrvā* (grass), wet cow-dung, courtesan, gold, silver, gem, *vacā*, white mustard, herbs, beans, weapons, sword, umbrella, throne, insignia of royalty, a dead body without (being followed by) mourners, fruit, ghee, curd, milk, unbroken rice, mirror, honey, conch, sugarcane, auspicious sentence, the instrumental music of the devotee, the loud sound of thunder and lightning are all auspicious. The satisfaction in the mind (of the person undertaking a journey is also auspicious.

CHAPTER TWO HUNDRED AND THIRTYONE

The good and bad auguries known from the sounds of animals and birds

Puṣkara said :

1. Birds let us know the good and bad indications for a man staying or leaving a country or town or (putting) a question.

2. All excited sounds are pointed out to indicate evil according to fortune-tellers and cooing sounds are said to indicate good results by fortune-tellers.

3. The excitements of birds are said to be of six kinds based on the divisions of time, direction, place, *karaṇa* (a division of the day), the sound and the species (of the bird).

4-6. Each preceding (item in the above list) should be known as more powerful. The nocturnal (bird) moving in the day-time and that of the day-time moving in the night (are known to be the excitement in time). One should know the malefic asterisms, ascendants and planets also as excited. It is known to be *dhūmitā* (obscured), *jvalitā* (burning) and *aṅgāritā* (burnt) if the sun goes to or stays or leaves (a particular quarter). These three are remembered to be the excited ones and the gentle (cooings) are of five kinds.

7-9. It is said to be agitated bird if it makes an excited sound in the direction that is (termed) agitated. Similar (appellations should be given) to wild (birds making sound) in the village and the village (birds) in the forest as well as on an inauspicious tree. O Foremost brahmin ! The *deśadīpta* (agitation in respect of a place) is known to be in inauspicious place. It is designated as *kriyādīpta* (excitement in respect of an action) if there is any action improper for one's own species. It is said to be the *rutadīpta* (excitement in respect of sound) making broken and harsh sounds. It is known to be the *jātidīpta* (excitement in respect of the species) in the case of the carnivorous species alone.

10. If the excited characteristics of different categories occur together it is stated to be good. If they are mixed the result is said to be mixed.

11. The cows, horses, camels, asses, dogs, (birds) *sārikā*, small house-lizards, sparrows, vultures and tortoises and others are said to be living in the villages.

12. Goats, black sheep, parrots, elephants, pig, buffalo and crow are said to be both domestic and wild. All other (birds and animals) are wild.

13. The cat and the cock are both domestic and wild. We know about them from the change in their characteristics.

14-16. The snakes, peacocks, ruddy geese, mules, pigeons, cows, light-brown horses, wild cocks, hawks, jackals, wag-tails, monkeys, *śataghna* (?), sparrows, cuckoos, blue jays, hawks, *kapiñjala*[1] the three, *tittiri* (francoline partridge), peacocks, pigeons, wag-tails, gallinules, parrots, cranes, cocks, skylarks and deer are known to be moving about during daytime.

17. The fowlers, owls, *śarabha-s*,[2] curlews, hares, turtles, jackals and *piṅgalikas* (a kind of owl) are said to be nocturnal.

18-19. Ganders, deer, cats, mongooses, bears, serpents, red dogs, lions, tigers, camels, domestic boars, men, dogs, porcupines, bulls, jackals, wolves, cuckoos, cranes, horses, men in ragged clothes and alligators wander day and night.

20. The above seen in a group in front (of the king) making an expedition with the forces are stated to bring victory and seen on the back cause defeat.

21-22. If the blue jay comes out of the house and makes the sound remaining in front, it indicates humiliation for the king and (making sound) on the left (indicates) quarrel and gaining food. It being sighted on the vehicle or on the right side of the body are commended. The peacock making an unusual sound conveys plundering by thieves.

23-29. O Rāma ! a deer (seen) in front of one that has set out would be (indicating) danger to life. O Rāma ! The bears, rats, jackals, tigers, lions, cats and asses (running away) in the opposite direction as well as mule braying strangely (would indicate the same result). The *kapiñjala* (bird) (seen) on the left or right is an excellent (augury). But it does not augur well (if seen) on the back. The *tittiri* (bird) (in any one of the above positions) is not commended. The black deer, boars and spotted antelopes crossing from the left to the right would always be beneficial and the contrary (movements) are condemned. The bulls, horses, jackals, tigers, lions, cats and asses are known to

1. The *cātaka* bird that is said to drink water directly from the rains.
2. A fabulous animal powerful than the lion.

confer the desired results if they move to the left from the right. The vixen, *śyāmānana* (?), *chucchū* (a kind of animal), *piṅgalā* (a kind of owl), house alligator, sow and a female cuckoo (are said to be) male (omens) if they are on one's left. The vulture, *rūṣa* (?) monkey, *śrīkarṇa* (antelope), and *citkarā* (?) are known as feminine (omens). The monkey, *śrīkarṇa*, *pipīlikā*, *ruru* (a kind of deer), and hawks (auger well seen) on the right. The sounds made by the bull that is born, the serpent, hare, hog and alligator are good.

30-33. Then it is not desirable to see the monkey and bear at the commencement of a work. The strong omen from a bird as one sets out on a day should be explained by wise men as bearing result on the same day. O Brahmin ! Mad ones, those concerned only with the prey, young ones, those mutually quarrelling and those separated by a distance should be known to bear no effect. The vixen howling alone or in groups of two or three or four forebode good. It is said to be not beneficial if five or six (vixen howl). It would be good if seven (vixen howl) and there would be no effect if more than that.

34. The volcano facing the sun that causes the horripilation in men should be known to bring ill luck to vehicles and increase the fear.

35-36. When an antelope is seen at a good place it would give good results. It would give bad results for the whole year for the man (if seen) at a bad (place). One may know the result for himself for the whole year as he had seen the deer on the first day.

CHAPTER TWO HUNDRED AND THIRTYTWO

Omens known from birds

Puṣkara said :

1. An army would take possession of a city that is under siege by that way through which many crows enter that city.

2. It indicates unfordable fear if a crow taking its abode in the place of the army goes about cawing with agitation and fear.

3. If (the crow) pecks at the shadow, body, vehicle, shoes, umbrella and clothes and other things (of a person, it indicates) death (for that person). If it honours (the person, he) will be honoured. If it gives something that it is fond of, (it augurs) good.

4-6. A crow going to and fro at the entrance (to a house, indicates) the return of the absentee owner of the house. It indicates destruction by fire (if the crow) throws a red or burnt thing inside the house. A red (thing) placed (by the crow) in front of a person indicates imprisonment. O Bhārgava (son of Bhṛgu), if (a crow) brings (to the house) a yellow substance, gold or silver, it would indicate the gain of that (substance). So also one should indicate the loss of that thing which (a crow) should take away.

7. (If a crow) vomits raw flesh in front (of a house) there would be gain of wealth. (There would be) gain of land if (a piece of) earth is thrown. (There would be gain of kingdom if a great gem is cast.

8. If the crow (flies) favourably to the person who undertakes a journey it bids welfare and he would be able to accomplish his task. But if (it flies) against him it should be known that the task would not be accomplished and would cause fear.

9. If the crow comes cawing loudly against (the person) it would be an impediment to the journey. A crow on the left is considered to be beneficial and causing destruction of the task if on the right.

10. (If the crow flies) on the left in the direction (of the person undertaking a journey), it is excellent and medium if on the right. (If it flies) against the direction of the traveller on the left, it would cause impediment to the movement.

11. If the crow comes to the house when the traveller is beginning to move it should be known that he can set out. (If a crow) stands on one leg and looks at the sun with a single eye it causes fear.

12. (If a crow) makes its habitat in a hollow of a tree there would be great misfortune. A crow (seen) in the saline soil is not for good. But (the same seen) as having its wings with mud is commendable.

13. A crow (seen) as having its mouth full of excreta accom-

plishes all things. O Son of Bhṛgu ! The other birds should also be known as (indicating the same results) as the crow.

14-20. Dogs (howling) on the right of a royal camp (indicate) the destruction of the brahmins. If they howl at the place of Indra in the palace, at the main entrance to the royal city and inside the house, it would augur the death of the lord of the house. It indicates the accomplishment of the task, if (a dog smells the left side of the body (of a man) and fear if (it smells) the right side of the body and the left arm. A dog coming against the traveller would be adverse to the journey. O Bhārgava (son of Bhṛgu) ! (a dog) obstructing the path (of a traveller) indicates robbers on the way. (A dog)holding a piece of bone in the mouth (being seen in front indicates) fruitlessness (of the effort). Similarly (a dog being seen) holding a rope or rag in the mouth is sinful. (A dog being seen) as holding the shoes as well as full of meat in the mouth is also beneficial. (A dog being seen) as holding the hair or any filthy substance in the mouth is inauspicious. (A dog) urinating and going in front (of the traveller) would bring fear. If (one sees a dog) urinating and going to an auspicious place or tree or to an auspicious substance (it indicates) the accomplishment of the task for that person. O Rāma (Paraśurāma) ! Jackals and other (animals) should also be known (to indicate) the same (result) as a dog.

21. The lowing of the cows should be known as auguring fear for the master. (If a cow lows) in the night it would be indicating fear from thieves. (If it) wails (it forebodes) death.

22. If a bull bellows in the night it would be for the welfare of the master. A bull let loose in the night would confer victory on the king.

23. The cows belonging to a person that were given as gift (indicate) security (if found) eating (as they wish). (The cows) that had withheld showing affection to the calves are known to be (indicating) miscarriage (in the family).

24. (The cows) that pound the earth with their feet and are frightened bring fear. (The cows) that have wet skin, horripilation and earth stuck to the horns are auspicious.

25-31. It should be told in the same way in the case of the she-buffalos and others by those knowing (the science). A saddled horse (being seen) as ridden by another (other than the appointed person) forebodes evil. (A horse being seen) as plunging into the water and tumbling over the ground is not desirable. A horse that (is seen) sleeping without a good cause causes misfortune. (If a horse) has aversion to barley and balls (of grains) all of a sudden it is not commended. Bleeding from the mouth and trembling of the body are also not commended. (If a horse) plays with cranes, pigeons and the *sārikās* (a species of birds), one should indicate death. A horse licking the leg with the tongue with tear-filled eyes forebodes ruin. (If a horse) scratches the earth with the left foot or sleeps during the day (lying) on the left side, it does not confer good. The horse that passes urine once (a day), that is looking drowsy, does not allow to be ridden and that returns home frantically if ridden upon, indicates impediment for the journey. (It indicates the same result) if it touches the left side (of its body). (The horse) that neighs (on seeing) the enemy warrior and touching its leg brings victory.

32-35. If an elephant courts (openly) in a village it would ruin the country. If a she-elephant after delivering a calf runs amuck (it forebodes) the death of the king. (If an elephant) does not allow itself to be ridden or frantically returns home after being ridden or ichor flows from the elephant, it foretells the death of the king. (An elephant) crossing its left foot with its right foot and entwining its right tusk with its trunk is auspicious. A bull or a horse or an elephant entering the enemy forces is inauspicious. If clouds get broken (suddenly) and rain excessively, (the king) would get his army routed.

36. The tumbling down of the umbrella at the time of a travel or during the war on account of adverse asterisms and planetary conditions or the wind blowing against (the forces) forebodes fear.

37. Contended men and favourable planets are the characteristics for (foreboding) victory. The warriors being attacked by the crows and demons (forebodes) the destruction of the army. The east, west, north-east and north are the excellent and auspicious directions.

CHAPTER TWO HUNDRED AND THIRTYTHREE

The propitious periods for undertaking an expedition

Puṣkara said :

1-3. I shall describe all kinds of journeys relating to a sovereign. A journey should be abandoned when the Venus has set or is in a weak house or debilitated or in the house of an enemy or retrograde or malefic. One should avoid a journey when the Mercury is retrograde, the presiding planet of the quarter or any other planet (in a similar position), is under the *vaidhṛti*[1], *vyatipāta*, *nāga*[2], *śakuna*, *catuṣpada* and *kintughna*.

4. One should avoid undertaking journey under (the influence of) *vipat* (*tāra*)[3], *naidhana*, *pratyari*, as well as the *janma*, the *gaṇḍa*[4] and the void lunar day.

5. The north and the east are said to be having the same virtues. In the same way the west and south are of the same virtues.

6. One should not cross the obstacle that has risen from the north-west to the south-east. Sundays, Mondays and Saturdays are not auspicious (for a journey).

7-10. (The asterisms) *kṛttikā* and others (for journey) in the east, (the asterisms) *maghā* and others (for journey) in the south, (the asterisms) *anurādhā* and others (for journey) in the west and (the asterisms) *jyeṣṭhā* and others (for journey) in the north are all commendable. I shall describe the measure of the shadows (cast by the sun on different days. It is said to be twenty for the Sun, sixteen for the Moon, fifteen for the Mars, fourteen for the Mercury, thirteen for the Jupiter, twelve for the Venus and eleven for the Saturn. These are said (to be valid) for all actions. One should not set out on a journey under his native ascendant and in the direction of the rainbow.

11. One should march on an expedition after meditating on lord Hari for victory if the omens and other things are good. I shall describe the circle (of twelve primary kings) to be thought about that would offer protection to the king.

---

1. This and the next one are among the twenty-seven *yogas* or combinations.
2. This and the following three are some of the eleven divisions of a day called *karaṇas*.
3. This and the next three are the astral indications.
4. This is one of the twentyseven *yogas*.

12. A kingdom is said to consist of seven constituents—the king, minister, fort, treasury, punishment (law), allies and township.

13. One should destroy all those who obstruct (the normal course) of the seven constituents of a kingdom. Efforts should be made by the king to make all these circles develop.

14-15. The kingdom over which a king exercises direct control would be the first circle. The feudatories of that kingdom should be known as the enemies. If they are attached (to the paramount lord they) should be known as friends. The next (circle is) the allies of the enemy. The next (circle) should be known as the ally of the ally. The next (circle would be) the enemy of the ally of the ally.

16-20. Those in front have been described. Tell me those who are behind. Then there would be the enemy in the rear. A king whose kingdom lies next but one is said to be the next one (friend in rear). A hostile king would be the next one (friend of the rear enemy). That which is adjacent to the former is said to be the next one (friend of rear friend). O Brahmin ! This is (the way of maintaining order) by an independent king that has an enemy and is desirous of conquering (the same). O Excellent among men ! It is not possible to declare that it is settled. One is said to be an intermediary that is capable of punishing and favouring. A mighty king that would be able to punish and favour all is said to be neutral. No one is really one's enemy or ally. One is an enemy or an ally on account of some reason. I have described these twelve circles relating to a king.

21-25. Enemies are known to be of three kinds—ancestral, personal and artificial. Each one of the preceding class among them are (known to be) stronger (than the succeeding ones). One that is a personal enemy is considered by me as artificial. An enemy in the rear of an enemy and his hostiles would be one's friends. A king should subdue his hostile king in the rear by means of strategies. The ancient authorities commend the extinction of an enemy with (the help of) an ally. An ally may become an enemy after being a feudal. A king wishing to vanquish an enemy should himself destroy him if it is possible for him to do. There will not be any fear from an enemy when the glory is waxing. A king desiring to conquer righteously should exercise control over the world in such a way that the people do not feel grief-stricken and trust him.

CHAPTER TWO HUNDRED AND THIRTYFOUR

The six expedients used by the king

Puṣkara said :

1. I have already described (the political expedients of) conciliatory measures, creating dissensions, bribery (to win the enemy) and punishment. I have described the punishment (to be made by the king) in his own country. I shall (now) describe (the punishment to be meted to a person living) in a foreign country.

2. Punishment is said to be of two types—public and private. Public punishment (consists of) looting and the destruction of villages (of the enemy country), destruction of the food grains and setting fire. (The private punishment consists of) killing by poisoning or setting fire or by engaging several men, dishonouring pious men and poisoning waters.

3-7. O Bhārgava (son of Bhṛgu) ! I have described the mode of executing the punishment. Listen ! I shall describe when (the king) should be indifferent. A king should make peace (with his enemy) if he thinks that by his battle in the battle-field there would be bad consequences. One maybe indifferent (when he would find) the conciliatory measures as securing the position (of the enemy), paying a bribe would be squandering money and creating dissension would have punishment as the consequence. One may resort to indifference (if he is sure) that 'this person is not capable of doing any harm to me' and 'I am not capable of causing any harm to him'. In that case the king should humiliate the enemy (by being indifferent).

8-14. I shall describe the strategies of illusion (to be practised by a king). The enemy should be agitated by false portents by sending extensive lighted torches (tied to) the tails of strong birds in the camp of the enemy. Then the fall of the meteor should be shown to them. In this way many other portents also should be shown. The enemies should thus be agitated by different (kinds of) deception. The astrologers and ascetics should proclaim the fall of the enemy. A king that desires to conquer the earth should agitate others by the above (proclamation). The favour of gods should also be proclaimed to others. A king should declare (to his men) "We have received increased strength and you strike without fear; all others have been routed", when the battle has begun. War-cry and great commotion should be made saying that the enemy has been routed. (It should also be proclaimed); "The king has been blessed by the gods profusely and is ready for the battle". I shall describe *Indrajāla* (a kind of stratagem in war).

15. A king should exhibit the four divisions of the army (such as the infantry, cavalry, men mounted on elephants and chariots) (to delude the enemy) that the gods had sent them for aid. Showers of blood should be shed on the enemy.

16. Severed heads of the enemy should be exhibited on (the terrace of) palaces. I shall describe six expedients, among which war and peace are most excellent.

17. Making peace, war, expedition, halt, seeking shelter and duplicity are said to be the six expedients.

18-25. Making peace is known to be a treaty. War is offending (the enemy). Expedition is said to be the march against the enemy by the one that desires to conquer. It is said to be 'the halt' when (a king) remains in his own territory (mobilising his forces) for the war. Mobilisation of half the army in the enemy country is said to be 'seeking shelter'. It is said to be duplicity on account of resorting to indifference or neutral position. A king should seek a treaty with an equal (person) or not of lower strength and more powerful. A powerful king should make a war with (a king of) inferior strength. In that case he should take a stronger (king) as an ally when he is not having an enemy in the rear. A king should mobilise his army when he could easily intercept the work of the enemy, though he is not free from an enemy in the rear. One who is strong enough could mobilise half of his army in the territory of the enemy even though he may have an enemy in the rear. An alliance with another king is said to be the worst of all expedients a king fighting with a stronger adversary is compelled to do. It is said to bring many a long and tedious marches, loss of many lives and expenditure. A king should have an alliance only when he would have great benefits later. Moreover, he should have an alliance only when he has been deprived of all his strength.

CHAPTER TWO HUNDRED AND THIRTYFIVE

The daily duties of a king

Puṣkara said :

1-2. I shall describe the perpetual daily duties of the king. The king should put an end to his sleep with the songs and music of the panegyrists when two *muhūrtas* (fortyeight minutes) are still left in the night. He should then see spies in such a way that they are not known as his own men by anybody.

3. He should then hear the report about the income and expenditure as laid down. After having eased, the king should. go to the bath-room.

4. The king should then bathe preceded by cleansing the teeth. After having done the twilight worship and the repetition (of the sacred syllables) (the king) should worship lord Vāsudeva (Viṣṇu's manifestation as Kṛṣṇa).

5. He should then offer unto the fire holy (twigs). Libations should be offered to the ancestors. Accompanied by the blessings of brahmins, he should then give a cow (as gift) together with gold.

6. He should then see his face in the mirror after having adorned himself and besmeared (his body with sandal-paste). (He should also then see his face in clarified butter kept together with gold. The king should then hear about (the nature of) the day etc.

7. (He should then take) medicines prescribed by the physicians. He should then touch the auspicious things. He should then see the preceptor and go to the court after having been blessed by him.

8. O Fortunate one ! He should then see brahmins, ministers, counsellors and others presented by the door-keeper.

9-13. After having heard the traditional history and things to be done, he should determine the business (to be done). He should then look into civil disputes and have counsel with the counsellors. He should not have the counsel with a single person or with many or ignorant men or untrustworthy men. He should also not make public the secret (counsel). The counsel he had should be given effect to promptly so that the state may not get affected. The secret counsel is considered to be guarded well by a king by his postures. Wise men gather secrets from the postures of others. A king gets prosperity by following the words of astrologers, physicians and connsellors, because they sustain the king. After having had the counsel (he should do) physical exercises with discs, chariot and weapon.

14. He should then bathe in tanks not inhabited by living creatures and see lord Viṣṇu that has already been worshipped. He should then see fire into which oblations have been made and also see brahmins that have been worshipped well.

15-17. After having adorned himself he should take food after having fed beings and after having tested the food duly. After having taken food, he should chew betels and rest lying on the left. He should then have inquiry in the sacred texts. After having met the warriors and seen the granary and the armoury he should do the evening twilight worship. He should then think of the tasks to be done, send spies, eat food and spend time in the harem with instrumental music and being guarded by others. A king should do thus daily.

CHAPTER TWO HUNDRED AND THIRTYSIX

The rites preceding the march of a king

Puṣkara said :

1-5. I shall describe rites to be performed before commencing a march. When a march of a king has to begin after seven days, (lords) Hari (Viṣṇu) and Śambhu (Śiva) should be worshipped as well as lord Vināyaka (the elephant-faced god, lord of impediments) with sweet balls and other things (on the first day). After having worshipped the guardian (deities) of (different) directions, (the priest) should lie down (on a bed). He should then worship gods either (remaining) on the bed or in front of them. He should then think of Manu. "Obeisance O Śambhu (conferer of good) ! to the three-eyed, dreadful and conferer of boons. Obeisance to the dwarf (manifestation of lord Viṣṇu), the formless lord of dreams. O Master ! Lord of the lords ! Bearer of the trident ! One riding the bull ! O Eternal one ! Let me know in my dream while I sleep, the good or evil (to befall me). (The impressions) in the waking state (maybe driven) far away." The priest should thus utter these sacred syllables (on the second day).

6. He should worship the guardian (deities) of the quarters, Rudras and the lords of directions on the third day, the planets on the fourth day and the two Aśvins (divine physicians) on the fifth day.

7-14. Then (the gods on the way (of expedition) and the sacred rivers (presided over) by those gods should be worshipped. Offerings (should be made) to gods dwelling in heavens, atmosphere and earth. The group of goblins and (gods) Vāsudeva and others should be worshipped in the night. (Worship should be) made to (goddesses) Bhadrakālī and Śrī. One should pray to all gods. "May gods Vāsudeva, Saṅkarṣaṇa, Pradyumna and Aniruddha,[1] Nārāyaṇa (Viṣṇu), Abjaja (born in the lotus, Brahmā), Viṣṇu, Nārasiṁha (man-lion form of lord Viṣṇu), the boar (manifestation of lord Viṣṇu), O Rāma ! Śiva, Īśa[2] (Īśāna), Tatpuruṣa, Aghora, Satyaja[3], the Sun, Moon, Mars, Mercury, Jupiter, Venus, Saturn, Rāhu, (the ascending node of Moon), Ketu (descending node of Moon), Gaṇapati (lord of goblins), Senānī (son of Śiva and Pārvatī) (leader of the celestials against the demon Tāraka), (goddesses) Caṇḍikā, Umā (consort of Śiva), Lakṣmī (consort of Viṣṇu), Sarasvatī (goddess of speech), Durgā a form of Pārvatī), Brahmāṇī (consort of Brahmā), the Rudras (forms of Śiva, eleven in number), (the celestials) Indra and others such as the

1. This and the preceding three are the four forms of lord Viṣṇu.
2. This and the next four are the five forms of Śiva.
3. Obviously a mistake for Sadyaja denoting Sadyojāta.

Fire-god, serpents, Tārkṣya (Eagle, vehicle of lord Viṣṇu) and other celestials dwelling in heavens, atmosphere and earth be for my victory. Let them crush the enemies in the battle after having accepted offerings (made by me). O Gods ! I have sought your refuge together with sons, mother and servants. Obeisance to you ! After going to the rear of the enemies destroy them. I will offer more than that I have given after returning from the battle".

15-21. On the sixth day, the king should bathe for victory just as the bath at the coronation. Lord Trivikrama (manifestation of lord Viṣṇu as a dwarf and taking three strides humiliating king Bali) should be worshipped on the seventh (day), the day of expedition. The weapons and vehicles should be worshipped with the sacred syllables prescribed for *nīrājana* (rite of purification). The following sacred syllable should be uttered (in the ear of the king) with the sounds of auspiciousness and victory. "May the celestials dwelling in heaven, atmosphere and earth be bestowers of longevity on you. May the success of gods be attained by you. Let your (expedition) be the expedition of gods. May all gods protect you". After having heard this, the king should proceed. After having taken the bow together with the arrow with (the recitation of the sacred syllable) *dhanurnāga*[1], (the king) should place his foot in the direction of his enemy after having repeated (the sacred syllable) *tad viṣṇoḥ*[2]. (After having set) his right foot, he should place thirty steps in different directions such as the east in due order. He should duly climb the elephant., chariot, horse and the animal carrying the burden. After having climbed he should move on along with the sounds of musical instruments without looking back. After having gone (a distance of) a *krośa* (two or two and a half miles) he should halt and worship gods and brahmins. He should move to the foreign country protecting his own army.

22-23. After having reached the alien country (enemy's domain) the king should protect the guardian (deity) of the country. He should worship deities and should not destroy their properties. He should not humiliate the natives of that

1. Could not be identified.
2. ṚV. 1.22.20.

country. After having returned to his metropolis again after having gained victory, the king should worship gods and make gifts.

24-27. If there is a battle on the second day, the elephant, horse etc. should be bathed and lord Nṛsiṁha (man-lion manifestation of lord Viṣṇu) should be worshipped. The royal insignia such as the umbrella etc., weapons and the goblins (should be worshipped) in the night. After having worshipped lord Nṛsiṁha and all vehicles in the morning, (the king) should see the sacrificial fire kindled by the priest. After having made oblations into the fire, the king should worship brahmins. After having taken the bow and arrow he should mount the elephant and move. He should walk in the country of the enemy without being noticed (by anybody) (and find) the nature (of the enemy). He should cause a small army of men spread extensively.

28-35. A small army as the mouth of a needle can stand against many. The arrangement of the army is of the form of animals and things such as the *garuḍa* (the king of birds), crocodile, circle, vulture, semi-circle, *vajravyūha* (a strong impenetrable array), cart (shaped), the *sarvato-bhadra* circular (array) and *sūcivyūha* (as a needle). An army in one of the above arrays should be arranged in five parts—the two composing its two principal wings, the two forming its sides to protect the wings and the fifth one would be the main body. A battle should be fought with one or two of the above parts. The remaining three parts should be stationed only for their protection. A king should never be in arrays. If the main force is destroyed, (the whole army) will be routed. A king should not himself fight. A king should remain at a *krośa* (about two or two and a quarter miles), behind the army. It is said that a broken army could be resustained by that. One's stay is not laid down if the main army has suffered a defeat. The soldiers in the array should not be set up too close or too wide apart, so that there may not be any clash of their weapons mutually.

36-43. One who wants to break the hostile army should do so only with collective strength. So also the enemy should protect it from being broken with the collective strength. That division of a hostile army among many divisions, should be first attacked and broken through (by the commander) as he desires. O Brahmin ! There should be four soldiers to guard each foot of an elephant. There should be four cavalry and an equal number of armoured soldiers for guarding a chariot. (There should be) an equal number of bow-men as the armoured soldiers in front of the armoured soldiers in the battle. Behind bow-men, the cavalry and the chariot-fighters and then the soldiers mounted on elephants should be set up by a king. He should look after the duties of the infantry, elephants and horses with effort. Bold men should be placed in front. Only a division of the army should be shown. Cowards should not be placed in front because that would break the work of driving away the enemy. The bold men remaining in the front would enthuse cowards in the battle. Men of tall stature with acquiline noses, not having squint eyes, with well-blended eye-brows, irascible, fond of quarrels, contented, happy and lustful are known to be bold.

44-48. Carrying the wounded and the dead from the battle-field, offering water to the elephants in each war, bringing weapons (to the soldiers) are said to be the work of the soldiers. Protecting their own army from the enemies desiring to break, breaking the collected force (of the enemies) are the works of armoured men. Making (the enemies) turn away from battle is the task of bow-men. It is said that the chariot of a wounded person should be led away to a distant place. It is stated that the work of the chariot-warriors is to frighten the enemy army. The duties of men mounted on elephants are to break through the collected force of the enemy, to gather soldiers got split in the army of the self and the destruction of walls, arches, battlements and trees.

49. The ground for the infantry to fight is known to be uneven and that for the cavalry and chariot as even. The battle-fields for the elephants are pointed out as wet.

50-55. After having arranged the arrays thus and having the Sun behind and the Venus, Saturn, guardian deities of the quarters and the gentle breeze being favourable, all the warriors should be encouraged by repeating their names and the (achievement of their) clans (and pointing out) gain of prosperity on success and gain of heaven for the dead. After conquest over the enemies one gets pleasures. There would be supreme position for the dead. There is no way of requital for the food taken from the master equal to (sacrificing in) the battle. They would be washed of their sins as blood flows from the bold warriors. The endurance of pain due to wounds is the excellent penance. Thousands of celestial women attend on a man killed in the battle. One's master gets (the result of) the deeds (done) by those who run away after being defeated (in battle). It is said that such people get the fruits of killing a brahmin at each one of their step. The gods would be lost for one who deserts his companions in the battle-field.

56-60. It is said that the brave who do not retreat in battle would get the benefit (of performing the sacrifice) of *aśvamedha*. If the king is righteous he would be victorious. He should fight with men of equal valour. Men mounted.on elephants should be fought by men mounted on elephants. Retreating men, spectators, those not having weapons and those that have fallen should not be killed. One should do treacherous warfare when one is fatigued, sleeping, is crossing half the river or forest and on bad days. Raising up arms one should cry that the enemies have been defeated. "We have got the ally with abundant strength. The king (of the enemy forces) and the commander have been slain or the (hostile) king had retreated." One may kill easily the retreating warriors.

61. O One well-versed in righteousness ! incense that stupefies the enemies should be burnt. The banners and other paraphernalia and the musical instruments making frightening sounds should be made use of.

62-65. After having gained victory in the battle, one should worship gods and brahmins. In a battle won by the minister, the gems (acquired by the minister) should be made over to the king. The wives of a defeated king would not belong to anyone else (but to that defeated king). The wives of the defeated king should be protected (by the conquering king). A king should honour a hostile king defeated in the battle and treat him as his own son. He should not fight with him again. He should honour the customs and manners (of that country). Then after having entered his native country, he should enter the palace when a fixed star is ruling. He should worship the deities etc. and protect the families of warriors. He should divide the booty got from the battle among his servants. The procedure for commencing a military expedition has thus been described to you. It gives sure success for the king.

CHAPTER TWO HUNDRED AND THIRTYSEVEN

A hymn in praise of goddess Śrī (Lakṣmī) for the sake of success

Puṣkara said :

1. Indra made the prayer to (the goddess Śrī (Lakṣmī) in days of yore for securing the kingdom. A king should similarly do that prayer for the sake of victory.

Indra said :

2. I make obeisance to the mother of all worlds, that is born of the ocean, the (goddess) Śrī (Fortune), that has eyes like the lotus that is waking up after sleep and that person dwelling on the chest of lord Viṣṇu.

3-4. O Goddess ! You are the success. You are the Svadhā (food offered to the manes), the Svāhā (oblations). You are ambrosia. (You are) the purifier of the world. You are the twilights, night, lustre, wealth, memory, faith and Sarasvatī (the goddess of speech). (You are) the sacrificial knowledge, supreme knowledge and secret knowledge. O Auspicious one ! O Goddess ! You are the knowledge of the soul and the conferer of the benefit of emancipation.

5. You are the metaphysics, the three *Vedas* and the science of administration. O Goddess ! The Beautiful ! This has been filled by your beautiful worldly forms.

6. O Goddess ! Who else other than you would rest in the body composed of all sacrifices of the mace-wielding Lord Nārāyaṇa, the god of gods whom the yogins contemplate.

7. O Goddess ! All the three worlds were forsaken by you and the Earth was almost lost and resuscitated by you now.

8. O Most Fortunate One ! Men would always get wives, sons, house, friends, grains, wealth etc. on account of your glances.

9. O Goddess ! It is not impossible for men seen by your

glances to get beauty, health, fortune, destruction of the enemy beside happiness.

10. You are the mother of all beings; and Lord Hari (Viṣṇu), the god of gods, is the father. O Mother ! This world of movable and immovable beings is pervaded by you and lord Viṣṇu.

11-12. O Purifier of all ! Do not forsake honour, treasury, granary, house, attendants, body and wife. One resting on the chest of lord Viṣṇu ! Do not desert children, circle of friends, cows and ornaments.

13. O Spotless one ! Those men forsaken by you would be forsaken at once by nobility, truth, purity and other qualities such as good conduct.

14. Men seen by you would atonce be endowed with all qualities such as good conduct, the fortune of good family etc. even though they be without good qualities.

15. O Goddess ! Whoever is seen by you would be praiseworthy, possessing good qualities, fortunate, belonging to a good family, wise, valiant and victorious.

16. O Consort of lord Viṣṇu ! The Sustainer of the universe ! All qualities such as good conduct shed their excellence at once in men from whom you have turned your face.

17. Even the tongue of Brahmā is not capable of describing your qualities. O Goddess Lotus-eyed ! Be gracious. Never forsake us.

Puṣkara said :

18-19. Being thus adored, (goddess) Śrī (Lakṣmī) conferred on Indra the desired boon (such as) firmness of sovereignty and success in the battle etc. It confers enjoyment and emancipation on those reciting or hearing the hymn. Hence one should always read and listen to the hymn on (goddess) Śrī (Lakṣmī).

CHAPTER TWO HUNDRED AND THIRTYEIGHT

The ethics narrated by Rāma

Agni said :

1. I have narrated the ethics told by Puṣkara. Listen. I shall now narrate the ethics narrated by Rāma to Lakṣmaṇa for victory and that would increase piety etc.

Rāma said :

2. Wealth should be acquired by rightful means. It should be developed and guarded. It should be given to a deserving person. These are the four obligatory acts of a king.

3. Humility is the cause of statesmanship. Humility is the resultant of determination from scriptures as well as the control of senses. The king should guard the earth endowed with these.

4-5. Scriptures, knowledge, fortitude, dexterity, proficiency, reticence, energy, eloquence, generosity, endurance at the time of distress, greatness, purity, amity, renunciation, truthfulness gratitude, good family, good conduct, self-control are the qualities for gaining fortune.

6. The elephant (in the form) of senses running uncontrolled in the forest of diverse pleasures should be controlled with the goad of knowledge.

7. A king should give up the aggregate of six things, namely, lust, anger, greed, delight, pride and arrogance. The king who rejects these would be happy.

8. A king being endowed with modesty should contemplate on metaphysics, the three *Vedas*, emissary and polity with those well-versed in these and those practising them.

9. The knowledge about true nature of things is got through metaphysics. Virtue and vice rest on the three *Vedas*. Material prosperity and misfortune depend on emissary and justice and injustice on polity.

10. Abstaining from killing or causing injury to beings, courteous language, truthfulness, purity, kindness, and forbearance are the general virtues of the religious students.

11-13. One should show compassion to all beings and practise codes of conduct. Courteous words, compassion, charity and protection of one that has sought refuge are the acts of good people agreeable to pious men. Which king would do impious acts for the sake of the body that is encompassed by misery and disease and that is liable to get destroyed today or tomorrow ? One should not oppress the poor people desiring his own happiness.

14-15. A poor man being oppressed kills the king by means of his anger. A king desiring his own good should conduct with more humility than that shown to a respectful kinsman with folded palms. One should always speak only in a pleasing manner to friends and foes.

16. Those who speak pleasingly are gods and those who speak harsh are animals. One should always worship gods with cleanliness and get purified with piety.

17-18. The preceptors (should be respected) as gods and friends as one's own selves. The preceptor (should be pleased) by bowing down. The favourable pious men (should be pleased) by doing true gestures and services. The gods (should be pleased) by good deeds. A friend should be attracted by courteousness and kinsmen by showing respect.

19-22. The wife and servants (should be pleased respectively) by (showing) affection and (making) gifts. The rest of the people (should be won) by (showing) compassion. Not reviling the acts of others, maintaining to do one's duties, kindness towards the poor, sweet words towards all, helping a true friend even by (sacrificing one's) life, receiving warmly the person that has come to the house, making a gift (according) to one's ability, forbearance, absence of pride in prosperity, not jealous at other's prosperity, not speaking words hurting (the feelings of) others, practising the vow of silence, maintaining the bondage with kinsmen, keeping even attitude towards one's own men and taking actions conducive to welfare are the acts of greatmen.

CHAPTER TWO HUNDRED AND THIRTYNINE

The duties of a king

Rāma said :

1. The king, ministry, kingdom, fort, treasury, army and allies helpful to one another are said to be the seven constituents of a kingdom,.

2-16. The sovereignty is the most important means of a kingdom. It should hence always be protected. Good descent, good conduct, (young in) years, good quality, compassion, quick action, consistency, truthfulness, service to the aged, gratefulness, being fortunate, intellect, possessing an unwicked retinue, able to exhibit his valour, faithfulness, foresightedness zeal, purity, generosity, modesty and virtuousness are the qualities of a pious man and a king. A king, seeking his own good, should make those belonging to a good family his attendants, be not cruel, but capable of winning the people and pure. A king should be eloquent, confident, possessing good memory, distinguished,strong, self-controlled, a leader, well-versed in polity and the different branches of fine arts, capable of facing an attack, capable of remedying all evils, one who knows the movements of hostiles, one who knows the principles of peace-making and war; capable of knowing the secret counsels (of the hostiles), knower of opportune time and place, one that takes goods in the proper way and distributes to the proper person, free from wrath, greed, fear, doing evil, haughtiness and fickleness, free from harassing others, calumny, jealousy, envy and untruth, fortunate (in getting) the counsel of the aged, able, showing his amiable manners and one that is fond of good qualities which are known to confer prosperity. Men of noble descent, virtuous, brave, learned, attached, those who would implement the rules of punishment should be the ministers of the king. The minister should moreover be having good physique, a native of the country, belonging to a good family, endowed with good conduct and knowledge in arts, eloquent, courageous, possessing good eye-sight, enthusiasm, discrimination, devoid of rigidity and ficklemindedness, friendly, capable of enduring hardship, virtuous, possessing (the qualities, of) truthfulness, good nature, firmness, perseverence, dignity, good health, able, having retentive memory, firm devotion (to the king) and not creating enmity (with other kings). Good memory, good application of the mind conducive to gain, decisive knowledge, firmness and guarding the secret counsels are the virtues of a minister. The royal priest should be profiicient in the *Vedas* and codes of punishment.

17-23. The priest should do the expiatory and welfare-yielding rites as laid down in *Atharvaveda*. The wise king should examine the fitness of these ministers with the help of experts. The two qualities of having a clear sight and skill should be examined. He should know about the family and the integrity from his own people. The three qualities—ability in service, knowledge and endurance should be examined. So also the boldness, and their pleasure in conversation should be known. Their eloquence, truthfulness, enthusiasm, greatness, endurance for hardship, firmness, loyalty and steadiness in distress should be noted. The king should know their devotion, friendship and honesty from their conduct. Likewise their strength, good nature, health, good conduct, not being fickleminded and not exhibiting their enmity (should be known) from their companions. Their gentleness and meanness should be known (from their acts) in his presence. Everywhere the virtues of them (practised) not in his presence should be gauged from results.

24-25. A region having good crops, meritorious, endowed with minerals, beneficial for cows, having plenty of water having holy cities, enchanting, abounding in elephants, having water courses and not depending on rains is commended for abundant prosperity.

26-27. It should abound with *śūdras*, artisans and merchants and have great enterprises and agriculturers. (It should abound with men) fondly attached (to the king), hating the hostile king, capable of enduring hardship. It should contain people who have come from different countries and who are pious, possessing cattle and strength. Such a country is commended. The head should be wise and not addicted to any vice.

28-30. The fortress should be built on hills having a river or desert or forest (as a boundary) covering a large area and having a deep moat, high walls and gateways. The fort should contain water, grains and treasures to stand a long siege. Those surrounded by water, mountain, forest, desert and archers are six (kinds of forts)[1]. The forts should be replete with choice things, righteously acquired since the time of forefathers that would stand a heavy drain for the furtherance of righteousness etc.

31-37. (The servants should be descendants) of their forefathers' (servants), subservient, salaried, known for their valour,

1. It mentions only five names.

belonging to a good family, able, possessing knowledge about omens. (The army of the king should be) armed with different kinds of weapons, conversant with different types of warfare, possessing varied kinds of warriors, having horses and elephants duly sanctified, which has endured hardships in battle and sufferings in expeditions etc. Those who administer justice should be undivided and mostly drawn from the *kṣatriya* community. One that is proficient in *yoga*, good-natured, possessing a strong army, conversing affectionately, able to wait patiently for the outcome, not divided and belonging to a good family should be befriended. Approaching from a distance, uttering words having clear meaning and agreeable to the heart and doing good deeds are the three ways of acquiring friendship. One gets three kinds of fruits such as piety, enjoyment and prosperity through the friend. The son of a friend, a newly acquired friend, an ancestral friend and one protected from distress are known to be the four kinds of friends. Truthfulness and other things and similar pleasure and pain are the qualities in the friend.

38-41. I shall describe the conduct of those who serve (the king). A servant should serve the king (to the best of his ability). Ability, good disposition, firmness, forbearance, ability to endure hardship, happiness, good conduct, enthusiasm are ornaments for the servants. A servant should serve the king to the best of his ability for the agreed period. He should give up visiting the place of enemies, doing cruel acts, haughtiness and jealousy. A servant should not exchange harsh words with his superiors. He should not publicise the confidential matters and the secret councils of his master. He should desire the prosperity of the affectionate king. He should desert a king that is not affectionate.

42. Dissuading the king from doing evil deeds and persuading him to do good deeds (are said to be) the good conduct in brief for the relatives, friends and servants.

43-45. The king, like the god of rain, should be sustainer of all good. He would take a part of the earnings from the sources of one's earning. He should employ efficient men to be in charge of all deeds. A good king should protect eight things such as agriculture, trade, fort, bridge, elephant stable, mines, ocean (the source of gems) and the abodes of the downcast and thus follow a good code of conduct.

46. There is danger for the subjects from the (following) five sources such as the soldiers, thieves, subjects, king's officers and the greed of the king.

47. The king should take tax after having taken note of this danger at the proper time. He has to protect his own body and the external body, the kingdom.

48. He should punish those deserving punishment and protect himself from poison as well as his wives and sons from the enemies. He should never trust them.

CHAPTER TWO HUNDRED AND FORTY

The six expedients used by a king

Rāma said :

1-5. A king should think mainly about the circle of twelve kings. The enemy, friend, ally of an enemy, ally of an ally, ally of an ally of the enemy are known to be at the front of the conqueror. An enemy in the rear, a king whose kingdom lies next but one, the allies of these two is the circle (of kings) of a king desiring to conquer. One who is beyond the enemy and the invader is the neutral. One is a master in favouring the united and the suppression of the divided. One who is beyond this circle of kings and possessing a greater strength is known to be a neutral. One is a lord in favouring the allies and the annihilation of the divided. I shall describe the treaty, battle, vehicle, seat etc.

6-9. One should make a treaty with the strongly opposed for one's welfare. Treaties are said to be sixteen—*kapāla*, *upahāra*, *santāna*, *saṅgata*, *upanyāsa*, *pratikāra*, *saṁyoga*, *puruṣāntara*, *adṛṣṭanara*, *ādiṣṭa*, *ātman*, *upagraha*, *parikrama*, *chinna*, *paradūṣaṇa* and *skandhopaneya*. Reciprocally beneficial, mutual amity, being related to each other and making presents (as token of friendship) are the four principal treaties.

10-14. One should not make treaties with the twenty people such as a child, an old man, one ill since a long time, an excommunicated relative, a coward, cowardly people, greedy people, one who has renounced the world, one excessively fond of worldly things, one devising many schemes, a despiser of gods and brahmins, an ill-fated one, one who speaks ill of fate, one suffering from famine, one having a discontented army, one having many enemies within the country and one who had become free in course of time and one swerved from adhering to truth and virtuous life. They should always be fought. A war is the result of mutual offence of men (hostile kings).

15-18. One aspiring the prosperity for himself, one being oppressed by another and one having favourable position, time and strength should begin war. Taking possession of kingdom, women, suzerainty, knowledge and strength, pride, honour, loss of fortune, destruction of knowledge, one's soul force and the virtue, that is due fate, dishonour on account of a friend, the destruction of a relative, cessation of the favour of (natural) elements, disturbance among the circle of monarchs, intense attachment for the sake of one are the causes for hostility.

19-24. Enmity is said to be of five kinds—through the co-wife, on account of one's abode, on account of wife, that arising from one's expression and that due to an offence. It should be amended by (suitable) expedients. A king should not engage in any of the following sixteen kinds of war, such as giving meagre result, yielding absolutely nil result, of uncertain result, that vitiating the existing order, proving fruitless in the long run that which affects in the long run and the existing order, with an army mobilised by enemy whose strength is not known, being undertaken for the sake of an ally or for the (recovery of a) woman or that (lasting) for a long time, or with brahmins, with one equipped with an untimely providence, with (an enemy) supported by a mighty friend, when it yields some result only at that moment but with no fruit in the long run and that which bears fruit in the long run but no benefit at that very moment. A king should undertake a task that would bear fruit at that moment and also in the long run.

25-32. One should wage war when one's forces are happy and strong and the enemy forces are of contrary nature. One should commence a battle when the friend, an ally and a neighbouring king are firmly attached to him and that of the enemy is the contrary. A military expedition is said to be of five kinds by experts such as an open foe, as an ally (If one of the combatants), as united force, as occasional and remaining neutral. Like the expedition, halt is also of five kinds according to the ability of mutually (combating forces) of the enemy and the invader. One should inform his arrival to (the commander of) the stronger of the two opposing forces remaining without taking the side of either of them and like the eye of the crow remain un-noticed. One should join the stronger one when the hostilities begin. When both of them suspect his feigned neutrality and would dislike the engagement, one should himself attack the enemy that is more antagonistic. When a king with his army is routed by the powerful enemy and does not find a strategy, he should practise truthfulness and noble virtues of the ancestors. He should visit the powerful ally frequently, stay by his side, view things as he does and show gratitude for the support extended. The code of conduct for those seeking refuge has been heard.

CHAPTER TWO HUNDRED AND FORTYONE

The four means conciliation etc.

Rāma said :

1. The power of counsel is commended than the power of greatness and enthusiasm. Kāvya (Śukra), the preceptor of demons), possessing greatness and enthusiasm was conquered by the priest of the celestials (Bṛhaspati).

2-4. One should not have a counsel with untrustworthy and foolish persons. How can a scheme that is impossible to begin be made to bear the fruit without toil. A counsel is laid down as of five kinds—knowledge of the unknown, ascertainment of that known (already), removal of doubt relating to an ambiguous matter in politics, (determination) of the right time and place of action and helpful means, and remedial measures against misfortunes.

5. The marks of success in the acts are the cheerfulness of the mind, faith, efficiency of the means, aid and effort.

6. Pride, negligence, lust, prattling in sleep and enjoying pleasures with the beloved women break the secret counsel.

7-13. A person who is bold, having good memory, eloquent well-versed in the (wielding of) weapons and in the sciences, and one accustomed with the work deserves to become a messenger of the king. A messenger is said to be of three types such as one that discharges duty efficiently, one that does moderately and one who just conveys the message. (Each one of the succeeding one) is inferior by a quarter based on the ability (of the respective ones). One should not enter the city of the enemy and his assembly without having (previous) acquaintance. One should abide the right time and should fall upon (the enemy) after knowing (the opportune moment). One should know the weakness of the enemy as well as his treasury, friends and strength. He should also know the likes and dislikes from the looks and gestures (of the enemy). (An enemy) should make four-fold eulogies of both the sides (i.e. the master and the enemy). He should live with good spies having the guise of ascetics. An ambassador would be an open spy. A spy in disguise is of two kinds. Spies would be in the guise of a merchant, agriculturer or mendicant and the like. When the effort of the messenger has become fruitless, the king should attack the distressed enemy. One should take into account the natural calamity (that has befallen the enemy) and fall upon him.

14-24. Because it destroys the good fortune on account of bad policy it is said to be misfortune. Conflagration, water, diseases (epidemics), famine and hell are the five calamities due to divine agency. The rest are due to human agency. The misfortune due to divine agency should be subdued by means of human effort and appeasing rites. The misfortune due to human agency should be removed by means of expedients based on the rightful living. Deliberation, the reaping of the fruits of deliberation, following a course of action for future contingencies, the income and expenditure of the state, enforcing laws, the prevention of (the encroachment by) the enemy, (taking) remedial steps for the calamity and the protection of kingdom and the king are the duties of a minister. Hence one beset with misfortune would ruin kingdom. Gold, grain, clothes and vehicle would be through the subjects. In the same way other things (are got through the subjects). If the subjects are having misfortune (all the above) are destroyed. Citizens of the city etc. help to protect subjects having misfortune as well as the treasury and law if it is sought. (The duties of feudatory chiefs) are to put down disturbance, help the sovereign in war, protection of people and taking note of the allies and foes. A king would perish on account of the fault of the vassals and suffer misfortune. Treasure enables a king to pay his servants, to win him friends and subjects, to aid the purposes of virtue and desire, to attend to the renovation of forts. If that is having misfortune, it would ruin the king. The king is dependent on the treasury. The enforcement of law is a means to create friends and foes, to acquire land and gold, to conquer enemies, to accomplish a work quickly that would take long time. If that is affected it would ruin the king. An ally would collect together allies, destroy the enemy and help him with money etc. If that is affected, that would destroy the king.

25-27. The king having a vice would destroy the affairs of the state. The vices of a king are the use of harsh words, (inflicting) cruel punishment, wasteful spending of revenue, drinking, (excessive enjoyment of the company of) women, hunting and gambling. Idleness, obstinacy, pride, intelligence and dupli city are the defects of a minister as already pointed out. Drought and epidemics etc. are the misfortunes of a country.

28. Shattered machines, walls and ditches not equipped with weapons and possessing a depleted army are the defects of a fort.

29. One nearly drained, not filled regularly, not being accounted, not accumulated, made waste and situated at a far off place are the defects in treasury.

30-33. Being obstructed, scattered, not honoured, disrespected, not existing, afflicted with disease, tired, arrived from a distant place, newly recruited, much reduced, disappointed, repulsed much, abound with hopes and disgust, deceived, having wives, having grievance within, break in the supply of provisions of different kinds, the base being made void, divided by the hostile (king), deprived of a leader and bribed by the hostile king at the rear are said to be the defects of an army.

34. An ally suffering adverse fate, attacked by the enemy forces, having lust, rage etc. and energy would be (considered as) an enemy.

35-41. Lavish spending of money, inflicting harsh words and punishment on account of anger, due to lust, hunting, gambling, drinking and women (are the vices of a king). Harsh words create the estrangement in the world and havoc. Punishment is a means (to achieve) things difficult to accomplish. A king should remove it with care. A king that inflicts punishment and harsh words would agitate the subjects. The agitated subjects resort to the enemy. Multiplication of enemies would be for your destruction. A wasteful expenditure of wealth to a greater extent in order to defile one is said to be extravagance in spending by the learned in political science. By drinking one becomes ignorant, by hunting one gets destroyed by the enemy. One should wander in the forest that is guarded doing hunting in order to remove hardships due to victory. The destruction of virtues, wealth, life and quarrels etc. would be on account of gambling. Delay and affliction to virtue and wealth would result from the defect of association with women. On account of the vice of drinking (there would be) destruction of life, indecision relating to things to be done and not to be done.

42-46. One who knows the (mode of) laying the capital and the opportune moments would conquer the enemy. The dwelling of the king alongwith the treasury should be in the midst of the royal capital. The artisans, friends, unhostile foresters and the main division of the army should be placed surrounding the royal dwelling. The army should be placed ready at a corner under the lead of the commander. They should roam about the quadrangular points in a circle during the nights. Information relating to one's self should be known (through spies) moving about the borders (of the country). All should leave and enter the city being noticed, The seven (political) expedients such as conciliation, gift, dissension, punishment indifference, conjuring and deceit should be instituted for accomplishing them.

47-51 Conciliation is of four kinds such as the expression of gratitude, recollection of the relationship between one another, use of soft words and seeing and submission of the self with the words "I am yours", when (the other person) had come. The making of a gift of wealth to one that has come (is of three kinds such as) excellent, medium and inferior. The making of a gift is of five kinds (such as) giving back (the gift), accepting (the gift) received, making a novel gift, accepting a gift by his own choice, giving and returning. Dissension is of three kinds by experts knowing dissension (such as) destroying amity, creating a thrill of fear, inducing dissension between the two. Punishment is of three kinds (such as) killing, confiscating the property, and imposing hardship.

52-53. (Punishment is also of two other kinds such as) public and secret. The public enemies (should be punished) in public. In cases in which the people would get agitated by killing in public, (killing by poisoning) the food is commended. The enemies (of the public should be killed) by employing special black rites or with weapons etc. A member of the brahmin community alone should not be killed even after being under control after conciliation.

54-58. A good person should do conciliation (speaking) sweet words as if besmearing the heart, looking (at the person) as if feasting and taking in his form as if ambrosia. One duped with false hopes, desirous (of getting) wealth, one being invited and insulted, one having contempt for the king, one superseded in honour, one thinking much about his virtue, one whose virtue, desire and riches have been cut off, one that is angry, one having self-respect, insulted, one rejected without any cause, appeased even though had enmity, one whose wealth and wife have been taken, one deserving to be honoured but not honoured and such men permanently remaining in the enemy camp and are to be suspected should be divided.

59-62. (A king) should honour those that have come (from the enemy side) with presents and pacify those on his own side. Winning affection by conciliatory measures, showing threats, and honouring and buying the allegiance of principal men are stated to be the means for dissension. One having a frustrated ally is ruined like the timber eaten by an insect. (A king) possessing the three kinds of regal power[1] and one who knows the proper place and time should subjugate his enemies by (means of) force. The ruler of a neighbouring country who is favourably disposed should be pacified in the event of his being befriended by mighty allies. The greedy and poor (should be won) by making a gift. Other friends (should be won by pointing out) danger from others. The wicked (should be won) by threats of punishment and the sons, brothers and others by conciliatory measures. The chieftains of the army, the warriors (and) the heads of provinces (should be controlled), the vassals and foresters by making gifts and (causing) dissension (among themselves). The offenders (should be put down) by (means of) dissension and punishment.

63-68. After having propitiated the images of gods the male should dress as the female and illusions should be made by men such as the forms of goblins, meteors, monsters and vixens, assuming the desired form, showering of weapons, fire, stones and water, (and showing) the divine phenomena such as darkness, wind, fire, and cloud. Bhīma (one of the Pāṇḍavas) killed Kīcaka (son of king of Virāṭa) assuming the form of a woman. It is said to be indifference when one does not dissuade another from unfair battle or plight just as Hiḍimbā (the demoness that married Bhīma) remained indifferent towards his brother (when he was fighting with Bhīma). Indrajāla (stratagem) such as clouds, darkness, rain, fire, mountain, wonders, the banners of a large army causing fright and mirage-like picture of being torn and spread should be shown in order to frighten the enemies.

CHAPTER TWO HUNDRED AND FORTYTWO

Statesmanship for a king

Rāma said :

1-6. After having worshipped gods and arranging six divisions of the army (the king) should march against the enemy. (The six divisions of the army are) the central force, the front, the rear, the auxiliary, hostile and the pioneer.

1. These are the supreme position of the king, the strength of a good council and energy.

Each (division) of the (above) forces are more important (than the succeeding ones). (The same holds good in the case of) reverses also. The commander-in-chief should go to such places as the rivers, mountains, forests and forts wherever there may be danger, with the army in array consisting of six divisions, machines, treasury, foot-soldiers, cavalry, chariots and elephants. The leader (of the forces) should march at its head being surrounded by best warriors. The queen, king, treasury and the excellent warriors of the army should be placed in the middle. The cavalrymen (should be) on the two sides, the chariots by the side of the cavalry and the elephants by the side of the chariots. The pioneer forces (should be by the side) of the elephants. Then the commander-in-chief should go slowly behind all with a fully equipped army encouraging the dejected.

7-13. A marching army should be set in (the array of) a crocodile and in (the array of) a hawk with raised wings or a *sūcī* or *vīravaktra*[1] in case of danger in the front. In case of fear behind, (an array in the form of) the cart (should be made). (In case of fear) on the sides, (an array) known as *vajra* (should be made). If there is danger on all sides one should set up (the array known as) *sarvatobhadra*. (A commander) should guard his army (while passing through) a cave, mountain forest, river and dense forest. (He should also guard) when the army has to go a long way, when it is tired, when it suffers hunger, thirst or adversity, when it is affected by ill-health, famine and epidemics, when attacked by robbers. (He should also protect the army) from marshy land, dust storm and watery place. He should see that they are neither scattered nor gathered together on the way. (He should also guard them) while sleeping, eating their food, while staying at an unfit place, when they are not well-placed, when they have been scared by robbers, fire and fear and when they have been struck by rains and wind. When the army of the enemy (is in a similar position) it should be struck. One should have an open encounter (with an enemy) only when the grounds and time are favourable and one is strong. On the contrary (one should do) treacherous warfare. When they (enemies) are attacking, the bewildered should be killed.

1. Types of arrangement of the army.

14-17. (An enemy) on another's soil (could be won) from staying in one's own soil. (An enemy) in one's own soil (could be won) by means of sowing seeds of dissension. (An enemy) subject to the wrath of his people should be made captive by employing the foresters and others and killed. They can also be conquered by employing extremely brave warriors. (One may also employ) dissension, bribe or (may) draw away. By appearing in front of (the enemy) the king would become a sure object of their aim. Then (the enemy) should be killed by extremely brave warriors by striking swiftly with a strong force. Brave warriors could be set in an array in front or at the back (and the enemy) could be killed. It has been explained by these two (methods) as to how to attack the two enemies on the adjacent sides in a treacherous warfare. If the front part (of the hostile army) is in an unfavourable land, the rear portion should be attacked swiftly.

18-22. If the front and rear are both unfavourable (one should strike) on the sides in the same way. After having fought with the vanguards, allies (of the enemy) and the pioneers, one should attack the fatigued, slow and the one whose aid has been cut off without causing fatigue for his force. In the alternative, one should defeat by emploiyng the pioneer force or the allies. Or, one should feign defeat and attack (the enemy) that is complacent that he has won by resorting to good counsel. One should destroy the enemy force when it is resting in the camps, barracks, villages, fields and among subjects without protection. Otherwise the cattle of the enemy should be seized and then the army on their way to reach the goal. Or the hostile army fatigued on account of overnight vigil fearing an attack and sleeping during the day overcome by sleep should be attacked (to gain victory).

23-27. In the alternative (a hostile army) sleeping during the night without any fear (should be attacked) by (employing) elephants or with men armed with swords. The functions of (men on) elephants are proceeding in front of the marching army, entry into forest fortification, division of the united (hostile) army, collecting together a divided army, causing right, breaking the doors (of the fort) and the protection of the treasury. Division of an undivided army and effecting the union of friendly forces are the task of (the men on) chariots. The functions of cavalry are to reconnoitre the forests, different directions and the highway, guard the transport of provisions, follow the retreating army, attend to tasks requiring quick action, follow the weak and attack the last columns and rear (of the hostile army). (The functions) of infantry are to bear always the weapons, inspecting the camps and the highways and to remove (obstructions).

28-33. The ground (suitable) for infantry should not be very uneven or abound with thick rows of trees, ant hills, bushes and thorns and should have (provision for) escape. The ground (suitable) for cavalry should have scanty trees, should be quickly traversible, firm, without sand and not be marshy and have (provision for) escape. The ground (suitable) for the chariot should not have trees, fields, mire, trees causing obstruction, creepers and mire. The ground for the elephant are hills difficult to cross having streams. (A king should march) setting the army in an array consisting of different (segments) such as chest etc. It is known as the rear of the army. It is capable of serving the needs of the king. An array not having this (the division) would appear as if it has been segmented. A wise king desiring to conquer should not fight without having (the array with) the divisions. The treasury would remain with the king. A kingship would be suzerainty over the treasure.

34-48. The soldiers should be paid (rewards) on gaining victory. It is not proper to give only a little. A lakh (should be given) on the death of (the enemy) king and half that when the son of that king is killed. Similarly (the soldiers) should be paid when the (enemy) commander-in-chief is killed or at the killing of the elephant etc. Otherwise (the soldiers) should fight in such a way that the infantry, cavalry, (men on) chariots and elephants do not get affected when the battle has been completed. (The soldiers) should fight without confusion. Confusion causes melee. One should employ an elephant in battles causing great confusion. Three infantry soldiers would be equal to fight a cavalryman. Three such cavalrymen should be employed (to combat) a single elephant (man). Fifteen infantry men would guard (each) foot (of the elephant). It is laid down that an arrangement known as an *anīka* (a unit) of the elephants should be made for (guarding) the chariot. There should be nine elephant men. The vulnerable point of such an army is said to be of five kinds. An array should be set by this division of the army. The chest, sides and wings are said to be (three) divisions. An array is said to have seven parts such as the chest, sides, wings, centre, back (hip), rear and the edge by those well acquainted with (the arrangement of) arrays. The array (called) *guru* consists of chest, sides and wings together with the rear. That of *śukra* is devoid of two sides. The commanders should remain being surrounded by excellent warriors. They should fight without any faction defending one another. Excellent warriors of the army (should be) at the centre. A commander (of an army) is the life of a battle. It would be destroyed if it is without a commander. The powerful elephants should be placed at the chest (of an array), the chariots on the sides and horses on the wings. This array is said to be breaking the central force. An army of horses at the centre, an army of chariots on the sides and an army of elephants on the wings is known to be an array of breaking the inner (force). Station the cavalry in the place of chariots, the infantry in the place of cavalry (in the above order) or place elephants everywhere in the array in the absence of chariots. (There is another view). If there is more than the required army it is said to be *ābādha*.

49-59. (An array called) *bhoga* consists of arranging (the army) in concentric circles. (An array called) *daṇḍa* is of many kinds. (I shall describe them) to you. Listen. (An array) spread horizontally would be (called) *daṇḍa*. (The array called) *maṇḍala bhoga* is in the form of a wave. (The array called) *maṇḍala* (would be) in perfect circle. The *asaṁhata* (class) (would be) in concentric circles. (The other arrays such as) the *pradara*, *dṛḍhaka*, *asahya*, *cāpa*, *kukṣi*, *pratiṣṭha*, *supratiṣṭha*, *śyena*, *vijaya*, *sañjaya*, *viśāla*, *vijaya*, *sūci*, *sthūṇākarṇa camūmukha*, *sarpāsya* and *valaya* are all invincible and modifications of (the array called) *daṇḍa*. They have the following characteristics—extending on both sides, extending on one side, extending in one wing, extending on both wings, three others of the contrary nature. (The array) *pratiṣṭha* extends on the wing and chest (and) the other *supratiṣṭha* is the contrary. (The arrays called) *sthūṇāpakṣa* and *dhanuḥ pakṣa*, *dvisthūṇa* and *daṇḍa* after that (are of) doubled units at the end or an additional wing or of the reverse of another. They should be known to have the characteristics of two or four columns of soldiers in order. (The arrays known as) *gomūtrikā*, *ahisañcārī*, *śakaṭa* and *makara* are said to be variations of the (array) *bhoga*. So also (the array called) *pāriplavaṅgaka*. (The array called) *yugorasya* (consists of) two wings in (the array) *daṇḍa*. (The array of the form of) cart is contrary to that. (The array of the name) crocodile is of mixed nature. (The array) *śeṣa* (is marked) by the rows of elephants. (The arrays) *sarvatobhadra* and *durjaya* are the modifications of the array (called) *maṇḍala*. That which has openings on all sides is the first one and that having the eight army units is the second one. (The arrays known as) *ardhacandraka* (of the shape of half the moon) and *ūrdhvāṅga* (elevated parts) (are formed) by the combinations of (different) divisions of (the class known as) the *vajra*. In the same way (the arrays known as) *karkaśṛṅgī* (the pincers of a crab), *kākapāda* (the feet of a crow) and *godhikā* (lizard) are known from their difference in shape (consisting) of three, four and five units of army.

60-67. Seventeen kinds of arrays could be formed from the (array called) *daṇḍa*. Two from the *maṇḍala* (class), six from the *asaṅghāta* and five from the *bhoga* (are combined) in a battle. (The structures of the abovesaid battle arrays) may be modified by omitting a wing or two wings. Otherwise (a squadron) may be taken from the chest (of the army) and placed around the edges. After having attacked the boundary army in the front with the army forming the wings, one should strike the army at the hip with (the army at) the boundaries and attack with that comprising the chest. The routed soldiers of a hostile army as well as the reserves should be completely destroyed and one's own should be expanded. The main part (of the hostile army) should be attacked with double that of the main and the reserve force (of the hostile army) with the main. A compact (hostile) army should be scattered with a strong contingent of elephants. If (the hostile army) is (in the array) *daṇḍaka* with the flanks, wings and chest (drawn up) then (a general) should employ the (array) *daṇḍa* and quickly show the position. (The array called) *pradāraka* would be by the addition of two wings to the *daṇḍa*. If it is added with wings and flanks it is known as *dṛḍha*. The array that is increased by (adding) two flanks is known to be asahya. The (array) *khātaka* (consists of) keeping the flanks and wings down and attacking with the troops at the chest.

68-72. The array *valaya* is said to be (the union of) two *daṇḍas* capable of breaking the enemy. The (array) *durjaya* (consists of) four *valayas* that is capable of routing the enemy forces. By changing the arrangement of elements (troops) on the flanks, wings and chest of (the array) *bhoga* (we get the arrays) *sarpacārī* and *gomūtrikā*. The array *śakaṭa* is of the shape of a cart. The reverse is said to be the array *amara* capable of destroying the enemies. The arrangement (of troops) on the sides, wings and chest would be in the same way as the (array) *maṇḍala*. The divisions (called) *cakra*, *padma* and others are variations of the *maṇḍala*. In the same way the arrays *sarvatobhadra*, the excellent *vajrākṣa*, the crow-shaped one, the half moon, *śṛṅgāṭaka* (resembling the junction of four roads) and *acala* of the forms corresponding to their names should be formed according to one's convenience that would prevent the enemy forces.

Fire-god said :

73. O Brahmin ! Rāma[1] reached Ayodhyā after killing (the demon) Rāvaṇa. Lakṣmaṇa (brother of Rāma) killed Indrajit (son of Rāvaṇa) in days of yore by means of statesmanship narrated by Rāma.

CHAPTER TWO HUNDRED AND FORTYTHREE

Physiognomy of men and their indications

Fire-god said :

1. O King ! Ethics were described by me to Rāma. I shall now describe the characteristics of men and women as described by Samudra to sage Garga formerly.

Samudra said :

2-7. I shall describe the good and bad characteristics of men and women. O Virtuous one ! A man having (the signs and features symbolised by the terms) *ekādhika*[2], *dviśukla* (two whites), *trigambhīra* (three depths), *tritrika* (three triads or nine virtues), *tripralamba* (three elongated organs), a spreading in three, threefolds (of skins), *trivinata* (having bends at three

1. One of the manifestations of lord Viṣṇu.
2. These terms are explained below in verses 7 ff.

places), *trikālajña* (knowing the three periods of time) and *trivipula* (broad organs at three places) would be possessing good characteristics. Similarly, (one possessing) four marks (on four different parts of the body), or four equal parts of the body, or cubits four frontal teeth (of commendable size), dark complexion of four, in four (parts of the body), sweet smells at the four (joints of the body) and four (specific organs) of short stature, five (parts of the body) small and long, six (parts) raised, eight bones (strong), seven (parts) glossy, nine (parts) clean, nine (parts like) the lotus, ten (parts like an) array and of the form of the fig tree, fourteen pairs (of parts) equal and sixteen eyes is commended.

8-15. (The term) *ekādhika* stands for virtue together with (the goals of life) righteousness, attainment of riches and pleasures. (The term) *dviśukla* (signifies) the whiteness of teeth and the eyes except the two pupils. (The term) *trigambhīra* (denotes) depth in the ear and navel and (the term) *tritrika* the virtues of absence of envy, compassion, forbearance, endowed with auspicious deeds, purity, desire, liberality, ease and valour known as one triad of virtue. (The term) *tripralamba* (denotes) a person that would have the testicles and arms long. One who has spread by his radiance, fame and fortune on the quarters, country and his own class (is said to be) *trikavyāpī*. A person that has three folds on the belly (is said to be) *trivalīmān*. Listen to me. I shall describe the man having three bends. (He is the person) that bows to the gods, brahmins and preceptors. One who knows the suitable time for (the practice of) virtues, attainment of riches and pleasure is said to be the knower of three periods. One who has a broad chest, forehead and face (is said to be) *trivistīrṇa*. The two hands and two feet bearing (the marks of) banners, umbrellas etc. (are deemed to be bringing good). The fingers, chest, back and hip that are equal are commendable. The commendable height (of the human figure is) four cubits. Four (frontal) teeth having moon-like lustre (is meant by *caturdaṁṣṭraḥ*). I shall describe the four black things. The two pupils of the eyes, the two eye-brows, the beard and hair (are the four) black (things).

16-26. The absence of bad smell in the nostril, mouth, perspiration and armpits (is *caturgandha*). The four short things are short penis, neck and the two shanks. The finger-joints nails, hair on the head, teeth and skin (are the five) minute, (parts). The two cheeks, two eyes, forehead, nose and the space between the breasts (are the five) long parts. The chest, shoulders, nails, nose, face and the back of neck (are the six) :aised parts. The seven parts that are glossy are the skin, hair on the head, teeth, hair on the body, one's sight nails and speech. (The eight bones that are strong are those in) the two knees, two thighs, back, bones of the hand and nose. The nine parts that are clean are the two eyes, two nostrils, two ears, penis, anus and face. The ten (parts of the body) of men of the lustre of a lotus that are commended are the tongue, two lips, palate, eyes, hands, feet, nails, tip of the penis and face. The hand, foot, face, neck, two ears, heart, head, forehead, belly and back, the ten that are broad (like an array) are praiseworthy. One is said to be of the form of a fig (tree) if the inter-space between the two middle and index fingers of the extended arms is equal to the height. The two feet, ankles, buttocks, sides, groins, testicles, breasts, ears, lips, thighs, shanks, hands, fore-arms and eyes are the pairs of fourteen organs that are equal in general for a man. One that sees with the fourteen branches of learning and the two eyes is said to be having sixteen eyes. One with extremely dry body with exposed veins and emaciated, smelling badly (is deemed to be) unfortunate. The person with contrary (characteristics) and pleasing look is commendable. The voice of a lucky man is sweet. His gait resembles that of an elephant in rut. He has two hairs from the same root. It gives protection from fear at once.

CHAPTER TWO HUNDRED AND FORTYFOUR

The characteristic features of women

Samudra said :

1-6. A woman that is beautiful in all her limbs, having the gait of an elephant in rut, having heavy thighs and hips and possessing a look like that of a longing pigeon is commendable. One that is having luxurious dark hair, slim, not having hairs on the body, beautiful, feet touching the ground evenly, and having a pair of breasts closely pressing each other (is also deemed to be lucky). The navel spiralling right to left, the private organ resembling the leaf of the fig (tree), ankles having a dip in the middle and (the dip in) the navel is of the measure of (the head of) a thumb (are also commendable). One that is not having an elongated abdomen (is also praiseworthy). One whose hairs are not soft is not good. One that is not having the name of an asterism, tree and river, one that is not fond of quarrels, one that is not greedy and one that does not speak harsh is auspicious and is honoured by the celestials. One that is having her cheeks of the colour of the *madhūka* flower, one that is not (having the body as) sinewy and abound with hairs, not having the eyebrows close to one another (is also commended). Even if one is crooked if she bestows her affection on the husband (she is deemed to be) the life of the husband even if the good characteristics are not present. If the quality of attraction is present other qualities (would also be present). One whose little toe does not touch the earth is verily the death itself.

CHAPTER TWO HUNDRED AND FORTYFIVE

The characteristics of the royal fan, bow and sword

Fire-god said :

1-6. The handle of (the royal) fan (should be of) gold. The royal umbrella made of the feathers of *haṁsa*, peacock, parrot or the feathers of crane is praised. It should not be made with mixed feathers,. (An umbrella) of a brahmin (should be) of square shape and that of a king (should be)circular and white. (There should be) three, four, five, six, seven or eight joints on the handle (of umbrella). The auspicious seat of the king (should be made) with (the wood of) the *kṣīra* trees of fifty inches long. Its breadth should be three cubits and decorated with gold and other things. O Excellent brahmin ! The bow (is made of three materials) iron, horn or wood. The three materials for the bow-string are the bamboo fibre, hide and wood. Four cubits would be the excellent measure of a bow. It is said to be mediocre if equal and inferior if less than that. Materials should be added at the middle part for the sake of the grip of the fist.

7-13. O Brahmin ! the tip of the bow made of horns or iron (should be having) minute edge (covered) by hides. The edge (should be) like the creeper, (like) the eye-brow of a beautiful damsel and should be fastened well. O Brahmin ! One should make the bow separately made of the horn or iron or (the two) mixed. A good bow should suitably be decorated with particles of gold. A bow that is crooked, broken and with incisions is not commended. Gold, silver, copper and black iron are remembered (to be the materials) in (making) a bow. A bow (made of) horns of a buffalo, a *śarabha* (a fabulous animal) or *rohiṣa* (a kind of deer) are auspicious. A bow (made of) sandal, cane, *sāla*, *dhavala* and *kakubha* (trees) (are good). The most excellent bow is that made of bamboos cut and collected in the autumn. The bow should be worshipped with the sacred syllables called *trailokyamohana* (captivating the three worlds) (used) for the swords. The arrows (may be made) of iron, bamboo or reeds. (They should be) straight and gold-coloured and bound by sinews. (They should have) good feathers. (They should have) gold feathers that are good. (They should) be cleaned with oil and be of good colour. One should worship weapons, bows and other things before starting an expedition or the royal consecration.

14-27. The king (should also worship) those carrying banners and weapons and the astrologers. Lord Brahmā performed a sacrifice on the banks of celestial Ganges on the peaks of the Meru (mountain). When he was contemplating at the sacrifice he saw the demon Loha (that causes) obstruction. As he was thinking about that, a great mighty form appeared from the fire in front of him. He bowed down to the lord (Brahmā) and the celestials greeted him with joy. Lord Hari took the sword (called) *Nandaka* from the demon as requested by the celestials. The lord seized it slowly and it became unsheathed. The sword was blue (in colour) with gem (studded) handle. Then the demon became (endowed with) hundred hands. That demon made the celestials run away in the battlefield by means of the mace. The body of the demon was cut by lord Hari with the sword and (the parts of) the body fell on the earth and all of them became pieces of iron on account of their contact with the (sword) *Nandaka*. After having killed him lord Hari gave him a boon (saying) "Your holy body would become (the material) for weapons on the earth". On account of the grace of lord Hari, Brahmā also worshipped lord Hari with the sacrifice without obstruction. Then I shall describe the characteristics of a sword. Swords that are produced at (the places) Khaṭī and Khaṭṭara are known to be worthy of being seen. Those belonging to (the region called) 'Ṛṣi' (would be capable of) cutting the body. Those produced from Sūrpāraka would be strong. Those got from Vaṅga are sharp and capable of cutting. Those produced from the country Aṅga are sharp. Sword (of the length) of fifty inches is said to be excellent. Half of that measure is known to be medium. One should not bear a sword shorter than that length. O Noblest one ! It is said to be extremely worthy to wear a sword that is long and that which makes a sweet sound like that of a bell. A sword having the tip resembling the lotus flower or round is commended. Swords having the colour of the tip of a *karavīra* leaf, the smell of ghee and the lustre of the sky (are also good). Spots at equal intervals of an inch on the swords are commendable as on the *liṅga*. Those resembling the colour of a crow or owl and of an uneven shape are not auspicious. One should not see his face reflected in the sword. One should not touch the sword after eating (without washing the mouth). One should not disclose the value and quality of a sword. One should not place the sword under the head in the night.

CHAPTER TWO HUNDRED AND FORTYSIX

The testing of gems

Fire-god said :

1-7. I shall describe the characteristics of gems. The gems that are to be worn by the kings are diamond, emerald, ruby, pearl, sapphire, *mahānīla* (a kind of sapphire), lapis lazuli, *gandhaśasyaka* (?), moon-stone, sun-stone, crystal, *pulaka, karketana*, topaz and the *jyotirasa*. Crystal, *rājapaṭṭa* (an inferior kind of diamond) and *rājamaya* are auspicious. O Brahmin ! Ruby, *gañjā*, conch-shell of a variety, *gomeda, rudhirākṣa* (holy beads and the marking nut (are auspicious). O Excellent brahmin ! *Dhūli* emerald, blue vitriol, lead, *pilu*, coral *girivajra* (?) the gem (found) in the serpents, auspicious diamond, *ṭiṭṭibha* (?), *piṇḍa* (?), *bhrāmara* (a kind of stone ?) and *utpala*—(these) gems set in gold (and worn) would confer prosperity and success. Inward lustre, free from impurities and good formation of the shape (are the characteristics of good gems).

8-15. Such gems could be worn. Those not having lustre, impure, cracked and containing pebbles inside should not at all be worn. It is commendable to wear the diamond. The diamond that could be carried away by water, that is unbreakable, without impurity, of hexagonal shape, has the lustre of the rainbow, light and (brilliant) like the sun is auspicious (to wear). Similarly an emerald possessing the hues of the plumes of a parrot, glossy, radiant, without impurity and containing minute particles resembling powdered gold is auspicious. The rubies got from crystal mines would be extremely red and spotless. Those got from (the place) Kuruvinda are naturally red. and those got from sulphur mines are of dark brown (colour). The pearls got from oysters are free from impurities. O Sage ! Those got from the conch-shells are superior to them. (The pearls) obtained from the tusks and temples of the elephants, those got from the boars and fish and those found in the bamboos and clouds are excellent. Rotundity, whiteness, transparency and heaviness are the (good) qualities in a pearl. A good sapphire shines in the milk, spreads more lustre and tinge of its own colour. It should be declared as invaluable. The lapis lazuli of red-blue (colour) is excellent and should be used in a necklace and other (ornaments).

CHAPTER TWO HUNDRED AND FORTYSEVEN

The characteristics of a site for building

Fire-god said :

1-3. I shall describe the characteristics of a building site for the brahmins and others. They are white, red, yellow and black (soil) in order (for the four castes). A building site should have the smell of ghee, blood, cooked rice and wine in order (for the four castes). (They should also) taste sweet, pungent and acid and other secondary tastes in order. (The ground) should be cleared of *kuśa*, reeds, *kāśa* (a kind of grass) and dūrvā (a kind of grass having razor-like edges) after having dug out pieces of iron etc. and worshipped the brahmins.

4-9. Sixty-four squares should be made. Lord Brahmā (occupies) the four central squares. The presiding deity (of the two squares) on the east of those (squares) is said to be lord Aryamā. God Vivasvān is (on the two squares) on the south. God Mitra is (on the two squares) on the west. Gods worshipped on the angular points are :) God Mahīdhara (Pṛthvīdhara) is on (the two squares on) the north. Āpas and (Āpa) Vatsa are on the south-east. God Sāvitra, Savitā, Jaya and Indra (are respectively) on the south-west and west. God Rudra and (personification of) disease are on the north-west. (The gods worshipped) outside on the east and other directions from the angular squares are Mahendra, Satya and Śeṣa on the east. Gṛhakṣata, Aryaman[1], Dhṛti and Gandharva on the south, Puṣpadanta, Asura Varuṇa and Yajña[2] on the west and Bhallāṭa Soma, Aditi[3] and Dhanada on the north. Nāga is the lord on north-east. Similarly, the first and the last are said to be the lords in each one of the eight directions.

10-15. Parjanya is the first god. The second one is Karagraha. (The other gods are) Mahendra, Ravi, Satya, Bhṛśa and Gagana. Pavana (should be worshipped) in the east, (gods) Antarīkṣa and Dhaneśvara in the south-east and the celestials Mṛga and Sugrīvaka in the south-west. Roga and Mukhya (should be worshipped) in the north-west, Puṣpa,

1. Yama and Bhṛṅgarāja in other texts.
2. Śeṣa in other texts.
3. Caraka, in other texts.

Kubera as well as Gṛhakṣata, Yama, Bhṛśa, Gandharva and Nāgapaitṛka on the south, Dauvārika, Sugrīva, Puṣpadanta, the demon, the (presidting deity of) water (should be worshipped) in the west. The pulmonary disease that emaciates (men) and Nāgarāja (the king of the serpents) (should be worshipped in the north). (The gods) Mukhya, Bhallāṭa, Moon, Aditi, Kubera, Nāga, Fire (god), the excellent Indra and Sun (god) (should be worshipped) in the east. Gṛhakṣata and puṣpa (are worshipped) in the south, the outstanding Sugrīva in the west and Puṣpadanta and Bhallāṭa at the northern door.

16-23. A stoneslab or a brick should be laid on the ground and worshipped with the mystic syllables (as follows) and the celestials should be worshipped. O Daughter of (the sage) Vasiṣṭha ! Gladden us with wealth and progeny. O Victorious one ! Heir of sage Bhārgava (Paraśurāma) ! Bring victory to the progeny. O Heir of (sage) Aṅgirasa ! The Satisfied one ! Fulfil my desires. O Auspicious one ! Heir of sage Kāśyapa ! Make my mind good. O One endowed with all seeds ! One surrounded by all gems and herbs ! O Bright one ! Rejoicing one ! Daughter of (sage) Vasiṣṭha ! Be pleased here. O Daughter of Prajāpati ! Goddess on the quadrangle on the earth. O Goddess of Good fortune and Good demeanour ! Auspicious one ! Daughter of (sage) Kāśyapa ! Be pleased in (this house). O One worshipped by great masters and adorned with incense and flowers ! O Goddess that makes one get prosperous ! O Daughter of (sage) Bhārgava ! May you be pleased in this house. One not mutilated ! Unbroken one ! Complete one ! Daughter of the sage Aṅgirasa ! I establish you on this brick. Confer on me the desired (things). One that is held by sovereigns, chieftains and owners of houses ! May you be one that increases the progeny, wealth, elephants, horses and cows. (A brick or) stone should similarly be laid at the entrance to the house (for the first time).

24-31. A *plakṣa* tree would be auspicious on the north and the *vaṭa* (tree) on the east of the house. *Udumbara* on the south and the *aśvattha* on the west are excellent. A garden should be laid on the left (of the house). Dwelling in such a house is good. The trees planted and grown should be watered morning and evening in the summer, alternate days in the winter and each night in the rainy season if the ground gets dried. They should be sprinkled with cold water mixed with the paste of *vidaṅga* (a medicinal herb used as a vermifuge). If the fruits get destroyed, (the trees should be sprinkled with water mixed) with (the paste of) horse-beans, black-gram, green gram, sesamum and barley. Sprinkling of cold water together with ghee is always (beneficial) for (the trees bearing) fruits and flowers. Sprinkling water with fish makes the trees grow. The powdered excrement of the sheep and goat (mixed with) the powdered barley and sesamum, beef and water should be buried in the ground for seven nights and then sprinkling that would make all the trees bear fruits and flowers abundantly. Sprinkling mango trees with cold water mixed with fish is commended. The gentle kick of the *aśoka* (tree) by women with their feet is also commended. Date palms, coconut and other trees grow well by (adding) salt. Sprinkling with water mixed with *vidaṅga* (herb) and fish would be beneficial for all trees.

CHAPTER TWO HUNDRED AND FORTYEIGHT

Benefit of worshipping lord Viṣṇu with flowers and leaves

Fire-god said :

1-6. (Lord) Viṣṇu would confer success in all ventures by worshipping (him) with flowers. (The flowers for worship are): *mālatī*, *mallikā*, *yūthī*, *pāṭalā*, *karavīraka*, *pāvanti*, *atimukta*, *karṇikāra*, *kuraṇṭaka*, *kubjaka*, *tagara*, *nīpa*, *vāṇa*, *barbara*, *mallikā*, *aśoka*, *tilaka*, *kunda* (and) *tamālaka* would be good for worship. The leaves of *bilva*, *śamī*, *bhṛṅgarāja*, *tulasī*, and *vāsaka* (are deemed good) for worship. The *ketakī* leaf and flower, lotus and red lotus and others (are also good). But the *arka*, *unmattaka*, *kāñcī*, *girimallikā*, *kauṭaja*, *śālmali* and *kaṇṭakārī* flowers are not at all good for the worship. The bathing of lord Viṣṇu with a *prastha* (measure) of ghee would be equal) to the benefit (of making a gift) of a crore of cows. (By doing so) with *āḍhaka* one would become a king. One would ascend heavens (by bathing) with ghee and milk.

CHAPTER TWO HUNDRED AND FORTYNINE

The science of archery

Fire-god said :

1-5. O Brahmin ! I shall describe the science of archery in four sections. It is said to be of five kinds resting on the warriors on chariots, elephant, cavalry and infantry. It is said to be of five kinds such as those projected by a machine, thrown by the hand, those cast (by hands) and retained, those permanently retained (in the hand) and boxing. (The weapons) are said to be of two kinds—ordinary weapons and missiles. They are again stated to be of two kinds by the divisions (such as) curved and conceit. (The weapons projected) by means of a sling or bow or other such contrivances are said to be projected by a machine. Stones and weapons such as the iron clubs are stated to be (weapons) thrown by the hand. (Weapons) such as the *prāsa* (dart) would be known as (the weapons) cast and retained. Swords and other (weapons) are those permanently retained. Personal combat without weapons (is the last one).

6-8. After surmounting the difficulties, (the king) desiring to fight should engage fit men (for the purpose). Battles (fought) with the bows (and arrows) are excellent, those with darts are mediocre, those with swords are inferior and those fought with hands are still inferior to them. A brahmin is said to be the preceptor in archery for two castes. A *śūdra* has the right to fight in case of an emergency if he had undergone training. The people of mixed castes belonging to that country should render assistance to the king in the battle.

9-19. If the thumbs, calves, palms and feet are kept closely pressed against each other, the position (is said to be) *samapada* from its characteristic feature. It is said to be *vaiśākha* if one stands on the outer toes and the two knees are held in a straight and motionless posture and the distance (between the two soles) is three *vitastis* (twelve *aṅgulas*). It is known as *maṇḍala* if the two knees look like a row of *haṁsas* and (the feet are) four *vitastis* apart. It is stated to be *āliḍha* when the right thigh and knee are held motionless and (appear) like the plough and are five *vitastis* apart. If the same is changed (to the left) it is known to be *pratyāliḍha*. If the left leg would be curved and the right would be straight and the two calves and the legs remain fifteen *aṅgulas* apart, the posture would be (known as) *jāta* (on the whole) extending to twelve *aṅgulas*. If the left knee would be straight and the right knee extended well or the right knee is curved and motionless and the feet together with the knee are four cubits apart, it is said to be *vikaṭa* extending to two cubits. If the knees (are kept down) twice (as much) and the two legs are raised, that posture is said to be *vikaṭa*. The feet are a little turned round, firm and equal to four cubits. It is properly seen to extend to sixteen *aṅgulas*. O Brahmin ! With this posture (known as) *svastika* one should first bow down holding the bow by the left hand and the arrow by the right hand.

20-29. One that loves his bow should remain in the (postures) *vaiśākha* or *jāta* or firm or extended and put the string on the bow. The lower tip of the bow and the striking part of the arrow should be fixed on the ground. O One practising good austerities ! it should be raised with the hands by means of the curved fore-arms. That bow and arrow of a person is excellent which has a space of twelve inches between the bow and the feathered part of the arrow. The string should be made neither too long nor too short. Holding the bow (in line) with the navel and the quiver on the back, the bow should be raised with the left hand between the eye and the ear. The arrow should be taken with the right fist to the edge of the breast. (Then the string) should be put on and quickly drawn to its full capacity. (It should not be stretched so much as to be) within or beyond or above or below or curbed or raised or shaking or extremely obstructed. It should be parallel, firm and straight like a rod. After having covered the mark with the right fist, the archer (should stand) with his chest raised and bent in the shape of a triangle, the shoulders stooping, the neck without motion, and the head poised erect as a peacock. The space between the fore head, nose, face, shoulder and the elbow should be equal. The space between the chin and shoulder is known to be three *aṅgulas*.

30-37. The interval between the chin and shoulder is said to be three *aṅgulas* in the first, two *aṅgulas* in the second and one *aṅgulas* in the third (kind of bow)1 After having taken the feathered end of an arrow with the thumb and the index finger and then with the ring and middle (finger of the right hand), it should be drawn fully such that the arrow gets completely stretched. After having begun in this way, the arrow should be released in the proper manner. O Man of good conduct ! The target that has been seen (by the eyes) and covered by the fist should be split with the arrow. After releasing (the arrow) the left hand should be thrown back quickly. O Brahmin ! It is known as excision. It should be known by you. An expert in the archery should keep the elbow down while drawing (an arrow), above while releasing and be in line with the target in the middle (state). Those who are well-versed in (the science of) archery know it as the excellent. The superior kind of arrow is known to be twelve *muṣṭis*[1], the mediocre of eleven *muṣṭis* and the inferior one of ten *muṣṭis*. A bow of four cubits is excellent, that of three and a half cubits is mediocre and that of three cubits is said to be inferior always by the infantry men. The same is said to be excellent in (the case of) cavalry, chariot and elephant.

CHAPTER TWO HUNDRED AND FIFTY

The science of archery

Fire-god said :

1-7. Then a brahmin should get ready the weapons such as the mace, bow etc., wash them well free from flesh and place them on the sacrificial ground. Then after having collected the arrow, furnishing himself with an armour and remaining composed he should get the quiver and bind it firmly on the right shoulder. Even though there may not be any definite aim, that arrow that has been placed in it in that position should be lifted from the quiver with the right hand. Then the arrow together with the hand that be lifted should be placed (on the bow) and held. The middle-part of the bow should be held with the left hand. After having made his mind diverted of all anxieties, the feathered end of the arrow should be placed on the string

1. The breadth of the clenched fist.

After holding firmly in the (position known as) *siṁhakarṇa* evenly with the feathered end, the fruit of the left that rested on the left ear should be borne (?) The covers should be borne with the left middle finger. One who knows the procedure should fix his mind on the target and (hold the arrow) with (the right) fist on the right side of the body and discharge covers.

8-12. (One that practises to shoot an arrow) should place a pole as the target in line with the fold on the forehead. The circular mark (of the extent) of sixteen *aṅgulas* should be struck after pulling (the arrow). After having discharged such an arrow, one should then practise (discharging) fire-brands with that. One should place the arrow again and again with the middle finger. One should strike from the quiver at the target perceived by the eye (imagining) as a square on the right. One that is in the first stage should practise to pierce (the target) in a square. Then he should practise to aim quickly, turning round and to pierce that below or above. When (the targets are) at the position of being pierced the bow (should be lifted) from its position and the hands should threaten with varied sounds of invincible (nature) (?)

13-19. O Brahmin ! Among those (objects) to be struck (by a bow-man), two (kinds) are known to be *dṛḍha* (requiring firm hand), two are known as Duṣkara (difficult to hit) and two as *citraduṣkara* (extremely difficult to hit). That which is not below and hard is stated to be requiring firm hand. That which is below as well as that which is above is said to be *duṣkara*. That which is between the head and the zenith is known as *citraduṣkara*. Thus after having known the position of the objects to be hit with the right and left, a hero (archer) should first make progress. Then one would be the conqueror of the target. This is said to be the rule that has been laid by those well-versed in that. It is said that one would have more mobility from that practice. The target that comes within the purview of the arrow should be aimed at firmly. One should strike at once, break, pierce and cause distress to that which is whirling round, that which is moving and that which is extremely steady. One who is well-versed in the performance of actions should practise this way after knowing that. One that has learnt the application would conquer (the lord of) death by means of his mind, eyes and look.

CHAPTER TWO HUNDRED AND FIFTYONE

The method of using a noose

Fire-god said :

1-6. One that has controlled the hand, conquered the mind and obtained proficiency in (hitting) the target perceived should board the chariot after getting the specified perfection. A noose should be ten cubits (long), round and such as to be held in the hand. The thread (of the noose) should be made either of cotton or *muñja* (grass), tendon, *arka* (plant) or hide. It may be made of any other strong (material) well twined with thirty (pieces). A wiseman should make the noose well-rounded. The instructors should always provide a place for that on the sides. Having gathered it with the left hand it should be lifted with the right-hand. After having made (the noose) into a loop, it should be whirled round the head and thrown quickly on a person covered by the armour and quiver. One that is well-trained should be employed after having made him proficient to use the noose on the (horsemen) galloping, capering and running away.

7-12. After having conquered the enemy, he should be made a captive in the proper manner. The sword should be hanging on the left side on the waist. (The sheath) should be held firmly by the left (hand) and (the sword) should be drawn out (from the scabbard) with the right hand. The circumference of a dart should be six *aṅgulas*, its height seven *hastas* and it (be made) of iron. Armours are of different kinds. It should be half the *hasta*, equal, spreading across and upwards. It should be fitted in the proper manner. Listen to me as I describe. After having made the person stand with the quiver and armour on his body, one should take the new, strong club in the right hand, move nine *aṅgulas* and strike. By this (blow) the head (of the enemy) would certainly be destroyed. (Otherwise) he may be struck down with both hands. After having done thus without strain, one is said to accomplish the death of the person. I have already described how to cause the distress of the arms for the sake of the movement.